D1571963

The Gambling Century

The Gambling Century

Commercial Gaming in Britain from Restoration to Regency

JOHN EGLIN

OXFORD
UNIVERSITY PRESS

Great Clarendon Street, Oxford, OX2 6DP,
United Kingdom

Oxford University Press is a department of the University of Oxford.
It furthers the University's objective of excellence in research, scholarship,
and education by publishing worldwide. Oxford is a registered trade mark of
Oxford University Press in the UK and in certain other countries

Published in the United States of America by Oxford University Press
198 Madison Avenue, New York, NY 10016, United States of America

British Library Cataloguing in Publication Data
Data available

Library of Congress Control Number: 2023938493

ISBN 978-0-19-288819-8

DOI: 10.1093/oso/9780192888198.001.0001

Printed and bound in the UK by
Clays Ltd, Elcograf S.p.A.

MIX
Paper | Supporting
responsible forestry
FSC® C018072

In Memoriam

Stuart Baker Eglin
22 February 1919–7 May 2007

Paula Louise Garrison Eglin
24 June 1930–30 June 2015

Contents

List of Illustrations

Introduction

The Gambling Century?

Within the well-upholstered and plushly carpeted precincts of Brooks's Club hangs evidence, in the form of engraved depictions of enthusiastic card and dice play of an earlier period, that the club was once a much less sedate place, with an atmosphere more consistent with blackjack tables on Fremont Street in Las Vegas than with the serene hush of Henry Holland's rooms. So it seemed to this author, then still a graduate student, having secured an invitation to examine the George Knapton Dilettanti portraits that decorate the library there. This memory resurfaced in research for a biography of Richard 'Beau' Nash, the self-styled 'Master of Ceremonies' at Bath and later Tunbridge Wells. When Nash complained of losing £500 one night to 'that damned bitch fortune,' the Earl of Chesterfield quickly put him in his place: 'I don't wonder at your losing money, Nash, but all the world is surprised where you get it to lose.'[1] The mystery was subsequently solved for contemporaries as a result of litigation that Nash filed in 1755 and 1757 in a desperate attempt to collect the proceeds from his partnerships in gaming tables at these resorts. Two such arrangements with the proprietors of assembly rooms at Bath and Tunbridge Wells became public knowledge, confirming charges that the Bath jeweller Thomas Goulding had levelled three decades earlier.[2] Nash was subsequently credited with the genesis of the modern casino,[3] a development that can be dated to the opening of Thomas Harrison's assembly rooms in Bath in 1708. The investigation into Nash's finances raised questions about the process through which gambling became a commercial venture, and in attempting to trace this evolution, it became clear that the commercialization of gambling was connected with the development of the cultural institutions that scholars of early modern Europe long associated with an emerging public sphere. It also became apparent, however, that the nature and structure of gaming ventures were not well understood by contemporaries, including polemicists who cast opprobrium on gaming,

---

[1] *The Works of Oliver Goldsmith*, ed. Arthur Friedman, 5 vols (Oxford: Oxford University Press, 1966), 3. 357.

[2] John Eglin, *The Imaginary Autocrat: Beau Nash and the Invention of Bath* (London: Profile, 2005), 122, 214–15.

[3] David Miers, *Regulating Commercial Gambling: Past, Present, and Future* (Oxford: Oxford University Press, 2004), 25; Thierry Depaulis, 'A Material History of Modern Gaming,' in Manfred Zollinger (ed.), *Random Riches: Gambling Past and Present* (London: Routledge, 2016), 49.

The Gambling Century: Commercial Gaming in Britain from Restoration to Regency. John Eglin, Oxford University Press.
© John Eglin 2023. DOI: 10.1093/oso/9780192888198.003.0001

and legislators and magistrates charged with policing it, nor had scholars of the period concerned themselves with the business of gaming as a commercial enterprise.

Gambling, of course, had been known from ancient times, and episodes of and allusions to games of chance were woven into the common cultural heritage that Europeans claimed. They had only to think of Julius Caesar's purported utterance on crossing the Rubicon, or of the lots thrown for Christ's garments. It has been argued that pre-modern gambling, for example that practised in ancient Rome by tossing *astragali,* the knuckle-bones of sheep, was an invitation to the intervention of indifferent providence, and that the different direction taken in early modernity stemmed from the application of mathematical principles to outcomes once thought to be utterly random or, if controlled, then only through the actions of supernatural beings. Today, clinical concern over social pathologies dialogues with anthropological respect for traditional cultural practices, such as the consumption of intoxicants or meat or saturated fats, or activities like gambling or hunting. Some of these are potentially addictive and therefore destructive, but all of them are global and multicultural phenomena of ancient provenance. The sociologist Gerda Reith asserts that gambling is 'a microcosm in which more general issues about the role of uncertainty and chance in human life are played out in concentrated form.'[4]

It was at the gaming table that a number of developments converged in the latter half of the seventeenth century in Europe. Court society was re-established after decades of civil and religious warfare, particularly in England and France, soon to emerge as the principal rivals for global hegemony. At the French court, high stakes gaming served to preoccupy a vestigially feudal aristocracy as it was repurposed into a service nobility under an absolute monarch. Across the Channel, gambling was not only a feature of a restored court but of a restored festive culture repressed under the puritanism ascendant during the Interregnum. The return of the court meant the return of theatre, in the particular form of royal patent theatres in the capital that catered to a new theatrical public there, as did a host of public accommodations newly freed from the strictures of Commonwealth and Protectorate. Later on, after the initial disruptions of the Dutch Wars, new comestible commodities—coffee, chocolate, and sugar to sweeten both—led to the rapid growth of venues for the on-premises consumption of the new stimulants. These establishments, as is now well known, were crucial sites for the consumption of a thriving print culture, including the new arrival, the newspaper. Like hot caffeinated beverages, commercial gambling was also new, enabled by many of the same developments that brought goods like coffee, tea, chocolate, tobacco, and cotton from Asia, Africa, and the Americas to European consumers

---

[4] Gerda Reith, *The Age of Chance: Gambling in Western Culture* (London: Routledge, 1999), 1.

in European market centres.[5] There was certainly more attention to gambling as one more aspect of a new public culture, akin to theatre, newly accessible to a wider public, as well as newspapers, periodicals, and other print culture, consumed along with newly available hot beverages in increasingly ubiquitous coffeehouses. The wider audience and demand for print culture led to its expansion, creating platforms on which cultural anxieties could be expressed and performed. Whether or not there was actually more gambling taking place, proportionally, is perhaps beyond the scope of any study to demonstrate. It is certainly true, however, that the public conversation about gambling changed, in large part because there were more venues for these conversations to take place. At the same time, courtly patronage of science, technology, engineering, and mathematics—manifested in the chartering of the Royal Society in England and the Académie des Sciences in France—fostered a new and unprecedented appreciation for mathematical probability and its applications.[6]

For generations, historians have echoed contemporary descriptions of unprecedented enthusiasm for gambling in Europe during the 'long eighteenth century,' as we call the period that encompasses the later seventeenth century as well as the first decades of the nineteenth. William Lecky's assessment that '[t]he passion for gambling' in Britain 'had been very prevalent since the Restoration' and 'attained its climax under the first two Georges' was repeated for over a century.[7] Gerda Reith locates what she thinks of as '[t]he unprecedented popularity of gambling in the seventeenth century' in the expansion of commerce, as the increasing affluence of a commercial and mercantile sector gave access to pastimes once confined to princely courts. The growth of an economy grounded in money, fuelled both by an influx of bullion from newly opened mines in the Americas and by the introduction of new financial instruments, was also crucial, creating 'a standardised universal measure of value.' The ensuing century witnessed 'a gradual demarcation of the gambling world into private and public leisure spheres' the latter of which came to take the form of 'a stratified network of commercial gaming houses,' a development that 'mirrored the commercialization and stratification of the world outside,' with the result that 'gambling was for the first time being carried on in a commercial environment.'[8] Jessica Richard asserts that 'gambling,' a term she applies with deliberate imprecision, 'played a foundational role... in the

---

[5] See, for example, Ross Jamieson, 'The Essence of Commodification: Caffeine Dependencies in the Early Modern World,' *Journal of Social History*, 35 (Winter 2001), 281–3.

[6] These applications are *mostly* beyond the scope of this study, except to the extent that they illustrate that the line dividing high finance and insurance on one hand from gambling on the other did not appear as clearly to contemporaries as it might to us.

[7] William E. H. Lecky, *A History of England in the Eighteenth Century*, 8 vols (London: Longman, 1878), 1. 521.

[8] Reith, *Age of Chance*, 59, 62, 68.

development of public credit and . . . early finance capitalism that transformed not only the British economy but culture at large."[9]

Playing the Field

Justine Crump noted in 2004 that while 'in the eighteenth century, people began to write about gambling in new ways and in connection with new topics, . . . [n]o comprehensive work on the subject of gambling in eighteenth-century Britain has yet been produced.'[10] Scholars of early modern France, blessed with thicker archival material generated by a more intrusive, energetic, and well-connected police apparatus across the Channel, have produced a much more extensive literature on gambling under the Ancien Régime.[11] In British studies, literary scholars have made an effort within the confines of that field, but Crump's observation still holds true for the discipline of history.[12] While Bob Harris's recent monograph aims at supplying this deficiency, it is largely (if quite usefully) concerned with lotteries and sports wagering. Games of chance are not treated at any length or in any detail, and indeed Harris comes very close to categorically excluding them from his analysis.[13] One obvious difficulty is that 'gambling' encompasses a wide range of practices, so that a comprehensive treatment even within the confines of a geographic or chronological frame is not really possible without drawing important distinctions. For the purposes of this book, I have adopted a terminology crafted by (among others) Nicholas Tosney and Donna Andrew, who distinguish 'gaming,' applied to games of pure chance, from 'gambling,' which can apply as well to games of skill (such as tennis, ninepins, billiards, or sociable card games like whist), lotteries, betting on racing and other sporting events, and

---

[9] Jessica Richard, *The Romance of Gambling in Eighteenth-Century Britain* (New York: Palgrave Macmillan, 2011), 4.

[10] Justine Crump, 'The Perils of Play: Eighteenth-Century Ideas about Gambling,' Centre for History and Economics, Cambridge University, April 2004, 4 and n. 4.

[11] See, for example, John Dunkley, *Gambling: A Social and Moral Problem in France, 1685–1792* (Oxford: Voltaire Foundation, 1985); Olivier Grussi, *La Vie Quotidienne des Joueurs sous l'Ancien Régime à Paris et à la Cour* (Paris: Hachette, 1985); Thomas Kavanagh, *Enlightenment and the Shadows of Chance: The Novel and the Culture of Gambling in Eighteenth-Century France* (Baltimore: Johns Hopkins University Press, 1993), and Thomas Kavanagh, Dice, Cards, Wheels: A Different History of French Culture (Philadelphia: University of Pennsylvania Press, 2005); Francis Freundlich, *Le Monde de Jeu à Paris 1715–1800* (Paris: Albin Michel, 1995); Élisabeth Belmas, *Jouer Autrefois: Essai sur le Jeu dans la France Moderne* (Seyssel: Champ Vallon, 2006).

[12] Apart from Jessica Richard's work already cited, there is Hope Donovan Cotton, 'Women and Risk: The Gambling Woman in Eighteenth-Century England,' unpublished Ph.D. dissertation, Auburn University, 1998; and Jesse Molesworth, *Chance and the Eighteenth-Century Novel: Realism, Probability, Magic* (Cambridge: Cambridge University Press, 2010), which is largely confined to lotteries and whist, understandably, given the voluminous contemporary literature on both.

[13] Bob Harris, *Gambling in Britain in the Long Eighteenth Century* (Cambridge: Cambridge University Press, 2022). I am very grateful to Professor Harris and to editors at Cambridge for affording me the opportunity to read the book manuscript in advance of its publication.

wagers on other sorts of outcomes, such as elections.[14] Janet Mullin argues that sociable games, whist in particular, played for modest sums, were 'very much within the financial and moral comfort zone of many middle-class people.' 'Carding' emphasized skill rather than risk, requiring 'greater concentration, focus, a good memory, and strategic thinking—all useful in the adult world and particularly in commerce.' Children could even participate in sociable play 'on the basis of teaching them their numbers and the importance of accounting for money lost and won.'[15] More than one admonitory writer carefully distinguished 'carding' from the social pathology of which they were warning the public:

> By Gaming the Author by no means includes the general recreation of cards, where the stake, according to the fortunes of the players, is just sufficient to excite attention, and not so large as to produce bad consequences either to individuals or to society.[16]

While play for high stakes at these games was certainly not unknown, it was comparatively rare. One consideration was that 'carding' frequently occurred in mixed company, as opposed to the homosocial atmosphere in which deep play generally took place. The Earl of Chesterfield advised his godson that he should '[n]ever sit down to play with men only, but let there always be a woman or two of the party, and then the loss or the gain cannot be considerable.'[17] Accounts of thousands of pounds won or lost in a single evening at whist or quadrille did not appear in any of over a thousand contemporary newspaper items reviewed. Of the hundreds of surveyed individuals summoned to Westminster sessions on charges of violating gaming statutes over the period, James Popjoy was the only respondent located who appeared for a sociable game, having won £30 at whist from Thomas Miller, probably on the premises of Richard Clarke, a victualler in Wardour Street,

---

[14] Nicholas Tosney, 'Gaming in England, c. 1540–1760,' unpublished Ph.D. dissertation, University of York, 2008, 10; Donna T. Andrew, *Aristocratic Vice: The Attack on Duelling, Suicide, Adultery, and Gambling in Eighteenth-Century England* (New Haven: Yale University Press, 2013), 175. The former *Daily Mail* reporter Rob Davies draws a similar distinction in his decidedly non-academic treatment of gambling in the contemporary UK, between 'wagering on real-world events like sport, where a degree of knowledge can be brought to bear to improve one's predictive ability,' and 'staking cash on games in which sensible styles of play may limit one's losses but where the odds are ultimately certain, in favour of the house.' Rob Davies, *Jackpot: How Gambling Conquered Britain* (London: Faber and Faber, 2022), 14.

[15] Janet E. Mullin, *A Sixpence at Whist: Gaming and the English Middle Classes 1680–1730* (Woodbridge and Rochester, NY: Boydell and Brewer, 2015), 4, 19, 31, 43.

[16] *Weekly Miscellany*, 7 (30 December 1776), 299.

[17] *The Letters of Philip Dormer Stanhope, Earl of Chesterfield*, ed. Philip Stanhope, Viscount Mahon, 5 vols (London: Richard Bentley, 1845), 2. 427. The presence of women at gaming tables, like the presence of women on stage, was an innovation that contemporaries remarked on from the middle of the seventeenth century, and it also drew public attention. In Paris of the earlier eighteenth century as in London of the later century, elite women were conspicuous as the hosts if not the proprietors of gaming concerns, as will be clear from subsequent chapters.

in 1783.[18] Generally, any money played for, as one writer advised, was 'considered in no other light than as mere counters, to reckon up the games won or lost; and for this innocent purpose, the smallest denominations of coin are sufficiently valuable.'[19]

It should be said that contemporaries were not always consistent themselves in making distinctions among or within terms such as 'gaming,' 'gambling,' or 'carding.' In contemporary usage, 'gaming' could be applied to polite games like whist or quadrille and to more plebeian amusements like skittles or ninepins, so that the term 'common gaming house' could denote, as it did in a memorandum of 1629, a premises fitted out for bowling and shovelboard.[20] 'Gambling,' as a term referring explicitly to games of pure chance, emerged relatively late in the period. A keyword search in the Burney collection reveals that 90 per cent of news items containing the word 'gambling,' as opposed to 'gaming,' appeared after the middle of April 1773, while 80 per cent appeared after the end of 1776, and three quarters appeared after the end of 1781; it first appeared in 1724. While a newspaper writer in 1756 arrived, by his own account, at the momentous conclusion that the two terms were actually synonymous, other observers would still write of 'gaming and gambling' as if distinctions were still drawn. Some of these uses suggested a distinction between polite 'gaming' and plebeian 'gambling.' Correspondents for the *Gazetteer* in the 1760s wrote of 'gambling' in outdoor venues, and 'gaming' in more elevated indoor settings like Carlisle House. Elsewhere the newer term was deployed with reference to financial speculation, although the *Morning Chronicle* (perhaps deliberately) swapped usages in asserting that '[t]he gaming table in Change Alley has ruined more families than all the gambling Coffee-Houses in London.' An item of January 1774 located the etymological origins of 'gambling,' which it called a 'modern term,' in a Scottish colloquialism referring to the trade in commodity futures for hops.[21]

Laying Odds

Two Acts of Parliament frame the period under examination. The Caroline Gaming Act of 1664 was the first such legislation to address games of chance specifically and elite gaming particularly; the Victorian Gaming Act of 1845 outlawed games of chance when played either in public or private for money, eliminating the obstacle that had hobbled previous legislative efforts. The legality or otherwise of gaming depended on the social standing of players and the accessibility of the

---

[18] LMA MJ/SR/3435, r 262.   [19] *Monthly Review*, 53 (December 1775), 522.
[20] TNA SP 16/146/106.
[21] *London Daily Advertiser*, 4558 (7 April 1756); *Gazetteer*, 10,986 (28 May 1764), 11,554 (24 March 1766); *Morning Chronicle*, 953 (12 June 1772); *London Evening Post*, 7034 (2 February 1773); *Public Advertiser*, 12,088 (19 January 1774).

venue, as embodied in the legal formulation of a 'common gaming house.' During Britain's long eighteenth century, however, boundaries between socioeconomic cohorts and between public and private realms were unsettled. Gaming as a commercial venture thrived in the institutions of social and cultural exchange that scholars of the period have described as a 'public sphere.' A chronology framed by legislation is also underpinned by three games: hazard in the first place, a dice game reportedly dating back to the Crusades; basset/faro, a seventeenth-century continental import; and finally E.O., a mid-eighteenth-century invention calculated to evade the language of proscriptive statutes. Each of these embody changing structures of gaming and incorporate assumptions about its cultural role in what some scholars have called a 'gambling century.'

Scholarship on eighteenth-century gaming in Britain in particular has focused on the tension between the irrational risk involved in gambling and the rational risk entailed in investment or insurance.[22] There was at least the possibility, however, of a rational risk opportunity in enabling the irrational risk of others through the establishment of a gaming enterprise. It has been gamblers rather than their enablers, however, who have captured the imagination, and thus they appear everywhere in print, visual, and literary culture. The development of the archetype of the 'gamester' is part of the history of commercial gaming, as it conditioned the response of media and the law to gaming operations. In literary, journalistic, and legal narratives, the bankers, dealers, and croupiers who formed the personnel of the 'house' are merely set decoration, like the cards, wheels, and dice themselves. Yet for the purposes of this book, theirs is the more interesting story. This study is less concerned with the reasons that people gambled than it is with the attraction of gaming to gaming entrepreneurs. It is also concerned with the literal and figurative spaces that gaming occupied, following it from the courtly to the commercial sector, from the Groom Porter's lodge into coffee-houses and 'ordinaries,' then back into relative sequestration in private clubs and 'at-homes,' all of which prefigure the quintessential and quintessentially modern gambling space, the casino.

We will be concerned throughout with the two bodies of law, one juridical and the other mathematical, that shaped the public discussion of gaming in Britain beginning in the middle of the seventeenth century. 'Unlawful games' had been targets of legislation from the Middle Ages, but these pastimes were not confined to those played for money, nor did play for money necessarily render a pastime illicit. Lotteries, as will be seen, entered a separate legal category that was never completely consolidated with other forms of gambling. Wagering notoriously eluded proscription for much of the period under examination, so that the same courts before which gaming debts were unenforceable heard litigation over the

---

[22] See, for example, Geoffrey Clark, *Betting on Lives: The Culture of Life Insurance in England, 1695–1775* (New York: St. Martin's, 1999).

results of bets, such as the famous wager over the sex of the Chevalier d'Eon. After the Restoration, statute law specifically addressed games of chance played for 'lucre and gain' for the first time. This statutory direction coincided with emerging awareness of mathematical probability, of the possibility that chance was governed by mathematical principles. Neither body of law as applied to gaming, however, was ever well understood outside the faculties of law and mathematics, and the mixed success of efforts to understand chance mathematically contributed to the frustration of efforts to tame it statutorily. Whether the laws in question were those of mathematical probability or those of statute, there was a disconnect between what the law understood and how the law was understood and applied. Both the probability of mathematicians and the statute and custom of legislators and jurists gave rise to fictions that promoted rather than hindered the expansion of commercial gaming.

There is ample cause as well to wonder how serious authorities were in their pursuit of gaming operations. Was gaming legitimately viewed as a serious threat to social order, or was public opprobrium merely another cudgel to use on political opposition? Was proscriptive legislation simply a strategy to enhance revenue? Just as there was no statutory definition of a 'gaming house,' as Howard Street put it,[23] there was no agreement, even among authorities, on any number of legal issues around gaming: whether or not gaming concerns could be licensed, how far exceptions to gaming statutes extended, whether gaming per se, even for high stakes, was lawful as long as it was not deceitful, or even whether, after decades of lax or otherwise problematic enforcement, gaming establishments were effectively legal de facto, and might legitimately contribute to public revenue.

Commercial gaming was fundamentally a metropolitan phenomenon, in the same way that participation in state lotteries was mostly metropolitan as well. To cite one provincial example, Nicholas Tosney found only twenty presentments for gaming offences before quarter sessions at York in the half century between 1707 and 1758, fourteen of which occurred after the opening of York's assembly rooms in 1735.[24] Gaming venues outside of London, at resorts like Bath and Brighton, and racecourses like Newmarket, tended to be run on a seasonal basis by metropolitan operators. Consequently, our attention is focused on London and Westminster, and the latter in particular. The legality of gaming was always murky in England, and nowhere more so than the City of Westminster, a patchwork of archaic, inchoate, and overlapping jurisdictions. It consisted of half a dozen urban parishes that had developed on property once attached to Westminster Abbey when it was a functioning Benedictine monastery on the outskirts of medieval London. Its manorial court, the Court of Burgesses, which answered to the Dean and Chapter of Westminster, still sat and exercised jurisdiction that often

---

[23]   Howard Street, *The Law of Gaming* (London: Sweet and Maxwell, 1937), 47.
[24]   Tosney, 'Gaming in England,' 103–4.

conflicted with Westminster's bench of magistrates, a subset of the Commission of the Peace for the county of Middlesex.[25] Westminster was also the site of one functioning royal palace (the Palace of St James) and two defunct and repurposed palaces: that of Westminster, which housed Parliament as well as the courts of King's Bench, Common Pleas, and the Exchequer; and Whitehall, which housed the Treasury and other government offices. Other putatively or residually 'royal' precincts in Westminster included the royal patent theatres in Haymarket, Drury Lane, and Covent Garden. As the nerve centre of government adjacent to the commercial centre that was the City of London proper, and as a centre of cultural production, Westminster boasted scores of the taverns and coffeehouses that were essential to the conduct of public and private business in Europe during the long eighteenth century. Many of these venues developed specialized functions.[26] Jonathan's and Garraway's, coffeehouses in the City, were exclusively the haunt of stockbrokers who traded securities in them, while Edward Lloyd's coffeehouse was the redoubt of 'underwriters' who insured ships' cargoes, essentially by booking wagers on them. Although it was illegal (strictly speaking), a number of public venues derived a significant portion of their profit margin from gaming. It was in Westminster in particular that the emergence of gaming tables as profit centres was to have profound consequences for the configuration of public space.

Hedging Bets

The reliability of print sources is a persistent issue in the study of early modernity, and especially so for that novelty of the period, the newspaper. News media of Britain's long eighteenth century were unabashedly partisan and polemical, and were notorious for their willingness to publish just about any news item that came through their letterboxes. Reportage was crowdsourced, and editorial curation minimal. This investigation has found, however, that newspaper accounts of the enforcement of gaming laws, to give one example, were generally reliable, the details of press accounts of arrests and indictments usually corroborated in documents among sessions rolls and sessions papers.[27] The regularity with which

---

[25] *An Account of the Endeavours that have been Used to Suppress Gaming Houses, and of the Discouragements that have been met with* (London: n.p., 1722), 9–10.

[26] See Brian Cowan, *The Social Life of Coffee* (New Haven: Yale University Press, 2005). The standard reference work on these establishments is Bryant Lillywhite, *London Coffee Houses* (London: George Allen and Unwin, 1963).

[27] Most actions against gaming venues were recorded in Westminster sessions rolls, as most of the venues were located in that jurisdiction, and consequently it is those rolls that I have examined systematically. It was not unknown, however, for offences in the City of Westminster to be referred to the Middlesex sessions, which sat monthly, as opposed to those for Westminster, which met at the traditional quarters. Two raids that Henry Fielding conducted on gaming operations in the Strand in the first months of 1750, for example, were widely reported in newspapers but not documented in the

raids on gaming venues documented in the sessions rolls were also adverted in newspapers does, however, raise other questions. Local authorities were clearly eager to publicize any efforts they made against this perceived social pathology.

There is also ample reason to be sceptical of one staple of the print culture around gaming, the innumerable anecdotal accounts of vast sums of money won and lost. Even contemporaries cocked an eyebrow at these stories, as Samuel Johnson did when James Boswell spoke of the 'desperate extent' of play at the newly opened Brooks's Club in 1776:

> Depend upon it, Sir, this is mere talk. *Who* is ruined by gaming? You will not find six instances in an age. There is a strange rout made against deep play: whereas you have many more people ruined by adventurous trade, and yet we do not hear such an outcry about it.[28]

According to one hostile account of faro from near the end of the century, a typical faro bank amounted to between 500 and 1,000 guineas, corresponding to a fictional French example, wherein the projectors of a bank in a Parisian hotel raise for the purpose the sum of 900 louis d'or.[29] Stakes, according to this account, were limited, usually to ten guineas; Almack's, the forerunner of Brooks's, the scene of any number of hyperbolic gaming anecdotes, boasted twenty-guinea and fifty-guinea tables. Given these limits, wins and losses in the tens of thousands of pounds were highly unlikely. The ability to absorb large losses with equanimity was a mark of status, and complaining of them the prerogative of elites. In consideration of these circumstances, it is probable that assertions of losses were often exaggerated. Justine Crump found it 'quite hard to find documented evidence of the rich and powerful absolutely ruined by gambling.' Janet Mullin similarly asserts that '[a]ccounts of high-stakes play in dark corners appear more often in novels and plays than in diaries and letters.'[30]

Anecdotes recounted in newspapers tend to follow tell-tale patterns. One tale type, to adopt a term from the anthropological study of folklore, concerned a fund allegedly maintained at one of the clubs of St James's for members who had gambled away their estates on the premises. *Lloyd's Evening Post* reported in April 1770 that a baronet who had sold his chariot, coach, and horses to settle a gaming debt contracted at 'a noted house, not many miles from St. James's-street' was retiring to the south of France to live on the pension that the club allotted to

Westminster rolls. Summonses, recognizances, and committals of the apprehended individuals were presumably processed for the next Middlesex sessions and bound with that roll.

[28] James Boswell, *The Life of Samuel Johnson*, ed. Marshall Waingrow, Bruce Redford, Elizabeth Goldring, and Thomas Bonnell, 4 vols (New Haven: Yale University Press, 1995–2020), 3. 20.

[29] *Faro and Rouge et Noir* (London: John Debrett, 1793), 30; Kavanagh, *Shadows of Chance*, 132.

[30] John Ashton, *The History of Gambling in England* (London: Duckworth, 1898), 91; Crump, 'Perils of Play,' 16; Mullin, *Sixpence at Whist*, 152.

'bankrupt gamesters.' In a report of June 1782, the club was identified as Brooks's and the recipient as a brewer, who had lost 'seventy thousand pounds, all his drays, dray-horses, coppers, casks, and waste butts, with his iron hoops, which were the last stake.' Charles James Fox, as keeper of the faro bank, was said then to have proposed to settle an annuity of £500 on the unlucky brewer 'to be paid out of the general fund,' and to be established in future for any member 'who should be *completely ruined* in that house,' provided they were never again admitted to play, a motion that the membership approved unanimously. The story was repeated *mostly* verbatim in April 1795, this time of an 'Hon. Mr. L—,' clearly *not* a brewer, who had lost the £70,000, again 'with his carriage, horses, &c, which was his last stake.' Fox again comes to the rescue, but with a much less generous pension of only £50 a year.[31] Such slippage of decimal points occurs elsewhere in the gaming anecdotes that were a staple of newspaper coverage. In March 1787, for example, the *Times* corrected an error, relating that Lord Duncannon lost £5,000 at faro one evening, and not £50,000 as it had previously reported.[32]

Crump cites three cases of quite large losses: Fox, whose losses by the end of his gaming career totalled £140,000; Hon. John Damer, who lost £60,000 and ended a suicide; and finally Lord Foley, who lost £20,000. She somehow omits to mention the Duchess of Devonshire, but we might nevertheless join her in wondering 'if it was not the comparative rarity of these events and the enormity of the sums involved' that so impressed contemporaries.[33] Even contemporaries were known to suspect hyperbolic accounts of wins and losses, as a writer in the *Gentleman's Magazine* did in 1763:

> You asked me whether it could be doubted there was such a thing as luck, when every company produced some glaring instance of a lucky man, who, without superior abilities, or unfair practices, was a perpetual winner; and, on the contrary, some example of another, who, though extremely skilful, was always a losing gamester.... the facts themselves are far from being so true as is usually imagined. Men of veracity, in every other particular, make no scruple to magnify their losses, and diminish their winnings.... every looker on at the gaming table will witness for me, that the losers generally declare they have lost more than the winners can or will account for.[34]

An item that appeared in newspapers in September 1781 recounted the annual expenses 'of a very well-known nobleman' with an estate worth £27,000 a year, who spent a third of this income on his stable, garden, kennel, and park,

[31] *Lloyd's Evening Post*, 1989 (2 April 1770); *Edinburgh Magazine*, 56 (20 June 1782), 334; *Town and Country Magazine*, 27 (April 1795), 133.
[32] Quoted in Andrew, *Aristocratic Vice*, 293 n. 5.   [33] Crump, 'Perils of Play,' 16.
[34] *Gentleman's Magazine*, 33 (November 1763), 534.

while another £5,800 was expended on his library and art collection. Gaming losses amounted to a scant £612.[35] When one witness before a parliamentary committee was asked in May 1844 if he had heard of anyone losing more than they could afford to pay at William Crockford's St James's Club, he replied, 'I have heard of their losing larger sums than they liked to pay, not more than they could pay.'[36]

Often the writers most likely to discuss gaming were those who understood it the least. Critics of gaming were frequently ignorant of its operations, thinking, for example, that hazard was played with cards, and in at least one case proudly admitting ignorance of the rules of faro. It is no surprise, then, that as Justine Crump points out, the authors of this admonitory literature:

> almost never condescend to describe the hum-drum reality of play as it must have happened in households, clubs, coffeehouses or taverns. The texts provide little information about who gambled—high or low, male or female—and hardly ever specify the stakes, if any, for which these gamesters might have played. The texts seldom mention which games were being played....

Clearly, then, Crump asserts, we cannot (for example) assume from these jeremiads that gaming was a dangerous social pathology in Georgian Britain.[37] In the case of gaming, it is particularly crucial to read printed sources against the grain and in light of what can be garnered from archival sources. It will often seem that the existence of commercial gaming in the eighteenth-century metropolis is extrapolated from these sources rather than positively demonstrated. There are a few cases, however, in which the arrangements that underlay gaming operations can be documented. To this end, the contemporary usage 'gaming house' has been avoided as much as possible, in recognition of circumstances that contemporary observers, and local authorities especially, did not comprehend either completely or consistently. Instead, terminology referring to gaming venues, operations, or concerns has been preferred. A gaming *venue* might consist of a public accommodation such as a tavern or a coffeehouse (terms that contemporaries often applied interchangeably), or a private subscription club (which could operate within a public accommodation, especially earlier in the period), or even a private residence. All of these were multipurpose facilities where a number of activities could be carried on, often simultaneously, including commercial gaming *operations*. These might be hazard tables supervised by staff known as 'box-keepers,' or tables for banking games like faro or E.O., in which the proprietor

---

[35]   *Caledonian Mercury*, 9371 (19 September 1781); the item also appeared in the *London Courant* (15 September 1781).

[36]   House of Commons, *Report from the Select Committee on Gaming* (London: House of Commons, 1844; facs. edn, Shannon: Irish University Press, 1968), 184.

[37]   Crump, 'Perils of Play', 4.

of the venue might be a partner. Gaming *concerns* might keep gaming operations in multiple venues, either simultaneously or on an itinerant basis.

Mains and Chances

Chapter 1 will address the reception of probability, and its application to gaming, in Restoration and Augustan England, while Chapter 2 will explore the ways that continental gaming established patterns that metropolitan gaming in England later followed. Chapter 3 will treat the gaming archetype of the 'sharper' as a construct of literary, journalistic, and legal fiction, and as an agent that shaped responses to commercial gaming. Chapter 4 will examine the trajectory of the Royal Oak Lottery, a game of chance played against a 'bank' that was promoted under a succession of royal patents, leading to the development of lotteries as a specific legal category of gaming under at least partial protection of the state. The emergence of commercial gaming venues in the metropolis will be treated in Chapter 5, while the relationship between courtly and commercial gaming in Augustan Westminster and elsewhere, and the real and perceived administrative anomalies that resulted, will be explored in Chapter 6. The efforts of authorities to contain the expansion of commercial gaming in public venues will be the subject of Chapter 7, while Chapter 8 will examine the different responses of gaming operators to aggressive legislative and judicial initiatives against gaming, involving the reconfiguration of public and private space and the introduction of new games grounded in a new faith in probability. For reasons that shall be seen, the emergence of private subscription clubs for gaming merits separate treatment in Chapter 9. The political fallout of renewed attention on elite gaming culture in the aftermath of the American Revolutionary War will be the focus of Chapter 10; Chapter 11 will continue that discussion with reference to commercial gaming operations that went forward in elite metropolitan households. Chapter 12 will address the consequences of increasing official and public awareness of the realities of gaming as a commercial enterprise. The concluding chapter will explore the context and consequences of the Victorian Gaming Act, which outlawed any and all games of chance played for money either in public or private for over a century, until the licensing of gaming venues became a reality from 1960.

On the Money

As the culture of gaming was tightly bound up with the culture of money, the complicated question of present-day equivalents of early modern sums inevitably arises. The most satisfactory results stem from the recognition that early modern currency took the form of bullion, and its units of exchange were often contiguous with units of weight. One pound sterling was so called because it was literally one troy pound of silver, consisting of twenty troy ounces denominated as 'shillings.' As research for this project was going forward, one troy ounce of silver generally traded for about £15, $20, or €18. The pound sterling in this period was a money of account, there being no unit of circulating 'hard' currency that equated to it. Gold coinage took the form of the guinea, a coin valued at twenty-one shillings, and the denomination customarily staked at the upmarket 'gold tables' at select gaming venues. Well into the twentieth century, the 'better sort' of artisans or retailers who catered to the 'carriage trade' presented their invoices, and were paid, in guineas, even after the guinea coin was supplanted by the gold 'sovereign,' valued at twenty shillings, early in the nineteenth century.

Debts of Honour

Scholars, including this one, have long been warned off the topic of gambling, which, in the words of Thomas Kavanagh, 'falls on the wrong side of scholarship's well-policed dividing line between the serious and the frivolous.'[38] For the very same reasons, of course, aspiring scholars have been discouraged from studying the eighteenth century (or, these days, any period at all before the advent of high modernity). I have no regrets at having ignored both warnings, and am all the more grateful for the support I have received. First and foremost, I must thank the Office of the Provost of the University of Montana for its award of sabbatical leave for the academic year 2020–2021, which not only afforded material support for the project, but spared me the ordeal of teaching under pandemic protocols. I also received travel grants from the university's Small Grant Program, and especially from the Faculty Development Fund of the Department of History, administered by my colleague Richard Drake. The University of Montana's Humanities Institute has also supported this project with a research grant awarded under the directorship of Nathaniel Levtow, as well as a Baldridge Subvention Grant under that of Gillian Glaes. Grant support also came in the form of the Huntington Library/British Academy Exchange Fellowship in 2009, a William Andrews Clark Library Fellowship in the summer of 2010, and an Eadington Fellowship at the Center for Gaming Research, housed in the Lied Library of the University of Nevada at Las Vegas, in the spring of 2021; in this last connection, I am particularly grateful for assistance from Peter Michel and Su Kim Chung. My work has benefited from conversations and other exchanges with Leon Jackson, Jessica Richard, Meghan Kobza, James Raven, Lawrence Klein, Gordon Turnbull, James Caudle, David Parrott, Olivier Grussi, Gregory Brown, Michael Mayer, the late

---

[38] Kavanagh, *Dice, Cards, Wheels*, 7.

Robert Oresko, and the late Marilyn Morris, as well as participants in the Eadington Colloquium of the Center for Gaming Research at UNLV, the Lockridge Seminar in my own department, and Jo Guldi, Thomas Kavanagh, Jesse Molesworth, and other participants in a panel at the meeting of the International Society for Eighteenth-Century Studies at the University of California at Los Angeles in 2003. At Oxford University Press, I would like to thank Karen Raith, my acquiring editor, for her interest in and support of the project; Luciana O'Flaherty, who seamlessly took it over; Imogene Haslam, who deftly steered the manuscript through pre-production, and finally OUP's eagle-eyed copy editor Sally Pelling-Deeves. Research and writing at various stages would have been impossible without the aid and hospitality of Daniel and Anne Clowers, Michael Eglin, Raquel Casas, Howard Gaass, Janet Doud, Betty Medeiros, John Camacho, and Mark Foley. I suppose I owe to a microbe, Coronavirus 19, a near complete freedom from distractions and the inability to travel for a year that was perforce devoted to writing.

1
Probability and its Discontents

[I]n Tables, man by faire casting Dice truly made, and in Cardes, by
shuffling & cutting, doth openly dispose the Dice and Cards so, as
whereby a variable event may follow: but it is onely and immediatly
of God that the Dice bee so cast, and the Cards so shuffled and cut, as
that this or that game followeth, except there be cogging and packing.
So that in faire play mans wit is not exercised in disposing the chance,
but in making the best of it being put.

As rector of St Olave's in Southwark, the Elizabethan cleric James Balmford was
more exposed than he would have liked to the gaming culture of the Tudor
metropolis, where, as in the rest of the realm, 'unlawful' games were forbidden to
those dependent on their labour for their living. Common law, however, left the
definition of 'unlawful' recreations to the determination of local magistrates. In
the case of games of chance, no more intrinsically unlawful than other pastimes,
the ground of illegality that Balmford advanced was based on an understanding
of chance episodes as manifestations of divine will. Since the Hebrews of the Old
Testament used lots to determine the will of God in connection to difficult questions, games of chance violated the third commandment as species of taking
God's name in vain.[1] For ordinary mortals, moreover, to apply their intellect to
derive any benefit from the disposition of chance was to tinker with divine providence. Whether or not they concurred with Balmford on the impiety of the critical analysis of chance, any number of contemporaries would have agreed with
him that consistent success at gaming was impossible without deceit.

As conventional as Balmford's position on games of chance was, it also suggests
that probability was not a novelty that sprang fully formed from the thought of
Pascal, Fermat, and Huygens in the middle of the seventeenth century. Ian
Hacking's assertion that an *enhanced* understanding of probability in Europe
emerged 'precisely . . . when theological views of divine foreknowledge were being
reinforced by the amazing success of mechanistic models' should not really surprise us.[2] Indeed, the Jesuit Joseph Sauveur's assertion in 1679 of the advantage of

---

[1] [James Balmford], *A Short and Plaine Dialogue Concerning the Unlawfulnes of Playing at Cards or
Tables* (London: Richard Boile, 1593), 8.
[2] Ian Hacking, *The Emergence of Probability* (2nd edn, Cambridge: Cambridge University Press,
2006), 2–3.

The Gambling Century: Commercial Gaming in Britain from Restoration to Regency. John Eglin, Oxford University Press.
© John Eglin 2023. DOI: 10.1093/oso/9780192888198.003.0002

the banker in the game of basset was cited only a few years later as proof that what passed for chance was actually divine providence.[3] Balmford, though his purpose was admonitory, had reconciled probability and providence, often assumed to be antithetical frames of reference to the early modern mind, much earlier. The limits of probability as applied to games were clear to an Anglican divine fully a century before the earliest probability study was published in English.

Since mathematicians, notably Pascal and Christian Huygens, began to study probability in the mid-seventeenth century, about the time that Louis XIV began to hold regular *appartements* for gaming at his court, and about the time that the newly restored Charles II resurrected the office of the Groom Porter at his re-established court, the history of probability has been linked with the history of gambling. There is an element of truth in the origin myth of mathematical probability, which hangs on the improbable encounter of the austere Jansenist Blaise Pascal with Antoine Gombaud, Chevalier de Méré.[4] Although stereotyped as a gaming enthusiast, no doubt on account of his title, Méré was in fact a writer and amateur mathematician who moved in the same intellectual circles as Pascal and Pierre de Fermat. When in 1654 Méré proposed a solution to the 'problem of the points,' an old mathematical conundrum concerning the equitable division of stakes after an interrupted game of dice between two players, Pascal wrote to Fermat, laying the foundation for the study of mathematical probability. Three years later appeared Christian Huygens' *De Ludo Aleae* ('of games of chance'), which became 'the standard text on probability theory for the next fifty years,'[5] and consequently the authority on which English interest in and investigation of probability was based.

It was not really the patronage of courtly gamblers, then, that provided the initial impetus for the study of probability, not least because gambling courtiers were not supposed to be interested in the money that they won or lost, as their gambling was a performance of the emotional distance from the vulgar preoccupations of emerging commercial interests. It has been suggested instead that the emergence of legal agreements known as 'aleatory contracts,' designed to enable lending at interest, generated a need to quantify the risk entailed in a loan, a necessary prerequisite to evade prohibitions on usury.[6] Games of chance, especially those involving dice, interested early writers on probability primarily as a source of simple and readily accessible examples suitable for the demonstration of

---

[3] Jean Frain du Tremblay, *Conversations Morales sur les Jeux et les Divertissements* (Paris: André Pralard, 1685), 77.

[4] Kavanagh, *Shadows of Chance*, 10–11; *Dice, Cards, Wheels*, 53.

[5] Anders Hald, *A History of Probability and Statistics and Their Applications before 1750* (New York: John Wiley and Sons, 1990), 42, 65.

[6] Gerd Gigerenzer, Zeno Swijtink, Theodore Porter, Lorraine Daston, John Beatty, and Lorenz Krüger, *The Empire of Chance: How Probability Changed Science and Everyday Life* (Cambridge: Cambridge University Press, 1989), 3–4.

complex mathematical principles with wider applications.[7] It was these utilitarian applications rather than any other preoccupation that drove probability writers to discuss games. John Arbuthnot, for example, hoped that none of the readers of his translation of Huygens would 'imagine I had so mean a Design in this, as to teach the Art of Playing at Dice.' Rather,

> the Calculation of the Quantity of Probability might be improved to a very useful and pleasant Speculation, and applied to a great many Events which are accidental, besides those of Games .... [A]ll the Politicks in the World are nothing else but a kind of Analysis of the Quantity of Probability in casual Events.[8]

What Ian Hacking understands as the fairly sudden 'emergence of probability' in the latter half of the seventeenth century has to be understood against a more basic reorientation to an entirely new epistemology of quantification. Before the middle of that century, contemporaries marked a distinction between 'probability' and 'chance,' the second expressed as a simple mathematical ratio and the first as an entirely non-numerical idea. By 1700, however, this distinction had been collapsed, so that the two terms were synonymous, as they have been since. Hacking locates the 'tipping point' at the publication of *De Ludo Aleae* in 1657. Responding to critics who pointed out concepts of numerical probability identified in ancient and medieval sources, he contends that while earlier writers may have noticed mathematical probability, it was not until after Huygens that there was a *use* for it, 'a use that spans morals, politics, economics and social affairs, and which engenders a new era of conjecturing on the one hand and a new mode of representing reality on the other.'[9] The new science of probability held the promise of a brave new world of numbers, making the compilation of statistics a worthwhile pursuit, and introducing the possibility of a variety of new products, especially various forms of insurance, which were at their basic level wagers on the likelihood of shipwreck, or fire, or untimely death. The application of probability to policy had already been dubbed 'political arithmetic' in the English jurist William Petty's tract by that title in 1690.[10]

Mathematicians who wrote on probability were not only uninterested in games of chance per se, they were actually sceptical that their findings would be useful to gamblers, however interested gamblers might be in the applications of mathematical probability to games of chance. John Arbuthnot, the 'Dr Arbuthnot' of Alexander Pope's famous epistle, attempted to manage their expectations in his

---

[7] Lorraine Daston, *Classical Probability in the Enlightenment* (Princeton: Princeton University Press, 1988), 114.

[8] [Christian Huygens], *Of the Laws of Chance, or, A Method of Calculating the Hazards of Game*, tr. attributed John Arbuthnot (London: Benjamin Motte for Randall Taylor, 1692).

[9] Quoted in Hald, *History of Probability*, 30–2.

[10] William Petty, *Political Arithmetick* (London: Robert Clavel and Henry Mortlock, 1690).

preface to his translation of Huygens. A gambler in the heat of play would not be able 'to calculate on which side there are most Chances' with any precision, and might only 'part with his Money with more content' after choosing 'the safer side' and losing anyway.[11] David Bellhouse was certainly correct to observe that 'the calculus of probability had very little impact on gambling practice until well into the eighteenth century,'[12] depending on how we define 'impact' and 'practice.' A series of questions might be posed here. What those concerned in gambling know about probability, when did they know it, and how did they use their knowledge? The interplay among the writings of mathematicians, the assumptions of gaming enthusiasts, and the activity of gaming entrepreneurs bears further exploration. Finally, if it was not the case that interest in games of chance spurred interest in and investigation of probability, was it understanding of probability that drove the proliferation of gaming as a commercial enterprise?

The Brave New World of Numbers

Even today, it is one thing to understand probability, but it is another thing to have faith in it. One sociological study of roulette players cited by Thomas Kavanagh noted that neither they nor casino management seemed to accept that the movements of the wheel were completely random. Players constructed complex 'systems' designed to predict outcomes, while management would have progressively senior staff take over a wheel that seemed to be running against the house. When confronted with the irrationality of this proceeding, one house manager readily acquiesced, offering only, 'we have to do *something*.'[13] A popular historian of and expert on card games, who presumably *does* understand probability, has quite seriously insisted in successive editions of his books that it is not merely a perception that certain decks of cards run for or against particular players or players collectively, but a well-established fact, and that players might legitimately demand that a deck be replaced on this account.[14] More than one scholar has pointed out the challenge that the law of large numbers poses to the individual gambler, what Kavanagh calls 'the challenge of the moment': it is of no use to gamblers to know what will *ultimately* occur if they cannot know what will happen *next*.[15] The only bet worth placing, in short, is that the law of large numbers

---

[11] [Huygens], *Laws of Chance*, tr. attributed Arbuthnot, n.p.

[12] David Bellhouse, 'The Role of Roguery in the History of Probability,' *Statistical Science*, 8 (November 1993), 417.

[13] Quoted in Kavanagh, *Dice, Cards, Wheels*, 9.

[14] David Parlett, *A-Z of Card Games* (Oxford: Oxford University Press, 1992), xi: 'It is a fact (not a superstition) that cards will sometimes run unfavourably to you for a long time. A traditional club rule is that anyone may call for new cards at any time in the session, but—also by tradition—at their own expense.'

[15] Kavanagh, *Shadows of Chance*, 15–17.

will prevail in the end, and only the 'house', its omnipresence embodied in the dealer and croupier, can place this bet, against the eternally shifting and changing assembly of punters.[16] Consequently, even a small mathematical advantage, such as that afforded by the 'house numbers' in roulette, can translate to gigantic profits. Essentially, the house wins because the house, alone among the individuals at the table, is not gambling, because to gamble, almost by definition, is to bet against the law of averages. 'This is the hell of all gamesters', a newspaper writer put it in 1757, by which time the 'house advantage' was more widely understood, especially by gaming operators; 'when they are at play, the board eats up all the money: for if there is £500 lost, there is never but £100 won.'[17]

It was nearly a century after the publication of Huygens' tract before the gaming entrepreneurs who were the progenitors of the 'house' fully absorbed the lesson of the law of large numbers and applied these to the commercial gaming that had begun to emerge at the same time as mathematical probability. As Bellhouse demonstrates, however, basic notions of probability were familiar outside of the small circle of mathematicians even before the earliest tracts appeared.[18] Dice players in baroque Europe did not need Christian Huygens to tell them that 'seven' was more likely to be rolled on two dice than any other number, as the thirty-six permutations of a throw of two dice had been tabulated as early as the tenth century.[19] It was just as well known, before Charles Cotton publicized it in 1674, that inexperienced players could be manoeuvred into accepting unfavourable odds. And it was in tracts devoted to recreational games, including games of chance, that English readers were first acquainted with probability. Huygens' work did not appear in English until Arbuthnot's translation of 1692, by which time Charles Cotton's *Compleat Gamester* (incorporating *Leathermore's Advice on Gaming*) had appeared in four editions. The crudity of seventeenth-century gamblers' ideas of probability is revealed in Cotton's remark that 'seven is *reputed* the best and easiest Main to be flung' on two dice, and even more so in his apparent belief that the odds of throwing four were equal to those of throwing five. While he corrected the common misconception of hazard players that the chances of throwing six, seven, or eight were equal, Cotton still accepted the convention of three permutations of each throw (when there are six permutations of seven, and only five of six or eight), arguing instead that the advantage of seven stemmed from the relative difficulty of throwing doubles, in this case two 'treys' or two 'quaters',[20] a contention preserved in contemporary casino parlance, in which doubles are 'hard' throws, while the other permutations of even numbers are 'easy'.

---

[16] Roger Caillois, *Man, Play and Games*, tr. Meyer Barash (Urbana: University of Illinois Press, 2001), 5, 117.

[17] *Read's Weekly Journal*, 3935 (16 July 1757).   [18] Bellhouse, 'Role of Roguery', 413–15.

[19] Gigerenzer et al., *Empire of Chance*, 2.

[20] Charles Cotton, *The Compleat Gamester* (London: R. Cutler and Henry Brome, 1674), 171–2; italics mine.

It is safe to say that while those concerned in gaming might have possessed basic notions of probability, their ideas remained rudimentary because their knowledge of even basic arithmetic was on par with that of a ten-year-old of the twenty-first century. Any more sophisticated understanding of probability was hampered by ignorance of basic arithmetic even among elites. The Restoration biographer John Aubrey 'knew young men of high birth who at the age of eighteen could not add up pounds, shillings, and pence,' and speculated that 'a Barreboy at an Alehouse will reckon better and readier than a Master of Arts in the University.'[21] Indeed, Samuel Pepys, holder of a Cambridge MA, did not master multiplication until he was nearly thirty, learning it under the tutelage of an ordinary merchant seaman. When John Arbuthnot and Abraham de Moivre wrote, it had only been relatively recently that merchants and retailers had begun keeping their accounts in Arabic numerals, in ink, and on paper. Quantification in the abstract, to say nothing of calculation, was fairly new. Until the later seventeenth century, even a simple operation like counting was sensory and organic, often employing visual and aural devices.[22] It did not help gamblers that when probability writers addressed games of chance, they did not do so in a systematic or accessible way. Arbuthnot's adaptation of Huygens obliged its readers to wade through thirty-odd pages of mathematical formulae unconnected to any discernible game before discussing very basic problems, like the odds of throwing twelve on two dice, and a reader was halfway through the tract before the odds of throwing the various mains at hazard were treated. It was still asserted as late as 1714 that calculations of 'the Proportions of Hazards in Gaming' were 'above the best Mathematicians to perform,' and certainly above the capacity of one sharper who 'not finding out the Art of at how many times one may undertake to throw 6 with one Dye,' condemned Huygens 'for as great a Blockhead as he was a Fool.'[23]

Real comprehension and application of the law of large numbers (not so named until well into the nineteenth century) depends on two other habits of mind that really did not take hold until the approach of high modernity. Understanding of aggregates and averages depends on the ability to quantify in the abstract, just as the concept of infinite series of chance episodes depends on a linear idea of time, as opposed to the cyclical notion that prevailed before the availability of mechanical clocks, and later pocket watches. It was not until the middle of the seventeenth century, according to Ian Hacking, that Europeans, even those who studied gambling from a mathematical perspective, showed any awareness at all that what we would recognize as the law of averages might impact the outcome of games of

[21] Quoted in Keith Thomas, 'Numeracy in Early Modern England,' *Transactions of the Royal Historical Society* 37 (1987), 109.

[22] Thomas, 'Numeracy in Early Modern England,' 111–12, 119–21, 128.

[23] Theophilus Lucas, *Memoirs of the Lives, Intrigues, and Comical Adventures of the Most Famous Gamesters* (London: Jonas Brown, 1714), reprinted in Cyril Hartmann (ed.), *Games and Gamesters of the Restoration* (London: Routledge, 1930), 203, 268.

chance, as even the concept of an 'average' was alien to the early modern mind.[24] Thus, for more than a century after Pascal and Huygens published their findings, operational understanding of probability remained elusive. Financiers, under-writers, and others involved in the calculation of risk struggled for decades to set returns and premiums that were both attractive to purchasers and profitable to vendors. For annuity brokers, maritime insurers, and gaming entrepreneurs, as one consortium of probability scholars has put it, '[t]he practice of risk was not simply astatistical; it was positively antistatistical in its focus on the individual case to the neglect of large numbers and the long term.' These 'practitioners of risk' conceived time to be as productive of increasing *uncertainty* as it approached eternity as it was of *certainty* for probability writers. Their embrace of probability would entail an entirely 'new conception of the world,' which is why they only accepted it gradually, if at all.[25] Consequently, it was well over a century after the earliest tracts appeared that probability was applied with any real acumen in any sort of enterprise, whether finance or public policy or, for that matter, gaming.

Banking on Infinity

The study of probability, and efforts to make it accessible to a reading public, took a great leap forward with the enunciation of what came to be known as the law of large numbers, of which the Swiss mathematician Jacob Bernoulli published the first proof in 1713. This principal stipulates that as the number of any series of chance events approaches infinity, the aggregate results will increasingly cleave to the mean of probability, meaning, for example, that an infinite succession of coin tosses will ultimately produce an exactly even ratio of 'heads' to 'tails,' or that 'seven,' already known to appear more frequently than any other number on two dice, would be rolled more and more closely to exactly one sixth of the time. Abraham de Moivre, the Huguenot émigré mathematician who popularized Bernoulli in England, drew out implications of Bernoulli's 'golden theorem' for the commercial gaming establishments that had already become conspicuous in metropolitan London. In a game of chance in which odds were evenly divided between two players, for example, neither player would ultimately win more than they individually staked. If, however, one player had a statistical advantage of as little as 2 to 3 per cent over the other, that player would ultimately win nearly all the money that was wagered, 'which will seem almost incredible, given the small-ness of the Odds.'[26] We might for a present-day example imagine ten robotic roulette players, each with one hundred pounds, or dollars, or euros, or any other

---

[24] Hacking, *Emergence of Probability*, 92.   [25] Gigerenzer et al., *Empire of Chance*, 24.
[26] Abraham de Moivre, *The Doctrine of Chances, or, A Method of Calculating the Probability of Events in Play* (London: W. Pearson, 1718), vi.

currency. If five robots are programmed to stake ten of any currency on red, and the other five to stake the same on black for every spin of the wheel, the bank will 'break even' for eighteen of nineteen spins. On the nineteenth spin, however, one of the green 'house numbers' will come up, allowing the bank to sweep the board of all the money staked. If we assume that an average casino roulette wheel will spin approximately one hundred times every three hours, in that amount of time, the bank will have won half of the funds the robots have available to stake, and in another three hours, it will have won all of it.

There were consequently two sets of implications of the application of probability to gaming, one for punters and the other for entrepreneurs. If the correspondence of Pascal and Méré was not what it appeared, the later and less well-known exchange between Joseph Sauveur and the Marquis de Dangeau was closer to the mark, and an important part of the story that is worth examining. It was the Duc de Saint-Simon who asserted that Louis XIV encouraged nobles to gamble as a means of controlling them, following the example of Cardinal Mazarin, who introduced high stakes gambling at the French court as a means of subverting the power of a nobility he hated. Saint-Simon regarded deep play at Versailles as socially disruptive, since *arrivistes* who played to win brought to courtly gaming tables those qualified only by their disposable cash. Saint-Simon's bête noire in this regard was Phillipe de Courcillon, a Huguenot by birth, who held the title Marquis de Dangeau in spite of what Saint-Simon considered an abbreviated lineage. Dangeau was a very successful gamester, winning, according to Madame de Sevigné, half a million livres over the course of six weeks. Even Saint-Simon admitted that Dangeau always played fairly, and was never accused or even suspected of cheating, having mastered the new science of probability.[27] Fontenelle, in his eulogy of the Jesuit mathematician Joseph Sauveur, related that Dangeau had asked Sauveur in 1678 to calculate the advantage to the banker at basset, then a game newly come into fashion at court, having been introduced by the Venetian envoy Giustiniani. Whatever their provenance, the results were published in the *Journal des Savants* the following February. Although the Abbé's finding that a basset banker indeed enjoyed a significant advantage over his punters was asserted rather than proven mathematically, Sauveur's conclusions apparently caused enough of a stir that he was summoned to present them before the King and Queen themselves.[28]

Pierre Rémond de Montmort supplied Sauveur's missing proof of the banker's advantage in basset in his *Essai d'Analyse sur les Jeux de Hazard* of 1708. Montmort, like de Moivre subsequently, independently arrived at many of Jacob Bernoulli's results. Most significantly, Montmort was the first probability writer to address games of chance specifically, and the first to address games of cards.

[27] Kavanagh, *Shadows of Chance*, 52–4.   [28] Hald, *History of Probability*, 192, 240.

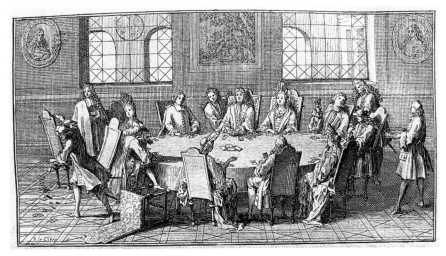

Figure 1.1 A game of basset, or possibly faro, from Pierre Rémond de Montmort, *Essai d'Analyse sur les Jeux de Hasard*, 1708. Trustees of the British Museum. Montmort was the first probability writer to address games of chance directly.

He advised readers that where the caster was at a disadvantage in games of dice, at card games like faro, basset, and lansquenet, all played against a bank, the dealer was at an advantage:

> It is almost as if those who invented these games never had any intention of making them entirely equal, or, that which appears more likely, they did not understand the nature of chance enough to distribute it equally. In most cases, the conditions are so unequal for the players that one is justified in thinking that one can neither win fairly, nor lose without being duped.[29]

Montmort, reportedly at the behest of several friends who had pressed him for some time, computed the advantage of the banker in faro (pharaon), which in France, at least, had overtaken basset in popularity (figure 1.1). He described two advantages of the banker, who won half of any stakes on a card that appeared twice in the same 'pull,' and who paid nothing on the last card dealt, which ordinarily would have won for punters. After over twenty pages of dense mathematical formulae, Montmort acknowledged the impatience of readers who might have

---

[29] Pierre Rémond de Montmort, *Essai d'Analyse sur les Jeux de Hazard* (Paris: Jacques Quillau, 1708), v, xii: 'Il est à croire que ceux qui ont inventé ces Jeux n'ont point prétendu les rendre entièrement égaux; ou, ce qui paroît plus vrai-semblable, qu'il n'en point assez connu la nature pour en bien distribuer les hazards. Dans la plupart les conditions sont si inégales pour les Joueurs, qu'on seroit bien fondé à soutenir qu'on ne peut y gagner avec justice, comme sans doute on ne peut y perdre sans être duppe.' Translations are my own.

noticed that he had not yet mentioned the opportunity of faro punters to defer collecting winning stakes to win three times or even seven times their initial bet, in making what was variously known as a *paroli* or *alpieu* by turning up the corner of the winning card. All these manoeuvres amounted to was sparing the banker, who already enjoyed a significant statistical advantage over punters, from having to pay winning stakes. Their provision was also occasion for punters to cheat, by making a surreptitious *alpieu de campagne* after a 'pull,' putting it in the banker's interest to engage a vigilant croupier. Like Edmund Hoyle later, Montmort gave players specific strategic advice to put them at the least disadvantage possible, such as staking less as the deck was depleted, and, by implication, to avoid *parolis* or *alpieus* altogether.[30]

Curiously, Montmort's treatise was never translated into English and published across the Channel, although Montmort had travelled there and was a fellow of the Royal Society. Nevertheless, English writers on games quickly followed his lead. The 1709 edition of Cotton's *Compleat Gamester* appended an account of basset, asserting that it was the first such description to appear in English of this 'French Game.' Here it was pointed out that even if no punter ever 'cocked' a card, the banker still had 'a greater prospect of gaining, than those that play,' so that 'the dimmest eye may easily see, without a pair of spectacles,' to say nothing of long series of equations, 'how much and considerable the design of this court game is in the favour of the *Talliere* [banker].'[31] Although mathematical demonstrations were difficult to follow even when 'adapted to the meanest capacity,' the explanatory literature on probability and gaming made the advantage to the 'house' in banking games like basset or faro clear to their readership.

Thinking Magically, Mathematically

By the second decade of the eighteenth century, popular treatises on probability as applied to games of chance began to appear in multiple printings and editions. Although de Moivre, a distinguished mathematician who like Montmort was a fellow of the Royal Society, was no more interested in gaming than Christian Huygens or John Arbuthnot, his *Doctrine of Chances* was widely known and circulated in gaming circles and, despite the inclusion of admonitory material in later editions, served to promote the idea that individual punters could master probability and use it to their advantage. Like Montmort, he dedicated discussions to basset and faro (pharaon), refraining as well from discussing the *paroli* or *alpieu,* or even acknowledging them. De Moivre also treated hazard, which Montmort had mentioned, but not discussed, out of a belief that it was unknown

---

[30] Montmort, *Essai d'Analyse*, 4, 27–9.
[31] Charles Cotton, *The Compleat Gamester* (London: Charles Brome, 1709), 183.

outside of England. The new and unprecedented analysis of hazard alone may have propelled the popularity of de Moivre's work. Writing of the several months he spent in England in 1737 and 1738, the Abbé Le Blanc allowed that while 'the great gamesters of this country... are not usually great geometricians' themselves, they had great regard for the study of probability, knowing 'the best of any men what are the mathematical principals of gaming,' and making recourse to expert opinion, no less a figure than de Moivre himself holding court at Slaughter's coffeehouse in St Martin's Lane for the purpose. Furthermore,

> Those who are gamesters by profession have tables ready calculated of all the different chances for laying or taking odds, and they who have not learned them by heart, carry them in their pockets. These tables are made for almost all games of hazard, which admit of infinite variety.[32]

De Moivre included diagrams like these for basset, faro, and hazard in his first edition, which was published to great fanfare, subscribers to his 'Book of Chances' being advised of the availability of their copies at Slaughter's in April 1718. Consequently, in the decades after the appearance of *The Doctrine of Chances*, de Moivre became a by-word for the application of mathematical probability to games of chance. The untimely deaths of both Montmort and Jacob Bernoulli left the field clear for him.[33]

De Moivre, however, was no more accessible to lay audiences than earlier probability writers had been. His tract careened chaotically from topic to topic, abruptly switching from dice to cards, whist to hazard, and back again. Moreover, de Moivre did not foreground games of chance in any way. His first edition of 1718 posed problems in probability involving dice and cards generally, computing the chances of four aces being dealt into a hand of eighteen cards, or of rolling particular numbers on two dice, which could then be applied to particular games; this was the pattern that Edmund Hoyle later adopted in addressing probability explicitly in 1754. Specific games that de Moivre addressed included sociable games like whist, quadrille, and picquet, generally played in private households for small stakes. Particular games of chance (basset, faro, and hazard) were also treated, but these discussions were not indexed in his table of contents. Consequently, '[t]he reception of de Moivre's work has been a puzzle to scholars,' Jesse Molesworth has pointed out, noting that the tract was cited both in Ephraim Chamber's *Cyclopedia* and in the *Britannica*, although 'it was remarkably slow to inspire extensions and applications.... Because de Moivre's work is exceptionally

---

[32] Jean-Bernard Le Blanc, *Letters on the English and French Nations*, 2 vols (London: J. Brindley, R. Franklin, C. Davis, and J. Hodges, 1747), 2. 307–9.

[33] De Moivre, *Doctrine of Chances* (1718), 38, 44, 174–5; *Post Man*, 16,452 (29 March 1718); Hald, *History of Probability*, 195.

dense, mastering it entirely would have tested even the most erudite of minds.'[34] Nevertheless, whatever its author's intention, and however opaque his analysis was to his readers, the tract was received as a handbook for professional gamblers. One writer advised losing gamesters in 1727 to 'study the Humour and Complexion of their Fortune' rather than 'amusing themselves by computing the Odds and Chances of the Game according to the Mathematick Laws of *Du Moivre*.' A less sympathetic observer two decades later wrote of 'that sordid animal the gamester' for whom '[f]ortune is his goddess, de Moivre his guide.' '[B]efore the Doctrine of Chances was laid open by *Demoivre*,' asserted one writer in 1768, gamblers 'who, by understanding where the Odds lay, were more fortunate in their Play than those who did not, were looked upon as Sharpers.'[35]

In his preface to the second edition of his work, de Moivre himself acknowledged that '[t]here are many People in the World who are prepossessed with an Opinion, that the Doctrine of Chances has a Tendency to promote Play.'[36] Like Edmund Hoyle later, writers on games were concerned with strategy, and tended to assume that readers were already familiar with polite games like ombre and quadrille. Their treatment of games of chance, however, reflected more of a concern to dissuade readers from playing these games than an effort to describe them accurately. It was possibly not until the *New Hoyle* of Charles Pigott, an experienced gambler, appeared in 1795 that a more or less accurate description of faro, or any other game of chance, was available.[37] In the same way that probability tracts treated games of chance peripherally, treatises on games initially avoided games of chance. As both probability writers and writers on games responded to market pressure to address games of chance explicitly, there was complementary pressure to deliver moral judgements about them. The focus on games of chance purely as exempla meant that writers on probability like de Moivre initially refrained from value judgements about gambling. Justine Crump points out that tracts that described rules of games and outlined gaming strategies, more often than not with reference to probability, had a far wider circulation than purely admonitory literature. For example, Hoyle's tract on whist appeared in twenty editions between 1742 and 1807; Charles Cotton appeared in six editions between 1674 and 1726; Richard Seymour appeared in five editions between 1719 and 1732. Such descriptions of game rules were 'cheap and prolific.' Even de Moivre's tract on probability, which was not exactly light reading, appeared in three editions in the eighteenth century. By marked contrast, most of the purely admonitory critiques of gaming that Crump discusses were only published in single

---

[34] Molesworth, *Chance and the Eighteenth-Century Novel*, 66.
[35] *London Journal*, 409 (3 June 1727); *London Magazine*, 18 (December 1749), 587; *Public Advertiser*, 10,363 (15 January 1768).
[36] Abraham de Moivre, *The Doctrine of Chances: or, A Method of Calculating the Probabilities of Events in Play* (2nd edn, London: Henry Woodfall, 1738), n.p.
[37] Charles Pigott, *New Hoyle, or the General Repository of Games* (London: James Ridgeway, 1795).

editions, with a typical run of four hundred to six hundred copies.[38] Importantly, however, tracts on games from Charles Cotton onward were uniformly critical of games of chance, a refrain taken up in later editions of probability tracts, particularly from the 1730s onward. Writers on games observed a distinction between games of chance and sociable games involving a degree of skill, which were considered innocent pastimes even when they were played for stakes. Opprobrium was reserved for games of pure chance, much of which took the form of extensive descriptions of cheating, of lapses in civility and decorum that this class of gaming seemed to occasion, and of the public nuisances that gaming establishments constituted. Treatments of cheating in gaming tracts tended to focus on 'private play' between individuals, creating an avenue of defence for commercial operators who subsequently asserted that their personnel assiduously excluded 'sharpers' who employed loaded or irregular dice, and took other measures, such as the employment of real or putative agents of the Groom Porter, to ensure that play on their premises was 'on the square.'

Richard Seymour's publication history is interesting in this regard. Initially, in 1718, he wrote only of picquet, ombre, and chess as the games most often played at court and in polite company.[39] In his 1732 edition, however, he included a censorious treatment of faro and basset, as well as a tract on probability by Giovanni Rizzetti, *The Knowledge of Play,* that featured a simple redaction of Bernoulli's law of large numbers, using the example of the drawing from an equal number of black and white ballots. This last tract does not appear in the *Compleat Gamester* of 1739, but treatments of basset and faro were included, as well as Cotton's account of hazard.[40] In 1738, new editions of de Moivre and of Arbuthnot's translation of Huygens appeared with chapters devoted to hazard, faro, basset, and Ace of Hearts, games proscribed as illegal lotteries in the first of the Georgian Gaming Acts passed in 1739. The new iteration of Huygens, for example, appended 'A Demonstration of the Gain of the Banker, In any Circumstance of the Game call'd Pharaon.'[41]

Whether probability writers looked askance at games of chance from inclination or compulsion, those who enabled commercial gaming were no more likely than their clientele to absorb the principles of mathematical probability, as dazzled as such enablers may have been by their mystique. The formula 'logically *x*, but *y*' that the sociologist David Oldman suggests as governing the behaviour of

---

[38] Crump, 'Perils of Play,' 3.

[39] Richard Seymour, *The Court Gamester* (London: Edmund Curll, 1718). Editions also appeared in 1719, 1720, and 1728.

[40] Richard Seymour, *The Court Gamester* (London: J. Wilford, 1732), 2. 1–69; Richard Seymour, *The Compleat Gamester* (London: Edmund Curll and J. Hodges, 1739).

[41] Abraham de Moivre, *The Doctrine of Chances: or, A Method of Calculating the Probabilities of Events in Play* (2nd edn, London: Henry Woodfall, 1738); Huygens, *The Laws of Chance* (4th edn, London: B. Motte and C. Bathurst, 1738), 53–73.

roulette players[42] and operators applied in a different way to gaming entrepreneurs in the long eighteenth century. Even after gaming operators understood their advantage in 'banking' games, they were still reluctant to place too much faith in the law of large numbers. They relied instead on the psychological lure of the larger payoffs that accompanied betting options with longer odds. The baroque iterations of the game variously known as basset, pharaon, pharo or faro, point to this persistent resistance to probability among gaming entrepreneurs. In these games, punters placed bets on the appearance of particular denominations of cards in one of two piles dealt by the banker, each 'pull' a ludic episode akin to a coin toss, with an even chance of an ace, for example, being dealt into the pile that won for the punters, or for the bank. Probability writers from the later seventeenth century onward had postulated that the bank's ability to collect on the first and last cards in faro would ultimately garner most of the stakes on the table even absent betting options with longer odds. Baroque faro, however, encouraged punters to defer collecting a winning stake by making *paroli* or *alpieu*, turning up successive corners of a card for the exponentially smaller chances of a particular denomination of card appearing in the winning pile up to six times in succession for correspondingly multiplied payouts. 'What tempts People so much to play at this Game,' according to one contemporary analysis of the baroque version of the game,

> is the great Benefit which accrues to the *Punter*, upon the coming up of some of the prime Chances. They are dazzled and deluded…with Chances which give them Seven, Fifteen, Thirty-three, or Sixty-seven Times the Value of their Stakes: Not considering how many Hundreds to one there is against them, every Time they attempt it, that they won't succeed; and that by the Laws of Chance they must lose those Sums many Times over, before they can expect to win them once. If Persons were to govern themselves by Reason, that which allures them to hazard their Money at this Game would deter them: I mean, the seeming Greatness of the Advantages, which is a certain Sign of the Difficulty of obtaining them. For no one can suppose, if a *Soissant et le va,* was as easy to obtain as a *Sept et le va,* that the Contriver of the Game (who it is plain has calculated it entirely for the benefit of the Banker) would have made the Value of it so much.[43]

In practice, it seems to have been uncommon for punters to press their luck beyond the second *paroli*, the *sept-et-le-va*. Outside of guides such as Cotton or Seymour, references to *quinze-* or *trente-et-le-va* simply do not appear. There are surprisingly few literary references. In the eclogue 'The Basset Table' from the *Court Poems* of 1716, no one seems to make more than one or two *alpieus*, one of

[42] Quoted in Kavanagh, *Dice, Cards, Wheels*, 10.
[43] Seymour, *The Court Gamester* (1732), 2. 64–5.

the punters lamenting that she has lost three *sept-et-le-vas*.[44] In *Marriage: A Satire* of 1728, Clodia leaves the basset table after failing to win even a single *paroli*.[45] A successful *sept-et-le-va* that won a French nobleman 400 guineas at the Portuguese embassy in Paris was noteworthy enough for the *Daily Courant* to mention in November of 1723.[46] Nevertheless, even if punters never ventured beyond a single *paroli*, the banker's advantage was still augmented considerably.

In dicing games such as hazard and passage (the ancestors of modern 'craps'), the house's profit centre consisted of 'box money,' a fee collected independently of individual punters' wins and losses. In hazard, a set sum was collected from a 'caster' for every three 'mains' (five, six, seven, eight, or nine) thrown on the dice. A tract of 1669 posited a scenario in which twenty punters brought £200 apiece to a hazard table and played three to four hours, every day for a year, after which it was estimated that 'the Box shall have fifteen hundred Pounds of the Money, and that eighteen of the twenty Persons shall be losers.' The author claimed by way of anecdote to 'have seen three persons sit down at twelve penny *In and In*,' a game played with four dice, 'and each draw forty shillings a piece in less than three hours;' of the £6 staked, 'the box hath had three pound, and all the three gamesters have been losers.'[47] De Moivre's second edition related that at a 'gold table,' half a guinea would be collected from a 'caster' who threw three 'mains' in a row, which was estimated to occur every fourteen throws.[48] Robert Hunstone, who ran a gaming operation in his ordinary in Bridges Street, Covent Garden, reported in 1707 an annual income from 'box money' of just over £400, a sum collected 'in such manner but not in so large proportion as is payd at the Groome Porters.'[49] Two decades later, an anonymous tract reported that a typical Covent Garden hazard operation would collect £30 per week in box money, or £1,500 a year; the writer claimed to have seen two hazard players pay seventy-two 'boxes' over the course of approximately nine hours.[50] From the perspective of gaming entrepreneurs, there was one additional advantage in that a hazard table could be operated with a relatively modest initial outlay, as it was not necessary to fund a bank. It is entirely credible, then, that Philip Palfreman, who died aged 100 in December 1768, would leave a fortune of £10,000 acquired, as his obituary asserted, 'by being formerly box-keeper to two noted gaming houses in Covent-garden,' although he was more likely the proprietor of a couple of tables.[51]

---

[44] *Court Poems* (London: J. Roberts, 1716), 3–9.

[45] *Marriage: A Satire* (London: J. Roberts, 1728), 20.

[46] *Daily Courant*, 6898 (29 November 1723).

[47] *Leathermore's Advice Concerning Gaming*, published as *The Nicker Nicked, or the Cheats of Gaming Discovered* (London: n.p., 1669), 8.

[48] De Moivre, *Doctrine of Chances* (2nd edn, 1738), 140.

[49] TNA, Chancery Proceedings. Six Clerks Series. C5/333/18: *Hunstone v. Bradbury*, 1707.

[50] *The Whole Art and Mystery of Modern Gaming Fully Expos'd and Detected* (London: J. Roberts and T. Cox, 1726), 25.

[51] *Gazetteer*, 12,415 (16 December 1768).

Until William Crockford introduced 'French hazard' in the Regency period, hazard was not played against a bank, but one writer, who combined confident mastery of mathematical probability and sophisticated knowledge of gaming operations with admonitory zeal, once again called attention in 1726 to the advantage of the 'setter' over the 'caster' in the game, as Arbuthnot and de Moivre had earlier. The setter's 'edge' was small, of course, on average 1.5 per cent, but thanks to de Moivre it was already common knowledge that in actual practice such a seemingly miniscule disparity could generate significant profit. For this reason, another tract averred, 'there are several Persons that never cast at Hazard,' who avoided the payment of 'box money' into the bargain.[52]

Awareness of probability unaccompanied by any real understanding of it may have led punters into 'magical thinking' about games of chance, so that a mystique of probability emerged before very many contemporaries mastered its applications. Jean de Préchac's treatment of basset testified to this attitude as early as 1679, writing of contemporaries who 'flattered themselves that they could win at basset by the rules of algebra, but experience has shown that these are very uncertain.'[53] The principles of probability, rather than persuading gamblers, as probability writers hoped, that they were more likely to lose than win, may instead have convinced them to rise to 'the challenge of the moment,' and read the law of large numbers to mean that a run of bad luck *must* turn at some point. The conclusions for those in position to keep the bank, however, were very different, and the proliferation of both licit and illicit gaming establishments in the capitals of Europe after the turn of the century suggests that these had been drawn. '[T]he Mathematicians have demonstrated,' a pamphleteer (possibly Daniel Defoe) asserted in 1719,

[t]hat whoever has the least Advantage in Gaming, will win all the Money he plays for (for less than one Farthing Advantage in a Guinea, is enough to win all the Money in the *Bank of England,* if it was infinitely greater) so consequently, he that has the least Odds or Disadvantage must lose all: But instead of discouraging this Vice, and informing the People what is just and right, we see Companies of Men running into it.[54]

Defoe referred to lotteries, but he could just as well have been speaking of the commercial gaming operations that had proliferated in the metropolis over the previous decade or so.

---

[52] *Whole Art and Mystery,* 22.

[53] Jean de Préchac, *La Noble Venitienne, ou La Bassette: Histoire Galante* (Paris: Claude Barbin, 1679), 126: 'Plusieurs personnes s'estoient flattés de gagner à la Bassette par les regles de l'Algebre; Mais l'experience a fait voir qu'elles sont fort incertaines.'

[54] *The Gamester: A Benefit-Ticket for All that are Concern'd in the Lotteries* (London: J. Roberts, 1719), 3.

While probability writers did not take into account the configurations of gaming that emerged in public settings, we might well ask what influence their findings had on entrepreneurs who opened commercial gaming operations. It was perhaps coincidental, especially given the projected revival of state lotteries, that the first judicial initiative specifically targeting commercial gaming establishments in metropolitan London, in response to a directive from Whitehall, followed de Moivre's publication by a matter of only several months, in the same way that the publication of de Moivre's second edition coincided with the first of the Georgian Gaming Acts, the first gaming legislation to cite mathematical probability as a justification for regulating (in this case, prohibiting) games of chance. This statute, however, and those that followed in quick succession, failed to take into account the structure of commercial enterprises that had emerged in replication of continental patterns, and was hostage to fictions that focused attention on the 'sharper,' the professional gambler who supposedly made a livelihood by cheating unwary players. These blind spots are the focus of the next chapters.

2

Court to City

Gaming in Baroque Europe

Early in 1713, John Robinson, Bishop of Bristol and Lord Privy Seal, met Thomas Wentworth, Earl of Strafford and Ambassador to the Hague, in Utrecht to negotiate the terms of Britain's controversial withdrawal from the War of the Spanish Succession. As 17 February was the Queen's birthday, Robinson threw an entertainment for the assembled diplomatic community at Strafford's residence. An estimated four hundred guests attended the 'noble and magnificent' gathering, described deferentially in several paragraphs taking up fully half the text of one newspaper in which it appeared, the same account not failing to note that the festive atmosphere did not prevent the British and Dutch plenipotentiaries from conferring on the preliminaries to negotiations for four hours. There was a masquerade ball followed by a buffet supper, where fish was served as an alternative selection, as it was a Friday. Finally, '[i]n order that every one might take his Diversion according to his Inclination,' there were two rooms furnished with faro and basset tables, where play continued until two in the morning.[1]

Much of gaming culture, then as now, was and is aspirationally upmarket, often cultivating a veneer of elite cosmopolitanism. Commercial gaming was well established in continental Europe, and exhaustively documented in the much more detailed records of a more pervasive police apparatus. In Europe, at least, gaming was part of the shared culture of an international elite. This elite included the diplomatic corps together with wealthy nationals of the states they represented, whom it was part of their brief to entertain. Gaming tables in embassies and other elite households were among the most important milieus, and occasionally the only ones, where diplomats could mingle with the ruling classes of their posting. For wealthy young men on tour, gaming in these settings was the most accessible means of inserting themselves into the select companies of courts and capitals, as one 'grand tour' veteran, tutor to a princely household in Germany, allowed, urging his charges while in Paris to prefer ombre to lansquenet or pharaon, to play only at assemblies, and only with individuals they knew at least by sight.[2]

---

[1] *Evening Post*, 553 (21 February 1713).
[2] Joachim Christoph Nemeitz, *Séjour de Paris* (Leiden: Jean van Abconde, 1727), 201, 204, 207–8.

The Gambling Century: Commercial Gaming in Britain from Restoration to Regency. John Eglin, Oxford University Press.
© John Eglin 2023. DOI: 10.1093/oso/9780192888198.003.0003

Just as gaming tables were an accepted feature of entertainments at embassies, they were a fixture of resorts that drew a multinational clientele, especially in the Holy Roman Empire, where, as Thierry Depaulis points out, a profusion of semi-autonomous territories with absolute rulers presented ample opportunity for gaming entrepreneurs to open venues. By 1738, Bad Schwalbach in Hesse Darmstadt boasted thirty gaming tables, including faro tables from a silver table with a ten schilling limit to a gold table with no limit; in October of 1762, the Prince Bishop of Liège licensed the city of Spa to run an assembly room for gaming.[3] These circumstances particularly applied in France, and especially in Paris, which furnishes an instructive parallel illustrating many of the patterns that commercial gaming followed across the Channel. In England, commercial gaming in the metropolis and its satellite cultures at resorts adopted continental models, which elite tourists and the diplomatic community had observed first-hand.

The Serene Ridotto

The term 'casino' referring to a gaming establishment had its origins in Venice. *Casini* were originally pied-à-terre houses where male patricians met for putatively homosocial gatherings outside of palazzi, their official family residences. Gambling was foremost among the activities that might occur there. By the early seventeenth century, individuals or groups were renting these premises purportedly for convivial gatherings, but possibly for other less licit activities, including gambling. There was fierce competition for the choicest venues. At one such casino that was prosecuted as a gambling den, twenty *patroni* 'kept' the casino, while more plebeian attendants, including a dealer, operated it. Apart from an expectation that visitors would pay 'card money,' there is no evidence of operators receiving a cut of the winnings. Over the succeeding decades, gambling in Venice was transformed from an activity confined to small groups in aristocratic circles 'to a major feature of the social life of the city.' The Venetian patriciate had recognized that the wholesale proscription of gambling had made gaming debts legally unenforceable, so that 'their recovery frequently involved violence or the threat of violence.'[4] Consequently, the government eventually legalized gambling (during Carnival) in venues like the *Ridotto Pubblico* in the Palazzo Dandolo in San Moisé, subsequently the subject of canvases by Canaletto and Pietro Longhi, which opened for Carnival in 1638 and remained in business until 1774.[5] By the eighteenth century, gambling, permitted during the Carnival observed from the

---

[3] Depaulis, 'Material History,' in Zollinger, 50.
[4] Jonathan Walker, 'Gambling and Venetian Noblemen c.1500–1700,' *Past and Present*, 162 (February 1999), 34–7, 40.
[5] Depaulis, 'Material History,' in Zollinger, 45.

Figure 2.1 Joseph Heintz the Younger (attributed), *Gambling at the Ridotto during the Venetian Carnival*. National Trust, Westwood Manor. Venetian elites were silent partners in gaming tables that operated in the Palazzo Dandolo and elsewhere.

feast of the Epiphany through Shrove Tuesday, was a major draw for foreign visitors, and short-term licences were available for gaming operations. The *Ridotto* in the Palazzo Dandolo was arguably the prototype of the modern casino (figure 2.1). It was both larger and more public than the original *casini,* which was crucial:

> if gambling took place in public and permanent institutions, then 'debts of honour' were more likely to be repaid, because possibilities for dishonour increased with the size and coherence of the audience.

The structure of gaming at the *Ridotto* also imposed a mediator in the form of a bank, 'which gave its judgements impassively, impersonally and instantaneously, or at least with minimum delay.' The banking games favoured at the *Ridotto* displaced any locus of aggression between players:

> With a banker in charge, the stakes could rise without the competition becoming personal or aggressive. Games played in *casini* reduced the contact between players, so that socialization took place mainly off the tables – that is, it took place *around* the players rather than *between* the players, who wagered in silence.

The game of choice at the *Ridotto Pubblico* was *bassetta* (basset), at which masked punters wearing the *domino* bet on cards dealt by *barnabotti,* impoverished nobles who resided in the hostel of San Barnabo and were permitted to support themselves as dealers at tables where wealthier nobles held the bank. The *barnabotti* dealt barefaced, their costume the black *vesta,* the Venetian rendition of a noble Roman's toga, their humiliation deepened by this reminder of their nominally noble status. In Venice, gambling was a means for young noblemen to make their way and be introduced and initiated into public life. The *ridotto* and *casino* filled particularly important functions in a republic that lacked a court. The *ridotto* was as important as the *broglio,* the morning and afternoon promenades of the nobility in front of the Ducal Palace; those who did not attend found it difficult to procure advancement into the offices that were the hallmarks of Venetian nobility.

Gambling expanded in step 'with the growing importance of Carnival in the social and economic life of Venice,' taking place in a wide variety of smaller venues, especially coffeehouses, which here as elsewhere in baroque Europe became increasingly prominent. However, 'organized' gambling in *ridotti* and *casini,* 'defined either by insistence on taking a predetermined cut of the stake or by organization under a "company," increasingly dominated the scene.'[6] Alexandre Toussaint Limojon de Saint-Didier, secretary to the French embassy in Venice in the early 1670s, wrote a detailed description of the basset banks at the *Ridotto* in the Palazzo Dandolo, remarking on the silence that prevailed in spite of crowds that made it difficult to pass through the rooms. Limojon also noted, intending *casini,* 'Places...where the *Venetian* Nobility keep an open Bank against all such as are desirous to try their Fortunes at Play,' adding that there were several of these kept year-round. 'The places which they call *Ridotti,*' another French observer, Maximilien Misson, related,

> are properly the Academies of *Basset:* They are open'd at the same time with the Theaters; there are none but Noble-men who cut. They dismiss the Gamesters when they please; and they have so much good Fortune joyn'd to their Privileges, and good Play, that the Bank is almost always Fortunate. There are Ten or Twelve Chambers on a Floor, with Gaming-Tables in all of them.

Limojon's account appeared in English translation in 1699, by which time a translation of Misson had appeared in a second edition. Edward Wright observed of the *Ridotto* that

> Generally he that keeps the Bank is the Winner; and it may be reasonably concluded, without inquiry into the Chances of the Game, that the Odds lie on the

---

⁶ Walker, 'Gambling and Venetian Noblemen,' 28, 52–3, 55–6, 60.

Banker's side; since the Noblemen secure that Privilege to themselves: Tho' 'tis possible for another to keep a Bank by Proxy, for there are noblemen that will do it for you for ten *per Cent* of the Winnings.[7]

Basset was reportedly introduced at the French court in the 1670s by the Venetian ambassador Marcantonio Giustiniani, subsequently Doge of Venice, and quickly came into fashion at Versailles.[8] It was in response to this development that the courtier and gaming enthusiast Philippe de Courcillon, Marquis de Dangeau, asked the Abbé Sauveur, a noted mathematician, to compute the odds in the game. Sauveur's finding of the advantage to the banker was reportedly presented to Louis XIV himself at the King's request before it was published in the *Journal des Savants*.[9] The same year that Sauveur's article appeared also witnessed the publication of Jean de Préchac's *roman-à-clef*, with the requisite key helpfully appended, *La Noble Venitienne, ou La Bassette*, which related by way of metaphor basset's Venetian origins, and testified to its immediate popularity:

There is almost no talk of any gallantry since basset came into fashion, and if two people whisper in each other's ear, it is certainly something to do with basset, and as there are many interested parties, letters are often written recounting what has passed at basset.[10]

A greater testament than any of those happenstances was the recourse of many noble households to faro and basset banks.

Tolerated, but not Permitted

In France, the court culture established under the Grand Monarch became the model for monarchial courts elsewhere in Europe. Courtly gaming as re-established in England after the Restoration was gaming on the French model, where play for high stakes had become an important facet of 'living nobly,' the modes through which a disarmed and domesticated aristocracy distinguished

[7] Alexandre Toussaint Limojon de Saint-Didier, *The City and Republick of Venice*, tr. unknown, 3 vols (London: Charles Brome, 1699), 3. 58–9; Maximilien Misson, *A New Voyage to Italy*, 2 vols (London: R. Bently, M. Wootton, T. Godwin, and S. Manship, 1695), 1. 194; Edward Wright, *Some Observations Made in Travelling through France, Italy, etc., in the Years 1720, 1721, and 1722*, 2 vols (London: T. Ward and E. Wicksteed, 1730), 1. 87.
[8] Limojon, *Venice*, 3. 59; Grussi, *Vie Quotidienne des Joueurs*, 110–1.
[9] [Joseph Sauveur], 'Supputation des avantages du banquier dans le jeu de bassette,' *Journal des Sçavans* 7 (1679): 44–51.
[10] Préchac, *Noble Venitienne*, 126: 'On n'entend Presque point d'aucune galanterie, dépuis que la Bassette est à la mode, & si deux Personnes se parlent à l'oreille, c'est assurement de quelque chose qui a raport à la Bassette, & comme il y a plusieurs personnes interesées, on s'écrit souvent des billets pour se render pour se render conte de ce qui s'est passe à la Bassette.'

itself from upwardly mobile social interlopers, and demonstrated contempt for an increasingly prevalent and invasive culture of money. French nobles pursued gaming at the court of the Sun King and on its periphery both as a means of social advancement and of receiving or recovering royal favour.[11] At Versailles, Louis XIV held *appartements du roi* for three hours, three days a week, just for gaming. Outside of court, however, the lid was ostensibly on, as the King was especially concerned to suppress gaming and other vice in Paris in particular. Even at court, the King had limits. By January 1679, he had stopped playing basset after a reported loss of nearly three and a half million livres. In March of that year, Madame de Montespan (the King's *maîtresse en titre*) lost three million livres in a single night at basset, and kept the banker up until eight the following morning to win it back. After the episode was reported to the King, basset was forbidden at court.[12]

High-stakes gaming, according to one source, was confined to the household of the King's brother, the Duc d'Orléans, at the Palais Royal, where the minimum stake at lansquenet was four louis d'or. Gaming at lansquenet, basset, and pharaon was central enough to courtly culture to migrate to other aristocratic hotels in Paris once the death of Louis XIV temporarily displaced the royal household as a cultural centre of gravity. Gaming in France was illegal according to the strict letter of the law, reinforced by thirty-two edicts issued between 1643 and 1777, 'whose very repetition testified to their futility.'[13] As was subsequently the case in Britain, the onus of regulation or proscription was on particular games. One English observer noted that lansquenet was preferred to the extensively regulated game of basset, which was reportedly forbidden outside of embassies; another anglophone source had basset in France restricted to silver tables kept exclusively by the younger sons of noble families.[14] After 1715, there were eight authorized *maisons de jeux* (gaming houses) where gambling was permitted at *jeux de commerce,* games like picquet or ombre thought to depend more on skill than chance and generally played for lower stakes, one writer estimating that players at ombre stood to win or lose fifteen or twenty *ecus* at most at one sitting.[15] More often than not, however, back rooms in the same establishments housed play at the much more profitable (and illegal) *jeux de hasard,* especially the banking games of basset, pharaon, and lansquenet. In France, edicts against games of chance routinely excepted gaming in private residences, which naturally proved to be a significant

[11] Grussi, Vie Quotidienne des Joueurs, 154–6.

[12] Grussi, *Vie Quotidienne des Joueurs,* 63, 81. One *livre tournois,* a money of account, was approximately equivalent to ten pence in pre-decimal British currency. A gold *louis d'or* was valued at twenty-four livres, making it equivalent to one pound sterling. Sums were also recounted in *ecus,* worth six livres and equivalent to the British 'crown' of five shillings.

[13] Kavanagh, *Shadows of Chance,* 30.

[14] Freundlich, *Le Monde de Jeu,* 27; *A View of Paris, and Places Adjoining* (London: John Nutt, 1701), 35; Lucas, *Lives of the Gamesters,* 271, 274.

[15] Nemeitz, *Séjour de Paris,* 208.

loophole. Gaming in private among families, for example, was explicitly excluded from prohibitions in 1727 and 1734, with boilerplate language to the effect that the decrees were not intended 'to forbid the honest recreations necessary to the relaxation of the tired mind and relief to the body worn down by working long hours,' and permitting any head of household to play 'in his own house with his family, relations, and friends' provided that there was no 'abuse,' and that 'all wisdom and moderation' was exercised.[16] High-stakes tables consequently flourished in the townhouses of the Parisian elite:

> The sight of the proprietors of sanctioned gambling houses making very considerable fortunes from them was a strong inducement to others to set up their own den.... [W]hile the act of gambling itself held a strong attraction, the virtual certainty of making greater quantities of money as a banker than as a punter held a far stronger one for many people.[17]

Gambling was thus akin to many other practices that were 'tolerated, but not permitted.'[18] During the reign of Louis XIV, the vicar of the Sainte Chapelle received notice to end his household gaming operation, as did Maître Lemaye, a *conseiller* of the Parlement de Paris, who issued threats sufficiently credible that the Marquis d'Argenson, the Lieutenant General de Police, was reluctant to proceed without assurances of support from the King.[19] In March of 1700, the King suspended the execution of a warrant against the Sieur Aubert notwithstanding his conviction that Aubert would continue to keep a faro table, 'since the general seizure of his property and the level of expenditure which he has assumed impose on him the necessity of it.' Requested to ascertain whether Aubert was indeed running a faro operation, the Lieutenant General de Police advised his superior that 'it will be difficult to prove this without the visit of a commissioner, whose visit will always seem derogatory to him, however honourably it is conducted.'[20] Additionally, it was difficult to find witnesses willing to inform on gaming operations who were not compromised in some way, particularly when the operators were people of rank and title, and the informants were often dismissed or otherwise disgruntled servants.[21]

---

[16] 'N'entendons néantmoins interdire les Récréations honnetes qui seront necessaires pur donner du relache à l'esprit fatigue, et du soulagement au corps abattu par un trop long travail, dont chaque Chef du famille pourra continuer l'usage comme par le passé, dans sa maison particuliere avec ses enfans, parens et amis, sans en abuser, et en y observant toute sagesse & moderation;' quoted in Dunkley, *Gambling*, 39–40.

[17] Dunkley, *Gambling*, 35.   [18] Kavanagh, *Shadows of Chance*, 30–44.

[19] Grussi, *Vie Quotidienne des Joueurs*, 181–2.

[20] René d'Argenson, *Notes*, ed. Lorédan Larchy and Émile Mabille (Paris: Émile Voitelain, 1866), 22: '...puisque la saisie générale de ses biens et l'air de dépense qu'il a pris lui en imposent la nécessité...la preuve en sera difficile sans la visite d'un commissaire dont la visite lui paroître toujours déobligeante, de quelque honnêteté qu'elle puisse être accompagnée.'

[21] *Rapports Inédits de René d'Argenson*, ed. Paul Cottin (Paris: Librairie Plon, 1891), 306–7.

Apart from gaming establishments licensed by the police, and those that operated in privileged enclaves like the Palais Royal, the Temple, and foreign embassies, the last years of Louis XIV and the regency of the Duc d'Orléans saw privileged nobles operating gaming concerns in their residences with tacit or explicit royal permission. Some of these had been French allies during the War of the Spanish Succession and forced to flee upon defeat, and for a government already burdened with enormous debt, granting gaming concessions was a more attractive option than awarding pensions. Thus it was that Ferenc Rákóczy, exiled Prince of Transylvania, was able to open a large gaming operation in what became the Hôtel de Transylvanie in 1716. Similarly, Mustafa Agha, who claimed to be an Ottoman prince, in 1719 received permission to keep gaming tables in his house in Paris in recognition of his military service, which lasted until he was obliged to flee the city two years later after the discovery of his imposture.[22] A number of officers' widows were permitted to keep tables until the privilege was revoked in 1727. A rumour circulated in the early 1720s that a set of 'entrepreneurs,' as they were termed in one account, had offered the court a considerable sum for the exclusive right to keep a particular, unspecified, game. Although the proposal came to naught, Blouin, the intendant of Versailles, received authorization to keep gaming tables at his residence.

Of the Parisian gaming concerns operated by French nobility, the two largest such establishments, the Hôtel de Gesvres and the Hôtel de Soissons, operated under royal privilege. The proprietor of the latter, the Prince de Carignan, was the brother of the King of Savoy. The Duc de Gesvres was conveniently enough the Governor of Paris, and netted a reported annual income of 130,000 livres from his gaming concession, which featured initially ten dice tables, with the subsequent addition of two apartments for pharaon and lansquenet. After a decade, however, the gaming assemblies at the Hôtel de Gesvres reportedly went into decline, one account relating that Paul Poisson, a celebrated actor of the Comédie, paid Gesvres only 1,000 livres per month for the privilege of keeping the tables there. Although officially tolerated, both venues were under constant police surveillance. At the highest levels, the police in Paris were staffed with men who mixed comfortably in elite social settings, and their surveillance of gaming produced and proceeded from a more sophisticated understanding of the arrangement of gaming operations. Carignan died in 1741, and operations at his residence had ceased by 1745. The Duc de Gesvres received generous compensation (100,000 livres in cash and 20,000 annually for life) for lost revenue after closing his tables voluntarily the same year. After Louis XIV's death, courtly gaming venues also multiplied in the households of the royal family. Until her untimely death in 1719, the Duchesse de Berry held assemblies three days a week

---

[22] Grussi, *Vie Quotidienne des Joueurs*, 19–20.

for lansquenet, pharaon, and other games at the Palais du Luxembourg; on the alternating days, the Duchesse d'Orléans kept the same games at the Palais Royal, which her daughter-in-law continued after the Duchesse's death in 1749.[23] Until 1722, *jeux d'argent* were also permitted at the annual fairs of Saint-Germain, from Candlemas to Palm Sunday, and Saint-Laurent, from the latter part of July to late September. These were so profitable to the operators that they were charged very high rents for their stalls, in some cases over 500 livres a day. The clientele was as elevated, and played as high, as at court or any of the *hôtels* of the *grand noblesse,* the Comte de Horn losing 12,000 livres at the Saint-Germain fair in 1720, and another observer asserting that punters at the two fairs thought nothing of staking tens of thousands of livres on a card or throw of the dice. It was perhaps because of the medium of these fairs that the finance minister Colbert apprehended in 1671 that games of chance introduced at court would filter into other socioeconomic cohorts, from bourgeois rentiers to merchants and artisans.[24]

Outside of the privileged premises of embassies and great aristocratic households, even the 'clandestine' gaming houses that fell under the jurisdiction of the police often boasted socially elevated proprietors, which created complications for law enforcement. Often the end result of painstaking police investigations was polite letters from the Lieutenant General de Police requesting that the recipients cease and desist from keeping gaming tables in their households, to which indignant protestations of innocence were the customary response. When the Comtesse de Monastérol received such a warning in the 1740s, she was deferentially assured that both of her letters denying the charges had been shown to the Secretary of State. In the case of less privileged operators, a warrant authorizing a raid could be issued, and when it was, raids were successful in nine cases out of ten, in spite of proprietors usually having some warning. As in London, however, convictions for gaming offences were relatively rare, Grussi only finding some two hundred of these in a period encompassing a century and a half. Players identified as *fripons* (the ever-elusive 'professional gambler') were the most likely to go to prison, constituting half of those imprisoned for gaming offences. Of the handful of proprietors who went to prison, almost all had disobeyed orders banishing them from Paris. Proprietors and bankers were more likely to be fined, typically about 3,000 livres in the case of the former, and 1,000 livres in the case of the latter. Recidivism, although common, did not result in heavier penalties, a Madame Godemart being fined seven times between 1720 and 1730, and a Madame de Pottonier four times between 1724 and 1729. Banishment a certain distance from the capital, or to a particular province or provincial city, typically for a period of just over two years, was another outcome of the relatively few convictions. Again, recidivism did not increase penalties, although the offender

---

[23] Grussi, *Vie Quotidienne des Joueurs,* 20–1, 90; Freundlich, *Le Monde de Jeu,* 30, 49.
[24] Grussi, *Vie Quotidienne des Joueurs,* 97–9, 121; Nemeitz, Séjour de Paris, 201.

would never be exiled to the same place twice; one Monsieur Berthelot was banished at least four times. The application of penalties illustrates an official attitude that proprietors of gaming operations, and those who kept banks within them, were respectable folk to be spared the social derogating experience of prison, while those who allegedly supported themselves playing at games of chance were not.[25] Francis Freundlich found that in Paris, 90 per cent of the proprietors of clandestine *tripots* were women, often the wives or widows of officers or professionals. Many were involved in retail trade oriented toward women, such as dressmaking or millinery. Many of these proprietors were in difficult financial straits, as military officers, for example, were not well compensated, a colonel making 6,000 livres annually, a captain 3,000, and a lieutenant 1,500.[26]

Fines, even when paid (which they often were not), were ineffectual deterrents, probably for the same reasons that obtained across the Channel. Proprietors could recoup the relatively paltry sum of cash involved, 3000 livres at most, in a single night. Even if orders of exile were enforced (and often they were not, with the banished person either never leaving Paris or returning very shortly), there was little to prevent gaming operators from setting up shop in another town.[27] In Paris as in London, petty corruption also hampered the enforcement of proscriptions against games of chance. It was in the material interest of rank-and-file police to turn a blind eye to gaming operations. There was an officer directly under the Lieutenant General who was responsible for the policing of gaming, a post which became desirable as it was potentially lucrative. Grussi cites the case of Pierre Pons, who very unenthusiastically and negligently pursued clandestine gaming operations in Paris from 1740 to 1745 until his superior received affidavits that he was taking bribes. A Madame de Neuville testified that she had agreed to pay Pons two louis d'or weekly to keep pharaon at her house, and a Monsieur du Monteil reported paying Pons twelve louis to expedite his return from banishment. After Pons was imprisoned, Madame de Neuville offered in his defence that while Pons had accepted her payments, he had not solicited them.

In Paris, the social stature of many proprietors made the equitable suppression of gaming a 'practical impossibility,' a term Grussi acknowledges using in preference to 'bad faith,' 'complicity,' or above all, 'corruption.' Many households were deemed too elevated to be subjected to the indignity of a raid. The clandestine gaming house kept by the Comtesse de Lignières was protected by an understanding with the Procurer General of the Parlement de Paris. Although Madame de la Bertinierre did not escape a raid on her premises, she was spared exile in consideration of her husband's position on the Grand Council, the judicial arm of the Conseil du Roi. Madame de Saint-Priest was shielded from prosecution by none

---

[25] Grussi, *Vie Quotidienne des Joueurs*, 180–2, 193–200.
[26] Freundlich, *Le Monde de Jeu*, 81–8.   [27] Grussi, *Vie Quotidienne des Joueurs*, 211–12.

other than the Duc de Gesvres, Governor of Paris and himself proprietor of one of the largest gaming concerns in the city. Sometimes indirect pressure could be applied through the arrest, exile, or imprisonment of subsidiary personnel such as bankers. The most that could be done in other cases was for letters to be dispatched from the Secretary of State of the Royal Household adverting the King's awareness that games of chance were unlawfully played in their houses. The Comte de Ponchartrain as Secretary of State was in the awkward position of making this declaration to the Marquis d'Argenson, the Lieutenant General de Police himself, concerning gaming kept by his wife and her sisters.[28]

The Great Game

The circumstances and arrangements of Parisian gaming were well known in elite circles across the Channel. Horace Walpole reported from Paris in 1739 that

> it is no dishonour to keep public gaming houses: there are at least an hundred and fifty people of the first quality in Paris who live by it. You may go into their houses at all hours of the night and find hazard, pharaoh, etc. The men who keep the hazard-table at the Duke de Gesvres' pay him twelve guineas each night for the privilege. Even the princesses of the blood are dirty enough to have shares in the banks kept at their houses.[29]

In 1753, twenty-two individuals named as gamblers in police dossiers were members of principal noble families, and played in four operations based in aristocratic households.[30] In 1759, one tract claimed that three quarters of respectable households in Paris derived significant income from gaming, and that there was no place for guests who did not play. By the 1770s, the servants of one Parisian *hôtel* were telling Jean Dusaulx that their employer had realized over 100,000 livres from gaming over the space of twenty years. Hers was among the hundred great households known to subsist at least in part on gaming revenue.[31] Gaming tables were also kept in foreign legations in Paris, and were according to one observer the only premises where the game of basset was allowed during the reign of the Grand Monarch. The Earl of Hertford reported in 1764 that to open a faro table for entertainments at the British Embassy, he would 'send to the

[28] Grussi, *Vie Quotidienne des Joueurs*, 207–10.
[29] HWC: *The Correspondence of Horace Walpole*, ed. Wilmarth Sheldon Lewis, 48 vols (New Haven: Yale University Press, 1937–1983), 13. 164–5.
[30] Freundlich, *Le Monde de Jeu*, 183.   [31] Grussi, *Vie Quotidienne des Joueurs*, 87.

lieutenant de police for a banker, and he sends you a very civil man, who is under the rod of the police of Paris if he offends.'[32]

England was an interesting case, as court society was never re-established after the seventeenth-century crisis on the same footing as elsewhere. Monarchs were never in position to build the splendid settings constructed on the Continent. Of Inigo Jones's ambitious project for Whitehall Palace, only the Banqueting House was built, as a tantalizing sample of what might have been. Toward the end of the century, there were relatively modest expansions built at Hampton Court and Kensington, but suitably regal settings had to wait until the nineteenth century. Continental-style courtly gaming, however, did establish a foothold, one observer reporting from court at the end of Charles II's reign that 'Play is grown the predominate passion even of the ladys as well as men prefers it to all divertions.' Although the trick-taking game of Comet was most in fashion, '*Bassette* still keeps in credit' with a number of prominent courtiers, including the Duke of Norfolk and the Duchess of Portsmouth, the most eminent of the King's mistresses.[33] Gaming continued to flourish at court even after the libertine Charles II had given way to the putatively dour Dutch Calvinist William III. Katherine Manners, Countess of Rutland, recalled being pressed to play basset at the court of William and Mary by both monarchs; the 'Mr Boucher' who dealt at the gold table, and was the only untitled person present, may have been Richard Boucher, who rated an entry in *Lives of the Gamesters*.[34] If so, it would not be the last time that an established gaming entrepreneur penetrated the periphery of court. Queen Anne was also a gaming enthusiast, requisitioning at least three gaming tables for the Palace of St James.[35] Did courtly practice in England move into metropolitan settings, as was clearly the case in France? Elite and elite-adjacent metropolites may have been familiar enough with continental practice to reproduce these arrangements in settings that were under the radar of local authorities, at least initially. Continental example might have been less apparent to ordinary readers of newspapers, who might read with admiration or apprehension of the efforts of absolute regimes to suppress the same species of gaming that persistently evaded the measures of both legislators and magistrates on their side of the Channel. A report in the *Daily Courant* in March 1710 described very strict provisions against gaming in a decree of the Parlement de Paris, forbidding anyone of any quality from playing or keeping tables for any game of chance, including faro, basset, or lansquenet. The same paper followed up several years later with another account from Paris of a royal edict against gaming that did not exclude even Princes of the Blood.[36]

[32] *A View of Paris*, 35; HWC, 38. 398.
[33] HMC *Rutland*: Historical Manuscripts Commission. *The Manuscripts of the Duke of Rutland, Preserved at Belvoir Castle*, 4 vols (London: HMSO, 1889), 2. 85.
[34] HMC *Rutland*, 2. 166.   [35] TNA LC 5/70, ff 289, 307.
[36] *Daily Courant*, 2615 (11 March 1710), 5044 (19 December 1717).

Observers of basset in England and on the continent noted that it was 'a very quiet game'; Mary Wortley Montagu noted its visual appeal as early as 1716:

> [O]f what Marble must that Breast be form'd,
> To gaze on *Basset,* and remain unwarm'd?
> When *Kings, Queens, Knaves,* are set in decent Rank;
> Expos'd in Glorious Heaps the *Tempting Bank,*
> *Guineas, Half-Guineas,* all the Shining Train;
> The *Winner's* Pleasure, and the *Loser's* Pain:
> In bright Confusion open *Rouleaus* lye,
> They strike the Soul, and glitter in the Eye.
> Fir'd by the Sight, all Reason I disdain....
> At the *Groom-Porter's,* batter'd Bullies play;
> Some DUKES at *Mary-Bone* bowl Time away.
> But who the *Bowl,* or ratt'ling *Dice* compares,
> To *Basset's* Heav'nly Joys, and pleasing Cares?[37]

Faro was substantially the same game as basset, with the elimination of the undoubtedly aggravating provision of basset that no card landing in either the punters' or the banker's pile could win or lose across two successive 'pulls.' It was known as 'pharaon' in France, where it was probably devised to evade restrictions, including outright proscription, imposed on basset. As it decreased the number of circumstances in which 'cocks' would have to 'retire,' it was more attractive to both punters and bankers, and appears to have completely supplanted basset by around 1730, after which basset is never mentioned. Curiously, lansquenet, cousin to both basset and faro, never caught on in England, although it was much in vogue in Paris. In lansquenet, it was the banker rather than the punters who had the option to defer collecting after a successful 'pull' for the chance of winning increased stakes, a provision that may have made the game less susceptible to commercialization.

There is literary evidence that basset in particular was played outside of court in elite residential settings by the late seventeenth century, following patterns of organization that obtained a century later, when Thomas Southerne's Lady Trickitt and Susanna Centlivre's Lady Reveller had non-fictional counterparts in the 'Faro Ladies' of St James's Square. In these gaming households, women might host the tables, but men held the bank. In Southerne's play, one of the male principals suggests that bankers chose hostesses most likely to attract male punters. 'There lies the secret,' he declares, '[w]hen you design a Bank, you first consider what

---

[37] Mary Wortley Montagu, 'The Basset Table, an Eclogue,' in *Court Poems* (London: J. Roberts, 1716), 7–9.

Beauties you shall get to draw in Custom.'³⁸ Anglophone readers of Jean de Préchac's *Disorders of Basset,* translated in 1688, were advised that the bank's advantage increased with the size of the company laying stakes. In this novel, Madame Landroze is persuaded to host a bank when the house edge is explained to her, following Montmort, without reference to *alpieus* or *parolis*:

> [A]t this very instant, People of the best Quality in all *Paris,* make no scruple of having *Bassett* at their Houses; and I know some of very good Fashion, that neither care for *Bassett,* or any other sort of Gameing, and yet are desirous to have it at their Houses for the Profit of the Card-money.

Her suitor is horrified at the thought:

> [T]o keep a Bank at her house, and make it a publick Gameing Ordinary, and Rendevouze for all sorts of People, where every Rake-helly Sharper of the Town, and common Strumpet, is Hail-fellow-well-met with Persons of the best Reputation and Quality, to expose her every Minute to a thousand Foolleries, and impertinent Disputes and Quarrels.³⁹

Just as Susanna Centlivre's *The Gamester* was based on Jean-François Regnard's *Le Joueur,* first performed in 1696,⁴⁰ *The Basset Table* of 1706 owes a significant debt to Préchac, for which reason we should perhaps resist its suggestion that by the first decade of the new century, gaming concerns were kept in private houses in London on the Franco-Venetian model, although these were certainly kept in public accommodations in the metropolis by then. The cast of *The Basset Table* features Lady Reveller, 'A Coquettish Widow, that keeps a *Basset-Table*' in the house of her uncle, Sir Richard Plainman, and Sir James Courtly, 'An airy Gentleman, given to Gaming.' Mrs Sago, the wife of an apothecary, affecting airs above her station, regularly plays, and loses, at Lady Reveller's, who remarks that 'a Citizen's Wife is not to be endur'd among Quality; had she not Money, 'twere impossible to receive her.' Early in the play, Sir Richard upbraids his niece for the chaos she has brought on his household:

> Can you that keep a Basset-Table, a publick Gaming-House, be insensible of the shame on't? I have often told you how much the vast concourse of People, which Day and Night make my House their Rendezvouze, incommode my Health; your Apartment is a Parade for Men of all Ranks, from the Duke to the Fidler....

³⁸ Thomas Southerne, *A Maid's Last Prayer, or Any, Rather than Fail* (London: R. Bentley and Jacob Tonson, 1693), 1.
³⁹ Susanna Centlivre, *The Gamester, A Comedy* (London: William Turner and William Davis, 1705); [Jean de Préchac], *The Disorders of Basset,* tr. unknown (London: John Newton, 1688), 17–19.
⁴⁰ Jean-François Regnard, *Le Joueur: Comedie en Vers* (Paris: Thomas Guillain, 1697).

Her cousin, Lady Lucy, taxes her with receiving 'such a Train of People … that my Lady *Reveller* is as noted as a publick Ordinary, where every Fool with Money finds a Welcome.' Lady Reveller's maid, Alpiew, defends her employer, asserting that 'my Lady keeps no Revels beneath her Quality,' and that 'my Lady's a Widdow, and Widdows are accountable to none for their Actions.' Centlivre, however, appears not to have understood the arrangements involved in 'keeping' a gaming concern. At the basset table of her title, Sir James deals, and Lady Reveller plays, taking her chances with the other players, apparently, and losing the fifty pounds that she had won the night before. Her loss makes her vulnerable, which Sir James is in a position to exploit. If Lady Reveller holds the bank and loses when she plays, she loses only to herself, suggesting that we are meant to understand that Sir James holds the bank, which Lady Reveller merely hosts. This construction is further supported when Sir James restores Mrs Sago's losses at the end of the play. Significantly, all of the gambling characters are redeemed in this play. Both Lady Reveller and Mrs Sago renounce gaming after facing threats to their status, sexual assault in Lady Reveller's case, and spousal desertion in Mrs Sago's.[41] Sir James abandons gaming as well, as Lady Reveller will no longer host the bank. In other words, the action of the play makes no sense to anyone familiar with the operational structure of the game. Nor was Centlivre's *Basset Table* the only literary expression of concern over an apparent social pathology, accompanied with critical misunderstanding of its mechanics. Fictions similar to Centlivre's would have an inordinate impact on the very non-fictional responses of authorities and others.

---

[41] Susanna Centlivre, *The Basset Table* (London: William Turner and J. Nutt, 1706), 3, 5, 7, 18, 50.

3

Sons of Hazard

The Sharper in Literature, Media, and Law

Tobias Smollett related of his picaresque character Ferdinand Count Fathom that dice 'had been one of his chief studies, and in which he had made such progress, that he could calculate all the chances with the utmost exactness and certainty.' The 'arithmetic' with which he initially fleeces one of his 'marks,' however, is no match for the manipulated dice that his opponent, who turns out to be a well-known sharper, introduces, whereupon the hapless Ferdinand loses everything he has.[1] Jessica Richard argues that unlike Smollett's Count Fathom, heroic gamblers in the eighteenth-century English novel set themselves at odds with probability:

> The romance of gambling is in the episode, as the gambler seeks this particular moment again and again and resists combining episodes into a longer narrative, a narrative that would perforce suggest walking away from the tables....Calculation worked against the episodic nature of gambling, encouraging the player to look beyond the game at hand to calculate odds and formulate long term strategy.[2]

We could pass this observation by as irrelevant to the historical analysis of gaming as a commercial enterprise, were it not the case that the narrative of the heroic gamester, and conversely that of the sharper, conditioned the response of the media and the law, effectively blinding both to the aspects of gaming that enabled commercial operations to proliferate in spite of concerted efforts to eradicate them.

Hazardous Scenarios

The original 'problem of the points' reflected assumptions about games of chance that probability writers shared with legislators, jurists, and journalists that games were by definition contests—the *agon*, to use Roger Caillois' terminology—between individuals or groups of them. The popularization of probability generated a

---

[1] Tobias Smollett, *The Adventures of Ferdinand, Count Fathom*, 2 vols (London: W. Johnston, 1753), 1. 165–7.
[2] Richard, *Romance of Gambling*, 46.

The Gambling Century: Commercial Gaming in Britain from Restoration to Regency. John Eglin, Oxford University Press.
© John Eglin 2023. DOI: 10.1093/oso/9780192888198.003.0004

perception that a sufficiently sophisticated gamester could gain the upper hand over a novice player in this contest, a convention that fed into the narrative of 'sharping.' Much anti-gaming polemic decries violent confrontations, including duels, arising among gaming individuals, and the preoccupation with cheating proceeded from the same assumption.

The prominence of the dicing game of hazard was certainly a factor in the proliferation of print around the sharper. In hazard, the *agon* among individual players was intact, and in tandem with a complex set of rules, there were conventions governing the behaviour and bearing of players. Making a figure at the hazard table meant mastering all of these, as might be surmised from the following exchange from George Colman's play *The Nabob,* in which a club waiter instructs the *arriviste* Sir Matthew Mite:

MITE: Main and Chance?
WAITER: Five to nine, please your honour.
MITE: I am at all that is set. How must I proceed?
WAITER: With a tap, as the chances are equal; then raise the box genteely and
    gently, with the finger and thumb.
MITE: Thus?
WAITER: Exactly, your honour. Cinque and quater: you're out.
MITE: What is next to be done?
WAITER: Flirt the bones with an air of indifference, and pay the money that's set.
MITE: Will that do?
WAITER: With a little more experience, your honour.
MITE: Then pass the box to my neighbour?
WAITER: Yes, or you make a back hand, if you please.[3]

Hazard was the ancestor of modern 'craps,' the name of which is a corruption of 'crabs,' the original term for the losing throws of two or three on two dice. The modern casino game is a simplification of 'French hazard,' introduced in the nineteenth century and adapted to be played against a bank. Baroque hazard was structured in the same way as 'street craps,' with players betting against each other. It differed from the modern iteration of the game in that the 'main' was not confined to seven (as in craps) but could be any number from five to nine 'called' by the 'setter,' which in a gaming establishment was a function that could be assumed by the box-keeper. The 'caster' instantly won all the money staked if the main were rolled immediately after it was called. If two or three were rolled, the caster immediately lost, and was obliged to pay all of the players who staked against them. Any other number on the initial roll was the caster's 'chance,' and

---

[3] George Colman, *The Nabob* (London: T. Cadell, 1778), 27.

usually won if it was rolled again before the main was rolled, depending on the main. An initial roll of twelve won if the main were six or eight but lost if the main were five, seven, or nine; eleven lost to any main but seven, in which case it won.

Hazard was necessarily a highly sociable game. The caster negotiated wagers and stakes with the other players in advance of the initial roll. Side bets unrelated to the caster's win or loss, set either with the caster or among the players looking on, were also common. There was constant banter around the hazard table, and occasional disputes, which could get heated. Much of the legal justification for the suppression of gaming venues stemmed from the noise and disturbance that could arise. Importantly, however, hazard was an outlier in this respect, as observers often remarked on the silence that accompanied play at other games of chance, especially 'banking' games. Because hazard was decidedly *not* a 'quiet game,' it was more often depicted, affording graphic artists like Hogarth and Rowlandson ample latitude to render a variety of physiognomies, postures, gestures, and expressions. Rowlandson's *Gaming Table* of 1801 (figure 3.1) depicts the dramatic moment when a young caster, having 'stamped' the dice box on the table, pauses to take last wagers from the other players before revealing the result of the cast. This assemblage is a relatively genteel crowd, the hatless box-keeper deferentially attending. The same artist's *Kick-Up at a Hazard Table* of 1787 (figure 3.2) shows a rougher crowd, in which military officers are prominent, as pistols are drawn, and candlesticks, bottles, and side chairs are raised to strike in a

Figure 3.1 Thomas Rowlandson, *The Gaming Table*, 1801. Yale Center for British Art, Paul Mellon Collection. Hazard was a highly sociable game, requiring constant interaction between the 'caster' and those who wagered on the throw.

Figure 3.2 Thomas Rowlandson, *A Kick-Up at a Hazard Table*, 1787. The Elisha Whittelsey Collection, The Elisha Whittelsey Fund, 1959, Metropolitan Museum of Art. Hazard could be boisterous, especially if foul play were suspected.

confrontation, probably over charges of cheating. There is no sign of a box-keeper with a characteristic croupier's rake, perhaps indicating the 'private play' that so many admonitory tracts warned against. Images by Rowlandson and others of analogous card games are relatively placid.

Hazard was also a masculine game. It was certainly not unknown for women to play, especially at resorts like Tunbridge Wells, where the Duchess of Dorset and the Countess of Bristol were spied rolling dice in 1730.[4] The latter was part of a small circle that played hazard at Bath in 1721, but only for silver, as Lady Bristol complained after she threw fifteen 'mains' and won only £50.[5] Writing of Bath in 1713, Richard Steele sarcastically remarked on 'the Opportunity [hazard] gives to display the well-turned Arm, and to scatter to Advantage the Rays of the Diamond.'[6] *The Bath Unmask'd*, Gabriel Odingsells' comedy of 1725, featured Lady Ambs-Ace, an abandoned 'female gamester' who vows she would not

[4] Letitia Cornwallis to Cassandra, Duchess of Chandos, 23 August 1730, Huntington Library, Stowe MSS STB 1(27).
[5] *Letter Books of John Hervey, First Earl of Bristol*, ed. Sydenham Hervey, 3 vols (Wells: Ernest Jackson, 1894), 2. 176, 203.
[6] Richard Steele, *The Guardian*, ed. John Calhoun Stephens (Lexington: University Press of Kentucky, 1982), 568.

exchange her 'Seat at the Gold Table...for a Throne.'[7] A visiting French diplomat was surprised to learn in May of 1720 of 'ladies of quality' dicing at 'one of the academies (gaming houses) near the theatre in Lincoln's Inn Fields,...among all sorts of people, a thing not seen before in town.'[8] Even toward the end of the century, a male commentator might still observe that 'the robust exercise of rattling a *dice-box,* and of calling across a table *"Seven's the main,"* can contribute to no pleasure which a fine woman should desire.'[9] Rowlandson's 1791 rendition of *A Gaming Table at Devonshire House,* showing the Duchess of Devonshire casting at hazard, was calculated to invite judgement. If there was a female equivalent of the sharper, it was the hostess who kept tables for banking games in her house, with the difference that these women entrepreneurs are as well represented in the archives as they are in print culture.

Having At All

By definition, a sharper was a professional gambler who made a livelihood from games of chance. An 'agony aunt' in one late seventeenth-century periodical was asked whether it was permissible for an honest and honourable person of either sex, in reduced circumstances, to earn a living by gaming, 'by Cards or Dice, playing on the Square justly and honestly, but by Skill being almost assured they shall be gainers?' Such a way of living, came the response, would make the individual angry and covetous in the worst cases, and in the best case would engender 'such a Levity of Mind as unfits him for a Virtuous Course of Life.' In sum, 'it is absolutely unlawful to make a Livelihood of what is only allowable sometimes to be used for the Refreshment of our selves, when tired with Business.'[10] Gaming was blameless when pursued recreationally and only occasionally, an assumption in keeping with a traditional festive culture that permitted games of chance at certain times of year, such as Christmastide in England, or Carnival on the Continent. For individuals to support themselves in this way would necessitate play for high stakes, which was also outside the bounds of the polite recreation countenanced, for example, in the earliest editions of Cotton's *Compleat Gamester.* Just as polite carding would never suffice to generate a comfortable income, neither would skill. Probability writers, as well as continental example, demonstrated the highly remunerative possibilities of banking games like basset or faro, but only to those in a position to make a significant initial capital investment. To the reading public

[7] Gabriel Odingsells, *The Bath Unmask'd: A Comedy* (London: John Walthoe, 1725), 64.

[8] TNA SP 35/21/117: ('[J]'ai apris aussi...que dans une des academies prez de la comedie de lincoln in-fields, ou y voir quelques dames de qualité & autres, qui y voir jouer aux dez, parmi toutes sorte de gens, chose que ne c'etois jamais vue en ville....').

[9] *Morning Herald,* 4382 (3 April 1793).   [10] *Athenian Mercury,* 6 (24 February 1694).

north of the Channel, many if not most of whom would never play for significant stakes, anyone who was a gambler by profession was a cheat by necessity.

At about the same time that a new gaming Act was being debated in the reign of Queen Anne, Richard Steele's *Tatler* waged a paper war not against gaming per se, but against sharpers who played unscrupulously and targeted wealthy young men. These, the *Tatler* warned in 1709, were found everywhere, moving easily 'among all Sorts of Assemblies and Companies,' and particularly in the venues associated with emerging public culture, where 'an unexperienc'd young Gentleman is as often ensnar'd by his Understanding as his Folly' upon hearing an articulate sharper 'debate the greatest Question of State in a common Chocolate or Coffee-house.'[11] The sharper was a cultural archetype who, while a socially liminal character, lived not on the margin of polite culture but at its epicentre. In literary works, they were often impostors, the Marquis of Hazard in Susanna Centlivre's *The Gamester* being exposed as a footman, and Count Basset, sporting a similarly spurious title in Vanbrugh and Cibber's *Provok'd Husband,* arguing that 'since modern Men of Quality are grown wise enough to be Sharpers, I think Sharpers are Fools that don't take up the Airs of Men of Quality.'[12] Nothing had changed by the middle of the century, when a writer in *The Connoisseur* allowed that readers would

> perhaps be startled...when I mention the excellencies of a Sharper; but a Gamester who makes a decent figure in the world, must be endued with many amiable qualities....In order to carry on the common business of his profession, he must be a man of quick and lively parts....As he is to live among the great, he must not want politeness and affability; he must be submissive, but not servile; he must be master of an ingenuous liberal air, and have a seeming openness of behaviour.[13]

Henry Fielding warned that 'sharpers of the lowest kind' had infiltrated 'several public Places (I might have said Gaming Places)' where 'too little Care is taken to prevent the promiscuous Union of Company.' Here, those engaged in cheating of a more figurative kind 'found admission to their Superiors, upon no other Pretence of Merit than that of a laced Coat, and with no other Stock than that of Assurance.' Sharpers, then, successfully represented themselves as established constituents of the polite world when they merely skulked on its fringes. Fielding asserted that this ruse was unsustainable, as once the sharper's

---

[11] Richard Steele, et al., *The Tatler*, ed. Donald Bond, 3 vols (Oxford: Oxford University Press, 1987), 1. 391.

[12] Susanna Centlivre, *The Gamester, A Comedy* (London: William Turner and William Davis, 1705), 69; John Vanbrugh and Colley Cibber, *The Provok'd Husband, or A Journey to London* (London: J. Watts, 1728), 72.

[13] *The Connoisseur*, 40 (31 October 1754), 237.

imposture was exposed, he would have no recourse but to 'take to the highway' for a life of crime.[14]

Sharpers were thought to be a special hazard at resorts, mineral springs in particular, where the composition of the clientele varied from season to season. John Macky, spying on Jacobites in Tunbridge Wells in 1714, wrote of sharpers 'whose Trade is to go Genteel, and mix themselves in all the diversions here.' They were easy to spot, however, from 'their more than ordinary Assiduity to Strangers,' and moreover their keenness to point out *other* sharpers.[15] Among the ways Richard Nash was supposed to have recommended himself to the company at Bath, according to Oliver Goldsmith's biography, was pointing out sharpers to visitors, particularly inexperienced young men, in the assembly rooms. 'I do not mind your playing in the rooms for guineas,' he reportedly told one young punter, warning, however, that he had made 'dangerous acquaintance' with known sharpers, 'and if you once meet them at a tavern you are sure to be undone.' Contemporaries might have asked why it was that the 'King of Bath' did not simply deploy his authority to bar known sharpers, and Nash's detractors certainly accused him of collusion, if not taxing him with being a sharper himself. Goldsmith himself admitted the peculiarity of 'a gamester thus employed, in detecting the frauds of gamesters.'[16] Nash, for much of his life, fit the description of a sharper as a conspicuous consumer without any apparent means of support; his first archival appearance in 1710 described him not supervising a minuet, but as a 'sporting Gentleman' playing hazard for high stakes, as much as '40 Ginnyes a Maine.' There were anecdotes of his having won the estates of grandees and then magnanimously returning them, in exchange for annual incomes out of rent rolls. Alongside these, however, were records of losses, and the insistence of Goldsmith's sources that Nash 'always played very fairly.' It was more likely that Nash was a gaming entrepreneur, the income from any number of silent partnerships being spent as soon as it was acquired.[17]

The literary scholars who have dominated the study of gaming in the long eighteenth century have understandably and quite usefully focused on sharper lore. Writers of fiction were drawn to gambling as it provided useful plot devices in the form of sudden reversals of fortune, and just as naturally they were drawn to the sharper, a colourful character operating under multiple false pretences, and a much more attractive and compelling story element than the shadowy personnel behind a faro bank. The *Tatler* suggested that sharpers were frequently foreign;[18] 'half-pay' reserve officers were also suspect, especially if they were Irish.

[14] Henry Fielding, *An Enquiry into the Causes of the Late Increase of Robbers and Other Writings*, ed. Malvin R. Zirker (Middletown, CT: Wesleyan University Press, 1988), 93.

[15] [John Macky], *A Journey through England in Familiar Letters* (London: J. Roberts, 1714), 58.

[16] *Works of Goldsmith*, ed. Friedman, 3. 389.   [17] Eglin, *Imaginary Autocrat*, 116–17.

[18] *Tatler,* ed. Bond, 1. 427, 488.

Nineteen of the twenty-six sharpers profiled in the *Lives of the Gamesters* of 'Theophilus Lucas' were army officers, or Irish, or foreign. Jacobites figured prominently, as did Roman Catholic recusants. The stereotype of the gaming officer reflected anxiety over an increasingly conspicuous military establishment, particularly in peacetime, when debates over a 'standing army' were prominent, as well as concerns over increasing entanglement in military adventures on the continent. 'Lucas' admitted as much in noting that demobilized officers 'did what they pleas'd,' and asserted that this liminal status left them open to the charge of sharping:

> [A] man of no employ, or any visible income, that appears and lives like a gentleman, and makes gaming his constant business, is always suspected of not playing for diversion only; and, in short, of knowing and practicing more than he should do.[19]

The novelist William Goodall essentially admitted in 1752 that much of his information about the sharpers at work 'from the Groom Porter's, to the Petty Alehouse' came from fiction, directing his reader to 'some usefull Passages on the dreadfull Malady of Gaming…in the History of *Roderick Random;* an excellent Comedy call'd the *Gamester;* [and] another call'd the *Provok'd-Husband.*'[20] Fiction writers like Goodall were not the only contemporaries to derive their information from fictional sources. Just as 'police procedural' dramas in our own time (whether fictional television series or putatively factual 'reality' series) have shaped not only public perceptions of crime and the police, but moulded the self-perceptions of agencies of law enforcement, so too did increasingly accessible print narratives, whether fictional or (putatively) factual, form public attitudes, including official attitudes, toward the problematic phenomenon that gaming constituted. The sharper was not merely a literary character, as he (invariably cast as male) appeared in other print culture such as newspapers, periodicals, and printed tracts, and most importantly in statute law. He was a fictional character in all of these, to varying degrees. The persistence of this stereotype throughout the period inhibited either authorities or the public at large from understanding the business model of commercial gaming.

Compendia of biographical profiles of celebrated gamblers, such as Charles Pigott's *Jockey Club* and the *Lives of the Gamesters,* were contemporary staples, and still inform much of the scholarship about gaming in this period. Instructively, much of Olivier Grussi's chapter on sharpers (*fripons*) in Old Regime Paris is drawn from sensational compendia of the period, such as Pierre Ange Goudar's

---

[19] Lucas, *Lives of the Gamesters,* in Hartmann (ed.), *Games and Gamesters,* 164.
[20] [William Goodall], *The Adventures of Captain Greenland,* 4 vols (London: R. Baldwin, 1752), 4. 68, 70–1.

Histoire des Grecs of 1758.[21] It is worth sorting out the fictive elements of these narratives from those that can be documented. Take, for example, one of the Lucas gamesters, a 'Monsieur Shevalier,' as he is rendered in the Lucas account, who according to that account was the son of a Norman noble family and a page to the Duchess of Orléans. The circumstances of his crossing the Channel are not discussed, 'Lucas' only offering that his continental sophistication 'recommended him to the favour of some persons of quality, who are too apt to prefer a foreigner before one of their own country' and landed him a commission in the Grenadier Guards. He became a fixture at the Groom Porter's lodge, where he won several hundred guineas from a prominent peer who offered a captaincy in the Grenadiers in lieu of immediate payment. He was killed at Sedgemoor in 1685, Lucas suggesting that his own troops shot him in the back.[22] 'Monsieur Shevalier' can be identified as Louis Mauguet, Chevalier de Mézières, who was commissioned an ensign in the Grenadiers in 1681 and promoted lieutenant the following year. By the date of the battle of Sedgemoor, he had just been appointed the regiment's second adjutant. His death at the battle is not recorded, and it is only noted that Mézières was 'out of the regiment' by November 1687. As for his winning a commission at hazard, his initial commission coincided with the appointment of the eighteen-year-old Duke of Grafton, second son of Charles II by Barbara Villiers, as the regiment's colonel-in-chief.[23]

Colonel Thomas Panton, one of the founding officers of the Grenadiers, was one of the best known of Lucas' gamesters, his entry in the Oxford Dictionary of National Biography relating that accounts of his exploits in print culture 'contributed to the construction of the myth of a libertine Restoration court'; as if to reinforce the point, the same entry quotes the *Lives of the Gamesters* more or less uncritically. Panton reportedly swore off gaming after winning an estate worth £1,500 a year, turning his attention to speculation in real estate, to which Panton Street between Haymarket and Leicester Square owes its name.[24] It is significant that so many of Lucas' gaming officers were affiliated with the Grenadier Guards, the regiment of the Household Division established to incorporate the royalist officers who returned from exile with Charles II in 1660. The initially mysterious Captain H—is the exception that proves the rule. This was very likely William Hewitt, who is only made anonymous to avoid confusion with Beau Hewitt, the last of Lucas' gamesters. William Hewitt alone was an officer of the Coldstream Regiment, the last remnant of Cromwell's New Model Army. This sharper's title of 'captain' was appropriately dubious, Lucas suggests, as it stemmed from a commission in a projected but ultimately abortive new regiment to be named in

[21] Grussi, *Vie Quotidienne des Joueurs*, 123–46.   [22] Lucas, *Lives of the Gamesters*, 163, 167.
[23] Charles Dalton, *English Army Lists and Commission Registers, 1661–1714*, 6 vols (London: Eyre and Spottiswoode, 1892–1904), 1. 287, 294, 316, 2. 19, 45.
[24] Dalton, *Army Lists*, 1. 1 and n. 5, 7, 37; Lucas, *Lives of the Gamesters*, 153–7; ODNB sv 'Panton, Thomas.'

honour of the infant Prince of Wales in 1688. Hewitt appears as a lieutenant in the Coldstream Regiment promoted in May 1684, and still holding that rank in 1687, but does not appear in regimental lists subsequently, which is consistent with the line of the Lucas narrative that Hewitt lost his commission on refusing the Oaths of Allegiance.[25]

Occam's Wager

Lucas' gamesters often serve merely as foils for descriptions of various games, and not always games of chance, together with detailed descriptions of methods of cheating, both plausible and otherwise. Lucas suggested that sharpers sufficiently skilled at hazard, for example, were capable of rolling any number on dice that they wished, a contention repeated in other literary sources. Mézières, according to Lucas, had 'such a command in the throwing, that chalking a circle on a table, with its circumference no bigger than a shilling, he would at above the distance of 3 foot throw a dice exactly into it, which should be either Ace, Deuce, Trey, or what he pleas'd.'[26] Fictional works promoted this possibility as well. In the scene at the hazard table in Centlivre's play *The Gamester,* the heroine Angelica, disguised in male dress, wins her miniature in its diamond-studded frame from her betrothed, Valere; until her arrival, Valere throws mains essentially on cue, an extraordinary run of luck that Angelica then repeats.[27] In George Colman's *The Nabob*, the title character receives a tutorial from a club waiter on throwing dice to obtain particular results:

> Seven, sir, is better nicked by a stamp.... When you want to throw a six and four, or two cinques, you must take the long gallery, and whirl the dice to the end of the table.... When your chance is low, as tray, ace, or two deuces, the best method is to dribble out the bones from the box.[28]

Even writers concerned to present serious statistical analyses of gaming succumbed to this and other figments of sharper lore. One tract, after several pages of calculations and tables demonstrating the advantage of the setter over the caster in hazard, declared that 'there are many Casters that can fling half a dozen Mains together without sweating or blushing.'[29]

There is ample evidence of cutting and pasting from other sources, the rules of hazard and other games appearing more than once. There are instances in which Lucas appears ignorant of the rules of the very same games that are described

---

[25] Dalton, *Army Lists*, 1. 327, 2. 130; Lucas, *Lives of the Gamesters*, 186.
[26] Lucas, *Lives of the Gamesters*, 165.   [27] Centlivre, *The Gamester*, 50–6.
[28] Colman, *The Nabob*, 27–9.   [29] *Whole Art and Mystery*, 14–19, 27.

elsewhere. Colonel Panton, for example, wins £1,100 of a Mrs Davis at basset by seating her in front of a mirror, enabling him to see 'her' cards, the writer apparently not realizing that players were not dealt individual 'hands' at basset, and that all cards were dealt face up in any case. More to the point, these characteristics of basset are clear in two different discussions of the game that appear elsewhere in the work.[30]

Few of the cheating methodologies described in sources like Lucas were really practicable. Cards could potentially be marked, so that the high-ranking 'honours' were conspicuous to the cheater who introduced the deck. Any marking, however, would have to be discrete, as until well into the nineteenth century the backs of cards were blank; they were often used as notecards, particularly after they were worn out, or became dirty or smudged, which happened quickly. Packs could reportedly be 'trimmed' so that high-value aces and 'court cards' were slightly wider than other cards, so that dexterous dealers skilled in legerdemain could dispose cards as they saw fit. These techniques, however, would only be useful in sociable games like quadrille or whist, which were not typically played for high stakes. Marked or trimmed cards would have been of little or no utility in basset or faro. In those games it was far easier for *punters* to cheat the bank, by surreptitiously increasing or decreasing the stakes on a card, or stealthily 'cocking' it, after a 'pull.'

Similarly, dice could be 'loaded' with mercury or lead to favour particular rolls, potentially useful at hazard if a 'setter' were able to introduce dice loaded to favour a particular 'main.' According to admonitory literature, dice could also be cut irregularly so as not to be perfectly cubical. The 'sharper' was stereotypically equipped with these 'fullums' or 'doctors.' One of the less plausible species of manipulated dice were pairs linked by a very fine chain, which Nicholas Tosney argues might not have been perceptible by candlelight. The rapid pace of hazard, and the attention required, would however have limited the practicality of manipulated dice. The advantage of a particular 'main' only applied on the initial roll; thereafter, the relative ease of rolling that number would become a liability. The rotation of the roles of 'setter' and 'caster' might be an additional complication. One attraction of commercial gaming concerns was the interposition of a third party, the box-keeper, to perform the function of the 'setter,' as was documented when Samuel Sprake was summoned in December 1720 for 'haunting and resorting to a Common Gameing House and there maintaining the same by proclaiming the Main & chance on the dice.' The mediation of the box-keeper minimized the possibility of players cheating each other, or making accusations of cheating, which could result in violent altercations. John Purcell found himself on trial for assault after one such round of hazard in October 1717, played

---

[30] Lucas, *Lives of the Gamesters*, 157, 178–9, 239–41.

privately at a tavern in Pall Mall 'to save the Expence of the Box-keepers at the Gaming Houses.'[31]

The alternatives to manipulated dice were various techniques of casting such as 'slurring' or 'topping,' legerdemain requiring a similarly implausible degree of dexterity. Take, for example, 'palming' dice, which required the cheating 'caster' to deposit only one die in the box, surreptitiously concealing the other in the palm of the hand, being careful to note the orientation of the die's faces. On casting the die from the box and noting the result, the cheat would then somehow manipulate the die in the palm to drop with the desired number.[32] All of these actions had to be performed with enough speed and fluidity to sustain the appearance of the simultaneous roll of two dice, which is very difficult to imagine, even assuming dimly lit premises and inebriated punters. Success at any of these methods of cheating would likely require the collusion of other players, and of the box-keeper or other personnel of the gaming venue, '[e]laborate ruses' that Tosney allows 'were perhaps not the norm, for the more complex a deception, the more likely it was that something could go wrong.'[33]

The lore of deceit in the admonitory literature on gaming depended on the confirmation bias of its readers. Among players, it was easy for those who suffered heavy losses to imagine that they had been cheated. '[A]n honest but rash adventurer often loses his temper with his money, and begins to suspect that the cards are packed, or the dice loaded,' particularly when primed with the stereotype of gaming venues 'filled with rogues in lace and sharpers in embroidery.'[34] A particularly illuminating tract appeared in 1726, which promised in its title to elucidate *The Whole Art and Mystery of Gaming*. While the customarily lengthy catalogue of methods of cheating was recounted here as well, especially for hazard, the writer subtly suggested that unwary players were more likely to be cozened into 'bubble bets,' dice wagers with unfavourable odds, than they were to fall victim to 'false' dice or legerdemain. The statistical advantage of the 'setter' over the 'caster' in hazard was sufficiently known to sharpers, for example, that many simply avoided ever throwing the dice. These stratagems, in this account, were made to appear easier and less detectable than the other manipulations that sharpers were said to practice. Dice that were 'loaded' or 'scooped,' for example, were easily detected on examination, which might be done by dropping a suspect pair into a pail of water several times, as 'false' dice would tend to land on the same faces. Another method purportedly in vogue at the beginning of the century involved waxing dice so that they adhered to the caster's fingers. This tactic, however, 'was soon known to the World' as '[t]he *Tatlers* or *Spectators,* I know not which, gave the Town an Account of it,' in describing a sharper who had recently

[31] LMA MJ/SR/2358, r 48; OBPO t17180110-63.   [32] Lucas, *Lives of the Gamesters,* 136.
[33] Tosney, 'Gaming in England,' 285.   [34] *The Connoisseur,* 31 (29 August 1754), 182.

gone to Bath, and was consequently shunned by the company there and 'obliged to fly to his old Quarters at *London*.' After carefully and minutely describing all of the various sleights of hand recounted in Lucas, and relating additional prestidigitations, the writer lamented that he was unable to perform any of them himself, wishing that someone more adept, perhaps a reformed sharper, would hold a public demonstration. 'For my part,' he finally admitted, 'I can believe many things that I have read and heard talk of, which I have never seen, tho' they appear seemingly high improbabilities.'

In similar fashion, *The Whole Art and Mystery* catalogued a series of ruses that a faro dealer might transact with the assistance of the two to three 'puffs' at the table, suggesting, for example, that dealers surreptitiously switching shuffled packs for 'stacked' ones accounted for a typical bank consuming a few thousand packs of cards in a year. With the aid of diagrams, the writer expanded on two methods of 'stacking,' which he insisted would defy the effects of shuffling, or its appearance, as the practice of 'sham shuffling' was mentioned, but not described. One system ensured that no card would win or lose more than once in succession, while the second, it was claimed, would consistently produce 'runs' of cards winning or losing four times in succession. Both systems required cards to be collated in a particular order, as illustrated in the diagrams, at the point of manufacture before the pack was sealed and stamped. Cardmakers, the tract asserted, would readily produce such packs to specifications, 'not knowing, I presume, the Use and Design of them; nor is it their Business to inquire, for many Reasons.' The collusion of croupiers was essential, as was that of strategically placed decoys among the punters. When, for example, the dealer needed to pull a card surreptitiously from the bottom of the pack, he would either step on the croupier's toe or exchange some prearranged signal with one of the decoys, 'so one of them readily puts his hand cross the Table' to distract the other punters, 'in which time the Card is drawn and the Mischief done.' These 'puffs,' thought to be ubiquitous, constituted another manifestation of the lore of the sharper, described as 'Gentlemen and Ladies of good Fortunes, who make a handsome Appearance and keep an Equipage,' and 'appear the very Pink of Honour and Civility to every one that is not in the Secret.' Here again, the writer of the tract felt obliged to acknowledge the sceptical reader:

> Perhaps you may fancy this difficult to be performed; but, by the Assistance of the Croupes and Puffs who know the Course of Cards as well as the Dealer, nothing is more easy: 'Tis the first thing they are taught to understand, and upon the least Notice given (by the Dealer) they immediately do their Duty; for you must know there is Order in this Society as well as in others; and in case any Miscarriage should happen through the Neglect or Carelessness of a Croupe or Puff, he certainly receives a severe Reprimand from the Commanding Officer....

After recounting all of these putatively infallible stratagems, it was nevertheless necessary for the author to point out that the bank was in as much danger of being cheated by punters, who were, he asserted, equally capable of imposing stacked decks, and of marking all the cards in a pack over the course of only two deals.[35]

Admonitory writers essentially admitted that players could not be cheated in commercial gaming venues absent the complicity of staff, and gaming insiders asserted that operators who tolerated such collusion would find their tables empty, as a correspondent who dated his letter from the notorious gaming venue of White's assumed in stating positively that 'in public Gaming no Frauds can be committed without Discovery.'[36] Lucas asserted that habitual cheats would eventually be discovered, and would have to relocate as they were increasingly excluded from play, an assessment that Tosney shares.[37] As Pierre Ange Goudar put it, '[u]n Grec connu est un homme perdu.'[38] This observation was sufficiently commonplace to appear in the moralist Jeremy Collier's *Essay on Gaming* of 1713, which noted that successful sharpers became so notorious 'that few have the Courage to engage them. Thus they are disabled by their Skill, and their Eminency breaks their Business.'[39] Habitual gamblers moved in rarefied circles in a face-to-face culture, and while there was seasonal recourse to mineral spas, they, like gaming operators, would necessarily have a metropolitan base. This circumstance accounts for another key feature of the picaresque, the necessity of constant movement. Few early modern Europeans were in a position to be itinerant to this degree, especially if their circumstances were as parlous as those of the archetypal sharper. Forced into an ever-narrower circuit, any 'knight of industry' would ultimately find, as a writer at mid-century asserted, that

[o]pportunities of fraud will not for ever present themselves. The false die cannot be constantly produced, nor the packed cards perpetually be placed upon the table. It is then our gamester is in the greatest danger.... he is in the power of fortune, and has nothing but meer luck and fair play on his side.[40]

Statutory Fiction

Accounts of cheating tend to come from fictional sources, from admonitory tracts, or, later in the period, from newspapers. The archival record is thinner,

---

[35] *Whole Art and Mystery*, 22, 29, 38–9, 45, 48–9, 62–71, 79.
[36] *Old England, or, The Constitutional Journal*, 101 (16 March 1745), 330.
[37] Lucas, *Lives of the Gamesters*, 242; Tosney, 'Gaming in England,' 263–4.
[38] Quoted in Grussi, *Vie Quotidienne des Joueurs*, 129.
[39] Jeremy Collier, *An Essay on Gaming, in a Dialogue* (London: John Morphew, 1713), 30.
[40] *The Connoisseur*, 40 (31 October 1754), 239.

unaccountably so, given the statutory apparatus that was constructed to identify and sanction deceitful play. In the middle of the seventeenth century, the picaresque character of the sharper made the leap from folklore into legislation. Late medieval and Tudor legislation aimed at confining gaming to elites; statutes of the later seventeenth century strove to protect these elite gamesters from excessive losses from either fair or foul play. As David Miers points out, 'its purpose was protective rather than proscriptive.'[41] The spectre of the sharper loomed large in this legislation that created new categories of illegality. The Cromwellian Gaming Act of 1657, although voided at the Restoration, set an important precedent for later legislation not only in focusing on stakes won, and invalidating bonds or contracts undertaken in satisfaction of gaming debts, but by referring in its preamble to 'lewd and dissolute Persons' who lived 'at very high Rates and Expences' with 'no visible Estate, Profession or Calling.'[42] Seven years later, the Caroline Gaming Act of 1664 (16 Carolus II c. 7) followed the Cromwellian statute closely, and was similarly predicated on the existence of 'sundry idle loose and disorderly persons' who pursued gaming 'as constant Trades or Callings to gaine a liveing or make unlawfull Advantage thereby,' and who had defrauded 'many of the younger sort both of the Nobility and Gentry' to the 'ruine of their Estates and Fortunes,' through gaming that the statute now defined as unlawful because it was 'excessive and deceitful.' It stipulated that anyone who won any sum of money by deceitful gaming forfeit three times the sum won, of which the loser could recover half provided they lodged a prosecution within six months. Subsequently, half the fine could be awarded to anyone else who prosecuted within a year, or eighteen months after the original offence. The revision of the statute under Queen Anne raised the penalty to five times the sum won 'by deceit, couzenage, or fraud,' with the addition of corporal punishment.[43]

Gaming was clearly deceitful if one or more players cheated, using, for example, loaded dice or marked cards. Indeed, gaming paraphernalia were liable to be seized as evidence when constables raided suspected gaming establishments, such as the three gaming tables, probably for E.O. or another prototype of roulette, confiscated in the Strand early in 1751 and found to be rigged with iron rollers and springs.[44] Another such wheel, alleged to have been used at Newmarket and seized before it could be dispatched to a race meeting at Salisbury in July 1785, was displayed in the magistrates' office in Bow Street.[45] Similarly, James Pattle, prosecuted in 1750 for cheating a victim of seventy-six guineas using a trimmed pack of cards, was discovered with two such packs on his person.[46] Curiously,

---

[41] Miers, *Regulating Commercial Gambling*, 29.
[42] Quoted in Tosney, 'Gaming in England,' 84.
[43] *Statutes of the Realm* (London: HMSO, 1819), 5. 523, 9. 477.
[44] *Gentleman's Magazine*, 21 (February 1751), 87.
[45] *Public Advertiser*, 15,958 (18 July 1785), 15,959 (19 July 1785).
[46] *Gentleman's Magazine*, 20 (July 1750), 239.

however, loaded dice and marked cards never similarly appear in sessions rolls, although there were a handful of complaints of *play* with false dice. A fairly exhaustive search of the Westminster sessions rolls turned up three such episodes: Abel Mitchell accused Richard Roger in February 1665; Robert Neale and John Hammond were committed to the New Prison at Clerkenwell on the oath of Ralph Robinson in January 1722, for having cheated Robinson, a labourer, of four and a half guineas with dice that may have been false, as alleged in the indictment, but were certainly unstamped, resulting in an additional charge. Both Neale and Hammond were ultimately apprehended, jailed for want of sureties, and indicted. Finally, Elizabeth Ward and Elizabeth Batterscumb were summoned in December 1721 'for enticing and encouraging Sarah Clarkson…to play with unlawfull Dice for Oranges.' Similarly, John Deier's presentation on the complaint of Charles Napier in December 1720 is the only instance of a charge of cheating at cards in the sessions rolls examined. All but two of the references to 'cheating' in these rolls applied to plebeian street gaming in Christmastide.[47] Nicholas Tosney, noting the disparity between anecdotal printed evidence and archival evidence of cheating, warns against assuming 'that legal records somehow provide a more "real" account of cheating in early modern England than do the pamphlets' while at the same time admitting to 'methodological difficulties reconciling the sources.' Nevertheless, absence of evidence for Tosney does not add up to evidence of absence. While 'few people attempted to prosecute sharpers in court,' there were a number of disincentives for doing so. *Qui tam* prosecutions were time-consuming and expensive, and the complicity of complainants, who had often been playing unlawfully themselves, was a further complicating factor. Cheating was difficult to prove, especially absent material evidence such as loaded dice or marked or trimmed cards. Finally, 'anyone bringing a prosecution would have to admit publicly that they had been cheated,' and it was arguably as damaging to personal credit to be cheated as it was to cheat.[48]

Stuart legislation decisively shaped the public discussion of gaming as a social problem. The 'deceit' and 'excess' stipulated in the language of the statutes subsequently featured conspicuously in the admonitory discourse around gaming, contributing to the vein of contemporary conventional wisdom that gaming was profitable because players were being cheated, and that large sums in the thousands of pounds were being quickly won and lost by individuals. The introduction of 'deceit' and 'excess' into the language of gaming statutes, however, did little to stem the proliferation of gaming. The issue of 'excess,' for example, was addressed with a threshold of £100 won or lost at a single sitting set in the Caroline Act, which was decreased to £10 under the Queen Anne Act in 1710. Gaming debts over these thresholds were legally unenforceable, any bonds or

[47] LMA MJ/SR/1303, r 194; MJ/SR/2379, pc; MJ/SR/2378.
[48] Tosney, 'Gaming in England,' 265–6, 286.

securities given for them were void, and any losses above the statutory limit, as well as losses accrued by deceitful gaming, were recoverable by civil action. David Miers argues that these provisions had the perverse effect of 'facilitating,' even 'liberating,' gaming. Punters gambled even more, under the assumption that debts were unenforceable and losses recoverable.[49]

Moreover, the later Stuart statutes may have enhanced the social cachet of gaming. In allowing the recovery of gaming losses by litigation, gaming Acts ratcheted up the social stakes of dealing with 'debts of honour' in an 'honourable' way. When a character in Susanna Centlivre's *The Gamester* refuses to pay his son's gaming debt, his servant warns that 'among Gentlemen, that debt is look'd upon as the most just of any; you may cheat Widows, Orphans, Tradesmen without a Blush—but a debt of Honour, Sir, must be paid.'[50] A plaintiff suing for recovery of losses would come off as mercenary and mean, and (more importantly) as impugning the defendant as a cheat. Moreover, the language of the statute created a definitional problem on the point of what constituted a 'single sitting': a marathon gaming session could be interpreted as several different sessions if the players interrupted play to take meals, or as two different sessions on two different days if a session lasted overnight. The last of the Georgian gaming Acts resolved this difficulty in 1744 by setting a further threshold of £20 won or lost within twenty-four hours, a provision of no use to the plaintiffs in a 1788 case in which the recovery of a £14 loss was disputed because the players stopped the game for an hour to have dinner; the court ruled that it was a single sitting because the players had remained in each other's company.[51] In a ruling of 1701, the Court of King's Bench held that promissory notes given for gaming debts contracted by an individual at one sitting to several other individuals were enforceable as long as each individual note was for no more than £100, even if the total debt exceeded £100.[52]

Enforcement of the Restoration statute was effectively a complaint-driven procedure, depending on *qui tam* prosecutions, probably initiated by one or another of the players, a reality that the statute acknowledged in allowing a portion of any fine collected to go to the 'prosecutor,' meaning the informant. Such informants were held in low regard among gamesters and critics of gaming alike. An extraordinary case in 1688 may have rendered the Caroline Act a dead letter. Sir Basil Firebrass, having lost £900 at hazard to a Mr Brett, took his opponent to quarter sessions on a charge of playing with false dice. When Brett was acquitted,

[49] Miers, *Regulating Commercial Gambling*, 29.   [50] Centlivre, *The Gamester*, 28.
[51] Miers, *Regulating Commercial Gambling*, 29.
[52] *Dickson v. Pawlett* (Michaelmas 13WmIII). Dickson sued to recover £106 lost at one sitting, but to two different individuals. The court ruled that a loss 'to several Persons at one Sitting, is not within the Statute, unless they go Shares fraudulently, and join in the Stakes: for then, as to the Chance of the Game, they are as one Person'; William Salkeld, *Reports of Cases Adjudg'd in the Court of King's Bench* (London: Elizabeth Nutt and R. Gosling for J. Walthoe, 1717), 345.

Firebrass filed suit in Chancery to recover his losses. Incredibly, the plaintiff lost, no less a person than Lord Chancellor King ruling that while the gaming in question was certainly excessive, it was not unlawful, presumably because magistrates had found that it wasn't deceitful.[53] To have any prospect of reimbursement, then, a plaintiff had to prove that the defendant had cheated. Additionally, while the equity courts that held jurisdiction in cases of fraud could void gaming debts or securities given for them, they could not (until the statute of 1744 permitted them) order remuneration of a gaming debt that had already been paid.

In a provision aimed at 'sharpers', the Queen Anne Act of 1710 (9 Anna c. 19) made it an offence for an individual to earn a living by gaming. It had been possible under the Henrician Act to seize individuals found in a gaming house operating unlawfully, but by the early eighteenth century, the stipulated fine of six shillings and eightpence was too modest to deter the committed professional gamblers that newspaper and periodical writers had convinced their reading public were legion. For the first time, under the Queen Anne Act, any two justices of the peace could warrant constables to seize individuals, whether found in gaming venues or not, who were suspected of having no other income apart from gaming. Those who could not satisfy the magistrates that they were not professional gamblers would have to find sureties, generally two individuals, who were liable for substantial sums to ensure the respondent's good behaviour for one year. If sureties were not immediately forthcoming, respondents could be jailed until they were, for up to one year. This provision accounted for a substantial increase in the business of the Westminster sessions related to gaming, as did its last provision, also a departure from the Caroline Act: a blanket exception for the royal household, the repercussions of which were extensive, as a later chapter will show.[54]

The revised provisions for 'excess' and the renewed prohibition of 'deceit' were no more effective on these scores than the Caroline statute had been. In January of 1714, John Dee appeared on the complaint of William Wood for cheating at cards, while John Sharman was summoned in December 1720 for having won £38 of John Peake 'fraudulently and by deceit.' Sharman's sureties were William Vanderman, proprietor of the eponymous gaming house near the Theatre Royal, and Humphrey Jones, who had been summoned ten years earlier for keeping a 'rowly-powly' table; Sharman was probably a faro dealer.[55] Charges of excess, absent deceit, were also rare, and similarly concentrated in the first few years that the Queen Anne statute was in effect. In December 1714, John Gancy complained of losing fifteen guineas at faro to David Bennett, who possibly dealt at Fryar's in the Haymarket, while the following September, a 'Count Venlo' filed charges after losing a total of thirty-five guineas to two individuals at Peter Vignier's

[53] Street, *Law of Gaming*, 364.   [54] *Statutes of the Realm*, 9. 476–7.
[55] LMA MJ/SR/2225, r 2; MJ/SR 2358, r 20; CLA/047/LJ/11/010; CLA/047/LJ/01/0533.

coffeehouse in Great Suffolk Street.[56] Nevertheless, the Queen Anne statute effectively encoded the archetype of the sharper, again placing the onus of gaming proscription on the individual gamester.

One manual for magistrates from 1745 provided a sample warrant of commitment for a professional gamester under the Queen Anne statute, which reiterated many of the provisions of the 1664 Act. The warrant describes the individual to be committed as 'a lewd and dissolute Person who lives at great Expences' with 'no visible Estate, Profession or Calling to maintain himself' who 'doth for the most Part support himself by Gaming' in the jurisdiction of the signatory magistrates. To avoid imprisonment, the accused was to present either evidence to the contrary, or sureties for good behaviour for twelve months. The amount of the surety, to be forfeited if the accused is found to have play again for over twenty shillings, was left to the discretion of the magistrate.[57] Since gaming was still a status offence, magistrates were obliged to record the names, addresses, and occupations of anyone seized in a gaming house raid, and anyone unable to 'give a proper account of themselves' would be presumed to be a sharper and be liable to be jailed. It was relatively rare, however, for 'common gamesters' seized in raids to be held for trial in this way. After one raid on a gaming house attached to the Rose Tavern in Covent Garden, only one of the box-keepers was not 'able to give any good Account of his Way of Living,' and was accordingly 'sent to Bridewell to beat Hemp.'[58] That so few punters saw the inside of the 'house of correction' persuaded Robert Shoemaker that most of them were 'respectable'; it might also suggest that the professional 'sharper,' the roving vagabond who made a living from gaming, was a myth.[59]

Were it otherwise, it would follow that sharpers, who were habitual gamblers, would routinely turn up in sessions rolls, and there were indeed individuals who appeared multiple times for gaming offences. In Westminster, however, it was more often gaming operators who made repeated appearances before justices on charges of 'keeping a common gaming house' than individual punters. The repeat appearances of the latter are few and far between. Philip Spooner was apprehended at Fryar's in the Haymarket in autumn of 1718, and again at the beginning of 1721, possibly at Fryar's, where he was also charged with obstructing the constables; finally, after a raid on the Phoenix (in the former premises of Fryar's) in March 1729, Spooner was committed to the Gatehouse. Spooner, identified on one recognizance slip as a common soldier in a Guards unit, was most likely hired as security detail for that gaming venue, as other enlisted military personnel were; in 1726, Robert Irwin, a grenadier who had been dismissed as doorkeeper at the

[56]   LMA MJ/SR/2240, r 94; MJ/SR/2255, rr 221–2, 228–9.
[57]   Theodore Barlow, *The Justice of Peace* (London: Henry Lintot, 1745), 264.
[58]   *London Evening Post*, 184 (6 February 1729).
[59]   Robert Shoemaker, *Prosecution and Punishment: Petty Crime and the Law in London and Rural Middlesex, c.1660–1725* (Cambridge: Cambridge University Press, 1991), 58, 203.

Phoenix in the Haymarket, attacked and killed Charles Piercy, his successor. There was also Anthony Balhash/Bolach/Bollash, a more likely suspect identified as a 'gentleman' with three different addresses to complement the three different spellings of his name, who ended up in the Gatehouse in company with Spooner. Metcalf Ashe, another 'gentleman,' was apprehended in the Phoenix in April 1725 and in another gaming house near the Rose Tavern in Covent Garden in February 1729.[60] Ashe, of course, was subsequently a defendant in Nash's E.O. suit, suggesting that he like Nash was a gaming entrepreneur of long standing.

Sessions records, then, do not turn up 'sharpers' of the sort found in contemporary print culture. More to the point, they buttress Shoemaker's suggestion that a critical mass of the clientele of gaming operations was 'respectable,' a finding that surfaces more than once in reportage. In December 1774, when Sir John Fielding questioned fourteen individuals found at a hazard table in the Royal Larder, Thomas Nelson's establishment in Gerard Street, Soho, 'it appeared the parties charged were persons of good characters, and not gamblers,' whereupon Fielding 'made every reasonable allowance.'[61] Acquittals stemmed not infrequently from a perception that many of those indicted for gaming were more respectable, reliable, and honest than the informers, often gamblers themselves, who stood to gain from a successful prosecution. Such was the case of Richard Haddock, charged as a proprietor of a gaming table at the Phoenix coffeehouse in the Haymarket in May of 1730. Although his character witnesses knew that Haddock had been a box-keeper at a hazard table in the Rose Tavern, Covent Garden, they all vouched for his honesty and good reputation.[62] This understanding informed a counter-current in contemporary commentary on gaming found in proposals to mine a revenue stream through schemes of taxation or licensing, and suggestions that 'public' gaming sponsored and overseen by commercial operators was self-regulating and less prone to abuses than the unmediated and spontaneous 'private' play in the dark unregulated corners of public culture.

A tract of 1722 by an anonymous Westminster magistrate provides an invaluable insider's account of efforts to enforce gaming legislation in the locality where it was most frequently challenged. Although the writer showed some awareness of the arrangements of gaming enterprises, mentioning faro banks and the partnerships that supported them, and describing how gaming interests infiltrated and corrupted the local justice system, the nuisance value of gaming was nevertheless located in the supposition that gentlemen of property were being fleeced, either directly by sharpers, or indirectly by servants who stole in order to gamble, and that gaming permitted undeserving plebeians to enjoy unjustifiable social

---

[60] LMA MJ/SR/2315, r 170; MJ/SR/2363, r 85; MJ/SR/2445; OBPO t17310908-46; MJ/SR/2517, rr 11, 19, 140.
[61] *Sentimental Magazine*, 2 (December 1774), 562.
[62] *Daily Journal*, 2909 (4 May 1730); OBPO t17300116-30.

mobility.[63] Another writer later in the decade, who showed the same degree of sophistication concerning the business arrangements that attended gaming operations, still located the primary danger of gaming in the presence of sharpers. Gaming, pursued professionally, according to this observer, would yield 'a yearly Income sufficient to support a Family to live much above the middle State of Life.' Although the denomination of 'gamester' might be applied to 'every Person that plays,' his tract confined the term to those 'that have no other visible way of living.' The best advice he could give those who chose to game 'to play only with such Persons whose Lives and Characters are well known to you, and not with such as make Gaming their Livelihood.'[64]

This misunderstanding persisted, as reflected in press accounts of gaming in Haymarket at mid-century. The E.O. table at the masquerades, one account ran, was 'the sole Motive and Temptation that induces Sharpers to attend those Meetings at a very great Expence for Dress.' E.O., of course, was a banking game, at which 'sharpers' were as liable to losses as any other punters. Nine 'notorious Sharpers,' named by an informant, had recently been seized in a raid on the Haymarket masquerade, including 'a fidler, formerly a tapster,...a broken publican,...a sausage merchant,' and 'a journeyman founder,' all of them 'dressed in rich cloaths and swords hired in Monmouth-street.' One newspaper account related that all nine 'sharpers' were jailed lacking sureties. However, recognizances for eight, with sureties, appear in the sessions roll; three were listed as 'gentleman,' while the remainder appeared as broker, victualler, goldsmith, wine merchant, and coach founder. Newspapers noted that none of the other punters at the E.O. table were seized, although they were equally culpable under the terms of the gaming statutes, nor was the table itself confiscated. Appropriately enough, the justice who accompanied the constables raiding the masquerade was Henry Fielding, whose novels traded on any number of picaresque archetypes, that of the sharper among them.[65]

It was a theatre critic who in October 1781 acknowledged the cognitive dissonance that literary treatments of gaming, in this case theatre pieces, had engendered. The writer listed a partial catalogue of plays dealing with gaming, including Thomas Holcroft's Duplicity, The Gamester by Edward Moore, Thomas O'Bierne's The Generous Impostor, George Colman's Oxonian in Town, and The Minor by Samuel Foote, as example of the theatre's efforts to 'afford a real and effectual antidote against gaming' that had 'failed in producing an effect by mistaking the object.' The plays mentioned had 'dissuaded with much earnestness from playing with sharpers, a caution with which most men who play deep are sufficiently

---

[63] Account of the Endeavours.   [64] Whole Art and Mystery, 3–4, 86.
[65] Public Advertiser, 6690 (1 April 1756); Read's Weekly Journal, 2357 (3 April 1756); London Daily Advertiser, 4558 (7 April 1756); LMA MJ/SR/3050, rr 196, 199, 221, 261, 271–3, 277.

armed.' Sums were won and lost 'not by cogged dies, or tricks in cutting cards,' but through 'the common chances and variations of fortune.'[66]

The character of the sharper, who confronts us in print culture, eludes us in archives. Just as other early modern scholars have asked 'were there really witches?,' we could ask the same question about 'sharpers,' and wonder if the term was less a reflection of actuality than an exclusively pejorative usage applied to third parties. That there were certainly individuals who fit the language of statutes in deriving their primary income from games of chance proceeds from the sources examined here, but two important considerations also follow. Cheating was difficult, and difficult to sustain, and ultimately counterproductive. Second, those we might call 'statutory sharpers' necessarily spent significant time in gaming venues and milieus, and would understand that the only certain source of regular income from gaming was partnership of some sort in a commercial operation, such as a faro bank or an E.O. table. *The Whole Art and Mystery of Gaming* suggested as much, in relating how adept sharpers were at luring punters to the faro table, where the personnel included 'puffs' who were customarily half-pay military officers in conformity to stereotype.[67] Correspondingly, it is gaming entrepreneurs who make repeated appearances in sessions rolls, and to whom we now turn our attention; picaresque rascals with loaded dice, on the other hand, seem to be confined to fiction and rumour.

---

[66] *Gazetteer*, 16,477 (16 October 1781).   [67] *Whole Art and Mystery*, 22, 60.

4

In the Shade of the Royal Oak

Commercial Gaming by Royal Patent

The first few years after Charles II's return to the thrones of the three kingdoms, what we might call the Restoration Moment, was a time of relief and hope, of resentment and apprehension, and above all, of opportunity. It promised, among other things, a return to the festive culture of 'Merry England' after two decades of puritan ascendancy. Official documents, dated with the regnal year, encoded the presumption that the new reign had in fact begun with the fall of the regicidal axe on 30 January 1649, the pen strokes of innumerable clerks bureaucratically erasing a decade of exile during which a dispossessed prince roamed the Continent dependent on the solicitude of others and accumulating debts of many different sorts. The spring of 1660 posed the challenge of recreating a court culture *de novo* after a hiatus of nearly two decades. Those who had served a royal refugee in his time of need would finally be able to collect on the obligations he had incurred.

It seems likely that the experience of exile had brought courtiers and others in royalist circles into contact with the commercial gaming concerns that were emerging on the Continent. We have seen how the Venetian patriciate pioneered operations with a business model that established banking games as a profit centre, together with anecdotal evidence of their transmission to elite circles in France through the medium of a Venetian embassy. There is direct documentary evidence that the agents of transmission into England were continental emigrants with connections to the French court or French officialdom who won office at the restored court of Charles II. One of these was Francesco Corbetta, a guitarist who had been a music tutor to the young Louis XIV. By February of 1661, Corbetta (who dutifully anglicized his name to Francis Corbett), was across the Channel as Groom of the Privy Chamber to Queen Catherine of Braganza, and received a royal patent to operate the game of L'Oca di Catalonia.[1] This 'board lottery' was of Catalan origin, called 'The Goose' after the geese that according to pious legend miraculously appeared after the martyrdom of Saint Eulalia, a local saint who was patron of the old cathedral of Barcelona. This game was played in France by 1659,

---

[1] Cecil L'Estrange Ewen, *Lotteries and Sweepstakes: An Historical, Legal, and Ethical Survey of their Introduction, Suppression and Re-Establishment in the British Isles* (London: Heath Cranton, 1932; reprint edn, New York: Benjamin Blom, 1972), 95–6.

The Gambling Century: Commercial Gaming in Britain from Restoration to Regency. John Eglin, Oxford University Press.
© John Eglin 2023. DOI: 10.1093/oso/9780192888198.003.0005

reportedly introduced by Italian emigrants in the retinue of Cardinal Mazarin, when it was described as 'L'Hoca de Catalogne' in an edition of a standard tract on rules of games. It was described there, perhaps facetiously, as 'an honest diversion' played 'at many of the most considerable households in Paris' in the hours before retiring, care being taken that no oaths or blasphemies were uttered, and that on Sundays and feast days, play was relegated to the late afternoon as not to interfere with divine service.[2] It was a 'true lottery' in the sense that lots were drawn, in this case beads numbered one to thirty, corresponding to numbers arranged in rows and columns on a betting cloth or 'board,' giving rise to the usage 'board lottery.' These betting boards were often richly decorated and colourfully illustrated, and some derivatives of L'Hoca, such as La Belle, Biribi, or Biribissi, remained popular in France and Italy into the nineteenth century. Players could stake on categories of illustrated items (men, women, flowers, fruits, birds, or coats of arms, to name some examples) as well as on numbers and combinations thereof. The culturally iconic Mexican *loteria* possibly derives from these; L'Oca, now shorn of its gambling associations, is still a children's game in Spain and Portugal.

By November of 1661, Corbett was complaining that another émigré, Giovanni Francesco Finocelli, whom Corbett had dismissed as a factor for his own patent, had partnered with James Roche, an army captain from an 'old English' family in Ireland, 'for a newly invented lottery called the Royal Oak.' Corbett indignantly asserted that this enterprise was essentially L'Oca di Catalonia under another name, while Roche and his partners countered that their lottery was 'invented by them in commemoration of the Royal Oak,' the Boscobel Oak in which Charles II had hidden after the Siege of Worcester in 1651.[3] Lotteries, established as fundraising mechanisms in England from at least the Elizabethan period, fell outside of gaming statutes, both the Tudor enactments aimed at enforcing time-work discipline on plebeians, and the Stuart legislation intended to contain rather than prohibit games of chance among more affluent players. Royal patents were granted for lotteries in support of public and private initiatives, such as the establishment of colonies in Virginia. Institutions as well as individuals purchased 'lots,' and the prizes were more often material goods such as plate or tapestries than sums of cash.

Like the other 'board lotteries' that imitated it, however, the Royal Oak was not a proper lottery in the sense that the term came to be understood in the next century and later, but something more akin to a casino game like roulette. Charles Cotton compared it to basset, indicating that even writers on games had to wrap their minds around the concept of a game played against a 'house' or a 'bank'

---

[2] *La Maison Academique, Contenant les Jeux* (Paris: Etienne Loison, 1659), 102–7.
[3] TNA SP 29/44/98.

Figure 4.1 Teetotum, marine ivory, seventeenth century. Charles Miller Ltd
Polyhedral dice like this one, with thirty-two facets, served as the randomization
devices for the Royal Oak Lottery.

rather than other individual players.[4] The game employed a 'teetotum', a small
ivory polyhedron with thirty-two facets, each painted with a number from one to
thirty-two (figure 4.1). These numbers were also represented on a large decorated
board, on which punters would lay their stakes. The lottery operator dropped the
'teetotum' into a vertical tube, which was possibly fashioned to represent the
eponymous oak tree and likely configured to ensure that the die made a sufficient
number of turns before landing on the betting cloth. Players could stake on a
'whole figure' (a single number out of thirty-two), a 'half figure' (two adjacent
numbers), or finally a 'quarter figure' (four adjacent numbers). The impossibility
of laying a stake on more than four numbers out of thirty-two, for a one-in-eight

---

[4] Cotton, *Compleat Gamester* (1709), in Hartmann (ed.), *Games and Gamesters*, 271.

chance of winning, meant that a Royal Oak operator enjoyed a steep advantage, even discounting that payouts on winning stakes were significantly less than what the mean of probability would have mandated.

The Royal Oak Lottery was the prototypical commercial gaming venture, setting the patterns and precedents that characterized subsequent enterprises. Although there is more evidence that it was played in open-air venues like markets and fairs than in public accommodations, the Royal Oak was an important gaming innovation in two respects, as it introduced the concept of an organized gaming syndicate that operated 'banks,' and introduced the Crown as an agency bestowing legitimacy on otherwise shady enterprises. Both developments were critical to the proliferation of commercial gaming in the metropolis, and in different ways complicated efforts to regulate, contain, or proscribe it.

The Polyhedral Face of Patronage

In their dispute with Corbett, Finocelli and Roche could point to the polyhedral teetotum as a randomization device entirely distinct from the numbered beads used in L'Oca as in Biribi and its derivatives later; the Royal Oak also afforded fewer and less generous betting options to players, as its predecessor enabled single stakes to be laid on as many as ten numbers out of thirty. Although the matter was initially decided in favour of Corbett, Roche was licensed to keep the Royal Oak, cited as his own invention, in Ireland less than a year later, a patent that was still operative near the end of the decade.[5] The rift was temporarily healed as Roche and Finocelli entered into partnership with Corbett, receiving a licence in August 1663 'to set up and exercise' the Royal Oak and a new lottery, the Queen's Nosegay, anywhere in England and Wales.[6] By the end of that year, two other émigré courtiers, Antoine Demarces and Laurent Dupuy, asserting that they had purchased the interest of Roche and Corbett in the lotteries operated in England and Wales, were granted a similar licence.[7] Demarces, a French postal official who had intercepted and copied correspondence posted from England for the exiled court during the Interregnum, arrived in England as a client of Clarendon and was promptly awarded a baronetcy.[8] Dupuy, described to Samuel Pepys as 'a knave and by quality but a tailor,' was Yeoman of the Robes to the Duke of York.[9] The two consortia of patentees were still at odds in January 1664, Demarces and

---

[5] *Calendar of State Papers Relating to Ireland [of the Reign of Charles II]*, ed. Robert Pentland Mahaffy, 4 vols (London: HMSO, 1905–1910), 1. 592, 3. 687.

[6] TNA SP 29/79/102.   [7] TNA SP 29/86/147; SP 29/86/154.

[8] Nadine Akkerman, *Invisible Agents: Women and Espionage in Seventeenth-Century Britain* (Oxford: Oxford University Press, 2018), 136; George Edward Cokayne, *Complete Baronetage 1611–1800*, 5 vols (Exeter: William Pollard, 1900–1909), 3. 24.

[9] *The Diary of Samuel Pepys*, ed. Robert Latham and William Matthews, 11 vols (Berkeley: University of California Press, 2000), 5. 279.

Dupuy complaining of Corbett and Finocelli selling them their patent, and then securing a licence for a new game, Il Trionfo Imperiale, which the complaint held was only the Royal Oak under another name.[10]

These claims and counter-claims as documented in the State Papers show a pattern of court officials, generally émigrés, obtaining licences to operate games of chance in the form of royal patents or warrants, selling these concessions for a lump sum, only to promote different 'board lotteries' under different names, but played on the same principles.[11] Among these documents is a memorandum attempting to establish the sequence of events relative to the Royal Oak, its antecedents, and its derivatives, among the various patentees, licensees, and partners, testifying to how confusing these claims became.[12] This dynamic, involving slight variations in games to evade the language of patents, or subsequently of statutes, would bedevil efforts to regulate commercial gaming ventures throughout the long eighteenth century. Whether these developments were infringements or misunderstandings, officials and their concessionaires were continuously at odds, disputes that royal councillors were called upon to resolve. Successive Royal Oak patentees continued to face difficulties in enforcing their patent, facing competition from imitators and from unauthorized operators right up until the Lottery Act of 1699 put all of the 'board lotteries,' licit or otherwise, out of business.

If this unseemly jockeying in high places tells us anything, it is that the Royal Oak Lottery and its competitors were highly profitable enterprises. A single operation at the Smithfield Fair with a £40 bank netted nearly that much per week, on average, in the autumn of 1663.[13] Corbett claimed a few months later that the patentees who had excluded him had realized about £1,000 apiece in about one year.[14] By the end of 1663, one of the principal partners in the Royal Oak was Joseph Williamson, secretary to Sir Henry Bennet, a principal Secretary of State. Williamson, who was notoriously quick to seize the financial opportunities that his office afforded him, purchased a 20 per cent share, and subsequently received regular accounts from Royal Oak 'farmers.'[15] As Undersecretary of State, he exerted pressure on reluctant local officials to allow the Royal Oak to operate. An alderman of Bristol wrote at the beginning of the new year of resistance to permitting the Royal Oak Lottery at their fair, 'which broke half the cashiers in Bristol when last there.' Within a week, the same alderman was writing that he had 'prevailed with the mayor... to allow the Royal Oak lottery during the eight days of the fair,' and perhaps longer, despite its having 'ruined' a number of young men during the five months it was in Bristol the previous year, the mayor's own son having lost £50. One month later, the mayor himself reported that the Royal Oak had been in operation in Bristol for three weeks, and would be permitted

---

[10] TNA SP 29/89/17; SP 29/91/65; SP 29/91/73.   [11] Ewen, *Lotteries and Sweepstakes*, 95.
[12] TNA SP 29/91/74.   [13] TNA SP 29/79/150.   [14] TNA SP 29/91/65.
[15] Ewen, *Lotteries and Sweepstakes*, 95–8.

somewhat longer, although he suspected 'they will soon be warped out.' Williamson's response brought the mayor's sheepish reply several days later that he would 'obey Mr. Secretary's commands about the Royal Oak lottery.'[16] In February of 1668, Sir John Skelton wrote to Williamson from Plymouth to tell him that Royal Oak operators there would

> not fayle of my Assistance wherein I can serve them (for your sake) but I much fear that ye Mayor will not permitt them to come into Towne, in regard they carried so vast a Sum[m]e out with them the last tyme they were here.

Skelton wrote subsequently of his continuing efforts to browbeat the mayor and corporation into submission over the lottery.[17]

One of the mechanisms through which officials nosed their way into the trough was for the lottery to be appropriated for philanthropic, charitable, or public works projects, the intended beneficiaries quickly dismayed to discover that these ostensibly laudable enterprises largely served to launder lottery proceeds, very few of which trickled into their hands. The Royal Oak was initially seized upon as a means of financing ventures such as the establishment of a herring fishery, under Crown oversight, to foster the recovery of trade after the Civil Wars, and to prevent the incursions of Dutch fishing vessels on the North Sea coast. The herring fishery was a favourite project of Sir Edward Ford, who surfaced in Corbett's complaint against Roche and Finocelli for authorizing their exercising the lottery in defiance of Corbett's warrant. In December 1663, Henry Bennet, having secured half interest in the Royal Oak, obtained for Demarces, Dupuy, and Richard Baddeley the licence for it and l'Oca di Catalonia, 'applying the whole profits to support the fishing trade only,' minus 'fit recompense for their trouble' and pensions to two of Bennet's clients.[18] Pepys, who sat on the committee overseeing the Fishery, consequently found himself ensnared in 'poor simple doings about the business of the Lottery,' and regretted 'that a thing so low and base should have any thing to do with so noble an undertaking.' He complained again within a few months of 'how superficially things are done in the business of the Lottery, which will be the disgrace of the Fishery, and without profit.'[19] The confounding profusion of overlapping patents and the dismaying number of hands in the till meant that it was probably no small relief to Pepys when the Fishery's grant of lottery proceeds expired at Easter in 1667.

After the collapse of the Clarendon ministry that year, lotteries were advanced as a means of funding pensions for 'the indigent and distressed officers' who had

[16] Ewen, *Lotteries and Sweepstakes*, 109; TNA SP 29/90/50, 83, 112; SP 29/92/151; SP 29/93/64.

[17] TNA SP 29/234/305; SP 29/235/135.

[18] TNA SP 29/86/148–152; CSPD Charles II: *Calendar of State Papers, Domestic Series, of the Reign of Charles II*, 28 vols (London: Public Record Office, 1860–1939), 2. 146, 3. 397.

[19] *Pepys' Diary*, 5. 323, 6. 53.

served the royalist cause during the Civil Wars, were dispossessed under the Interregnum, and were left with little prospect of other relief under the terms of the Restoration settlement. A consortium of 'Loyal and Indigent Officers' was granted a monopoly of plate lotteries, essentially raffles of luxury household goods, by royal warrant in August 1668. By the following April, they had been granted the concession of all lotteries, including the Royal Oak. There were complaints from the beginning, however, that very few of the proceeds of the concessions reached pensioners. Charles Hammond estimated that there were two hundred-odd former royalist officers 'that had no Imployments, nor Subsistance of a Livelihood' who were allotted one quarter of the proceeds of the lottery, which had so far amounted to the equivalent of eleven days' wages for a commissioned officer.[20] From June of 1672, the proceeds of the Royal Oak were directed to be divided evenly between the pensioners, including 300 widows and orphans, and the trustees of the Loyal and Indigent Officers.[21] The patentees paid £4,000 per annum for the ability to grant concessions or 'farms' to individual operators, who in turn purchased the grants from the patentee; the patents typically ran for thirteen years. Although the Royal Oak's intended beneficiaries had changed, the same senior officials continued to have a stake and apply pressure to allow the lottery to proliferate. In July 1675, Williamson, by now Secretary of State for the Northern Department, wrote to the Vice Chancellor of Oxford on behalf of Royal Oak farmers to request his permission to operate the lottery during Trinity Term, and for 'as long as well the matter will bear,' noting that the Chancellor had already recommended this course of action, and that his own permission as a principal Secretary of State would be given as a matter of course.[22]

Unlicensed operators were a perennial obstacle to the patentees' ability to enforce their monopoly. It was perhaps from this concern that Finocelli wrote to Demarces in November 1666 with 'several new descriptions of lottery games.'[23] The patentees were also embroiled as third parties in jurisdictional disputes at court between the Master of the Revels and the Groom Porter. In June of 1675, a number of 'loyal indigent officers,' who claimed to have a patent for thirteen years for all lotteries except for the Royal Oak, petitioned the Lord Keeper to prevent the Groom Porter, Thomas Offley, and the Master of the Revels, Thomas Killigrew, 'from the exercise or creating of any lotteries.' Offley and his successor Thomas Neale contended that the Royal Oak and its variants were 'games,' entailing the expenditure of time, rather than 'lotteries,' and thus fell within the purview of their office. Orders in Council issued that month requested that a settlement be reached among the parties, the officers contending that an 'Indian Game and

---

[20] [Charles Hammond], *The Loyal Indigent Officer* (London: E.C., 1670), 5–7.
[21] Ewen, *Lotteries and Sweepstakes*, 112–17.   [22] TNA SP 44/43/23; CSPD Charles II, 17. 194.
[23] TNA SP 29/179/19; CSPD Charles II, 6. 281.

Twirling Board' that the Groom Porter had licensed was a lottery, and thus an infringement of their patent. Offley countered that this was not a 'lottery,' but a 'game,' played with dice, invented and introduced after he came into office, and belonged to him under his patent. The Groom Porter refused to yield, 'the right of his place [being] so much concerned.'[24] The matter was still unsettled in 1683, when Offley's successor as Groom Porter, Thomas Neale, petitioned that the Royal Oak and other 'dice' lotteries fell within his remit, and that their concession to third parties had deprived him of £400 to £500 in annual revenue. Neale also called attention to the dwindling number of beneficiaries among the Loyal Indigent Officers, proposing instead that proceeds be directed to what was to become the Royal Hospital at Chelsea.[25]

By the Board

If Neale's intention was to require Royal Oak operators to procure licences from his office, his projections of the proceeds suggests that there were anywhere from eight hundred to one thousand Royal Oak operations going forward in England and Wales in any given year. Many of these seem to have been itinerant and ephemeral, popping up at seasonal events such as fairs. Joseph Williamson received weekly accounts of lottery proceeds from Norwich and Exeter in letters that mention results of capital trials, suggesting that the Royal Oak visited county towns when the assizes were sitting.[26] A tract entitled *The Pleasures of Matrimony* suggested that a young man with 'an Opportunity to carry his Mistress to *Bartholomew*-Fair, or *Southwark*-Fair...forgets not to carry her to the Royal-Oak Lottery, and to throw away forty or fifty Shillings to learn her the manner of the Game.' The satirist Edward Ward located the Royal Oak at the seasonal resort of Tunbridge Wells and also at Islington, a haven for Londoners seeking a respite from urban noise, dirt, and crowds; Epsom and Lambeth Wells were also mentioned in connection with Royal Oak operations, as were coffee and chocolate houses in St James's, Westminster. Another contemporary writer mentioned 'the *Royal-Oake-Lottery* in *Suffolk street*,' which seems to have been a more permanent fixture, whether it was located between Leicester Fields and the Haymarket, or south of the Thames, near the Mint. Since lottery projectors were dependent on networks of distributors, it is possible that those listed for the ticket lottery licensed under the Royal Oak patent in 1695 were venues where the Royal Oak

---

[24] CSPD Charles II, 17. 147, 211; Ewen, *Lotteries and Sweepstakes*, 117–18.
[25] TNA SP 29/423/68.   [26] TNA SP 29/265/25, 82–3.

Lottery was kept. The majority of these were taverns and coffeehouses in London and Westminster, the single exception a mercer in Oxford.[27] Whether exercised legitimately by agents of the patentees or illicitly by others, the Royal Oak and its variants developed an unsavoury reputation, and there were repeated calls for their abolition. When its operators descended on Bristol in 1663, the mayor recounted that 'the cry of the poorer sort of people was very great against them,' on account, he claimed, of the Royal Oak's dubious legality.[28] Under the Henrician statute, unlawful games were those that drew workers away from their employment. Lotteries, on the other hand, seemed to some contemporaries to present a different category. Board lotteries such as the Royal Oak were played at fairs with the permission of local authorities and were often associated with charitable or other public-spirited fundraising initiatives. The Royal Oak arguably fell outside the language of existing gaming statutes, even the newest Gaming Act, provided that artisans, labourers, servants, and apprentices were barred, and provided that no player was permitted to win or lose more than £100 at a sitting, which last provision would protect the operators from excessive losses. Nevertheless, in April of 1664, the lottery agent John Poyntz was summoned before the Westminster sessions on a complaint that he had fraudulently received payments from several individuals 'pr[e]tending to grant them Lycenses for ye keeping of unlawfull Games in their houses.' Poyntz was clerk comptroller to the Master of the Revels, and was very likely the 'Captain Poyntz' with whom Samuel Pepys conferred in September of that year about a prospective lottery to support a Royal Fishery.[29] Nicholas Wood, one of Williamson's agents for the Royal Oak, requested an order to leave Norwich in June of 1669, as 'the Merchants and better sort of people will not Come at it.'[30]

The modest weekly yields reported from Norwich in September 1669, just under six pounds one week and under three pounds the next, suggest that many operations were pitched low. Toward the end of the century, Edward Ward described punters playing for pennies at Tunbridge Wells.[31] Royal Oak operators promoted the lottery aggressively, either misrepresenting or glossing over the considerable advantage of the 'bank.' One advertisement from around 1695 noted the continuation of the patent under William and Mary,

> by reason this *Lottery* consists purely of *Chance & Fortune*, contrived in so excellent a manner, that every Person that considers but the following *Rules*,

---

[27] *The Pleasures of Matrimony* (London: Henry Rhodes, 1688), 19; Edward Ward, *A Walk to Islington* (London: n.p., 1699), 11–12; Edward Ward, *The World Bewitch'd* (London: n.p., 1699), 23; *The Arraignment, Trial, and Condemnation of Squire Lottery, Alias Royal-Oak Lottery* (London: A. Baldwin, 1699), 34–5, 37; *The Character of the Beaux* (London: n.p., 1696), 22; *Collection for Improvement of Husbandry and Trade*, 138 (1695).

[28] TNA SP 29/92/151.   [29] LMA MJ/SR/1285, r 76; *Pepys' Diary*, 5. 276.

[30] TNA SP 29/261/107.   [31] TNA SP 29/265/25, 82; Ward, *A Walk to Islington*, 12.

may clearly see, that it is impossible for any that ventures their Money at it, either to deceive or be deceived; as is often practic'd at play upon Cards & Dice.

This broadside echoed language applied to L'Oca di Catalonia decades earlier, touted as 'a game of pure fortune' that 'everyone may play without the least apprehension or suspicion of deceit.' The promotion further asserted that the 'genteel & pleasant' game had gained 'a general approbation in the principal Courts & Cities of Christendom; where person of all Ranks & Qualities of both Sexes, disdain not to assemble together, and daily divert themselves with this Princely Recreation.'[32]

Contemporary commentary on the Royal Oak Lottery anticipated many of the grounds of anxiety that informed the critique of gaming over the course of the next century. The involvement of women alarmed many observers, as did the participation not only of plebeians, but also of 'the middling sort.' A tract that appeared the year that the Lottery Act was finally enacted lamented that that 'many an honest Gentleman and Citizen has been seduc'd' by the Royal Oak. Operators kept 'an open Table' so that 'a Person that has twenty or thirty pound in his Pocket to lose with 'em at Night, may dine with 'em at any time.' The author noted the popularity of the Royal Oak among women, especially those from urban mercantile and commercial households: 'I have seen, my self,' the writer averred, 'an ordinary Citizen's Wife lose her Seven or Eight Pieces in a Morning, and at the same time swear solemnly she has had the same bad Fortune for a Month together successively.'[33] Edward Ward also suggested that operators particularly targeted women, describing in his verses the proposal of a 'Cunning Projector' for

A New Royal-Oak with two Balls, and the Cheat
Will be thought twice as Fair, yet be doubly as great.
And why with two Balls? Cause it's very well known,
A Pair pleases Ladies, much better than One.[34]

Years after the last of the Royal Oak patents expired, De Moivre described how 'lottery men' took advantage of the mathematical ignorance that prevailed among the public at large:

When the Play of the Royal Oak was still in use, some Persons who lost considerably by it, had their Losses chiefly occasioned by an Argument of which they could not perceive the Fallacy. The Odds against any particular Point of the Ball

---

[32] *The Rules of the Royal Money Lottery*, Amsterdam, c. 1695.
[33] *The Country Gentleman's Vade Mecum* (London: John Harris, 1699), 80–1, 84.
[34] Ward, *A Walk to Islington*, 12.

were one and Thirty to One, which intituled the Adventurers, in case they were winners, to have thirty two Stakes returned, including their own; instead of which they having but eight and Twenty, it was very plain that on the Single account of the disadvantage of the Play, they lost one eighth part of all the Money they played for. But the Master of the Ball maintained that they had no Reason to complain; since he would undertake that any particular point should come up in two and Twenty Throws; of this he would offer to lay a Wager, and actually laid it when required. The seeming contradiction...so perplexed the Adventurers, that they began to think the Advantage was on their side; for which reason they play'd on and continued to lose.[35]

Arbuthnot, in addenda to his translation of Huygens, had actually argued that the odds of throwing a particular number on the polyhedral 'teetotum' were slightly better than the mean in twenty-two casts, but slightly worse in only twenty casts. The reason for this anomaly, as Arbuthnot indicated, was the impossibility of a polyhedron with thirty-two sides of perfectly equal surface area.[36] One writer asserted near the end of the century that not even the Royal Oak operators perceived the extent of their statistical advantage.[37]

Oaks and Oranges

By 1687, the patentees paid 4,000 guineas (£4,200) annually for the right to grant concessions to 'farmers,' as lottery operators were termed, for a period of thirteen years. 'Farms' of this lottery were highly profitable to the concessionaires, so much so that there were efforts to establish a Royal Oak operation on Barbados. The Lieutenant Governor of the island lamented in March 1688 that 'our poverty, together with the disorders and rudenesses of certain persons, forced the person who managed it to give it over.' There were hopes, however, that the Royal Oak projectors there would try the lottery again at Easter, 'and if they succeed sufficiently to be worth your notice,' the Lord President Sunderland was told, 'they will ask for your patronage and favour.'[38] In 1692, Henry Bulstrode, a gentleman usher to William and Mary, petitioned to establish the Royal Oak on Barbados

---

[35] De Moivre, *Doctrine of Chances* (1718), iii–iv.

[36] [Huygens], *Laws of Chance*, tr. attributed Arbuthnot, 58–9; David R. Bellhouse, 'A Manuscript on Chance Written by John Arbuthnot,' *International Statistical Review*, 57 (December 1989), 251. The thirty-two panels of a black and white soccer ball illustrate the problem neatly, with twenty hexagons joined with twelve pentagons.

[37] *Country Gentleman's Vade Mecum*, 79–80.

[38] *Calendar of State Papers, Colonial Series, America and West Indies*, 1685–1688, ed. J. W. Fortescue (London: HMSO, 1899), 521.

and Jamaica, professing himself 'willing to make ye Experiment at his owne hazard.'[39]

The language of the patent issued in 1687 enjoined local authorities 'to give all just and necessary Protection, Encouragement, Aid, and Assistance' to the patentees and their concessionaires, including the apprehension of any unauthorized operators infringing on the patent, and furthermore 'not to molest, trouble or disquiet them,' notwithstanding any existing gaming statutes, all of which were inventoried in the patent.[40] Nevertheless, in common with the semi-official deputies of the Groom Porter in the next century, agents of the Royal Oak patentees were on occasion 'molested, troubled, or disquieted' by challenges to the legality of their activities. There continued to be public harassment of Royal Oak operators, which by the tempestuous reign of James II may have had ideological overtones, given the lottery's association with the royalist cause. The conduct of what some observers deemed an intrinsically deceitful enterprise under royal patents might be constructed as an abuse of the royal prerogative akin to those that heightened the aggravation that finally erupted in the Civil Wars, and that were an increasing source of grievance in the reign of James II. In March of 1688, the Treasury lords themselves summoned the lowly City constable John Faircloth to answer complaints that he had disturbed Royal Oak operators 'in the quiet exercise of said lottery in contempt of the King's patent and proclamation.' During the tense summer that followed, the Royal Oak farmers twice petitioned for troops to protect lottery operators from harassment 'by several lewd and disorderly persons,' which had reached a point that operators were 'forced to shut up their banks.'[41] The events of the ensuing year, however, as tumultuous as they were otherwise, incredibly enough saw no disruption in the operation of the Royal Oak. The patentees continued in possession for the rest of their term, which did not expire until 1691, and the comptroller appointed to oversee their accounts continued in office under the new monarchs, who were 'well satisfied in his fidelity and circumspection therein.'[42] By the 1690s, the Royal Oak Lottery had gravitated to the Netherlands, where as the 'Koniglyke Gelt-Lottery' was kept at the Golden Crown near the Stadthuis from six to nine-thirty every evening, according to a broadside from the middle of the decade (figure 4.2). It, as well as basset 'and other Games of this nature,' were similarly found in other 'Publick Houses' in Amsterdam, so that by 1697 the city government 'prohibited these Games upon severe penalties.'[43]

[39] TNA SP 44/235/305.

[40] *His Majesties Letters Patent Granted to Randolph Ashenhurst, Esquire, Stephen Hales, Michael Cope, and Thomas Ashenhurst, Gentlemen, for the Sole Exercise of the Royal-Oak Lottery, Raffling, and all other Lotteries*, London 1687, 12, 14–15, 20.

[41] *Calendar of Treasury Books*, ed. William A. Shaw, 32 vols (London: HMSO, 1904–1961), 8. 1801, 2030–1.

[42] *Calendar of Treasury Books*, 9. 204.

[43] *The Rules of the Royal Money Lottery*, Amsterdam, c. 1695; *Post Man*, 289 (6–9 March 1697).

Figure 4.2 *The Royal Money Lottery*, printed broadside, c. 1695. After the succession of the Dutch stadtholder William of Orange to the British thrones, the Royal Oak Lottery was introduced in Amsterdam.

Local officials were also enjoined to protect the patentees and the concessions they granted from imitators, such as the Marble Lottery mentioned elsewhere, which was only one among a number of 'new invented lotteries and games resembling those granted to them' of which the Loyal Indigent Officers complained in July 1686. The Attorney General Sir Robert Sawyer supported this complaint, reporting illicit operations in London and Westminster and particularly at Bartholomew Fair, and recommending that magistrates be ordered to suppress these and punish offenders. William Perkins and Francis Queenborough were accused in October 1686 as the promoters of a 'Marble Figure Board Lottery,... a perfect Resemblance of the Royal Oak Lottery,' in violation of the patent of the Loyal Indigent Officers.[44] Individuals were still presented at sessions for operating the Marble Lottery for over a decade afterward. The Crown, however, sent mixed signals. Not quite one year after reporting on the Loyal Indigent Officers'

---

[44] *London Gazette*, 2180 (7–11 October 1686).

complaint, Sawyer advised two projectors of a new lottery that its design was 'distinct in nature from the Royal Oak Lottery, and not comprised within the prohibition contained in the grant thereof,' although he left it to the Commissioners of the Treasury to determine if it infringed on any other lottery patents in force.[45]

In England, legislation was drafted to prohibit any lottery in name or form 'by dice, lots, cards, balls, or any numbers or figures' from Lady Day (25 March) of 1693, on pain of a fine of £500 for operators and forty shillings per offence, up to a maximum of £20, for those who played. Importantly, the statute located the unlawfulness of lotteries in their inherent fraudulence, fraud that was both individual and institutional. The 1693 legislation was a direct attack on the Royal Oak Lottery, cited as 'more grievous and mischievous than any of the rest,' noting that its projectors had obtained from the beginning of the reign of Charles II onward 'several Patents or Grants under the Great Seal' in order 'the better to cover and perpetrate their said evil practice.' For all of this rhetorical posturing, including outrage over 'riots and murders... committed by reason of quarrels happening at the said unlawful games,' the Lottery Bill was probably intended to eliminate competition for the first of the state lotteries drawn the following year. The bill ultimately foundered over questions of compensating pensioners dependent on the income from the Royal Oak patent, and patentees for payments already made under its terms.[46]

In May of 1693, the Treasury agreed to publish a notice to the effect that the Royal Oak and other lotteries

> are lately reduced to so small a number and under such regulations as hath been by experience found the most effectual way and means to suppress all such as act without any authority (who are far the greater number) and whose actings have occasioned the common prejudice so generally conceived against the Lotteries.[47]

Soon afterward, unable to bring the Royal Oak under the purview of his office, and confronted with the failure of the Lottery Bill, the Groom Porter Thomas Neale projected an entirely new venture. Neale's 'Million Lottery' was the first of the state lotteries, introduced in March 1694, not coincidentally the same year that the Bank of England was chartered to facilitate the funding of an expanded military and naval establishment through the institution of a national debt. The 'Million Lottery' was a fiscal experiment along the same lines, prompted by the new demands of a foreign policy that involved the nation in a protracted series of continental wars. Neale's venture was unlike any lottery that had been drawn before. Subscribers paid £10 for an annuity of £1 per year for sixteen years, in

---

[45] LMA MJ/SR/1841, r 49; MJ/SR/1902, i 18; TNA SP 31/3/229–30; SP 44/71/342.
[46] Ewen, *Lotteries and Sweepstakes*, 125–6, 176–7.   [47] *Calendar of Treasury Books*, 10. 205.

addition to a chance at a greater annual sum, ranging from £10 to £1,000. Unlike 'blanks' in other 'ticket lotteries,' which were wastepaper, these were government bonds, and as such 'remained a tradable commodity after the draw,' or even before it. As early as March 1694, eight months before the November drawing, enterprising investors were offering to purchase tickets at second hand from ticket holders with sufficiently cold feet or compromised cash flow to swallow a 30 per cent discount.

Purchasers seem to have been socioeconomically heterogeneous. There are anecdotal accounts in printed sources of titled aristocrats purchasing blocks of tickets, while humbler folk bought single tickets in consortia. The top prize of £1,000 per annum was split among four Huguenot émigrés, who were fairly well-to-do, as one had been a President of the Parlement de Paris. The multiple second prizes of £500 annually were shared among consortia that included a silk-thrower, a stationer, a hosier, and a stonecutter. The initial success of the 'Million Lottery' set the pattern for the state lotteries drawn until 1769, which are explored in greater depth in a later chapter. It also opened the floodgates for a profusion of private lotteries, a number of which had to be withdrawn when market saturation resulted in an unsustainable number of unsold tickets.[48] The Royal Oak patentees themselves sponsored a ticket lottery the very next year, issuing 40,000 tickets for 4,004 cash prizes ranging from £3 to £1,000. Criticism of the Royal Oak, and the near brush with suppression in Parliament two years earlier, likely led the promoters to disclose scrupulously the number of tickets and prizes, the ratio of 'blanks' to prizes, and the procedures for the drawing, which in common with continental lotteries employed purportedly innocent and incorruptible young boys to pull the tickets. As a further assurance of transparency, all tickets were drawn, including the 'blanks,' and a prize of £100 awarded to the first and last tickets drawn.[49]

As a result of continuing competition from this and other lotteries, Neale's state lottery ran into trouble. Within a few years, the government found itself hard pressed to pay the annuities from the Million Lottery, which were soon in arrears. Desperately short of cash near the end of 'King William's War,' the government promoted a second lottery in 1697, called the Malt Lottery as annuities were to be payable from the excise on that commodity. The bad publicity over the Million Lottery annuities resulted in only 1,763 tickets being purchased for its successor, with the embarrassing result that the Exchequer was reduced to paying government contractors in unsold tickets in lieu of cash. The Navy Victualling Board was able to refuse them; the Middlesex innkeepers who were stabling cavalry

---

[48] Ewen, *Lotteries and Sweepstakes*, 127–8, 172–3; Anne L. Murphy, 'Lotteries in the 1690s: Investment or Gamble?,' *Financial History Review*, 12 (2005), 230–2, 234, 239.

[49] *Collection for Improvement of Husbandry and Trade*, 138 (1695); this lottery seems to have escaped Ewen's notice.

horses could only complain bitterly.[50] The fiscal experiment of state-sponsored lotteries was such an abject failure that it was not attempted again until 1710, and only after the passage of legislation designed to manage some forms of competition and prohibit others outright.

A revised Lottery Act was finally passed in 1699. Its preamble was notably ameliorated from the 1693 bill, eliminating any derogatory references to the Royal Oak, while asserting that 'evill-disposed Persons' had for a number of years 'unjustly and fraudulently gott to themselves great Sums of Money' from the dependents of both elite and middling-sort households 'and from other unwary Persons... by Colour of severall Patents or Grants under the Great Seale of England,' which could be understood to refer only to the Royal Oak's imitators such as the 'Marble Figure Board.'[51] Under this Act, the Royal Oak was explicitly permitted to continue until the expiration of its patent at Michaelmas (29 September) 1703, a provision for which a number of pension recipients had petitioned. By this time, however, there were only about three dozen Royal Oak pensioners remaining, the median annual pension standing at £20.[52] The Royal Oak concessionaires for six south-eastern counties petitioned the Privy Council in April 1702 after magistrates shut down the lottery in Norwich, Yarmouth, and Lynn, indicating that operations were aggressively pursued, in both senses of the word, until the last patent ran its course.[53]

The Royal Oak Lottery set a precedent for the complicity of the Crown in the establishment of commercial gaming ventures, so it was perhaps fitting that its prohibition created the mechanism through which gaming would be attacked subsequently. It was only in 1739, when the first of the Georgian Gaming Acts classified hazard, basset, and Ace of Hearts as illegal lotteries as defined in the Lottery Act of 1699, that any statutory distinction emerged between games of chance and other games. The statute located the unlawfulness of lotteries in the inability of players to determine the odds of winning or losing, recommending, in effect, that mathematical probability be legally defined as beyond the comprehension of the general public. The closing of one set of loopholes, however, had the effect of opening others. In the meantime, the Royal Oak stood as an example of a business model that metropolitan gaming entrepreneurs quickly adopted.

---

[50] Murphy, 'Lotteries in the 1690s,' 233; Ewen, *Lotteries and Sweepstakes*, 133.
[51] *Statutes of the Realm*, 7. 532; italics mine.
[52] *Journal of the House of Commons*, 85 vols (London: HMSO, 1802–1830), 12. 645–9.
[53] TNA PC 1/14/8.

5

Making Bank

The Emergence of Metropolitan Gaming Concerns

In the months before and after the Restoration in 1660, one Abraham Cornish, an informant and possibly a parish constable, submitted twenty-one petitions to the Westminster sessions for a portion of the fines levied on victuallers for violations of a statute enacted in 1541, 33 Henricus VIII c. 9, against 'unlawful gaming.' Among these, Maria Howes was summoned in July 'for keeping unlawfull games in her house,' as was Thomas Lovejoy of Holborn in August 'for suffering unlawfull games to be used in his house,' and William Kempster of the same parish the following January for allowing unlawful gaming in his alehouse. A victualler of Clerkenwell was presented for keeping a 'common' gaming house 'and for dice tables cardes & shove groate' as well as a bowling alley, for at least forty days between 1 August 1659 and 13 July 1660, which last detail allowed the maximum fine of £80 to be imposed. The varying ways that these and other similar offences were denominated is worth noting. The inventory of dice, tables, cards, shove-groat, and ninepins, for example, was formulaic, appearing verbatim in a number of recognizances and petitions in sessions rolls from this year, and corresponding to language in the statute that listed bowling, quoits, and tennis along with dice and cards as games prohibited under prior statutes.[1]

Cornish possibly viewed these petitions as his last chance to cash in as the Protectorate sounded its death rattle. Popular recreations of the sort comprehended within this and other statutes had been bones of contention throughout the century, and had been particular targets of the Interregnum regimes. The Book of Sports, for example, had permitted games to be played on Sunday, provided these were not games of chance played for money. Whether money was staked or not, however, for much of the century, the law operated from an entirely different set of objectives from those that obtained later when it pursued games of chance and those who facilitated them.

---

[1] LMA MJ/SR/1214, rr 210, 313–315, 326–328; MJ/SR/1217, r 109; MJ/SR/1220, rr 335–345, 360–362; MJ/SR/1222, r 180.

The Gambling Century: Commercial Gaming in Britain from Restoration to Regency. John Eglin, Oxford University Press.
© John Eglin 2023. DOI: 10.1093/oso/9780192888198.003.0006

Lawful Recreation

Common law did not distinguish games of chance from other games, including athletic contests, and held all games to be lawful; unlawful games were defined as such by statute.[2] The first such statute, enacted in 1388, forbade handball, football, quoits, dice, bowling, and skittles to 'servants and laborers of husbandry, and laborers and servants of artificers,' in the interest of having these workers devote their spare time to practising the defence-essential skill of archery. This prohibition, and the justification for it, was reiterated in statute of 1541, legislation that seemed fairly prohibitive at first glance. No one, of any 'degree, quality, or condition,' was permitted either by themselves or through 'factors, deputies or servants,' to keep any premises where games were played for the 'gain, lucre, or living' of the occupant. Violators were to be fined forty shillings for every day the games in question were in operation, and customers taken while gaming were fined a silver 'mark,' or six shillings and eightpence, one third of one pound sterling. In 1541, of course, these were still substantial sums of money. Forty shillings, or two pounds sterling, was literally two troy pounds of silver, a much more valuable commodity before the vast mineral wealth of the Americas began to be exploited. By the time that the first of the Georgian Gaming Acts raised fines substantially for play at specific games re-classified as illegal lotteries, two centuries of inflation had taken its toll.

The Henrician Act also contained a litany of exceptions. The statute permitted gaming to all from Christmas Day to Twelfth Night. Nobility and gentry, the latter defined as freeholders with an annual landed income of at least £100, could keep all of the enumerated games, including those with cards or dice, in their residences. More importantly, they could also license their servants to play, either with their employer, or their employer's guests, with the permission of the former and for the entertainment of the latter.[3] The Tudor enactments, then, proscribed only plebeian gaming. There was as much concern in the Henrician statute, and in the Marian revision passed in 1555, for loss of time as loss of money, and the considerable exceptions that were carved out testify to a concern that plebeian recreation should be carefully supervised. Elite gaming, including courtly gaming, was well outside the provisions of these statutes. The loophole that permitted householders to license their servants to game proved so useful to gaming entrepreneurs from the mid-eighteenth century onward that it was specifically repealed under the Victorian Gaming Act of 1845, the first statute to recognize the reality of commercial gaming.[4] Although it was supplemented by half a dozen other

---

[2] The most comprehensive treatment of gaming legislation in Britain before the twentieth century is still Howard Street, *The Law of Gaming* (London: Sweet and Maxwell, 1937). Tosney provides a useful précis in 'Gaming in England,' 78–87.
[3] *Statutes of the Realm*, 3. 839–41.   [4] Street, *Law of Gaming*, 8, 25–6.

statutes over the next two centuries, most gaming was prosecuted under the Henrician Act, meaning that gaming was essentially a status offence, its illegality consisting in the socioeconomic status of those gaming rather than in the practice of gaming itself. The loss of work hours to employers was as great a concern as loss of money from workers' pocketbooks, a circumstance reflected in the anomalous legality, and legal enforceability, of wagering, as well as the eventual need to carve out a separate legal category for lotteries.

33 Henricus VIII c. 9 also allowed for public accommodations to be licensed for gaming within the limitations of the statute. Licensees were enjoined to keep order on their premises, on pain of a charge of 'keeping a disorderly house,' and specifically to disallow gaming by anyone 'dependent on their labor for their bread.' The Marian Gaming Act of 1555 (2&3 Phillipus et Maria c. 9) invalidated all such licences, but it was never clear whether the statute only applied to licences issued up to that point, or disallowed the licensing of gaming thenceforward. While a tract of 1708 asserted the latter, Roger L'Estrange suggested that licensing placards could be seen in gaming venues in 1686.[5] Instructively, the patent of James I's Groom Porter permitted him to license forty gaming houses, billiard parlours, and bowling greens in London, Westminster, and Southwark.[6] When Thomas Morecock, who kept the Three Diamonds in Hosier Lane in the City parish of Saint Sepulchre, was reported for operating a gaming house in March of 1674, he claimed to hold 'a Lycense for Gameing from ye Groome Porter' for which he had paid ten shillings.[7] In May of 1683, Elizabeth Dudley obtained a Groom Porter's licence to keep 'a shoffel board...and a Billiard Table' at her establishment, the Hen and Chickens; she was enjoined 'only to use the sayd Games for the moderate Recreation of such persons whose livelihood depends not on their labours,' and specifically not to permit 'any Labourer, Journeyman, Apprentice, or Servant to play...', whereby not only their Money may be expended, but their time lost.'[8] These licences may or may not have been legitimate, given that in July of 1684, William Browne of Cripplegate was summoned to the Westminster sessions for 'extorting sivirall sumes of money from divers p[er]sons by forcing upon them Lycences to keepe gameinge houses.'[9]

The language of the Henrician statute specifically forbade keepers of public accommodations to profit from gaming, from keeping 'a house or place' for gaming for their own 'gain, lucre, or living,' phrasing that found its way into the boilerplate of indictments as victuallers, vintners, coffee-sellers, and others were returned for allowing, aiding, abetting, and encouraging gaming on their premises. The Tudor statutes did not necessarily contemplate proprietors of public

---

[5] *The Gamester's Law* (London: Arthur Collins and Samuel Butler, 1708), 4; [Roger L'Estrange], *Observator in Dialogue*, 3 (April 1686), 1733.

[6] Tosney, 'Gaming in England,' 133.   [7] LMA COL/WD/02/038.

[8] TNA SP29/423/f103.   [9] LMA MJ/SR/1653, r 101.

accommodations either operating or sharing in the proceeds of games of chance on their premises, nor did the parliaments that enacted them anticipate that 'gain, lucre, or living' would be derived from gaming in that way. Games could be a means of moving product if patrons of public houses, for example, played skittles or ninepins for pots of ale. Correspondingly, contemporaries noted that it was difficult to let premises for alehouses that did not have bowling greens or other such amenities attached.[10] A tract of 1708 noted a judicial understanding 'that if the Guests in any Inn or Tavern, call for a pair of Dice or Tables, and for their Recreation play with them,...that this is not within the Statute, for these Houses are not kept for Lucre or Gain.' Furthermore, if play at cards or dice was unlawful in itself, then no one could be licensed to manufacture these items.[11] The Tudor statutes were clearly applied as much to games of skill, like ninepins, skittles, shuffleboard, and tennis, as to games of chance played with cards or dice like hazard, basset, and faro. The Henrician Gaming Act classified bowling alleys and tennis courts as venues that might be kept unlawfully for the 'gain lucre or living' of the proprietor, putting them in the same category as public facilities for dicing (which might include backgammon) or carding. To operate within the statute, the same licensing was required for tennis courts and bowling alleys as for any games of cards and dice. It was still the case in the later seventeenth century that both licences for 'games' and prosecutions of 'gaming' reflected the concerns of the Henrician statute.

It is safe to say that the entities designated 'common gaming houses' in the sixteenth century, and much of the seventeenth century, were not the commercial gaming enterprises targeted in prosecutions later. As early as 1668, however, there were printed descriptions of a very different sort of establishment, in which the facilitation of games of chance was a critical source of profit. *Leathermore's Advice* of that year and the *Compleat Gamester* six years later described a typical 'ordinary,' citing the example of Speering's in Bell Yard, Lincoln's Inn Fields,

> a handsom house, where every day, about the hour of twelve, a good Dinner is prepared..., with all other accommodations fit for that purpose, whereby many gentlemen of great estates and good repute, make this place their resort, who after play a while for recreation both moderately and commonly without deserving reproof.

As day wore into night, however, the clientele and character of the ordinary changed as dedicated gamblers turned up, to the evident delight of the management, for 'if the house find you free to the box and a constant caster, you shall be treated with suppers at night, and a cawdle in the morning, and have the honour

---

[10] *Gazetteer*, 11,780 (6 December 1766).   [11] *The Gamester's Law*, 5–7.

to be stiled a lover of the house, whilst your money lasts.'[12] In recognizing not just the existence but even the possibility of commercial gaming in the guise of a 'house' that derived revenue from gaming (from the 'box' in dicing games, in this case), these Restoration writers on games were ahead of experts on probability, as well as magistrates, for that matter. Probability writers operated from the presumption of adversarial contests between individual players. As elusive as the practice of individual gamblers may be (one of the reasons they are outside the scope of this investigation), it is nevertheless significant that so many of the scenarios found in popularizations of probability are dicing wagers between individual gamblers, or 'side bets' that were common features of games like hazard. The possibility of a collective entity, identified as the 'bank' or 'house,' did not enter into these calculations. That collective, manifested in a commercial gaming venture, *did* appear in the work of writers on games such as Charles Cotton and Richard Seymour. Attention to probability as applied to games of chance, although taking the form of assertions supported by anecdote rather than mathematical proof, also suggests that it occurred to at least some contemporaries that there was profit to be made in gaming entrepreneurship, based in a more diverse and specialized range of public accommodations. The increasing prominence of the commercial gaming establishment in print culture supports this suggestion.

On the House

The emergence of the 'house' created a different gaming dynamic that neither punters nor proprietors nor the probabilists themselves recognized. The advantage that an omnipresent operator would enjoy did not occur to early modern mathematicians, in part because of their disinterest in gaming per se, but also because the 'house' or 'bank,' in short the commercial gaming enterprise, did not yet exist conceptually. The emergence of the institutionalized gaming space coincided with the development of other institutional and cultural spaces, and the reconfiguration of existing ones. In 1700, Thomas Brown, through the foil of an Asian visitor to London, described basset/faro as it was played in a chocolate house in Covent Garden:

> In this Place there is a great Altar to be seen, built round and covered with a Green *Wachum,* lighted in the midst, and encompassed by several Persons in a sitting Posture.... [O]ne of those, who I supposed was the *Priest,* spread upon the Altar certain Leaves which he took out of a little Book that he held in his Hand.... [I]n proportion as they were distributed round, each one of the

[12] Cotton, *Compleat Gamester* (1674), 4, 17.

Assistants made an Offering to it, greater, or less, according to his Devotion.... At last every Leaf which he returns to them, these unmoveable Assistants are all of them in their Turn possest by different Agitations, according to the *Spirit* which happens to seize them.... [S]carce has the Priest returned a certain Leaf, but he is likewise seised by the same Fury with the rest.[13]

As whimsical as Brown's tract may be, it does suggest that banking games were being played in public accommodations in the metropolis by the turn of the eighteenth century. The relatively few returns for gaming to Westminster sessions in the rest of the decade of the 1660s were generally directed at street gaming, such as dice played on wheelbarrows for small sums or articles of little value, or alehouse keepers who allowed plebeian customers to play at dice, bowls, or billiards on their premises. Presentments for gaming were still few and far between in the 1680s, the odd victualler or vintner summoned periodically for 'keeping a common gaming house.'

After 1700, however, presentments for keeping gaming houses became more frequent, and became the norm for gaming prosecutions. The language of charges became more precise, the phrase 'gaming house' appearing more frequently, and formulaic inventories of unlawful games kept in an accommodation or permitted by the proprietor cropping up less often, replaced with language focused on games of chance played with dice or cards. This development argues for a shifting connotation of the term 'gaming house' toward the specific comprehension of a venue specializing in games of chance. In July 1705, John Corderey was summoned 'for keeping two or more Roomes for playing at Cards Dice & other unlawfull Games' in Pall Mall, and was bound in recognizance not to 'use keepe or occupy any such House Roomes or places.' In September of the following year, however, Corderey appeared again with John Andrews 'for keeping a Com[m]on Gaming house,' again in Pall Mall. Richard Martin, a coffeeman of the same address, stood surety in both cases, raising the possibility that the rooms in question were on his premises and leased to Corderey.[14] The justice before whom Corderey made his second appearance was apparently unaware of his earlier appearance before a different justice with a different clerk, a pattern often repeated in the enforcement of gaming statutes in Westminster. Between July 1707 and October 1709, a period for which there are detailed minutes of the Westminster Court of Burgesses, eleven individuals were fined specifically for keeping gaming houses, one of whom was explicitly cited for a hazard table. Not included in this number are four men 'amerced' for keeping billiards or ninepins, whose entries appear on the same date as men cited for gaming houses, suggesting that a

---

[13] Thomas Brown, *Amusements Serious and Comical, Calculated for the Meridian of London* (London: John Nutt, 1700), 101–4.
[14] LMA MJ/SR/2057, r 82; MJ/SR/2078, r 3.

distinction was made between games of chance and other games, akin to that subsequently drawn in a grand jury charge for the Westminster sessions. The establishments in question included Tom's and Will's coffeehouses, as well as the Rose Tavern, all in Covent Garden, public accommodations that were closely associated with gaming in print culture.[15] By 1714 and 1715, recognizances issued after raids on gaming houses begin to list specific games, such as hazard, faro, or 'rowley-powley,' the last possibly an iteration of the seventeenth-century 'Marble Lottery.' Games of chance were becoming more conspicuous to authorities, who now differentiated them from other games that also qualified as 'unlawful.' The disproportionate number of demobilized military personnel seized in these cases may explain much of the concern for specificity.

It is still difficult to know when prosecutions were specifically targeted at games of chance as profit centres for the proprietors of establishments. When fourteen victuallers of Shoreditch stood indicted for keeping gaming houses in 1708, the constables, churchwardens, and overseers of the poor of the parish of St Leonard's petitioned for the prosecutions to be dropped, asserting 'that upon strict search and enquiry by us made, were never found or heard of any disorders kept in their respective houses,' and that the accused were 'very honest, industrious, persons (though but in mean conditions).' These appear not to have been commercial gaming operators, but fairly modest publicans with bowling greens or skittles grounds or other such facilities. One of them, Andrew Whitehead, pleaded a licence from the Groom Porter.[16] As Queen Anne's Parliament debated a revision of gaming statutes in 1709, a petition against the legislation asserted that a prohibition of gaming in "'All Publick Rooms and Places of Gaming...tho' for never so small a Sum' would result in 'the Ruin of many Thousand Families, that never had Gaming for any Thing considerable.'"[17] Such a bald statement in a petition addressed to Parliament indicates that the legality of games of chance in England (and elsewhere) continued to be murky. This lack of clarity became problematic in the first decades of the eighteenth century, as commercial ventures that featured gaming tables as profit centres began to emerge in metropolitan London. These were very different public spaces from those envisioned in either common or statute law.

By this time gaming, like other commercial concerns (stockbroking, maritime insurance), was embedded in the definitive 'public sphere' institution, the coffeehouse. John Macky in 1714 described Little Man's coffeehouse in St James as the redoubt of serious gamesters, where he 'saw two or three tables full at faro,

---

[15]   Westminster City Archives, WCBG/WCB 3: Minutes of the Court of Burgesses, 1705–1709.

[16]   Shoemaker, *Prosecution and Punishment,* 307–8; LMA MJ/SP/1708/001, 6–9, 53, 54; MJ/SP/1709/001, 3.

[17]   Hampshire Record Office 44M69/G2/188, quoted in Janet E. Mullin, 'Cards on the Table: The Middling Sort as Suppliers and Consumers of English Leisure Culture in the Eighteenth Century,' *Canadian Journal of History,* 45 (Spring/Summer 2010), 56 n. 30.

and was surrounded by a set of sharp faces that I was afraid would have devoured me with their eyes,' so much so that he felt pressured to lose six or seven shillings 'at faro to get off with a clear skin: and was overjoyed I so got rid of them.'[18] It is noteworthy that these were 'silver tables' for punters of moderate means. In December of that year, David Bennett of Suffolk Street was summoned on the complaint of John Gancy 'for unlawfully playing & winning from him at the Game of Faroe fifteen Guineas.' Again, Claude Porter, a coffeeman listed at the same address, stood surety, suggesting that Bennett kept a faro table in Porter's establishment, or perhaps that of the other surety, James Goddard, a vintner in nearby Warwick Street. In March 1716, there was another important departure when John Bernard Linster, a coffeeman in Haymarket, was summoned to the Westminster sessions on the complaint of the constables 'for keeping a Gameing table Called a Bank.' One of his sureties, William Miller, with an address in the Strand, appeared that August as complainant in another charge against Linster, as well as informing on Philip Wiseman, his neighbour in the Strand, and Henry Cole of Bishopsgate, both summoned 'for keeping a Gameing Bank.'[19] The commercial gaming venture had emerged in the archives.

Games People Play

In his charge to the grand jurors of Middlesex in October 1718, Whitelocke Bulstrode, as chair of the Commission of the Peace, distinguished two classifications of 'gaming houses,' the first consisting of 'Alehouses that have Shovel-board Tables, Nine-pins, and Bowling-Alleys belonging to them.' These catered to labourers, servants, artisans, and apprentices, who might, it was speculated, lose a week's wages in the course of an evening. Bulstrode adverted that several such houses 'in the upper part of Westminster' had been presented at the last sessions. 'The other sort of Gaming-Houses help to undo Persons of the first Quality, and young Gentleman of Estates'; Belsize House in Hampstead, operated by the gaming entrepreneur William Howell, was cited by way of example.[20] In spite of an increasing recognition among local authorities of gaming establishments aimed at a more affluent clientele, enforcement was necessarily tailored toward the first sort of accommodation as that was the direction of the applicable statutes. One guidebook published for the use of parish constables the same year as Bulstrode's

---

[18] Macky, *Journey through England*, 108.

[19] LMA MJ/SR/2240, r 94; MJ/SR/2265, r 129; MJ/SR/2275, rr 110–112; MJ/SR/2315, rr 170, 172. Significantly, Cole and Wiseman were permitted to stand as sureties for each other. Similarly, Edward Courtney, the box-keeper at Fryar's in the Haymarket seized there in September 1718, was a surety for Philip Spooner, apprehended in the same raid.

[20] *The Second Charge of Whitelocke Bulstrode, Esq., to the Grand Jury and Other Juries of the County of Middlesex* (London: Elizabeth Nutt and R. Gosling, 1718), 24.

charge included sample language for a variety of presentments, including one for the proprietor of 'an unlawful Gaming House' who had 'permitted Servants, Apprentices, & c. to play at Cards, Dice, and other Games prohibited by Law, to the great Encouragement of Vice, and Disturbance of the Neighbourhood there.'[21] Bulstrode's charge, supported by directives from Whitehall, refocused attention on commercial gaming establishments, as raids on these venues proliferated from November 1718, according to both sessions records and newspaper reports. During the previous decade, there had typically been one such raid per session.

The differentiation of gaming venues put forward in this grand jury charge was reinforced in September 1719, when a party of men, including officers of the Grenadier Guards, entered the Mitre coffeehouse in King Street, Whitehall, removed the dice and box from a backgammon table, and began to play, probably at hazard. The landlady, a Mrs Carter, then intervened, informing the group 'that she did not suffer any Gaming in her House.' The incident made the newspapers, and the Old Bailey proceedings, as the result of swordplay that later erupted, leaving one of the officers dead and another seriously wounded.[22] What is noteworthy for our purposes here is the proprietor of a public accommodation using the term 'gaming' in a way that drew a distinction between games of pure chance played for money, on one hand, and other permissible and presumably 'lawful' games, in this case backgammon, anticipating the line drawn in the 1740 Gaming Act between backgammon and any other games played with dice.

A memorandum sent anonymously to Charles Townshend sometime in the following decade urged a revision of policy toward gaming that distinguished *among* games of chance:

[A]s to the Pharo banks, and the Lights they put out at noon day, They were a burning Shame, and ought to be Extinguished, but as to Hazzard I think as I hope your Lordship will, that it may be revived, and over looked as other things are of greater Consequence and more pernicious a thousand times to ye good and well fare of the nation.

Hazard, as we have already seen, was favoured as an 'English game' that was 'fairer' than its competitors, generally continental imports. Casters at hazard knew against whom they played, and did not necessarily have to accept all of the wagers set. Neither circumstance held in foreign introductions like faro, played against a bank put up by an unknown number of silent partners. For the writer of this memorandum, hazard was a game in the same class with ninepins that drew

[21] [Jacob Giles], *The Compleat Parish Officer* (London: Elizabeth Nutt and R. Gosling for Bernard Lintot and W. Mears, 1718), 37.
[22] OBPO t17191014-23; *Evening Post*, 1583 (22 September 1719); *Weekly Journal*, 148 (3 October 1719).

custom to public accommodations to purchase commodities subject to excise duties. '[T]he putting down of public play,' it was alleged, had resulted in revenue lost to the Crown in the amount of £30,000 to £40,000 annually, as 'play for these last two or three years has been the only stimulus for the Circulation of the little money left.'[23]

Nicholas Tosney usefully asks whether we can assume that the contemporary usage 'gaming house' comprehended what he terms 'specialized gaming establishments,' posing a distinction between venues devoted to gaming, and venues where gaming took place. In the long eighteenth century, however, very few such establishments were 'specialized' for *any* purpose. The multi-purposing of public accommodations was possibly the single defining characteristic of the 'public sphere' that Jürgen Habermas described. The modern casino, which informs the comparative dimension of Tosney's work, belongs to a very different epoch. Tosney argues that specialized gaming houses were restricted to London and resorts like Bath, contending that even in London, they were relatively few in number and concentrated in particular areas, such as Covent Garden. He further suggests that most 'gaming houses' that appear in sessions rolls were in fact public accommodations in which individuals were caught gaming. While authorities did not carefully distinguish between those who kept tables and those who played at them, applying the epithet of 'common gamester' to both, Tosney plausibly suggests that many gamesters cited multiple times may actually have been gaming entrepreneurs, running gaming operations such as hazard tables or faro banks, since it was probably easier to prove that an individual had punted than it was to prove that householders had profited from gaming conducted on their premises.[24]

In 1722, a tract by a frustrated Westminster JP included a fanciful inventory of the personnel of a typical gaming house, including:

A *Commissioner,* always a Proprietor, who looks in of a Night, and the Week's Accompt is audited by him, and two others of the Proprietors....An *Operator,* who deals the Cards at a Cheating Game called *Faroe.* Two *Crowpees,* who watch the Cards, and gather the Money for the Bank....A *Flasher,* to swear how often the Bank has been stript.

This list subsequently had a long career in print culture, appearing again in the inaugural issue of the *Gentleman's Magazine* in 1731, and in newspapers well into

---

[23] TNA SP 35/66/76.
[24] Tosney, 'Gaming in England,' 101 n. 118, 128. Tosney relies on Robert Shoemaker's necessarily selective overview of the Middlesex and Westminster sessions rolls, although he has clearly examined some of these documents himself.

the 1790s.[25] Its hyperbolic inventions, while not to be taken at face value, do illustrate increased understanding of gaming operations as commercial enterprises. A tract of 1726 spoke explicitly not only of faro banks, but of the partnerships that underwrote them and the expenses involved in establishing them. The author seems to have had a specific operation in mind in cataloguing the expenditure and personnel of a faro bank 'when it was in its meridian Splendor.' The partners paid £100 annually '[f]or a Dog-kennel, or a Room before uninhabited, in the Play-house Passage next *Bridges-street Covent-garden*,' which was then decorated and furnished 'to insnare the best Company, before the Shop could be in Order for the Proprietors to lay down an hundred Guineas for a Bank.' No effort was spared in creating the atmosphere of a luxury accommodation; £150 would be budgeted annually for drink, including champagne, burgundy, claret, and brandy punch. Box-keepers were well-spoken and deferential, even in demanding to inspect dice to ensure that false ones were not introduced. At faro tables, 'the Gentleman that deals to you is commonly a polite well-bred Man.' Besides the two 'principals,' two junior partners were allowed smaller shares to manage the venue, 'the Principals being above acting themselves.'[26] In 1727, an observer remarked of White's, then still a public accommodation, that

> Conversation is not known here; the enquiries after news turn chiefly upon what happened last night at the Groom Porters. The business of the place is…above all, to solicit a share in the direction of the moneyed interests which is established here under the name of a Faro Bank.[27]

A French visitor to London had remarked in 1720 that 'more than half of the people in this city play at games of chance' and that gaming operations were 'established in all places where there is good company.'[28] An opposition newspaper argued in 1729 that gaming had become so pervasive among all classes 'that in some Measure, every *Tavern, Coffee-house*, and *Ale-house* in *London* and *Westminster* is more or less tainted.'[29] That decade had witnessed the first concerted effort to contain commercial gaming in the metropolis. Greater London's stature as Britain's 'royal metropolis' and the seat of central government contributed in no small degree to the multiplicity of gaming enterprises there, as did the intervention or intercession of the Crown, the court, or courts of different sorts, intentionally and otherwise.

---

[25] The list first appeared in *London Journal*, 129 (13 January 1722), and then later that year in *Account of the Endeavours*, 36; it ran again in *Gentleman's Magazine*, 1 (January 1731), 25, as well as *Read's Weekly Journal*, 3935 (16 July 1757), and the *True Briton*, 1477 (18 September 1797), to name a few examples.
[26] *Whole Art and Mystery*, 58–60.   [27] Quoted in Lillywhite, *London Coffee Houses*, 641.
[28] TNA SP 35/21/117 ('[P]lus de la moitié de gens de cette ville jouent aux jeux de hazard….on etablir…des academies dans tous les endroits ou il y a bonne compagnie….').
[29] *Fog's Weekly Journal*, 40 (28 June 1729).

The Stamp of Approval

Jurists and reformers failed to stem the emergence and rise of commercial gaming because they persistently failed to understand its nature and structure. It was not simply that magistrates, to give one example, did not know that faro was played with cards, and not with dice. They persisted in the belief that gaming enterprises turned profits by cheating unwary punters, rather than realizing, as other contemporary observers occasionally noted, that gaming proprietors hardly needed to cheat when they had mathematics on their side. In fact, legislation facilitated rather than hindered the growth of commercial gaming, illustrated by new legislative efforts to address gaming as a social pathology in the reign of Queen Anne. The first in a series of Stamp Acts imposed a duty of sixpence per pack on cards and dice, neither of which could be 'sold or exposed to Sale or used in Play in any public gaming House' unless enclosed in stamped wrappers. Officers of the Stamp Office were empowered to enter any manufactory or retailer or 'any Publick Gameing-house Roome or Place' to ensure that cards and dice were stamped.[30] Stamp duty was designed in large part to keep cards and dice out of the hands of the same working people that the Henrician statute debarred from gaming in public accommodations. The levy of sixpence put even the cheapest cards out of their reach. The cardmaker Richard Tustian petitioned for a temporary exemption from the duty in 1711, as he was unlucky enough to have on hand when the duty was imposed nearly two hundred of his cheapest packs, which retailed for as little as pence and halfpence, and which an additional sixpence would render unsaleable.[31] These impositions never produced a significant revenue stream, the duty on cards taking in around £10,000 annually in the last several years before it was raised to a shilling. The proceeds of the duty on dice were even lower, its annual revenue averaging just over £500 between 1712 and 1724, the first twelve years it was collected.[32]

Stamp duty on cards was widely evaded, given that the Stamp Office was critically understaffed, its clerks overburdened, and their pay often in arrears. In 1724, there were nine officers to stamp cards and one to stamp dice; eight of the ten drew an annual salary of £45. This circumstance made them susceptible to bribery, and there were suggestions that Stamp officers were induced to stamp more packs than duty had been paid for.[33] From 1744, and possibly from as early as 1720, the wrappers used were required to be those printed for and provided by the Stamp Office. This wrapper would be pasted over the wrapping that the manufacturer tied over the cards. The cards could not be unpacked without breaking

[30] *Statutes of the Realm*, 9. 634–6.   [31] TNA IR 72/38, f 139.
[32] TNA T1/431/98; T1/431/104; Cholmondely Houghton MSS, Cambridge University Library, Ch(H) 34/5.
[33] TNA IR 72/38, ff 153–154, 160, 207; CUL Ch(H) 34/5; Nicholas Tosney, 'The Playing Card Trade in Early Modern England,' *Historical Research*, 84 (November 2011), 637.

the seal, and thus seals could not be re-used. The duty was steep, tripling the retail cost of a pack of cards. Nevertheless, demand for cards and dice continued to increase, as a correspondent in the *Connoisseur* noted, quoting a Stamp Office official that revenue from these duties had increased sixfold from their inception.[34] In the case of cards, the actual coefficient was closer to ninefold, while the revenue from dice was always comparatively small. When the duty on a pack of cards was raised to a shilling in 1756, half was levied on the wrapper, and half on the ace of spades, meaning that those cards had to be printed at the Stamp Office, using paper provided by the manufacturer, giving rise to the ornate 'revenue ace' that still survives in packs of cards today. The publisher of one newspaper, explaining its 'not having *proposed* or *applauded* the *Tax* upon *Cards* and *Dice*,' asserted 'that *Multiplication* is a Rule of *little Use* in *Revenue* Arithmetick, and that many a Tax has been *halved* by *doubling* it.'[35] Annual revenue from card duty indeed decreased, by about 25 per cent.

Far from inhibiting high-stakes play, the stamping regime afforded gaming entrepreneurs a means of establishing the integrity of their operations, as the cards or dice in a sealed and stamped pack were presumably not stacked, marked, trimmed, loaded, or otherwise tampered with.[36] Dice, like cards, were sold in stamped wrappers; in addition, newly manufactured dice were required to be deposited at the Stamp Office, where each die would be incised on the 'six' face with a sharp metal punch bearing the royal cipher, the resulting stamp then being picked out in indelible red ink. Forged stamps on dice were easily detected, as in most cases the forgers only went to the trouble of painting the red ink cipher on the surface of the die.[37] This officially sponsored guarantee of integrity may explain why the stamping apparatus remained so watertight that in the first fifty years that stamp duties were due on cards and dice, there was only a single charge brought for forged stamps on dice (against Anthony Walraven, acquitted in July of 1724) and likewise only one case of forging stamps on cards (Thomas Hill, convicted in 1744, having 'passed' some five thousand packs).[38] Another card manufacturer was prosecuted in 1761 for illicitly obtaining stamps, by which means 'he cheated ye Revenue of between £3000 or £4000.'[39] The presumption of security did not stop one writer from asserting that it was possible 'to loosen the Stamp and Seal which inclose a Pack of Cards, by holding the Cover, which is usually fastened by Paste, over the Steam of a boiling Water issuing out of the Spout of a Tea Kettle.' Servants were rumoured to sell the stamps thus removed from packs

---

[34] *The Connoisseur*, 15 (9 May 1754), 85.   [35] *London Evening Post*, 4422 (11 March 1756).
[36] Richard, *Romance of Gambling*, 49.
[37] John Berry, *Taxation on Playing Cards in England from 1711 to 1960* (Colchester: International Playing Card Society, 2001), 13–14; Henry Dagnall, *Making a Good Impression: Three Hundred Years of the Stamp Office and Stamp Duties* (London: HMSO, 1994), 23, 26.
[38] OBPO t17240708-68, t17440223-19.
[39] TNA T1/431/98.

in their employers' possession.[40] Increasing the duty to a shilling, then two shillings, and finally half a crown by the next century, only testified to the futility of taxation as a deterrent to gaming ventures, which continued under the cover of private clubs and ostensibly private entertainments.[41] Jonathan Swift asserted that domestic servants did a brisk business surreptitiously selling pilfered packs of second-hand cards to coffeehouses.[42] It was surely significant as well that the language of the statute acknowledged the existence of gaming houses that were operating sufficiently within the law that Stamp officers would need a statutory warrant to enter and inspect them. To that end, an inspector of gaming houses and vendors of cards, dice, and pamphlets was appointed under the Treasury, one more way in which the institutions of central government sent conflicting signals about the legality of gaming establishments.[43] Lotteries, over which the state asserted a monopoly in 1699, were another, as more than one contemporary noted. These, however, gave the government a material interest in identifying and containing commercial gaming.

Drawing a Blank

The first state lottery in Britain had been drawn in 1694 under the auspices of the Groom Porter Thomas Neale. From the beginning, and until well into the next century, these lotteries (unlike modern lotteries like the National Lottery in the United Kingdom or the 'Powerball' in the United States) were 'clearly developed investment schemes. Buying a lottery ticket was akin to buying government bonds.' In exchange for a lower return on investment, generally 3 to 4 per cent, the ticket holder had a chance of a bonus annual return many times the size of the initial outlay. In most lotteries before 1769, ticket holders did not lose the purchase price of the ticket. Lotteries varied enormously in their terms; some allowed ticket holders to be remunerated immediately, while others stipulated a term of one 'life,' i.e. thirty-two years.[44] Tickets for state lotteries were expensive, typically costing £10 apiece, significantly the limit placed on winnings in the Queen Anne Gaming Act. The least expensive tickets ever offered were £3, and the most expensive £100, thus it was common for lottery agents to sell multiple shares in single tickets. The proceeds were often used to fund specific public works, such as the Thames Water and the construction of Westminster Bridge, taking such projects

---

[40] *Public Advertiser*, 14,043 (4 October 1774).
[41] For stamp duties on playing cards, see Tosney, 'Playing Card Trade,' 637–56.
[42] Jonathan Swift, *Directions to Servants* (London: Hesperus, 2003), 22.
[43] *Calendar of Treasury Books and Papers*, ed. William A. Shaw, 5 vols (London: HMSO, 1900), 1. 611, 3. 289; *Whitehall Evening Post* 247, (10 September 1747).
[44] James Raven, 'Debating the Lottery in Britain c. 1750–1830,' in Zollinger (ed.), *Random Riches*, 90–1.

'off the books' of the ministry. They were attractive to the 'middling sort,' a demographic that now needed to be dissuaded from frequenting middle-range gaming houses with 'silver tables.' Consequently, new gaming legislation, and judicial campaigns against gaming mandated at the national level, tended to coincide with revivals of the state lottery. The lottery of 1710, the first state lottery in thirteen years, was preceded by legislation imposing steep duties on cards and dice, and lowering the threshold for 'excessive' gaming subject to fine and recoverable by civil action from £100 at a sitting to £10, coincidentally or not the price of a lottery ticket.

In his treatment of these lotteries, Bob Harris usefully points out that the mechanisms we now associate with the 'fiscal military state' were not considered certain to succeed when they were introduced. There was a scramble for methods to raise money and service the resulting debt, and lotteries were only one of a number of mechanisms tried out in an era of fiscal experimentation. Ministries realized that lotteries would be effective fiscal mechanisms if sales of tickets could be guaranteed. Consequently, there was a tendency not to discourage speculation in lottery tickets, if not to encourage 'scalping' outright, as it resulted in tickets being sold.[45] As Robert Walpole in the last years of his ministry was backed into war with Spain and ultimately France, lotteries proved essential to the financing of wartime deficit spending, and as the state lottery expanded, direct taxation receded, especially the land tax, which Walpole had earlier attempted to supplant with expanded excise duties. The lottery was as critical as the expansion of the excise to the development of the fiscal military state. Within two decades of the last of the Georgian Gaming Acts, 'it was noted that more people subscribed to the lottery than to any other government fund.'[46] One periodical suggested in 1756 that gaming legislation had done its work, as lotteries were 'the only *lawful* method of gaming left.'[47]

The evidence for the social background of lottery participants, while limited, is nonetheless intriguing. Among the 1,300-odd winners of the 'classis' lotteries drawn in 1711 and 1712, for which tickets cost £100 apiece, 70 per cent were from the landed or commercial elite. Just under 10 per cent of the winning tickets were purchased by institutions. The remainder of winners, however, just over 20 per cent, were 'middling sort' or lower, over half consisting of tradesmen and shopkeepers such as mercers, linen drapers, grocers, and distillers, and the remainder evenly divided between professionals, whether legal, medical, clerical, or military, and artisans. Although there were efforts to discourage the practice, lottery agents frequently sold shares of tickets to humbler folk, and publicized their modest backgrounds when they won, as occurred in the case of a prize of £5,000 shared among a journeyman oilman, a chambermaid, and a maidservant. Perhaps most

---

[45] Harris, *Gambling in Britain*, 126–8, 136–8.   [46] Raven, 'Debating the Lottery,' 91–2.
[47] *Universal Visiter and Monthly Memorialist*, 9 (September 1756), 422–3.

significantly, 90 per cent of winning tickets drawn in 1711 and 1712 were purchased in London, Westminster, and the 'home counties' around the metropolis. The lotteries revived under Queen Anne, according to Bob Harris, 'played a significant role in luring a wide range of people into investing in financial products...including many who had not previously bought company stocks or government debt.'[48] The socioeconomic profile of this cohort closely matches that of individuals apprehended in gaming venues and bound in recognizance. A large number of these were self-identified 'gentlemen,' a designation which had expanded in common parlance by this time to comprehend commercial elites, professionals, and respectable tradesmen.[49] It was rare for punters apprehended in raids to be detained until the sessions met, meaning that most of them could satisfy magistrates that they had means of support other than gaming, and that they could find sureties, suggesting that the clientele of gaming houses were largely 'respectable' men of the 'middling sort.' Shoemaker's study of misdemeanour prosecutions in Middlesex in the late seventeenth and early eighteenth centuries found that one quarter of gaming defendants identified themselves as 'gentlemen,' and that magistrates accepted them as such, while the majority (60 per cent) were in respectable trades and crafts.[50] These observations are in keeping with the lament of an oppositionist writer in 1729 that gaming had attracted 'the Trading Part of our Nation,...so that if you want a Merchant on a Post Night, you'll be surer to find him with a Pack of Cards than a Parcel of Letters before him.'[51] From the point of view of the state, money that might be parlayed into what were essentially municipal bonds for middle-income investors ought not to be frittered away at 'silver tables' in Covent Garden. To those who frequented those tables, however, the lotteries might not have appeared as the only protected species of gambling in the metropolis.

---

[48] Bob Harris, 'Lottery Adventuring in Britain, c.1710-1760,' *English Historical Review*, 133 (April 2018), 299–302, 309, 314.

[49] Alexandra Shepard, *Accounting for Oneself: Worth, Status, and the Social Order in Early Modern England* (Oxford: Oxford University Press, 2015), 271.

[50] Robert Shoemaker, 'Crime, Courts and Community: The Prosecution of Misdemeanors in Middlesex County, 1663–1723,' unpublished Ph.D. dissertation, Stanford University, 1986, 571.

[51] *Fog's Weekly Journal*, 40 (28 June 1729).

6

The Groom Porter's Dodge

The Court and Commercial Gaming

Consumers of metropolitan print media in London were confronted with a bewildering succession of reports in the first several weeks of 1731. Early in the new year, the high constable of Holborn raided a reputed gaming house in Gray's Inn Walks, seizing two men, one a common soldier, both bound in recognizances 'not to frequent gaming houses nor play at unlawful games.' Only days later, Twelfth Night was observed at court, with the royal family, following long-established custom, playing hazard for the benefit of the Groom Porter, a court official whose perquisites included keeping gaming tables in his 'grace and favour' apartments. Both items appeared on the same page of the *Gentleman's Magazine*.[1] Similarly, in the middle of February, 'several Persons of Quality and Distinction' were reported playing for high stakes 'at the Groom Porter's Lodge,' while only a week later came the report of the latest in a series of raids on another reputed gaming house, the Phoenix, a coffeehouse/tavern in the Haymarket Theatre complex. The same newspaper, the *Daily Courant*, carried both items.[2] All the previous summer, a war of nerves was conducted in the *Daily Journal* between Thomas Archer, the incumbent Groom Porter, and Captain William Bradbury, his former deputy. Bradbury, dissatisfied with his severance package, threatened to publish an exposé of Archer's conduct in courtly office, with a view to 'prevent the Groom Porter from taking a greater Liberty than the Law allows him,' declaring that Archer's abuse of his position was an open secret in the corridors of power. Apparently, Bradbury neither made good on his threat nor collected the disputed severance pay that occasioned it, as Archer was still challenging him to produce his evidence nearly two years later. The closest Bradbury may have come to making disclosure was a broadside satire entitled *The Gaming House*, provocatively 'dedicated to the Lord Protector of the Dice,' advertised in December 1735.[3] As no copy has survived, however, it is only speculation that Archer was its target or that Bradbury was involved in its publication.

---

[1] *Gentleman's Magazine*, 1 (January 1731), 25.
[2] *Daily Courant*, 9159 (15 February 1731), 9165 (22 February 1731); LMA MJ/SR/2551, rr 191, 193, 283.
[3] *Daily Journal*, 2983 (29 July 1730), 2987 (3 August 1730), 2988 (4 August 1730), and 3511 (6 April 1732); *London Daily Post*, 340 (4 December 1735).

The Gambling Century: Commercial Gaming in Britain from Restoration to Regency. John Eglin, Oxford University Press.
© John Eglin 2023. DOI: 10.1093/oso/9780192888198.003.0007

In the metropolis, at least, much of the uncertainty contributing to the nebulous status of gaming emanated from the peculiar status of gaming in the royal household. In Britain as on the Continent, gaming was often inflected with courtly privilege, which could overlap or create friction with the institutions and initiatives of government at both the national and local level. The coexistence of licit gaming in the Groom Porter's lodge in Whitehall Palace and illicit gaming only a few streets away reflected unsettled jurisdictions, contested spaces, and problematic boundaries between public and private.

Grace and Favour

The Groom Porter was a minor court official who answered to the Lord Chamberlain of the Household; his position was, according to one historian of the Georgian court, one of the 'most attractive' posts in the Lord Chamberlain's department.[4] He was responsible for furnishing and firing the royal palaces, including those of Westminster and Whitehall, as well as St James and Hampton Court, Kensington, and Windsor. Fireplaces, their cleaning, repair, maintenance, and apparatus, were ostensibly his particular concern, and his emolument took the form of quarterly disbursements for his expenses in this area. The office was generally filled from the ranks of the lesser gentry, and carried an estimated income between £500 and £1,000 per annum. It was very largely a sinecure; surviving records of the Lord Chamberlain's department do not indicate that it was very demanding. In one of the few surviving directives, the Groom Porter Thomas Neale was called upon in August of 1688 to furnish the apartments at Windsor Castle set aside for the infant Prince of Wales, and to house a troupe of French comedians who were performing there, unusual directives issued under unusual circumstances, arrangements that Neale was probably unable to complete, given the imminent flight of the Stuart court.[5] When the office came under scrutiny, as it did under Charles II in the 1670s, it was not the functions of the office that engaged the attention of the inquiring officials, but rather to whose patronage it properly belonged.[6] Neale, who occupied the post under William III, had ample time to pursue any number of other undertakings, while Thomas Archer was a busy architect whose surviving papers do not indicate any activity in his courtly position.

In addition to fireplaces, the Groom Porter equipped tennis courts and bowling greens, and provided other incidentals of entertainment, including cards and dice and gaming tables covered with the characteristic green felt. These last articles

---

[4] John Beattie, *The English Court in the Reign of George I* (Cambridge: Cambridge University Press, 1967), 52.

[5] TNA LC 5/17/64–65.   [6] TNA SP 29/366/225–228.

also gave the Groom Porter jurisdiction over play, and he was expected to be sufficiently conversant with the rules of all games to adjudicate disagreements. This capacity to understand and manage gaming was a key qualification for the post, if we are to judge from correspondence relating to candidates deemed *unqualified* to serve. In 1699, the deceased Groom Porter's heir claimed to have a patent for the reversion of his father's office, but his bid was ultimately declined. 'I fear Mr. Neale so unqualified for the place,' Sir John Stanley wrote to the Lord Chamberlain, 'that...the King's service will suffer by his carelessness in providing the King's houses, *and his own fortune too,* in not knowing how to manage play.'[7]

Traditionally, the Groom Porter oversaw the gaming at court that took place between Christmas and Twelfth Night, and under Charles II, at least, these delimitations seem to have been observed. Both Samuel Pepys and John Evelyn left wondering (Pepys) and dyspeptic (Evelyn) accounts of deep play for high stakes in the Groom Porter's apartments in Whitehall Palace. On New Year's Day in 1668, Pepys marvelled at

> the formality of the Groome-porter, who is their judge of all disputes in play and all quarrels that may arise therein; and how his under-officers are there to observe true play at each table and to give new dice, is a consideration I never could have thought had been in the world, had I not now seen it.

Exactly one week later, Evelyn 'saw deepe & prodigious gaming at the *Groome-porters,* vast heaps of Gold squandered away in a vaine & profuse manner: This I looked on as a horrid vice, & unsuitable to a *Christian Court.*'[8] Thomas Neale expanded the ambit of the Groom Porter's office by his promotion of lotteries, but there is no indication that he sought to expand or exploit the jurisdiction of his office otherwise. He was probably far too occupied with his numerous real estate projects, such as the Seven Dials development in Covent Garden. Nevertheless, a tract of 1699 cited the Groom Porter's lodge as 'the most Reputable and Convenient Place in Town' for gaming at hazard, noting that metropolitan 'ordinaries' were subsidiaries of the Groom Porter's privileged operation, operating under his licence and often overseen by one of his deputies.[9] Developments in the aftermath of 1689 increasingly removed the court as a centre of social gravity, as the rhythm of the London season took its cues from the sessions of Parliament, and as a succession of uncharismatic monarchs served to diffuse the topography

[7] HMC *Buccleuch*: Historical Manuscripts Commission. *Report on the Manuscripts of the Duke of Buccleuch and Queensberry, Preserved at Montagu House, Whitehall,* 3 vols (London: HMSO, 1899–1903), 2. 631, 634; italics mine.

[8] *Pepys' Diary,* 9. 4; *The Diary of John Evelyn,* ed. Esmond Samuel de Beer, 6 vols (Oxford: Clarendon Press, 1955), 3. 504.

[9] *Country Gentleman's Vade Mecum,* 69, 72.

of elite sociability in the metropolis. Perhaps alone of court officials, the Groom Porter was positioned to turn this diffusion to advantage.

Slings and Arrows

Thomas Archer held this position from 1705 until his death in 1743, making him easily the longest serving occupant of the post. Not much is known about Archer's social milieu, or how enthusiastic or knowledgeable a gamester he was. He appears to have farmed out the gaming functions of his office to a factor, in this case a much more shadowy figure, Captain William Bradbury. This was most likely the William Bradbury who was promoted Captain Lieutenant in the First Marine Regiment of Foot in March of 1695, and then Captain a year later. He transferred to Thomas Stringer's Regiment of Foot in March 1702, and was out of the regiment before 1708.[10] Bradbury's post as deputy Groom Porter was informal and unofficial; his name never appears in the records of the Lord Chamberlain's department, and he answered, it seems, to Archer alone. Whether through Archer's initiative or that of his deputy, from the beginning of Archer's tenure as Groom Porter the privileges and perquisites of his office were pursued, and their definition expanded, to an unprecedented extent. Importantly, both Pepys and Evelyn visited the Groom Porter's lodge during Christmastide. An unusual, undated and unfinished drawing attributed to Hogarth, but possibly by Philip Mercier, and now in the Royal Collection (figure 6.1), shows a socially august set of five hazard players, including a clergyman (possibly a bishop), a man wearing an order of chivalry (probably the Order of the Bath), and two women; a box-keeper stands behind. It is tempting to speculate from this elevated *staffage* that the sketch is a study for a conversation piece set at the Groom Porter's benefit on Twelfth Night. Under Archer, however, gaming in the Groom Porter's lodge took place essentially year-round. John Macky reported in February of 1714 that the Groom Porter hosted the only legal play at dice in England, the only restriction being play 'for ready money only,' and as we have seen, newspapers similarly reported high-stakes play there outside of Christmastide in 1731. Alexander Pope, in a footnote in the *Dunciad,* related that gaming had continued at the Groom Porter's lodge 'all the Summer the Court was at *Kensington*.'[11]

Soon after the accession of George II, the Lord Chamberlain's warrant books began to enumerate more or less semi-annual payments to Archer, averaging just under £300 per year, ostensibly for articles outside of his contract as Groom Porter, specifically chimney furniture, 'Grates, Fenders, Bellows, fine Brushes,

---

[10] Dalton, *Army Lists*, 4. 101, 146.
[11] Macky, *Journey through England*, 143; Alexander Pope, *Dunciad*, i. 309–10 and nn., in *The Poems of Alexander Pope,* ed. John Butt (New Haven: Yale University Press, 1963), 734.

Figure 6.1 William Hogarth, or possibly Philip Mercier (attributed), *The Hazard Table*. Royal Collection Trust/©His Majesty King Charles III 2023. The presence of clergy, and of women, at a dice table was highly unusual. Could this sketch represent the Groom Porter's Benefit on Twelfth Night?

&ca,' in royal palaces, typically St James's, Kensington, Hampton Court, and Windsor. Even considering the heavy use of fireplaces before the age of central gas heating, and the vast number of them across a half dozen royal residences, it is not really plausible that their fittings and furnishings would have to be replaced twice a year. Indeed, other recorded disbursements from the Lord Chamberlain's department suggest that payments to Archer served another purpose, possibly to launder box money collected in the Groom Porter's lodge. To cite one example, in the same period for which Archer was paid a total of £444 17s. 4d. 'for Grates, Tables, ffenders and Bellows &c' at Hampton Court and Kensington, a John Walker was paid a total of £18 7s. for six fenders in the King's apartments in Hampton Court.[12] The timing of the inception of these payments suggests an additional possibility. George II's antipathy to courtly gaming was recounted in a number of sources, Lord Chesterfield, for example, citing it as a reason for Charles Stanhope to avoid high play if he sought higher office.[13] Newspaper correspondence after the King's death assured readers that the monarch's participation at the Groom Porter's benefit on Twelfth Night was completely perfunctory and

---

[12] TNA LC 5/18, ff 46, 160, 243, 269, 323.   [13] *Chesterfield Letters*, 2. 269.

ceremonial, given his late Majesty's well-known aversion to gaming.[14] If Archer was being compensated for income understood to be lost from gaming tables that he was supposed to have discontinued, it would explain the King's anger that hazard continued unabated in the Groom Porter's apartments.

The increased activity of the Groom Porter's office reverberated beyond the court as well. The formulaic warrant for the post, issued over the Lord Chamberlain's signature, granted the holder 'by himselfe or sufficient Deputy or Deputys' oversight not only over gaming at court, but the right to license gaming houses in the cities of London and Westminster and the borough of Southwark, and to investigate and suppress all breaches of his privileges.[15] Archer's warrant was initially issued in 1705, and was renewed twice thereafter, on the succession of each of the first two Georges, and on each occasion was published in the *London Gazette* and other papers.[16] His customary rights, then, were well understood, certainly in the media-saturated environment of the metropolis. Soon after Archer's inauguration and Bradbury's installation as his deputy, the Groom Porter's privileges began to be enforced energetically. Robert Hunstone, the confessed keeper of a gaming house in Bridges Street, Covent Garden, sued Bradbury in 1707, charging that Bradbury, acting or claiming to act as deputy Groom Porter, had threatened to present him before the Westminster sessions if Bradbury were not made a partner in his venture. Bradbury indignantly denied the allegation, and the plaintiff was nonsuited, his cause not being helped by his filing from the Queen's Bench Prison on other undisclosed charges. Hunstone, significantly, was a signatory with one Thomas Minshull on one of the only surviving examples of a Groom Porter's licence, issued to John Stock of Southwark in September 1705.[17] Later in the same year as Hunstone's suit, Andrew Whitehead, another gaming house keeper, pleaded before the Middlesex sessions that he had a licence from the Groom Porter for his enterprise.[18] Soon afterward victuallers, vintners, and coffeemen in Covent Garden and Haymarket complained of extortion by individuals who represented themselves as agents of the Groom Porter and threatened prosecution unless licences were purchased from them. In 1709 Bradbury was obliged to place advertisements noting that 'neither the Groom Porter, nor any of his deputies' ever issued licences to gaming houses.[19]

[14] *Morning Post*, 1636 (17 January 1778) contained the account of a former courtier 'as to the celebrating *Twelfth-Day* at Court in the former reign: *King George the Second* was no friend to *gaming*: he discouraged it on all occasions in the most essential way; discountenanced all who did it; and had not in all his household a *gamester* for his servant....He kept up all the dignity, and forms of a Court; and in compliance to *them*, he played on the *Twelfth-Night* with the Royal Family, and some of the great Officers; many of his subjects came on that night, who did not presume on any other; but there was no riot; the King retired before midnight, and all dispersed.'
[15] TNA LC 5/154/48.
[16] *London Gazette*, 4181 (3 December 1705), 5291, (1–4 January 1715); TNA LC 3/63/9, 3/64/55.
[17] TNA, Chancery Proceedings, Six Clerks Series, C5/333/18: *Hunstone v. Bradbury*, 1707; C110/182/1705: Documents in the case of *Stock v. Jeffreys*.
[18] LMA MJ/SP/1707/July/77; quoted in Tosney, 'Gaming in England,' 114.
[19] *London Gazette*, 4525 (21 March 1709); 4533 (18 April 1709).

In spite of this disclaimer, Bradbury apparently continued in his office, but only apparently, as his appointment was always *sub rosa,* and his relationship with Archer governed by plausible deniability. Hunstone's suit, for example, asserted that Bradbury might only have 'pretended' to be Archer's deputy, and the only evidence that he was so in fact was the absence of any public denial from Archer. Bradbury himself was indicted at least twice for keeping gaming houses, in partnership with others. By November of 1706, he had been summoned for a hazard operation in conjunction with Bartholomew Whiting and John Philpot, and as one of three partners in the gaming venue in Bridges Street, with John Jefferies, who had purchased Hunstone's interest, and Benjamin Goss (or Gorst). Of these last three, only Jefferies had appeared to plead to the indictment by the beginning of 1709.[20] In 1710, Bradbury was 'amerced' twice in the Court of Burgesses of Westminster, but the clerk did not record the offence; Bradbury possibly managed to have his two sessional indictments heard in the Court Leet, a medieval holdover as the manorial court of the Dean and Chapter of Westminster Abbey, which fined unlawful gaming venues at the rate of one silver mark per day of operation, one sixth the already nominal rate of forty shillings a day stipulated in the Tudor statute.[21]

Those who acted for Archer, or at least claimed to do so, soon found other expedients than peddling gaming licences. Printed sources suggest that the Groom Porter's office ran a brisk consulting business at assemblies, masquerades, and resorts, ensuring that gaming in these milieus was conducted honestly, perhaps by running the tables themselves. An anonymous pamphlet of 1726 asserted that while

> [t]he Learned in the Law are of Opinion, that the Groom-Porter has no right to keep a Gaming-house in any Place except in the Court where the PRINCE resides,...his Servants are hackney'd up and down the Countries every Year to *Newmarket, Bath* and *Tunbridge-Wells,* as if they had a Licence for it.[22]

When one Mrs Bowes advertised the opening of her assembly rooms in St James's Street on New Year's Day in 1730, there was no explicit mention of gaming, but only 'a fine Concert of Musick, by the best Hands,' twice a week, to which men would be admitted for a crown, and women free of charge. During the season, the rooms would be open 'every Night for the Gentlemen, *the Groom Porter having Servants who attend there constantly.*'[23]

It was possibly unwelcome attention to the Groom Porter's office that led to William Bradbury's dismissal by the summer of 1730. Ultimately Francis Buller, another half-pay officer, was announced in the newspapers in February 1735 as the new deputy Groom Porter, as was his reputed emolument of £400 per annum,

[20] LMA WJ/SP/1709/01/043.   [21] WCA WCBG/WCB 3.
[22] *Whole Art and Mystery,* 24.   [23] *Daily Journal,* 2800 (27 December 1729); italics mine.

publicity that contrasted significantly with the obscurity around Bradbury's appointment.[24] This gesture toward transparency did not dispel the rumours that continued to swirl around the Groom Porter's office, and in April 1740 Archer was once again obliged to make a public declaration:

> Some Gentlemen having been induced to play at the Masquerade this Winter, under a mistaken Notion that the Groom-Porter's Servants attended there, *as they had formerly used to do*, Publick Notice is hereby given, That the Groom-Porter hath never suffered any of his Servants to attend at the Masquerades, or at Bath, Tunbridge, Epsom, or any other such Publick Place, *since the Commencement of the Act against Gaming*.[25]

As the legislation in question had only recently gone into effect, it appears that Archer's deputies had continued to facilitate commercial gaming ventures in public venues after Bradbury's departure.

Agents of the Groom Porter, then, were directly involved in commercial gaming ventures in the City of Westminster and beyond. If they were not (illicitly) issuing licences, they could be partners in gaming ventures or even proprietors; alternatively, they could oversee operations, ostensibly as guarantors of fair play, aligning with the function of the Groom Porter at court. The involvement of the Groom Porter's deputies allowed gaming entrepreneurs to promote the integrity of their operations, and assisted them in militating against the notion that gaming was intrinsically deceitful. Moreover, the Groom Porter's lodge was itself a commercial gaming venue located in the City of Westminster, but not subject to its jurisdiction. By working around and in the interstices of legal prohibitions, the Groom Porter's lodge pointed the way for other commercial gaming ventures to flourish with a semblance of legality. The activity of the Groom Porter fostered a set of legal fictions that combined with official misunderstanding of the changing nature of gaming to create a space in which gaming entrepreneurs could initiate commercial gaming ventures. A writer in the oppositionist paper *The Craftsman* declared that

> the bad Examples of *Men in Authority*, have…introduced a Spirit of *Gaming* amongst all Ranks of People. I cannot tell when the Office of *Groom-Porter* was first instituted, or how far it is *legal*, as it hath been lately exercised. But…whilst *Persons of Rank* indulge Themselves in *this Vice*, and a *publick Officer* is kept up for that Purpose, the *common People* will think it very hard to be restrain'd, and take every convenient Opportunity of imitating their *Superiors*.[26]

---

[24] *Universal Spectator*, 331 (February 1735), 409.
[25] *Daily Gazetteer* 1509, (21 April 1740); italics mine.
[26] *Craftsman*, 633 (26 August 1738).

In Ireland, the viceregal court at Dublin Castle also featured a Groom Porter with similar prerogatives to those belonging to his equivalent in Whitehall. When legislation 'for suppressing Lotteries and Gaming-Tables' was before the Dublin Parliament, John Knightly, the incumbent Groom Porter, requested exceptions that would preserve his privileges.[27] Accordingly, the statute in question classified as public nuisances gaming tables in any public house 'other than the Groom-Porter's Table, kept within the Walls of the *Castle*, or other House where the Chief Governor shall actually reside, and no longer.' Five years later, Irish statute law on gaming was brought into line with the English law, again excepting Dublin Castle while the Lord Lieutenant was in residence.[28] Among the Dublin elite, the Groom Porter's lodge was both more conspicuous and a cause of greater concern than its metropolitan analogue. 'The town is under great uneasiness for there being such a place of rendezvous as the Groom-Porters,' the Bishop of Kildare advised the Duke of Ormonde in 1706, adverting the vacancy of the post from the violent death of the previous incumbent, and advising the Lord Lieutenant 'to consider what you may think fit to do in it.'[29] The Groom Porter appeared before a Dublin grand jury in 1717 after a duel on his premises resulted in a fatality.[30] In 1725 appeared verses, attributed to Jonathan Swift, 'on the Erecting a Groom-Porter's House Adjoining to the Chapple, in the Castle of Dublin,' where

> a Wall only Hinders Union
> Between the Dice and the Communion,
> And but a thin Partition Guards
> The Common Pray'r Book from the Cards...[31]

In March of 1746, the Earl of Chesterfield as Lord Lieutenant suppressed the office, compensating John Bickerstaff, the dispossessed occupant, with a pension.[32]

On the Verge

The few years after Archer's appointment saw new legislation enacted with a view toward curtailing commercial gaming. In the same way that the stamping regime that accompanied the imposition of heavy taxation on cards and dice played into

[27] *Daily Courant*, 1698 (24 July 1707).
[28] Edward Hunt, *An Abridgement of all the Statutes in Ireland, in the Reigns of Queen Anne and King George, in Force and Use* (Dublin: A. Rhames and E. Dobson, 1718), 89, 94.
[29] HMC *Ormonde*: Historical Manuscripts Commission. *The Manuscripts of the Marquis of Ormonde, Preserved at the Castle, Kilkenny*, 2 vols (London: HMSO, 1895–1899), 1. 64.
[30] *Weekly Journal or Saturday's Post*, 39 (6 September 1717).
[31] *A Poem on the Erecting a Groom-Porter's House Adjoining to the Chapple, in the Castle of Dublin* (Dublin, n.p., 1725).
[32] *London Evening Post*, 2866 (18 March 1746).

the hands of commercial operators, so did the revision of the Restoration gaming statute a year later. Courtly gaming was not comprehended under either of the Tudor statutes, of course, and for reasons already described, was not curtailed under the Caroline Act. A new statute passed in 1710 lowered the threshold for 'excessive' gaming to ten pounds, but as this standard was likely to put a damper on the amusements of the court, a provision was inserted that for the first time explicitly exempted the royal household:

> [N]othing in this Act contained shall extend to prevent or hinder any Person or Persons from Gaming or Playing at any of the Games aforesaid, within any of her Majesties Palaces of Saint James or Whitehall, during such time as Her Majesty, Her Heirs or Successors, shall be actually Resident at either of the said Two Palaces, or in any other Royal Palace, where Her Majesty, Her Heirs or Successors, shall be actually Resident..., and so as such Playing be for Ready Money only.[33]

Although this exemption was not supposed to extend to any part of palace precincts of which the freehold was alienated from the Crown, in practice it presented a persistent definitional problem, which judicial rulings did not really resolve in the public's mind. For a number of reasons, it could be very hard to tell where the royal household began and ended. Unlike baroque courts on the Continent, those of the later Stuarts and earlier Georgians lacked imposing, architecturally outstanding edifices, or distinctive spaces within these.[34] The Palace of St James does not appear particularly palatial even today, and was even less so in the eighteenth century; built in the (by then) unfashionable Tudor/ Jacobean style, it was, according to one newspaper writer later in the century, 'dirty and sombre, and resembled more an hospital' than the 'palace of the monarch.'[35] Whitehall Palace, where the Groom Porter's lodge was situated for at least part of this period, lacked even architectural unity, consisting as it did of a warren of buildings haphazardly constructed and agglomerated over a period of two centuries. As is clear from Canaletto's London townscapes, the 'palace' blended seamlessly with buildings around it, so that it would not have been clear to any contemporary visitor where its precincts began or ended. Kensington Palace, on the outskirts of the metropolis, was newer, but was less impressive than any number of aristocratic townhouses in the capital. Consequently, where continental courts stood apart from and above the wider society of their respective realms, those of British monarchs were much more contiguous with the culture

---

[33] *Statutes of the Realm*, 9. 476–7.
[34] See Linda Colley's elaboration of this point in *Britons: Forging the Nation* (New Haven: Yale University Press, 1992), 196–200.
[35] *Whitehall Evening Post*, 6227 (5 April 1787).

of the metropolis, necessarily so, once the political consequences of the post-revolutionary settlement took hold and the court was less and less an exclusive centre of cultural gravity. The oppositionist paper *The Craftsman* put the problem neatly soon after the passage of a new Gaming Act in 1739:

> Whether the *Verge of the Court* is included in *this Exemption,* is not expressly declared; but if the *Palace* is understood to include the *Verge,* or any Rooms adjoining to the *Court,* we hope the *proper Officers* will not protect them; because the same Frauds may be practis'd there, and set a worse Example, than in any *other Place.*[36]

The concept of 'the verge of the court' was sufficiently misunderstood that the patent theatres, for example, could quite easily be comprehended as royal precincts, especially as they lay under the jurisdiction of the Lord Chamberlain, the senior official of the royal household. The anonymous Westminster magistrate who penned a pamphlet describing the anti-gaming efforts there noted that gaming entrepreneurs particularly sought commercial properties in the vicinity of the theatres.[37] A number of the gaming houses raided during first decades of the eighteenth century were adjacent to one of the patent theatres, often in buildings that shared walls or circulation space with them, and even in buildings on which the patentee paid parish rates, as was the case with the Phoenix in the Haymarket.[38] Later in the century, gaming operations proliferated in the vicinity of Leicester Fields (now Leicester Square), the site of Leicester House, the long disused residence of the heirs apparent. The exemption granted to the royal household, then, created disputed liminal spaces in which commercial gaming ventures could lodge, defying repeated revisions of gaming statutes. Tosney points to 'a common but erroneous belief on both sides of the law that certain situations were exempt from the gaming statutes.'[39] There were other such purlieus enjoying exemptions in what we might call legal folklore; the author of a 1726 tract felt obliged to point out 'that the *Court of Requests* and *St. Mary le Bone* are not privileg'd Places for *Gaming,* as the World imagines.'[40] The liminality afforded by the 'verge of the court' was periodically reinforced in the public's mind. In November 1728, eighteen individuals were seized at a gaming table in the house of a Mrs Bresson in one of the narrow lanes that ran south of the Strand to the west of Somerset House. This location placed the house within the boundaries of the Savoy, a tract of property belonging to the duchy of Lancaster, the largest and most prominent of the estates of the Crown. Consequently, it was not the Westminster justices who admitted Mrs Bresson and her punters to bail, but the Board of Green Cloth, over which

---

[36] *Craftsman,* 679 (14 July 1739).   [37] *Account of the Endeavours,* 20.
[38] WCA Overseers Accounts, St. James Piccadilly, D 26–32, 1718–1724.
[39] Tosney, 'Gaming in England,' 83 n. 26.   [40] *Whole Art and Mystery,* 24.

the Lord Steward of the household presided in St James's Palace.[41] In 1748, well after the passage of the last of the Georgian Gaming Acts, a gaming house was found to be operating in the former premises of the Fountain Tavern in the Strand, one street from the Savoy Chapel.[42]

Whether from frustration at the inefficacy of existing gaming statutes, or from a politically opportunistic impetus to expose social corruption which could be associated with the increasingly embattled administration of Robert Walpole, or from a renewed concern to eliminate competition for state lotteries, Parliament enacted three Gaming Acts in rapid succession between 1738 and 1744. Unlike previous legislation, these statutes classified specific games as illegal lotteries; the last of these outlawed as inherently deceitful any games of chance involving wagers on numbers or figures, and corrected a longstanding defect of gaming legislation in empowering equity courts to issue decrees for the repayment of gaming losses over £10.[43] The Georgian Gaming Acts, however, like the Queen Anne Act, specifically exempted the royal household, defined as any royal residence that the monarch, his or her consort, or the heir apparent occupied.

While the Groom Porter and his deputies were obliged to pay public deference to the revised statutes, it was Archer's death rather than renewed legislative efforts that had a greater impact on gaming culture in the metropolis. Archer's successor was Charles Fitzroy, a 'natural' kinsman of the Lord Chamberlain, the Duke of Grafton. While Fitzroy continued to collect 'reimbursements' for equipping and servicing fireplaces year-round, including high summer, there is no evidence that he sought to assert the privileges enumerated in his warrant to the extent that Archer clearly had. The office fell into particularly marked decline after the scrupulously upright George III, who chided the Archbishop of Canterbury for holding card parties in Lambeth Palace, ascended to the throne in 1760. For the first Twelfth Night observance of the new reign that was not under a court mourning, there was neither a ball nor gaming at St James's in the evening, 'it being his Majesty's Pleasure that ill Precedents should not be given at his Royal Palace.' That the long-time deputy Groom Porter Francis Buller, who had been a half-pay officer like Bradbury, succeeded his supervisor after Fitzroy's death in 1763 is probably a clue that the stature of the post had diminished. The office turned over rapidly in the new reign; Buller and his successor, Robert Wood, lasted only a year apiece. George III ended the practice of gaming on Twelfth Night in 1772, opting instead to pay the Groom Porter an annual gratuity.[44] At the death of

[41] *London Evening Post*, 152 (26 November 1728); *Daily Journal*, 2463 (29 November 1728).

[42] LMA MJ/SR/2894, pc, rr 81–114.

[43] *Reflexions on Gaming, and Observations on the Laws Relating Thereto* (London: J. Barnes and R. Corbett, 1751), 37.

[44] *London Evening Post*, 5332 (5 January 1762); *Annual Register for the Year 1772* (London: J. Dodsley, 1773), 65.

George Powlett, the last holder of the office, in 1782, no successor was appointed, and the office was formally abolished.

By that time, however, 'groom porters,' modelled on the courtly office, were found among the staff of clubs in St James's and Pall Mall, as well as those of gaming operations at race meetings such as Epsom and Newmarket, and resorts like Brighton.[45] Nor were these the only expressions of nostalgia for the office; as gaming culture expanded undeterred by legislation, the occasional writer advocated reopening the Groom Porter's lodge. 'I can see no better Remedy,' began one 'Citizen of London,'

> but that the Groom-Porter, as usual, should open his Mad-house at *St. James's*,...and that he should be permitted by his Deputy, to keep one Hazard Table at *Bath, Tunbridge, &c*....[S]uch Regulations might be made at such Tables, as might prevent all Suspicion of Fraud, and their being resorted to by Tradesmen, or Mechanicks.[46]

Another writer suggested some years later

> that if the *groom porter's public play* were permitted now as formerly, under certain regulations, and all private play suppressed under the severest penalties, there would be less mischief done than there is at present.[47]

'[P]utting a stop to public games of chance has greatly increased the more dangerous evil, private games of chance,' opined a third observer in 1781, who also proposed 'the admitting of public games of chance, under the direction of a groom porter, or some such officer.'[48] All of these commentators posited that gaming had moved from public spaces into private ones, and assumed a sharp distinction between the two. In fact, gaming entrepreneurs, having adapted to survive in the legal netherworld between court and city, were by then thriving in the still nebulous territory between public and private.

---

[45] *Monthly Review*, 34 (April 1766), 321; *Whitehall Evening Post*, 5516 (21 August 1781); *Morning Herald*, 472 (4 May 1782).

[46] *The Vices of the Cities of London and Westminster* (Dublin: G. Faulkner and R. James, 1751), 25–6.

[47] *Town and Country Magazine*, 1 (December 1769), 652.

[48] *London Courant and Westminster Chronicle* (28 July 1781).

7

The Bench Versus the Banks

Policing Gaming in Westminster

No sooner had Parliament enacted the bill for the first of the new lotteries in 1718 than a charge was read next door in Westminster Hall to the Middlesex grand jury. These charges, issued by the head of the Commission of the Peace, were routine items of business drawn up and read for every quarter sessions, but Whitelocke Bulstrode, the chair, took the unusual and unprecedented step of publishing them. The first set of charges, issued in April, instructed the grand jurors to present licensees who kept 'Shovelboard Tables, Bowling-Alleys, and Nine-Pins; for these allurements keep Gentlemens Servants and Apprentices too long from their Master's Service' and encouraged pilfering, as well as '[a]ll *Gaming-Houses* and other *disorderly Houses,*...and all common Gamesters that draw in young Gentlemen of Fortune.'[1] In his second charge issued six months later, Bulstrode was gratified that several keepers of the first sort of accommodation had been brought to book, but implied that more serious gaming operations had been neglected.[2] Soon thereafter, not only was there augmented enforcement of gaming statutes reflected in the Westminster sessions rolls, there was also increased coverage in the London press. This new initiative specifically targeted commercial gaming establishments, particularly significant given that de Moivre's *Doctrine of Chances,* which laid out for lay audiences the statistical advantage to the 'house' in the banking games that these operations promoted, had appeared earlier that year. At the end of November, thirty-five gaming houses were reportedly presented at the Westminster sessions, and in January, the Society for the Reformation of Manners in the Cities of London and Westminster asserted they had presented eight keepers of gaming houses over the course of the previous year.[3]

Given the prominence of that organization in the policing of vice in the metropolis, the last number might have been expected to be higher, considering that over the same period, the Society prosecuted thirty-one brothels, as well as 492 sabbatarian violations and 1,253 cases of miscellaneous 'Lewd and Disorderly

---

[1] *The Charge of Whitelocke Bulstrode, Esq., to the Grand Jury and Other Juries of the County of Middlesex* (London: J. Browne, 1718), 34, 36.
[2] *Second Charge of Whitelocke Bulstrode,* 24–8.
[3] *Weekly Journal,* 103 (29 November 1718); *Whitehall Evening Post,* 52 (13 January 1719).

The Gambling Century: Commercial Gaming in Britain from Restoration to Regency. John Eglin, Oxford University Press.
© John Eglin 2023. DOI: 10.1093/oso/9780192888198.003.0008

Practices.'[4] As things stood, however, the metropolitan police apparatus that bore the brunt of the enforcement of gaming statutes faced a number of structural challenges in carrying out its mandate. We might legitimately wonder if these realities created an atmosphere similar to continental capitals where commercial gaming was 'tolerated, but not permitted.' The motivations that drove however much policing of gaming was actually effected are worth exploring.

Outrageous Fortune

The bench for Middlesex and Westminster was large, with some eighty-odd just-ices, and heterogeneous, with great officers of state sitting *ex officio* alongside humble shopkeepers, and increasingly busy, the Middlesex sessions sitting every month in addition to the Westminster justices holding the customary 'quarter sessions' four times a year. Parishes in the county adjacent to the City of London were overwhelmed with an exploding population from in-migration. The unchar-itable task of 'resettling' relief applicants in the parish of their birth, for example, became such a large item of business that special forms were printed to spare par-ish clerks the drudgery of repeatedly copying out the requisite formulae by hand. The lot of a constable or justice, then, was not uniformly happy. A commentator protested at mid-century

> I cannot without indignation hear a rich tradesman, or a rich country 'squire, complaining of the non-execution of our laws, when, to my knowledge, the for-mer never serv'd in person the office of constable, nor did the other ever attend a quarter sessions, or endeavour to qualify himself for serving his country as a justice of the peace.[5]

In complaining of the laxity of law enforcement, these critics might well have referred to the comparatively few prosecutions for gaming. There were both practical and dispositional barriers to the policing of gaming houses. Pursuing a complaint against a gaming operation could be an expensive undertaking. If the complaint proceeded as far as a bill of indictment, the complainant was liable for fees up to a crown, and more if the services of a solicitor were required, the fees in one such case rising to £2 5s. Furthermore, a well-lawyered defendant could obtain a writ of certiorari transferring the case into the Court of King's Bench, where the complainant would have to engage an even more expensive barrister if

---

[4] Robert Shoemaker, 'Reforming the City: The Reformation of Manners Campaign in London, 1690–1738,' in Lee Davison, Tim Hitchcock, Tim Keirn, and Robert Shoemaker (eds.), *Stilling the Grumbling Hive: The Response to Social and Economic Problems in England, 1689–1750* (New York: St. Martin's Press, 1992), 105.

[5] *Magazine of Magazines* (April 1751), 338.

the prosecution were to proceed. Not surprisingly, many *qui tam* prosecutors abandoned their cases if a defendant got certiorari, and consequently these writs were frequently pursued 'as a vexatious tactic to obstruct prosecutors.'[6]

A single justice could convict offenders in summary judgment provided there were credible witnesses to the offence, but this outcome was rare in cases of gaming. Seized players, it was thought, could not give reliable testimony against gaming operators or proprietors because such players had violated the statute as well, a barrier that the last of the Georgian statutes explicitly lifted. Moreover, since informants were entitled to one third of the fine levied, the law did not allow them to serve as witnesses, since they would profit from a conviction.[7] '[I]t were to be wished that the statute of George II had required no more than one Witness to the Information,' Henry Fielding lamented in 1751, 'for even one Witness, as I have found by Experience, is very difficult to be procured.'[8] Most often, the only sanction that a gaming operator or a punter taken in a gaming house would face was a recognizance for good behaviour. Ordinarily, the power to bind individuals in such recognizance was one of the most effective weapons in a magistrate's arsenal, and would appear especially so as applied to gaming offences. A justice could demand a recognizance even if he merely thought it *likely* that an individual would offend, and anyone could be bound in recognizance for 'good behaviour' without the necessity of a third-party complaint.[9] A seized gambler would have to pledge a significant sum of money as security that he would not gamble or frequent gaming houses, and he—apprehended gamesters were overwhelmingly male—would have to find 'sureties,' generally two individuals known to him who would jointly pledge an equivalent sum to ensure his good behaviour. The amount pledged—£40 from the respondent was typical, with £20 from each of the sureties—was considerably more than the (by then nominal) forty shilling fine.

Recognizances for good behaviour were seen as means of abating nuisances, but their effectiveness depended on the vigilance of complainants, often constables, who were not usually in a position to surveil respondents with any regularity. At mid-century, Fielding dismissed recognizances as 'a mere Bugbear, unless the party who breaks it, should be sued thereon; which, as it is attended with great Expence, is never done.' Shoemaker found that '22% of those accused of keeping or frequenting gaming houses initially failed to appear in court,' and that 'defendants accused of gambling...were disproportionately likely to fail to appear in court or to have their cases continued to a subsequent sessions at the request of dissatisfied plaintiffs.' In Shoemaker's sample for 1720–22, there were sixty-three recognizances for gaming that did not result in indictments, and

---

[6] Shoemaker, *Prosecution and Punishment*, 140–4.

[7] Norma Landau, *The Justices of the Peace, 1679–1760* (Berkeley: University of California Press, 1984), 349.

[8] Fielding, *An Enquiry*, 96.   [9] Landau, *Justices of the Peace*, 24.

forty-four indictments for gaming, an unusually high number reflecting the results of the Westminster Commission's concerted effort against gaming in those years. Grand juries were significantly less likely to find 'true bills' for gaming indictments compared to those for other offences. The money pledged in recognizance was supposed to be forfeited if the terms of a recognizance were violated, the forfeiture triggered in a process known as 'estreat' that referred the recognizance to the Court of the Exchequer, which was empowered to collect. In the best-case scenario, it was generally several months before an estreated recognizance would be collected, and Fielding asserted that 'not a single Example of an Estreat hath been made within my Remembrance'.[10] He had only served three years on the bench at that point, but sessions rolls corroborate his observation. These documents bear witness to multiple cases of individuals bound in recognizance neither to game nor frequent gaming houses being seized and bound subsequently for the same offence, as might easily occur when different constables brought the same offender in front of different justices with different clerks.

It will become clear that when magistrates moved against gaming operations, they did so under pressure from above. The intersection of the Middlesex and Westminster bench with the highest levels of national government meant that the activity—or inactivity—of magistrates was unusually conspicuous and subject to oversight from the loftiest perches in Whitehall. During the Pelham ministry, for example, the keeper of the rolls for Middlesex was none other than the Duke of Newcastle, the elder of the two Pelham brothers. When raids on gaming houses occurred, reflected in the sessions rolls by runs of recognizance slips and the very occasional bill of indictment, there were also accounts in the press. Given a possible ulterior motivation of eliminating or managing competition for state lotteries, the question arises of what ostensible concerns drove authorities to focus on activities about which there seems to have been little actual public complaint. The formulae of charges and indictments frequently cite the disturbance that gaming venues, the scenes of boisterous disputes at late hours, might generate in their neighbourhoods, although contemporaries might well have asked when Covent Garden, for example, was ever quiet. The complaint that gaming houses were 'nurseries of crime,' generating highwaymen and subsequently harbouring them, was well known and later given voice in Henry Fielding's tract *On the Late Increase of Robbers*. Gaming, along with swearing, drinking, and fornication, was fixed in the boilerplate litany of bad behaviour catalogued in scores of the admonitory biographies of condemned felons found in the *Newgate Calendar* and documented in sessions rolls. The most persistent thread, however, in keeping with the direction of the Stuart gaming legislation, was the threat that gaming appeared to pose to the socioeconomic order. A draft memorandum that

---

[10] Shoemaker, *Prosecution and Punishment*, 26, 58, 115, 147, 220; Fielding, *An Enquiry*, 96.

somehow found its way to the office of Charles, Viscount Townshend, Secretary of State, complained of twenty-two gaming houses in Covent Garden and vicinity, a statistic that later appeared in newspapers, and related that 'Common Gamesters' who had worked as 'Drawers Perrywig makers footmen and Chairmen' had acquired fortunes of £20,000 to £30,000, or even as much as £80,000 in one case.[11] This chord of resentment of sudden, unjustifiable social mobility was repeated in the charges to grand juries published over the course of the decade. 'How many...of mean Originals,' Samuel Ryder asked in 1726, 'have, in a few Years raised uncommon Fortunes upon the Ruin of their Betters[?]'[12] Gaming was, Westminster justice Sir John Gonson thundered in 1729,

[a] Wheel of Fortune which with her preposterous Whirl raises the mean low born Wretch; adorns those choppy Hands with shining Diamonds, whose proper Use Nature designed to tug the Cable and the Oar, to hold the Plough, and dig their Bread from out of hardened Furrows: Whilst those born great and noble, with the same Whirl she forces to descend, losing all that their shining Ancestors by glorious War, or the more glorious Liberal Arts, obtained: For in Gaming all Distinction is lost; the Witty and the Weak are upon an equal Foot, for that admits of no Conversation. The illiterate Blockhead and the sparkling well taught polished Man, whose Learning and Genius would in every other Place procure him Admiration, are here upon a Level!

Gonson cited the specific example of 'a man dressed in Velvet,' arrested in a 'notorious Gaming House in *Covent Garden*...who not many Months before drove a common Hackney Coach.'[13]

The threat of individuals rising above their station assumed particular clarity for local magistrates in Augustan England, given the changing social composition of the bench. Appointment as a justice of the peace was once a hallmark of local status reserved for locally eminent families in town and countryside, but the annual sessions of Parliament occasioned after 1688 increasingly made national government and its adjuncts the foundations of social standing, so that the recruitment of local magistracies entailed seeking the service of members of humbler socioeconomic cohorts. This development was especially marked in the metropolis itself. From 1711, the property qualification for justices of the peace was the same as for that for members of the House of Commons, an estate worth £300 per year, although 'estate' was defined more loosely in the case of JPs; by 1720, however, there were proposals to lower the qualification to £200; in 1732, by

---

[11] TNA SP 35/27/247.

[12] Samuel Ryder, *The Charge to the Grand Jury of the City and Liberty of Westminster* (London: J. Roberts, 1726), 8.

[13] John Gonson, *A Charge to the Grand Jury of the City and Liberty of Westminster* (London: J. Lewis, 1729), 35.

which time the difficulty of recruitment had become impossible to ignore, the threshold was set at £100 per annum, which could proceed from any sort of real estate, or office, or benefice, or tithes, or 'what else.' One scholar of the local magistracy has remarked that '[e]ven the dubious gentility of the justices of Middlesex would have survived the test.'[14] As one complainant wrote of the Westminster bench to a Secretary of State, 'I can not believe that yor Lordship can think that men of such birth such meen Educations, such slender fortunes, and reprobate lives can or will act anything for ye preservation or good of his ffellow creatures.'[15] The stature not only of the magistracy but of the entire legal profession of the metropolis seemed to be at issue, given a second grievance of reformist justices that there were so many attorneys willing to provide gaming operators with legal counsel.

In Playhouse Passage

The justices of Westminster ran into a series of additional roadblocks in their efforts to curtail commercial gaming operations in their jurisdiction. The Court of King's Bench ruled in 1720 that individuals apprehended for gaming violations could not be compelled to find sureties unless the justice seeking to bind them in recognizance had observed the violation at first hand, for which reason it was necessary for justices to accompany constables on raids.[16] That ruling was one motivation for a consortium of justices to begin holding petty sessions specifically to address commercial gaming in October 1720. The reintroduction of state lotteries after a hiatus of five years was possibly another. Importantly, where the Queen Anne lotteries had been remarkably generous, as they 'bore the full burden of raising long term loans for the government,' the lotteries revived under George I were markedly less so. The first of these in 1719 paid nothing for 'blanks,' while those from 1721 to 1724 refunded only a portion of the purchase price, with or without a further 4 per cent annuity.[17] Another conspicuous, if unstated, impetus was the bursting of the South Sea Bubble. Company stock had reached its peak in early August of 1720, with the share price at £1,000; by the end of September it had plummeted to £150, and reached its initial public offering price of £100 by the end of the year. This debacle and the public outrage that accompanied it may have informed the concerted vigilance of this portion of the Westminster bench, but it may also have grounded much of the resistance that they met from a variety of quarters.

---

[14] Landau, *Justices of the Peace*, 140–1, 159–60, 162.   [15] TNA SP 35/66/76.

[16] Samuel and Nathaniel Blackerby, *The Justice of Peace his Companion*, 2 vols (London: E. and R. Nutt and R. Gosling, 1734), 2. 175–6.

[17] Harris, 'Lottery Adventuring,' 293–4; Ewen, *Lotteries and Sweepstakes*, 163.

Much of this resistance was internal. There were constables of St Paul's Covent Garden who overtly refused to serve warrants, such as one John Thomas, a mercer, who appeared at quarter sessions for refusing to serve a warrant and two summonses, 'fflinging Part of them in the Dirt swearing by God he would not serve them.' The high constable of the parish was no more trustworthy, often failing to attend sessions, so that by the end of November 1720 the justices resolved not to issue more warrants through him. This was James Steadman, who apprehended and presented fourteen punters on 12 October 1720, his name unusually appearing on the recognizance slips, possibly in an effort to document his diligence. He was removed in January, at least as high constable, as his name appears on a recognizance dated in March.[18]

While justices meeting in petty sessions were empowered to conduct raids on gaming and other 'disorderly houses,' they ran into obstacles even with a cooperative constabulary. On 17 December 1720, justices meeting in petty sessions at the Bedford Head Tavern were informed of a gaming table kept by the gaming entrepreneur William Howell at a tavern near Temple Bar. Howell, known as the 'Welsh Ambassador,' was associated with a number of operations in the City of Westminster, as well as Belsize House in Hampstead. In the ensuing raid, nine individuals were arrested. These included a half-pay lieutenant, along with another self-identified 'gentleman,' both of whom were released on their own recognizance; the rest were jailed on their inability to make bail. These consisted of two servants, a student of the Temple, an apothecary, and a clockmaker, along with the box-keeper and his assistant. After this session, however, the petty sessions were adjourned *sine die,* the justices believing that it was impossible to have their warrants enforced. Once the prosecutions were effectively dropped, the justices themselves faced lawsuits from the keepers of gaming houses 'for disturbing them in their Habitations, and their Occupations.' Counsel had advised these defendants 'that the Laws were either deficient against them, or at least so intricate, that the Gamesters could not be easily convicted.'[19] These circumstances help to explain William Howell's lack of concern at being summoned to sessions the morning after hosting a ball for the anniversary of the coronation, at which '[t]here was a very handsome Appearance both of Gentlemen and Ladies.' When the constable arrived with the summons, Howell reportedly 'gave his Duty to the Court, that he was indispos'd, and could not wait on them by reason of last Night's Fatigue,' adding that 'for his part he had forgiven all Offences, and hop'd they would do the like.'[20]

---

[18] *Account of the Endeavours,* 9; *Daily Post,* 402 (13 January 1721); LMA MJ/SR/2358, rr 33–47; MJ/SR/2363, r 149.

[19] *Account of the Endeavours,* 11–12; LMA MJ/SR/2358, rr 121–123, 173–177; Howell was among six men and three women indicted for keeping gaming houses in July of 1721 (MJ/SR/2368, ii 10, 24–30).

[20] *Weekly Journal,* 100 (8 November 1718).

An additional complication was that the high and petty constables weren't answerable to the Westminster justices, but to another court, the Leet Court of the Dean and Chapter of Westminster, also known as the Court of Burgesses. It was the bailiffs of the Court of Burgesses who summoned the juries for the quarter sessions, paying £20 annually to the High Bailiff of Westminster for the privilege. They were thus able to pack juries, for example, with employees of the defendants.[21] A memorandum in the State Papers made an identical allegation, noting that fourteen grand jurors were appointed by a bailiff named Cobley, a butcher whose customers included 'several of the Gaming houses.' All fourteen 'lived near the playhouses' in the parish of St Clement Danes, but they were listed as residents of different parishes 'on purpose that the Justices might not take notice that they were Neighbours friends and Acquaintance of the Gamesters.' The document asserted as well that the High Bailiff collected £2,000 annually in bribes from gaming venues and brothels.[22]

In the autumn of 1721, the Commission of the Peace again moved against gaming establishments through a policy of 'broken windows policing,' targeting offences not comprehended under the Gaming Act, but that occurred at gaming houses, such as disturbing the peace, fraud, receiving stolen goods, or harbouring fugitives. This initiative explains the absence of any presentations for gaming at the October sessions. The eighteen Westminster justices engaged in the suppression effort also began to be more secretive about their deliberations and the places and times of their meetings. Since magistrates' clerks were known to give notice to gaming operators that petty sessions were meeting and warrants were being issued, it was recommended that they not 'be Employed in this Matter.' The times and locations of petty sessions were left entirely to the chairman of the Commission of the Peace, 'to prevent Gentlemen (whom there might be cause to suspect) from coming to the Meeting for the future, either as Advocates or Sollicitors for the Gamesters, or as pretended Friends to the Commission.' These meetings were at venues like the Fountain in the Strand, itself the site of an illicit gaming operation some years later.[23]

Ultimately, the full bench decided to focus on Covent Garden, believed to house more gaming operations than any other parish, and issued orders for the v there to convene weekly petty sessions to apprehend and present both the keepers of gaming houses and those resorting to them. Justices of other parishes were asked to assist, and those of St Martin in the Fields and St Clement Danes were directed to attend the initial petty sessions on 17 October.[24] Relatively few arrests resulted from this renewed vigilance, save for the episode that precipitated *The Account of the Endeavours,* the fracas that occurred in the Playhouse Passage near

---

[21] *Account of the Endeavours,* 9–10.   [22] TNA SP 35/27/247.
[23] TNA SP 35/27/248; *Account of the Endeavours,* 14.   [24] LMA WJ/OC/001/26.

Drury Lane a few days before Christmas in 1721. A 'riot,' legally defined since the fifteenth century as any disturbance perpetrated by more than two individuals, was no rarity in that part of the metropolis, occurring every other day in greater London during the single year of 1720.[25] The criminal prosecutions that arose from this particular 'riot,' however, furnish possibly the only extensive and detailed eyewitness accounts of a gaming house raid, particularly valuable evidence given the multiple perspectives of deponents.

Four constables were dispatched under a warrant to the premises of William Vanderman, identified as a stay maker, but who had been previously summoned as proprietor of a gaming house, a case that had proceeded to a grand jury, which had declined to issue an indictment. His premises was in Playhouse Passage, a blind alley leading from Drury Lane to the green room and storage facilities of the Theatre Royal. One of Vanderman's box-keepers, corroborated by a second witness, said that the venue had been kept for gaming at hazard for the past eight to nine years. The raiding party proceeded under a warrant over the signatures of ten justices, and had raided at least two suspected brothels before arriving at Vanderman's; they held an additional warrant for the arrest of three men suspected of cheating a fourth of over £600.[26] The initial foray into Vanderman's, however, erupted into chaos. The constables, with an unspecified number of deputized *posse comitatus,* found twenty punters at Vanderman's, who then resisted arrest, drawing weapons, and forcing the constables out into the passage. A large and unruly crowd gathered, a memorandum subsequently alleging that gaming venues employed 'such Numbers of servants and Officers that 500 as Desperate men can be drawn together out of these Houses in half an hour.' This 'riotous assembly' prompted the head constable to request the assistance of guards posted at Somerset House. Five guardsmen arrived, under instruction to ensure that their firearms were unloaded. The ensuing riot lasted three hours, necessitating the intervention of two sets of guards. When the Somerset House contingent was unable to restore order, application was made to the Leicester House guard, where the commanding officer dispatched a serjeant and twelve guardsmen. By the time they arrived, however, the Riot Act had been read (allegedly), shots had been fired (certainly), and the crowd had dispersed. One of the Somerset House guardsmen had apparently torn off his brass buttons and loaded them in his musket; Henry Bowes, a tailor who acted as a box-keeper at hazard tables, was killed, surgeons reportedly removing two brass buttons from his corpse.[27]

Two criminal prosecutions resulted. Edward Vaughn JP and Philip Cholmondely, the high constable of Holborn, stood trial for Bowes' death in the

[25] Robert Shoemaker, 'The London "Mob" in the Early Eighteenth Century,' *Journal of British Studies,* 26 (July 1987), 276.
[26] LMA MJ/SR/2356, r 195; MJ/SR/2358, i77; MJ/SR/2379.
[27] TNA SP 35/27/247; *Account of the Endeavours,* 21–6; *Evening Post,* 1936 (26 December 1721); *Daily Journal,* 287 (25 December 1721).

middle of January 1722. The prosecution insinuated that the brass buttons removed from the corpse came from Vaughn's coat. Two witnesses testified to hearing Vaughn pledge to indemnify the guardsman if he fired on the crowd. Vaughn and Cholmondely were acquitted.[28] At the end of February, Charles MacCave, Edward Dun, and Edward Galloway appeared at the Old Bailey for 'Riotously assaulting several Constables, in the execution of their Office.' Parish constables contended that it was the punters in Vanderman's who had opened the window, and thrown brickbats, tankards, and a full chamber pot through it onto the raiding party. Constable Thomas Burt related that when the order to disperse mandated under the Riot Act was read, 'those within cry'd A T[ur]d of your Proclamation.' All three defendants in this case were convicted, MacCave receiving a sentence of five years' imprisonment and a fine of £100, and the others one year in prison and fines of £50.[29]

The riot in Playhouse Passage was only one particularly aggravated instance among multiple accounts of resistance to gaming enforcement. Significantly, eye-witnesses who lived or worked in the immediate vicinity of Vanderman's gave testimony uniformly hostile to the constables. These witnesses, referring to the raiding party as a 'mob,' did not testify to hearing the Riot Act read, but claimed to hear Cholmondely order Vanderman's to be set on fire, and Vaughn order the guardsman to fire. Admittedly, the first of these witnesses, Walter Hartshorn, had been apprehended for gaming at the George's Head near Temple Bar a year earlier, and was committed to the Gatehouse after being taken at Belsize House in March of 1723. There are no such compromising records, however, for Andrew Meal, whose cheese shop was across the passage, nor for Ann Lander, who also lived opposite Vanderman's, nor even George Ireland, who as a vintner whose shop adjoined the raided premises was certainly suspect.[30] The incident in Playhouse Passage was hardly the only instance of physical resistance to constables executing a warrant on a gaming operation, either. The previous January, four men were jailed in large part 'for Opposing the High and petty Constables' dispatched to search Fryar's in the Haymarket, having 'made such opposition against the Constables & peace Officers that they were obliged to get a file of Musketary to suppress them.' Two others, both guardsmen, were bound in recognizances for the same offence. A month later, James Cornwall was summoned for assaulting, resisting, and insulting constables 'when they were searching a reputed common gameing house.' Only two days before the raid on Vanderman's, Thomas Ramsdell had been jailed for assaulting the constable George Cartwright and his assistants 'and hindring them entrance into an unlawful Common Gameing house,' John Gooding's establishment in Bridges Street, Covent Garden, 'by which means severall Gamesters made their Escape.' Gooding's daughters, Amy and

[28] OBPO t17220112-43.   [29] OBPO t17220228-65.
[30] OBPO t17220112-43; LMA MJ/SR/2359, r 140; MJ/SR/2404, pc.

Lucy, were also implicated as participants in the assault.[31] Episodes like these raise the question of what grievances were in play.

An Information Economy

A persistent problem in the policing of vice then as now is that for any number of reasons, those likely to observe proscribed behaviour are unlikely to report it, and those likely to report it are correspondingly unlikely to observe it. This conundrum as it related to gaming explains the recourse to 'informing constables,' essentially undercover police, or other informants, often unsavoury figures seized for other offences or acting out of grievance or animus against gaming operators. Both sets of prospective prosecutors stood to benefit from convictions, as they were by statute entitled to a portion of any fines collected. Convictions for gaming were rare, however, and a more certain income could be derived from bribery and extortion. Informants, including 'informing constables,' were always held in low regard on both sides of the law and by the public at large, for these reasons.

The unique ability of gaming operators to corrupt the administration of justice must have informed some of the alarm in select quarters of the Westminster bench. These magistrates were heavily invested in the reputation for integrity that they believed should adhere to the Commission of the Peace as a whole, but in common with other incorporated groups with similar commitment to the same sort of corporate ethos, they were as liable to conceal the official malfeasance of their colleagues as they were to expose and address it, especially if they found that misconduct was pervasive. The frustration of the reforming Westminster magistrates was registered in a lengthy pamphlet that appeared in 1722, in the form of 'a letter to a noble lord,' who was almost certainly Charles, Viscount Townshend, the Secretary of State for the Northern Department. The response of the Commission of the Peace to *An Account of the Endeavours* was curious to say the least, reflecting as much anxiety for the reputation of the bench as for its (in)efficacy in sniffing out and snuffing out gaming operations. The tract was clearly the work of one of their number, or by someone else with privileged access to inside information, as entries in the sessions rolls corroborated many of its assertions of fact. An ad hoc investigative committee of eighteen justices was established to discern the identity of the author 'and in case of such discovery to consider by what legall ways or means they or any of them may be presented or proceeded against.' There was a particular worry that the pseudonymous author of what the Commission characterized as a 'fraudulent' tract was

---

[31] LMA MJ/SR/2363, rr 62, 66, 84–85, 184; MJ/SR/2378.

insinuating as if some Justices of the peace of this County who have seemed
most zealous & warm to suppress gameing houses, are Under hand ffavourers of
Gamesters & ffrequenters of gaming houses, and are for defending or at least
skreening of such.[32]

The Commission thought better of including this speculation, recorded in the
sessions papers, in the final draft of its orders, and it was deleted. The final report
of the ad hoc committee asserted 'that the s[ai]d pamphlett is calculated to lessen
the authority & respect due to the Commission of the peace,' and that the suggestion that particular justices were undermining the policing of commercial gaming was 'false scandalous and malicious.' They professed to be unable to determine
either the author or printer of the tract, although they must have been aware of
the very real possibility that the culprit, certainly a colleague on the bench, was
sitting among them.[33] William Cowper, who corresponded with Townshend's
office about the prosecution of gaming operators, and accompanied two of the
four raids described in the pamphlet, may have been responsible; another candidate is Daniel Combes, Joseph Addison's brother-in-law, who was an attending
justice on three of the raids.

This committee would have been interested, or possibly alarmed, to learn of an
anonymous memorandum sent to the Secretary of State that outlined many of the
concerns elaborated in the *Account of the Endeavours*. Thomas Jones's information on John Metcalfe, described below, was mentioned here, suggesting that
Metcalfe's case may have informed the pamphlet's remarks on the duplicity of
some Westminster justices. Also noted was Henry Brice, who threatened a fellow
justice for hearing an information against Brice's clerk; it was Brice who several
years earlier had allowed two accused gaming operators to stand as sureties for
each other. Most astonishing was the presence of an autograph manuscript of
what was very likely an initial draft of the list of gaming house personnel that
subsequently became a staple of admonitory literature. The author possibly
attempted to appeal to Townshend privately before resorting to print, prompted
from a concern that '[t]he Method the Justices are now taking will End only in a
Squabble and Quarrells among themselves Especially if it be Expected that the
Justices be Informers and prosecutors,' both functions beneath the dignity of the
bench. Even more curiously, the memorandum appears to be a draft, with

---

[32] LMA WJ/OC/001/40: 1 March 1722; MJ/SP/1722/02/22; the passage in question, from *Account
of the Endeavours*, 31, ran as follows: 'When there is any Method enter'd into for Suppressing this Evil,
every Body in Power seems equally zealous; and I fear that of late some, who have seemed most zealous and warm, and have taken the Lead, have done it to shew Thieves the Value of their Friendship;
and when they have made their Terms, they have continued with the same seeming Zeal, but grow to
be such Lovers of Form, that they obstruct all Prosecutions that are undertaken; they pretend to be
equally willing to suppress Thieves, and at the same time are against every thing that is propos'd
against them.'
[33] LMA MJ/SP/1722/04/50.

sentences that were left uncompleted, and an advisory that 'no persons ought particularly to be named in this Memoriall but that inquiry be left to the Wisdom of the Governmt, to whom it will be very Easy to find out the truth of what is here Asserted and the persons herein described.'[34] The presence of these documents in the State Papers, in the possession of Townshend's office, suggests that not only was the *Account of the Endeavours* addressed to the Secretary of State, it originated in his office, as a means of exerting pressure on the Westminster justices, or on the Lord Chancellor, the Earl of Macclesfield, to purge the bench. High politics may have figured here, as Macclesfield was a holdover from the ministry of Stanhope and Sunderland, a personal favourite of the King, and an adherent of Lord Carteret, the most prominent political rival of Walpole and Townshend.

The reputation for corruption that dogged justices and constables was undoubtedly a crucial factor that frustrated efforts to police gaming. The 'trading justice' and the 'informing constable' were archetypes well represented in Westminster's apparatus of local government. Until 1792, when Parliament established stipendiary magistracies for metropolitan London, JPs could collect fees for certain proceedings, and the Westminster and Middlesex benches were notoriously full of such 'trading justices.' Complainants might be charged a shilling for a recognizance binding a respondent; a respondent, in turn, could pay a shilling to have the recognizance lifted. 'If these worthy magistrates would issue out Discharges, and supersede Warrants, and do the other business of a justice *gratis*,' one commentator noted in 1731, it would redound as much to their honour, as anything they have yet done.' What Norma Landau termed 'the trading justice's trade' reflected poorly on the magistrates of Westminster in their efforts to suppress gaming houses.[35]

Townshend's office in Whitehall received far worse reports of the Westminster bench than newspapers did. An undated memorandum, purporting to be an abstract of a letter left in Button's coffeehouse, contained scathing assessments both of the magistrates themselves and their approach to policing commercial gaming. 'Its true they have put down a few Pharo banks in Cov[e]nt Garden,' the correspondent allowed,

> but what then they have left open Whites, Ozendoes,…and ye ridottos where there is more mischiefe done in one week, then ever there was in Cov[en]t Garden since it was a parish. Its true they have put down a Hazzard table or two but what then they have left open a good many others, nay they have left open the groom porters and all the Taverns Even those they use ym selves to all manner of play without controle.

[34] LMA MJ/SR/2275, rr 110, 112; TNA SP 35/27/247–249.
[35] *Weekly Register*, 47 (6 March 1731); *Grub Street Journal*, 57 (4 February 1731); Norma Landau, 'The Trading Justice's Trade,' in Norma Landau (ed.), *Law, Crime, and English Society, 1660–1830* (Cambridge: Cambridge University Press, 2002), 46–64.

None of these anomalies were surprising, the memorandum continued, considering that graft from gaming operations supplied 'trading justices' with most of their income, so that they were 'assuredly in fee with ye above named places as they are alive.'[36] It was not unknown for justices to allow apprehended punters to stand as sureties for each other, as Henry Brice JP did when he allowed Philip Wiseman and Henry Cole to post surety for each other in August 1716. Justice Crake allowed Edward Courtney, presented as a 'box-keeper' at Fryar's in the Haymarket, to stand for Philip Spooner in September 1718. Similarly, Justice Saunders permitted Peter Joiner to stand surety for two punters taken on the same premises near Long Acre where Joiner was charged with keeping a gaming house at the beginning of the next year. William Luffingham, well known to the bench as a gaming entrepreneur, was a surety for John Andrews, seized in the same raid.[37] In June of 1720, the high constable of Holborn, Thomas Jones, lodged an information concerning John Metcalfe, a Westminster justice who had asked Jones to take no action against the hazard tables on the premises of Cymbert Conyers, who was Metcalfe's tenant to the tune of £150 annually. This astronomical rent, three times the going rate for houses of that size in that vicinity, would according to Jones have been impossible to charge had Metcalfe not been a magistrate living nearby, and, as Metcalfe told Jones himself, would have been impossible for Conyers to pay 'if Gentlemen were not allowed to play there.' When Jones nevertheless persisted in efforts to investigate Conyers' establishment, he was refused entry, until finally he and a watchman were assaulted by three porters of Gray's Inn, where Metcalfe was a principal and used his position to impede the ensuing search for the offenders.[38] It comes as no surprise that Metcalfe's signature never appears on any recognizances for gaming offences, nor was he part of the committee of magistrates formed to police gaming. He was ultimately unable to protect Conyers, who in September 1722 pled guilty to an indictment of keeping a disorderly house, and was fined £10, sentenced to thirty days in Newgate, and bound to find sureties for good behaviour for two years, which sessions papers indicate he performed punctually.[39]

In the same way that gaming operators solicited the complicity of constables, sessions clerks and justices, Westminster magistrates were forced to rely on the cooperation of informants whose hands were not clean. In July of 1722, Townshend applied to the solicitor of the Treasury to pay the expenses of Daniel Underhill, Joshua Glassington, and Richard Williams, who had lodged prosecutions in the Playhouse Passage riot. In August of 1716, Underhill, identified as a 'gentleman of the Inner Temple,' had stood surety for Bernard Linster when he

[36] TNA SP 35/66/76.
[37] LMA MJ/SR/2275, rr 111–112; MJ/SR/2315, rr 170, 172; MJ/SR/2320, rr 124–126, 128.
[38] TNA SP 35/21/129.
[39] *Weekly Journal*, (15 September 1722); LMA MSP 1722 Oct/144, Dec/62; 1723 Jan/89, Feb/48, Ap/80, May/48, Jun/83/Aug/56; 1724 Feb/55, Oct/141.

stood before Henry Brice as the keeper of a faro bank, and in June 1721, Glassington was a surety for Katherine Roadhouse, summoned to 'answer two severall Indictments for Keeping a Common gameing Table.' Both Underhill and Glassington were likely clients of gaming venues. Members of the Inns of Court were stereotypically notorious gamblers. Glassington was a butcher in Clare Market whose subsequent archival traces suggest that he may have gambled compulsively. He appears several times in the vestry minutes of his parish, St Clement Danes, for failure to pay rates; his son and namesake, also a butcher, gave up the premises he inherited in 1760, and appeared as a pauper in 1769. Williams, called as a witness in the trials over the riot, admittedly may or may not have been the same Richard Williams, identified as a victualler in King Street near Whitehall, who was presented before Theodore Delafaye in May 1713 '[f]or allowing unlawfull gaming in his house.'[40] In the aftermath of the trials from the riot at Vanderman's, an informant named John Hallin, who seems to have been a merchant marine captain, came forward with a list of purported gaming houses and proprietors still operating in Westminster. His letters to Townshend, Townshend's deputy Charles Delafaye, and the chair of the Commission of the Peace, William Cowper, soliciting compensation for this information all survive, but any list that Hallin provided does not. No gaming proprietors appear in any of the corresponding sessions rolls, and there is no recognizance binding Hallin to lodge prosecutions. In April 1723, however, Hallin related that he had been bound over to the Westminster sessions after being taken in a gaming house two years earlier; in light of the information he had disclosed, he petitioned the Commission to be discharged from his recognizance. Thirteen justices, including William Cowper and John Gonson, signed a memorandum affirming the value of Hallin's testimony, and that some consideration, not specified, was due him.[41] In November 1722, Cowper requested that Townshend secure a discharge for John Elfick, a Grenadier Guardsman who was reportedly 'capable, & willing to discover several important matters' pertinent to the effort to suppress gaming operations. Three months later, however, Elfick was bound in recognizance as a 'common gamester,' still identified as a soldier, suggesting that his discharge was not granted.[42] Philip Cholmondely's obituary in March 1739 identified him as high constable of Holborn and 'one of the chief of those *honest* People call'd *Informing Constables*.' After his acquittal in the death of Henry Bowes, the notice related, Cholmondely

[40] TNA SP 35/32/42–43; LMA MJ/SR/2275, r 109; MJ/SR/2368, r 25; WCA St. Clement Danes Vestry Minutes 3 August 1739, 13 April 1747, 1 November 1749, 26 September 1750, 4 October 1750, 22 April 1751, 25 March 1752, 11 March 1756, 25 April 1757; LMA SM/PS October 1760; WCA St. Clement Danes Examination Papers 9 January 1769; MJ/SR/2211, r 89.
[41] TNA SP 35/41/1/34, SP 35/41/2/54, SP 35/42/1/79, SP 35/66/2/7–8; LMA WSP/1723/Ap/2–3.
[42] TNA SP 35/34/14; LMA MJ/SR/2401, r 76.

received a number of threatening letters, which he was suspected of having manu-factured himself.[43]

Westminster justices would not act against gaming operations absent any impetus from the Crown, and parish constables, volunteers who were policing their neighbours, were subject to pressure and inducements of various kinds. If newspapers were correct that twenty-two gaming establishments operating in Covent Garden in 1722 raked in between £40 and £100 a night, the paltry fine of forty shillings per documented day of operation, for which the arresting constable could petition for a share, was no match for the bribes that a gaming operator was able to offer, especially given that it could seldom be proven that gaming had gone forward in a presented establishment on dates other than the date of a raid. The Westminster justice Saunders Welch adverted this difficulty when he advised constables

> if you present, upon your own knowledge, either bawdy or gaming houses, men-tion the time they have been kept, and let your presentment be absolute. If only upon the reports of others, then mention them as only reputed so.[44]

In July, ostensibly congratulatory letters, exchanged between Secretary of State Townshend and the Commission of the Peace, were published in newspapers. Certain passages of Townshend's letter, delivered to the justices as they assembled for quarter sessions, were particularly pointed when read in the context of the documents that had come to the attention of his office, in addition to the *Account of the Endeavours*. The King, according to Townshend, commended the efforts of the Westminster bench against 'unlawful Gaming' while noting at the same time that it had 'increased in a most extraordinary & scandalous manner.' The justices were directed to deliver periodic reports on their progress, 'taking particular Notice of the Difficultys and Obstructions you meet with from whatever Quarter they may arise,' and to provide their subordinates 'all fitting Countenance and protection.' Townshend advised the justices that those of them who acted 'with Unanimity and Vigour' would be 'particularly entitled to His Majesty's Favour.'[45] Read against information in the Northern Department's possession, including the names of refractory justices, Townshend's missive might read like a veiled threat, and was perhaps intended as such.

For the remainder of 1722, the Westminster justices pursued a public rela-tions strategy of declaring victory in the press. In November it was reported that constables dispatched to determine if there were any gaming houses still

---

[43] *Universal Spectator*, 544 (10 March 1739).

[44] *Evening Post*, 1943 (9 January 1722); Saunders Welch, *Observations on the Office of Constable* (London: Andrew Millar, 1754), 30.

[45] *London Gazette*, 6076 (10 July 1722); *Daily Courant*, 6469 (16 July 1722); TNA SP 35/32/6–8.

operating in the parish of Covent Garden discovered only one, 'which was kept by Mrs. Barrow, and formerly by Mrs. Lloyd her Daughter, (sometime since committed to the Gate-house for keeping the same).' In December, not quite one year after the Playhouse Passage incident, came the pronouncement that '[a]ll the Gaming-Houses in Westminster are now entirely suppress'd.' The new year had barely begun, however, when another item related twenty-nine Westminster justices had signed a memorandum drawn up for presentation to the House of Commons, 'complaining of the great Number of Gaming and other disorderly Houses in the City and Liberties of Westminster, which it is not in their Power to quash in the present Situation of Affairs in that City.'[46] In the third and last of his charges, published later that year, Bulstrode, the chair of the Commission of the Peace, threw up his hands in despair. After reviewing the extant gaming statutes, he wondered

> what do all these excellent Laws signify, unless there was so much *Honesty* in the Subject to *Obey* them? . . . The *Magistrates* in this County, to their *eternal Honour*, have not been wanting, on their parts, to put the Laws in execution. But if the *Government* make ever so many Laws, . . . *Gentlemen and Ladies, and ev'n Men in Trade, Shop-keepers, will Game publickly, and that for Excessive Sums, in spite of all Laws.*[47]

Westminster justices had pursued a strategy of targeting particular gaming venues, typically staging a single high-profile raid in advance of any given quarter sessions. One such target was the purported 'Female Gaming-House' that Elizabeth Crosset kept in Theobald's Row, where five women and three men were seized in September 1722.[48] The Phoenix in the Haymarket was raided four times in the space of two years, while the Spread Eagle in Bridges Street was presented at least three times between 1720 and 1730. The Phoenix was conspicuous because of its location in the Haymarket Theatre complex, and it drew a socially heterogeneous clientele, a raid in April 1725 apprehending seventeen punters including a shoemaker, a surgeon, a member of the Middle Temple, a porter, a clock engraver, a wigmaker, a blacksmith, a journeyman in 'the Picture-Shop in Pall Mall,' and four self-described 'gentlemen,' including one Metcalf Ashe, who appears in Westminster rolls multiple times for gaming offences, and who decades later was concerned in gaming operations in Tunbridge Wells.[49] The Spread Eagle, on the

[46] *British Journal*, 7 (3 November 1722); *Evening Post*, 2087 (11 December 1722); *London Journal*, 180 (5 January 1723).

[47] *The Third Charge of Whitelocke Bulstrode, Esq., to the Grand Jury and Other Juries of the County of Middlesex* (London: D. Brown and R. Gosling, 1723), 26; italics in original.

[48] LMA MJ/SR/2392, rr 18–25; *Daily Journal*, 522 (25 September 1722).

[49] LMA MJ/SR/2445, rr 148–156, 173–175, 186–188, 191–192, 196; MJ/SR/2517, rr 13, 17, 57, 139–141; MJ/SR/2534, r 180; MJ/SR/2551, rr 191–193; *Daily Post*, 998 (10 December 1722); *Daily Journal*, 2563 (26 March 1729); *Universal Spectator*, 82 (2 May 1730).

other hand, was kept for over three decades by a Sephardic Jewish family, initially Abraham Nassau (variantly Norsa) and then Joshua Bassan; they also kept the Cocoa Tree, a much more select venue in St James's Street. The Spread Eagle's hazard tables were still in operation in January 1754, when it was raided under a warrant from Benjamin Cox, who subsequently petitioned the Crown for relief from vexatious litigation. '[T]he present Artfull and Crafty Schemes of the Gaming race of Men,' Cox complained, 'is scarcely to be Coped with by the Magistrates or Suppressed by the Civill Power without being thus Mollested.'[50]

The justices of Middlesex and Westminster also turned their attention to operators like William Howell and William Luffingham, who were proprietors of gaming concerns in Hampstead as well as Covent Garden. Belsize House was on the Belsize Estate, property of the Dean and Chapter of Westminster leased to successive Earls of Chesterfield, who were slow to recognize its real estate value as a location of genteel villas, so that income from the estate was negligible next to other Chesterfield properties in Nottinghamshire and Derbyshire. Charles Povey, a retired coal merchant, was technically Chesterfield's under-tenant. Povey in turn sublet Belsize House to William Howell, the 'Welsh Ambassador,' who, in the words of Francis Thompson, converted Belsize House 'into one of the most notorious pleasure gardens of the day.'[51] A French visitor in May 1720 wrote of

> a tavern with a handsome bowling green, lovely walks, and a lovely park; it is therefore here where crowds of gamesters have begun to go, in Hampstead, and to several other places, as each goes where there is good company, above all to new places.[52]

Luffingham, proprietor of gaming venues in Bridges Street and the Piazza, had an increasing stake in Hampstead Wells, whose proprietor John Duffield ultimately granted him a twenty-one year lease in 1719.[53] Both venues had come to the attention of magistrates a few years earlier, when their proprietors, as well as those of Sadler's Wells, Pancras Wells, and London Spa, Clerkenwell, were summoned to a meeting of the Commission of the Peace, the chairman of which later mentioned inquiries made about the 'Long Room' at Hampstead Wells, and a young man who had lost all his money there. In May of 1722, the justices issued an order

[50] LMA MJ/SR/2358, r 108; MJ/SR/2421, rr 25–26; MJ/SR/2529, rr 45, 149–153; WCA Overseers Receipt Book, St. Paul's Covent Garden, H8/24, H512/35; *London Evening Post*, 353 (12 March 1730); *Grub Street Journal*, 11 (19 March 1730); TNA SP 36/155/103–104.

[51] Francis Michael Longstreth Thompson, *Hampstead: Building a Borough, 1650–1964* (London: Routledge and Kegan Paul, 1974), 33–5.

[52] TNA SP 35/21/117 ('...une taverne ou il y a un beau bowlin-green, de belles promenades, & un trez beau parc; c'est donc la ou les joueurs commancent d'aller en foule, a hampstead, & a plusieurs autres endroits, car un chacun va ou il y a bonne compagnie, surtout dans les nouveaux endroits....').

[53] *Victoria County History: Middlesex*, 12 vols (London: Institute for Historical Research, 1989), 9. 82.

against both of the Hampstead properties. In July, Povey was jailed for 'for keeping an unlawfull gaming house…and raising a Mobb and Riot' on the high constable of Holborn and his assistants, 'and also for refusing to find sufficient sureties.' This raid seems to have achieved its objective, as a newspaper notice ran in August that Povey as proprietor of Belsize had 'prohibited all sorts of Gaming, which were so much practised there, and is willing to suffer the Peace-Officers to go round the House at all Hours, to see that there is no Play, nor any other Disorder.' In December, Luffingham, listed as sub-tenant of the tavern at Hampstead Wells, was indicted for keeping 'A com[m]on Gameing Table' from 4 August, alongside Edward Higgs, Duffield's tenant at the coffeehouse, charged with keeping a common gaming house from 4 June.[54] The Covent Garden concerns of these operators continued unabated. Luffingham's establishment under the Piazza, which he had occupied since at least 1715, was raided in July 1724. Although Howell was listed as a bankrupt in November 1723, he was operating a gaming house in Bridges Street when it was raided in December 1727, unsuccessfully as Howell had been alerted. His obituary in March 1736 noted that he 'formerly kept Bellsize House, and several noted Gaming-houses in and about Covent-Garden.'[55]

Authorities confronted an additional challenge in that gaming operations vested in 'banks' were portable, and could migrate from venue to venue, as one newspaper writer had recognized by May of 1723:

Our Reformers meet with much Difficulty in the Suppression of the Gaming Houses, for as fast as they are put down in one Place they spring up in another, and they are come into Methods of managing them in so private a manner that they elude all the Care of the Magistracy to find them out.[56]

These realities might have occurred to magistrates as well. Those arrested and indicted for keeping gaming tables were not always one and the same with the proprietors of venues where a gaming operation was going forward. The Haymarket coffeeman John Bernard Linster had already been charged for one gaming operation when he appeared again five months later in August 1716 for another, alongside Philip Wiseman and Henry Cole.[57] In March 1721, Edward Boucher was '*taken* in a comon Gameing house' in which he confessed he had kept a faro table.[58] The gaming entrepreneur William Howell, known by common report as the proprietor of the gaming house called by his name in Covent Garden

[54] LMA MJ/SP/1718/05/008–011; MJ/SR/2389, pc; MJ/SR/2392, ii 113–114; *Weekly Journal*, 182 (26 May 1722); *St. James's Journal*, 17 (23 August 1722).
[55] WCA Overseer's Receipt Book, St. Paul's Covent Garden, H19/1715/34; LMA MJ/SR/2430, rr 192–197; *British Journal*, 94 (4 July 1724); *Universal Spectator*, 387 (March 1736), 801.
[56] *London Journal*, 198 (11 May 1723).   [57] LMA MJ/SR/2275, rr 109–112.
[58] LMA MJ/SR/2363, r 150; italics mine.

Piazza, never paid rates on any property at that address, nor did he ever appear as the ratepayer on any property in the parish. In July of 1721, he was indicted for keeping a gaming *table* at the King George's Head without Temple Bar, along with John Parker, who may have been the tavern's proprietor.[59] Proprietors of public accommodations could plausibly plead ignorance that 'unlawful games' were played under their roof, or assert that gaming tables, recognizably configured to contain wheels, or featuring 'cut-outs' for dealers and croupiers, had been innocently found on a premises that they had taken over from a previous tenant, as William Dawson, who kept a coffeehouse near the corner of Queen Street and Long Ditch, pleaded in 1718. Dawson was nevertheless bound the following January not to allow 'unlawfull Games' to be played 'in his house Yard or Ally.'[60] It was common for gaming operations to surface in venues that were abandoned, or vacant, or past their prime, or fallen out of fashion. In the early 1720s, the Fountain Tavern in the Strand had hosted the petty sessions called to target gaming houses; two decades later, the vacant premises hosted a gaming concern of particular notoriety.[61]

Game and Match

In Westminster, the unique interrelation of local politics with the highest level of national politics meant that reconfigurations in the central government could decisively redirect local policy. Early in 1725, the Earl of Macclesfield, who had relied on royal favour to retain office, and who as an ally of Lord Carteret was no friend to Walpole or Townshend, resigned as Lord Chancellor amid accusations of malfeasance, for which he faced impeachment that spring. In May, as Macclesfield appeared for trial at the bar of the House of Lords, orders in court were issued at quarter sessions that no one keeping a gaming house, or even a victualling house or cook shop, or engaged in the retail sale of distilled spirits could be empanelled as a grand juror for Middlesex or Westminster. Viscount Townshend, as holder of the office that evolved into that of the Home Secretary, appeared frequently in connection with anti-gaming initiatives on the Westminster bench. It was Townshend, for example, who put up the reward of £50 for information leading to the arrest of the three fugitives concerned in the Playhouse Passage riot, and who put up the same reward later in the year when the Westminster justice Sir John Gonson received anonymous threats. In January of 1722, Townshend directed the Attorney General to render every possible assistance to the magistrates of Westminster and Middlesex in their effort to

---

[59] LMA MJ/SR/2358, r 177; MJ/SR/2368, i 10.
[60] LMA WJ/SP/1718/10/001; MJ/SR/2320, r 129.
[61] LMA MJ/SR/2894, pc, rr 81–114; MJ/SR/2897, pc, rr 159–161.

suppress gaming houses. In July of 1722, in addition to the commendatory letter he wrote to the justices for their efforts to suppress gaming operations, which was reprinted in several papers, he also authorized the payment of the legal expenses of three men who lodged prosecutions arising from the Playhouse Passage disturbance. His interest in the proscription of commercial gaming was sufficiently known for him to receive an anonymous report on the failure of the Westminster bench to close White's in Covent Garden, and also to receive a solicitation for a reward from an informant. It was also Townshend who issued new exhortations to the justices toward the end of the decade, when it was clear that gaming concerns in the jurisdiction had 'revived to a great Degree.'[62]

Thus it was that a growing rift between Townshend and his brother-in-law, Robert Walpole, did not bode well for the effort against gaming establishments in Westminster. The charge that William Cowper delivered to the grand jury in April 1730 sounded notes of bravado without any overtones of apprehension. He warned them not to relax their vigilance against gaming venues from anticipation that 'any Accession of Power given to the Magistracy' for that purpose would take these and other public nuisances out of the grand jury's purview. Cowper reiterated the determination of the consortium of anti-gaming justices to continue in the efforts of the previous ten years:

> [I]f any kind of Force, or Resolution in the Offenders, if Obloquy, either publick, or private, from their Abettors, and sometimes their Partners in Iniquity, or from Persons acted by any Motives inconsistent with Publick Spirit, could have prevailed, to deter them from the Course they are set in, it had been effected Long ago; for nothing of the kind has been wanting: But these Attempts will always prove, and they have hitherto been, in vain....[63]

In May of 1730, however, Townshend resigned from the ministry and from public life, returning to Raynham in Norfolk to promote the cultivation of turnips. Only two days before his resignation came a plea from the Westminster justices concerned in the suppression of commercial gaming asking for the renewal of an order that a Crown attorney 'defend at the public expense any actions or suits brought against the constables' in either the execution of warrants or any prosecutions of gaming operations, citing in particular constables who had been indicted in connection with a raid on the Phoenix in the Haymarket. 'This order enabled them to go on with great success in putting down so many of these

[62] TNA SP 35/30/9, ff 23–24; SP 35/32/22, ff 42–43; SP 35/66/76, part 1, f 94; SP35/66/102, part 2, ff 7–8; *London Gazette*, 6031 (3 February 1722), 6073 (30 June 1722), 6076 (10 July 1722), 6730 (26 November 1728).

[63] *The Charge Delivered by the Honorable William Cowper at the Sessions of the Peace and Oyer and Terminer to the Grand Jury and Other Juries of the County of Middlesex* (London: J. Stagg, 1730), 17–18.

pernicious houses and encouraged the officers to do their duty without fear.'[64] Charges to grand juries for Middlesex and Westminster, which had been published on average at least once a year from 1718, ceased to be published after April 1730 until Henry Fielding published the charge he issued in 1749. The purpose of publishing these charges was made clear in one justice's remark that the suppression of gaming houses to the extent that had been managed would not have been possible absent private individuals voluntarily assisting constables.[65]

While Townshend was in office, the King and royal family had played ombre for the Twelfth Night benefit for the Groom Porter, eschewing the customary play at hazard, perhaps by way of setting a public example, the exemption of the royal household from existing statutes notwithstanding. No sooner was Townshend out of office, however, than hazard resumed on Twelfth Night at court, with the King, Queen, Prince of Wales, and the three princesses winning nearly a thousand guineas among themselves in January 1731, and the Earl of Portmore and the Duke of Grafton, the Lord Chamberlain, winning 'several thousands.' Hazard continued as the game of preference as Twelfth Night was observed at court for at least the next decade, even after the Georgian Gaming Acts outlawed it as an illegal lottery.[66]

Absent material support from the Crown, magistrates opted to prosecute individual gamesters in response to third-party complaints, rather than attempting to raid gaming houses, which had proved impracticable. The Phoenix was raided once again in February 1731, but was then left unmolested.[67] In May 1732, the recovery of around £300 belonging to a City merchant that his nineteen-year-old apprentice had stolen and then gambled away, provided a gaming anecdote with a rare happy ending when the young man confessed to Sir John Gonson, who issued arrest warrants for the offenders under the Queen Anne statute.[68] At the beginning of June in 1735, constables of St Martin's in the Fields seized several Italian expatriates on the premises of a vintner, also an Italian, playing at games that were unidentified, but identifiably unlawful to the constables.[69] Between June of 1735 and October 1747, however, there were no recognizances for gaming, and no indictments of gaming houses in any of the Westminster sessions rolls, nor were there any newspaper accounts of raids in the jurisdiction in the same period.

---

[64]   TNA SP/36/18/197, ff 197–198.

[65]   *The Charge of Sir Daniel Dolins, Kt., to the Grand Jury and Other Juries of the County of Middlesex* (London: Samuel Chandler, 1725), 25.

[66]   *Weekly Packet*, 132 (8 January 1715); *Weekly Journal*, 108 (10 January 1719); *London Journal*, 77 (14 January 1721), 129 (13 January 1722); *Daily Journal*, 611 (7 January 1723); *Weekly Journal*, 272 (11 January 1724); *Daily Journal*, 1246 (16 January 1725), 1866 (6 January 1727); *Daily Post*, 2588 (8 January 1728); *Gentleman's Magazine*, 1 (January 1731), 25; *London Journal*, 759 (12 January 1734); *Read's Weekly Journal*, 592 (10 January 1736); *London Daily Post*, 1309 (8 January 1739); *General Evening Post*, 981 (8 January 1740).

[67]   LMA MJ/SR/2551; *Daily Courant*, 9165 (22 February 1731).

[68]   *London Evening Post*, 703 (30 May 1732).   [69]   LMA MJ/SR/2637, rr 237, 312–317.

The Societies for the Reformation of Manners apparently stopped initiating gaming v after 1730.[70] Only three recognizances for gaming appear in the Westminster rolls for the three years prior to June 1735.[71] It should be noted that eight of the Westminster rolls for this period are in extremely poor condition and unfit for consultation. In tandem with the paucity of newspaper accounts, however, is the similar pattern that obtained in the City. While a handful of individuals were presented for street gaming, no gaming houses were presented from 1728 until January 1739, when the coffeeman John Morris was summoned 'for keeping an ill govern'd disorderly house by suffering Unlawful Games to be Used therein at unseasonable hours to the disturbance of the Neighbourhood.' A raid on a 'roly-poly' table in Ludgate Hill in the City was reported in October 1745.[72]

The 'joint stock' lottery drawn in 1731 was the first state lottery in five years, and the last until the first Westminster Bridge lottery in 1737. The lapse in the policing of gaming coincided with the relative dormancy of lotteries, just as earlier drives for aggressive enforcement of gaming statutes coincided with the introduction of 'gaming' lotteries, which unlike annuity lotteries awarded either no payout on blanks, like those of 1719, or only a partial refund on the purchase price, as was the case with the Malt Lotteries of 1723 and 1724. Similarly, the revival of 'gaming' lotteries at the end of the decade of the 1730s preceded a wave of legislation targeted at games of chance. While the holder of a blank in the 1731 drawing still drew a small annuity, venturers in the first Westminster Bridge lottery collected nothing on the losing tickets for which they paid £5, as was the case for the third, fourth, and fifth lotteries held from 1739 to 1741; the second lottery refunded only £6 9s. of the £10 paid for a 'blank.' A writer in the *Grub Street Journal* pointed out that the purchaser of a lottery ticket 'is gaming at the same disadvantage, as he who is to throw five on the dice against seven,' the odds standing at three-to-one against the caster.[73]

'All Endeavours of remedy will be fruitless,' the government had been advised about the suppression of gaming in Westminster in 1722, 'untill all Justices of the peace be removed out of the Commission who receive any Advantage from these Gaming houses, or who play at them, or have discouraged and threatened the Constables.' The *Account of the Endeavours* described '[o]ne of the great Proprietors of the Faroe-Tables,' worth a reported £60,000, who actually managed to be appointed to the Commission of the Peace. When the Lord Chancellor was informed three or four days later that this new justice had been a drawer in a tavern in Pall Mall and been employed as a faro dealer at the Spanish Embassy, he was removed, although the Commission was not informed of that fact before

[70] Shoemaker, 'Reforming the City,' 105.
[71] LMA MJ/SR/2576, r 189; MJ/SR/2591, r 238; MJ/SR/2602, r 469.
[72] LMA CLA/047/LJ/11/012–013; CLA/047/LJ/01/0760; *General Evening Post*, 1887 (29 October 1745); *London Evening Post*, 2807 (31 October 1745); *St. James's Evening Post*, 5585 (31 October 1745).
[73] Ewen, *Lotteries and Sweepstakes*, 143–7, 163; *Grub Street Journal*, 397 (4 August 1737).

their quondam colleague appeared for the sessions at the Old Bailey and took a seat among them. He was induced to leave the court once the justices learned of his dismissal, but not without a scene.[74] In August of 1738, Lord Chancellor Hardwicke took the extraordinary step of removing seventy-five Middlesex justices from the bench.[75] Soon after his appointment, Hardwicke was informed of the Middlesex justice William Morrice, who as High Bailiff of Westminster 'acted in that Office in a very Vile & scandalous manner taking yearly pentions of Gaming Houses & Bawdy Houses to remit their fines when Convicted at the Sessions.'[76] Then there was Robert Midford, who lived in Wild Court near Drury Lane, who reportedly kept gaming houses while sitting as a justice for Middlesex and Westminster. Lord Chancellor Peter King removed him from the bench for 'vile practices,' but Midford was then reinstated 'to the great surprise of allmost Every body' ten months later, very likely after King's death in July 1734; he was once again sitting and issuing recognizances by October 1735. Under Hardwicke, Midford was removed from the bench a second time. In 1747 he was said to be keeping four gaming tables at Cuper's Gardens in Surrey.[77] In January of 1739, the Commission of the Peace for Middlesex and Westminster petitioned the Duke of Newcastle, the Lord Lieutenant, that several new gaming operations had once again emerged in the City of Westminster, particularly in the vicinity of the theatres in Covent Garden and Drury Lane. The justices reminded Newcastle that in 1722, gaming concerns had been prosecuted at the expense of the Crown.[78] By that point it had become clear that the metropolitan magistracy was not to be relied on. If commercial gaming was to be contained, new legislation would be necessary.

---

[74] *Account of the Endeavours*, 33.
[75] TNA SP/35/27/248; Landau, *Justices of the Peace*, 126–7.   [76] BL Add. MSS 35,601, f 261.
[77] BL Add. MSS 25,604, f 382; LMA MJ/SR/2643; TNA SP 44/85, ff 18–19.
[78] TNA SP 36/47/1/42.

8

Commercial Gaming in the Wake of the Georgian Statutes

In March 1742, a few weeks after Robert Walpole's resignation, verses appeared metaphorically casting the newly displaced Prime Minister as a faro dealer in a Covent Garden gaming house, who 'with a strange, uninterrupted Run, Against the Players, every Taily won.' After winning twenty successive deals, standing for twenty sessions of Parliament, he is discovered to be dealing from a deck in which over half the cards are marked. Here, of course, the metaphor collapses, as marked cards were of little or no utility in faro; nonetheless, the master of the house, representing William Pulteney or George Carteret or both, promises a new dealer with new cards, but the 'Company' quickly perceives '[m]ost of the *old, mark'd* Cards, still passing round.'[1]

As a series of political setbacks sent the Walpole ministry into its downward spiral, a sequence of statutes specifically targeting commercialized games of chance was introduced. Given the lax enforcement of existing statutes over much of the 1730s, the motivations for this new legislative initiative are important to explore. James Raven has called attention to the 'mathematical engine,' the invention of Thomas Foubert, a jeweller and goldsmith in King Street near Golden Square. This numerical randomization device, which Foubert called 'Patent Mathematical Circles,' consisted of four wheels, with the ten Arabic digits inscribed on their edges, mounted on gears that were turned with a single pull of an attached cord. It would not turn up the same four-digit combination twice over the course of ten thousand rotations. In January 1735, Foubert advertised what he asserted was the third of his raffles for plate and jewels, probably his surplus inventory, for which tickets were a little over a crown apiece. It was a great success, if the dramatic augmentation of the value and nature of commodities put up as prizes in subsequent drawings was any indication. Plate and jewels gave way by 1738 to real estate in larger and larger parcels, the ownership of which was a cornerstone of status in the established political order. Foubert's raffles were already brazen violations of the Lottery Act, their advertisements decorated with illustrations of the 'Mathematical Circles,' but they had crossed an important line in offering exactly the sort of instant and undeserved social mobility that critics

[1] *Champion*, 366 (16 March 1742).

The Gambling Century: Commercial Gaming in Britain from Restoration to Regency. John Eglin, Oxford University Press.
© John Eglin 2023. DOI: 10.1093/oso/9780192888198.003.0009

of the culture of chance had always deplored.[2] In fairly short order, the first of the Georgian gaming statutes, like its sequels, was enacted with little or no debate or opposition.

Perhaps the embattled ministry sought to banish its reputation as a bastion of oligarchic graft by attacking a conspicuous species of local corruption, or perhaps it wished to undercut oppositionist efforts to associate it with gaming operators who had gamed the system. The same concerns may have motivated the 'Broad Bottom' administration that succeeded Walpole's to promote or acquiesce in the last of these statutes in 1744. Whatever objectives were in view, the wave of legislation aimed at prohibiting commercialized games of chance as 'unlawful lotteries' was met with a variety of stratagems aimed at evading the language of statute, with varying degrees of success. Other innovations demonstrated a newfound faith in the science of probability.

Parliament Doubles Down

The first of the Georgian Gaming Acts, which went into effect in 1739, was in part an amendment of the 1699 Lottery Act, which categorically outlawed any lotteries other than those sponsored by the Crown and established by Act of Parliament. It closed any loopholes that Foubert and other operators may have found in the earlier statute by explicitly forbidding the sale of lots for 'Houses, Lands, Advowsons, Presentations to Livings, Plate, Jewels, Ships, Goods, or other Things.' The provisions of the Lottery Act were now to apply to the games of faro and basset, newly classified as unlawful lotteries along with hazard and the Ace of Hearts.[3] This last game, also known as Fair Chance, seems to have been a 'board lottery' similar enough to the Royal Oak and its imitators for some contemporaries to believe that it and 'roly-poly' were already comprehended under the statute of 1699. The Ace of Hearts board was decorated with representations of playing cards and fitted with a device called a 'worm,' into which an ivory ball was dropped, making a circuit of the board until it fell into one of the indentations cut into the card images. A punter who staked on a winning 'card' received twenty-three to twenty-eight times the wager, depending on the number of options, which was generally twenty-five or thirty-one. As in the Royal Oak Lottery, the house percentage subtracted from the statistically suggested payout was hardly necessary to secure the bank a profit, one observer calling the Ace of Hearts

---

[2] Ewen, *Lotteries and Sweepstakes*, 194–5; .Raven, 'Debating the Lottery,' 100; *London Evening Post*, 1123 (28–30 January 1735), 1145 (25–27 March 1735), 1700 (5–7 October 1738); *London Daily Post*, 1110 (10 October 1738), 1165 (24 July 1738), 1268 (21 November 1738); *Craftsman*, 498 (17 January 1736), 674 (9 June 1739).

[3] 12 George II c. 20, *An Act for the More Effectual Preventing of Excessive and Deceitful Gaming* (London: John Baskett, 1739).

'as notoriously unjust and unfair a Game as was ever set up,' the odds against punters appearing so clearly as to render explanation unnecessary.[4]

There was support for this first statute across the political spectrum, the ministerialist *Daily Gazetteer* commenting on largely positive coverage in the oppositionist *Craftsman,* and also noting that the bill had passed in a matter of hours, rather than the days that passing legislation normally involved.[5] None of the debate over the Act registered in Cobbett's *Parliamentary History,* which records the near complete preoccupation of that session with the preliminaries of the War of Jenkin's Ear.[6] All parties recognized, and Robert Walpole most of all, that hostilities with Spain would place new demands on revenue, and necessitate recourse to special fiscal measures, which might include lotteries. The statute departed from the Lottery Act, and any previous gaming legislation, in declaring that the deceit in these four prohibited games stemmed from players' ignorance 'of the great Disadvantages Adventurers in the said Games and Lotteries...are under, subject, and liable to.'

For the first time, the statute stipulated a fine of £10 on magistrates who failed to enforce the laws in effect against gaming, the proceeds to be divided evenly between the complainant and the overseers of the poor in the parish in question, as long as the complaint was made to 'any of His Majesty's Courts of Record' within six months of the offence. It increased the fines on operators of faro, hazard, basset, and the Ace of Hearts to £200, and £50 on players, creating new incentives for informants, who were entitled to a third of the proceeds. The 1739 Act also decreed that certiorari could not be granted to gaming defendants until their cases had first been tried at sessions. The statute of 1740 added passage to the list of proscribed games, along with all other games (other than backgammon) played with dice, a provision that had been proposed and seriously debated in 1728, but never enacted.[7] The third statute in 1745 disallowed 'roulet,' also known as 'roly-poly,' which was not the modern game played on a wheel, but a 'board lottery' in which a marble was rolled across an indented or perforated surface. It also addressed procedural difficulties that had hampered gaming prosecutions under the older statutes. The threshold for excessive gaming set in 1709, £10 won or lost at a single sitting, was expanded to include £20 won or lost in a period of twenty-four hours. For the first time, equity courts were empowered to order

---

[4] *Whole Art and Mystery,* 80–2; the only description found of this game is in John Ham's fourth edition of *The Laws of Chance,* Arbuthnot's translation of Huygens (London: B. Motte and C. Bathurst, 1738), 74.

[5] *Daily Gazetteer,* 1274 (21 July 1739).

[6] William Cobbett, *Parliamentary History of England,* 36 vols (London: T.C. Hansard, 1806–1820), 10. 874–1424.

[7] Gonson, *Charge to the Grand Jury,* 34–5; 13 George II, c. 19, *An Act to Restrain and Prevent the Excessive Increase of Horse Races, and for Amending an Act Made in the Last Session of Parliament, Entitled 'An Act for the More Effectual Preventing of Excessive and Deceitful Gaming'* (London: John Baskett, 1740).

the repayment of gaming losses challenged under the Queen Anne statute. More controversially, from 1745, justices could subpoena witnesses to the fact of gaming, such as wait staff, on pain of a fine of £50, witnesses who could not be disqualified by the fact of having gamed themselves, and, provided they had no prior convictions for gaming, could be granted immunity from prosecution in exchange for their testimony.[8]

Such 'a severe penal Statute,' one critic of this last of the Georgian Gaming Acts complained, not only constituted 'a Restraint on Liberty,' but 'subjects the most innocent Person to the Villainy of a perjured Informer.'[9] However, despite well-publicized crackdowns, especially those in Bath at mid-century, within a decade these statutes appeared as 'lame and deficient' as we shall see William Blackstone was to characterize them in his *Commentaries on the Laws of England*. What, then, went wrong?

When a Lady has a Piazza

Gaming entrepreneurs were quick to discover other expedients once the new gaming statutes, and personnel changes in the royal household, effectively removed the fig leaf of courtly protection. Members of the House of Commons and *most* peers of the realm, for example, could claim parliamentary privilege, exempting them and members of their family and household from civil actions or prosecution for misdemeanours. This privilege was notoriously asserted for a house at 12 Covent Garden Piazza, where a considerable gaming operation went forward under a succession of three different entrepreneurs who claimed, however tenuously or speciously, the protection of the peerage.[10] The initial tenant of the house under the Piazza was George Douglas, fourth Lord Mordington in the peerage of Scotland, who had been a prisoner for debt when he succeeded to the title in 1706. Two years earlier, he had married Mary Dillon, an Irish catholic, but a year after coming into the estate, he deserted her and repudiated the marriage, although she continued to claim the title, much to Mordington's annoyance. He took 12 Covent Garden Piazza, strategically located immediately adjacent to the Theatre Royal Covent Garden, in 1736, and lived there until his death in June of 1741; his acknowledged spouse, the daughter of a Hertfordshire clergyman, followed him to the grave only days later. It is not clear whether the gaming house known as 'Lord Mordington's' (figure 8.1) was the house in the Piazza, or the house in Haymarket opened under the auspices of the former Mary Dillon by

[8] 18 George II, c. 34, *An Act to Explain, Amend, and make more Effectual the Laws in Being, to Prevent Excessive and Deceitful Gaming, and to Restrain and Prevent the Excessive Increase of Horse Races* (London: Thomas Baskett, 1745).
[9] *Old England, or, The Constitutional Journal*, 101 (16 March 1745), 331.
[10] Ashton, *Gambling in England*, 60.

Figure 8.1 James Hulett, *L[or]d M[ordingto]n's Divertion*, 1746. ©Trustees of the British Museum. This print also appeared over the title 'Covent Garden Gaming House'; Mordington's was the most notorious of these.

February 1737, or if there were competing gaming operations in both locations.[11] Mary Dillon subsequently alleged that both her former husband and the next tenant of number 12, Lady Casillis, were 'fronts' for the gaming syndicate that operated there; John Bright, one of the servants named in her claim of privilege,

---

[11] George Edward Cokayne and Vicary Gibbs (eds.), *The Complete Peerage of England, Scotland, Great Britain and the United Kingdom*, 12 vols (London: St. Catherine's Press, 1910–1959), 9. 206; WCA Overseers Receipt Book, St. Paul's Covent Garden, H514/1736, f 41; *Daily Gazetteer*, 513 (16 February 1737); *London Evening Post*, 2119 (9–11 June 1741); *London Daily Post*, 2073 (15 June 1741).

disclosed in his information that the four individuals that Lady Mordington named as her 'managers' paid his weekly wages of five shillings, and also allowed Bright 'several other Perquisites arising from the said Gaming Table.' Lady Mordington admitted that she kept 'an Assembly to Certify I was not dead (as reported) likewise for ye honour of a Noble family.... as other persons of Quality are forced to.'[12]

After the death of Lord Mordington and his acknowledged consort, Mary Dillon (continuing to claim the title of Lady Mordington) took another house in the Piazza, at the corner of Russell Street.[13] Gaming was still going forward at number 12 under the Piazza under its next tenant, the dowager Countess of Casillis, who had taken the house by 1743. Born Mary Fox in the parish of St Giles in the Fields, she was briefly married to the seventh Earl of Casillis, who had died in 1701.[14] Both concerns, which the Westminster Commission of the Peace called 'the two most notorious common gaming houses within this City and Liberty,' operated within the imagined legal immunity thought to apply to the 'verge of the court' and to the households of peers of the realm. Strictly speaking, of course, both grounds of immunity were dubious at best. Judicial opinion held the royal household exemption to apply only to royal residences while occupied by the monarch or senior royals. The privilege of peers was actually parliamentary privilege that applied only while Parliament was sitting, and even then not to Scottish peers like Mordington and Casillis, who were not Scots representative peers and who lacked English titles. After she and Lady Casillis were presented by the grand jury of Middlesex for keeping common gaming houses, Mary Dillon filed a claim of privilege before the House of Lords, asserting that she held her house in the Piazza 'for and as an Assembly, where all persons of credit are at liberty to frequent and play at such diversions as are used at other Assemblys.' She named ten servants, including four 'box-keepers,' as under her protection, and demanded from the Commission of the Peace 'all those privileges that belong to me, as a Peeress of Great Britain, appertaining to my said Assembly.'[15]

As thin as this armour was, it was effective, at least initially. In January of 1745, the Westminster magistrates expressed (or affected) uncertainty whether they could proceed against the gaming concerns in the Piazza 'without incurring a breach of the priviledge of the peers and peeresses of Great Britain to which those Ladys claim title.'[16] While the claims of privilege were still pending in the House of Lords, three parish constables gave depositions attesting to their reluctance to

[12] TNA SP 36/64/3/66; BL Add. MSS 32,704, f 409.
[13] *Daily Advertiser*, 3960 (7 September 1743).
[14] WCA Overseers Receipt Book, St. Paul's Covent Garden, H521/1743, f 40; *Complete Peerage*, 3. 77.
[15] Quoted in Ashton, *Gambling in England*, 61.
[16] LMA Westminster Sessions, Orders of Court, January 1745, f 49.

execute warrants on these venues, given that the occupants asserted immunity from the jurisdiction of local authorities. Daniel Carnes, the high constable, was dispatched to Lady Casillis's door to make formal inquiry 'by what power she kept a Common Gameing house,' and heard the dowager Countess herself insist on her right, as a peeress of Great Britain, 'to keep such House, and to protect all persons who should frequent it (so as they behave themselves therein) and to protect her servants who should attend them.' While the Covent Garden constabulary demurred acting in an official capacity, leaving it to their betters to decide the question of privilege, they were not deterred from visiting to investigate the pretence that these were assemblies of nobility, gentry, and other people of quality. John Mangar and Samuel Barnes made off-duty visits to both houses, and reported seeing 'some Young Gentlemen' along with 'reputed Common Gamesters,' and others 'who had the appearance of Tradesmen, and many Persons of inferior Rank, and several of them of bad Character and Reputation.' Carnes's incognito visits to Lady Casillis's turned up only 'Tradesmen, journeymen, and other persons of Inferior and of very mean appearance.'[17]

During the 1740s, the gaming operations associated with Ladies Mordington and Casillis in Covent Garden Piazza were particularly notorious, rating eight mentions in the Old Bailey proceedings over a period of five years. On two occasions, stolen goods were 'fenced' there. On another, a French servant, charged with stealing a number of valuable goods from his employer, confessed that he did so in hopes of defraying gaming losses sustained at one of 'two houses in Covent-garden, one that goes by the name of My Lord's, and the other, My Lady's.' A first-time highwayman threw himself on the mercy of the court, relating that 'he had lost a hundred Pounds the Night before at my Lady Mordington's.' When Lord Mordington's cook Henry Corner brought charges of robbery and extortion, one of the witnesses for the defendants cited Corner's 'very indifferent Character in the Neighbourhood' stemming from his connection 'to a Gaming Table in the Piazza.'[18] The Mordington and Casillis operations routinely appeared as well in directions from Whitehall and in grand jury charges. In May 1744, the Middlesex grand jury chaired by Sir Roger Newdigate requested that magistrates and constables suppress both houses, as well as act against 'the proprietors of the avenues to the two Play-houses,' where gaming venues still proliferated.[19] After the Gaming Act of 1744 went into effect, disallowing pleas of parliamentary privilege in prosecutions for gaming, Lady Mordington launched a desperate plea to the Duke of Newcastle in June of 1745:

[17] TNA SP 36/65/158–159.   [18] OBPO t17410514-16, t17431207-17, t17441205-42.
[19] Benjamin Sedgly, *Observations on Mr Fielding's Enquiry into the Causes of the Late Increase in Robbers* (London: John Newbery, 1751), 35.

[B]y order from Your Grace, I ly at ye mercy of ye Common majestrate, by whose sanction ye high Constable, with a file of Musquiteers, broke open my house, carried away some of my servants, & Insulted me in bed, In so much, yt by ye freight, I have not been able to go out Since; they even broke down ye partition between my house & an other, so yt ye Mob entered at pleasure, & I exposed to their Indignities, whilest my maids, my only attendants left, were so frighted, yt I could gett no relief, or Service from them: Therefore, I beg Your Grace would Consider, yt I'm obliged to keep an Assembly, as other persons of Quality are forced to, as well as my self; & pleas give order to Sir Thos: Deveil, yt I may no more be molested....

At this point, however, she forthrightly denied 'protecting a publick gameing house, which I'm sensible no Peir, or Peires can do.'[20]

The third gaming entrepreneur to occupy the house was, at least, an actual peer of the realm. Francis, fifth Lord Oliphant, orphaned in childhood and neglected by his remaining family, was living on the street in Edinburgh until the Countess of Marischal took him in to be raised and educated. Succeeding to his title by the death of his uncle in 1728, Oliphant continued to live in poverty, his sole means of support a small pension he had managed to secure from the Crown.[21] Oliphant's tenure in the house under the Piazza was very brief, but long enough to be raided by constables under the direction of the justice Thomas Burdus. In September 1747, constables found four gaming tables on the premises, all on the second floor above the ground floor, one of which was identified by a notice posted on a door as a 'gold table.' No punters were apprehended on either night the premises was raided, as the house was found empty, except for Lady Oliphant and her maids, notwithstanding information that several punters had been playing there within two hours of the raid. This raid occurred in response to a directive from the Earl of Chesterfield, Secretary of State for the Northern Department, ordering a crackdown on gaming houses and other resorts of 'idle and disorderly persons,' recommending that JPs periodically accompany constables on their raids, and requesting that no licences be given to public houses 'where Gaming of any sort is carried on.' Accordingly, Chesterfield received a copy of the minutes of the petty sessions that preceded the raid. There were two raids the following February and March on the Fountain Tavern in the Strand, apparently untenanted at that point, which seized tables for the game of 'Gold and Silver.'[22] Chesterfield's directives were followed through when the Duke of Bedford succeeded him in the Northern Department the following year. Once again, as in the case of the Mordington and Casillis operations, the Westminster bench was under pressure from central government at the highest levels to prosecute gaming establishments such as

[20] BL Add. MSS 32,704, f 409.   [21] *Complete Peerage*, 10. 58.   [22] TNA SP 44/85, ff 6–8.

Oliphant's. Measures against all three establishments are documented in sessions papers and rolls, as expected, but also in the State Papers.

Privilege of Parliament had been disallowed by statute, as the Mordington, Casillis, and Oliphant households had ultimately been forced to acknowledge, although there were other forms of privilege that might be asserted. The assemblies that ambassadors kept in capitals on the Continent were notoriously havens for gaming concerns, but for some reason that pattern seems not to have obtained among the legations accredited to the Court of Saint James. Nevertheless, an anonymous and undated memorandum reported gaming operations either in preparation or in progress under the protection of diplomatic representatives, all of them, incidentally, serving states of the Holy Roman Empire in the 1740s. One was 'fitting up' in Great Suffolk Street near Haymarket, 'said to be for the Assembly of Monsr. Sambony Minister from the Prince of Hesse Darmstadt,' while another was projected in Golden Square under colour of the regular reception of Baron von Haszlang, the envoy of the Elector of Bavaria. Meanwhile in the Strand, a reported three hundred visitors every night over the course of three weeks played at three silver tables and one gold table at the residence of the Chevalier de Champigny, the representative of the Elector Archbishop of Cologne. The company, like the guests of Ladies Casillis and Mordington, consisted of 'some of the better sort of Tradesmen and Common Gamesters, far below a person in his Excellency's character to admitt.'[23] It appears that in the middle to later 1740s, gaming entrepreneurs, confronted with new legislation and deprived of the avenue of parliamentary privilege, may have sought the cover of diplomatic immunity and approached envoys for central European microstates, some of whose finances were shadowy. Giovanni Giacomo Zamboni, for example, had been established in London for several years before his diplomatic appointment, weathering a bankruptcy in 1715 and handling the sale of manuscripts to Robert Harley in 1725.[24] Haszlang, the longest serving of these three, was subsequently rumoured to have pawned the candlesticks from the Bavarian embassy chapel.[25] As there is no other archival trace of their actual or projected gaming operations, and no newspaper reports, it is probable that this initiative was quickly snuffed out.

---

[23] TNA SP 37/7/306. The approximate date of 1770 assigned to this document in the Calendar of State Papers cannot be correct, as Zamboni, appointed resident for the Landgrave of Hesse Darmstadt in November 1739, died in April 1753, his address listed as Great Marlborough Street. Josef Franz Xaver von Haszlang (c. 1700–1783) presented his credentials in February 1741, and had been elevated to Count (Graf) by autumn of 1746, when Lord Augustus Hervey referred to him by that title. The Bavarian embassy relocated to 23–24 Golden Square in 1747, when the Portuguese ambassador moved out. Charles Joseph François de Hennezel, Chevalier de Champigny (1710–1787), accredited as envoy for the Elector of Cologne in March 1744, departed in June 1748. Friedrich Hausmann, ed., *Repertorium der Diplomatischen Vertreter aller Länder*, 3 vols (Zurich: Fretz und Wasmuth, 1950), 2. 11, 181, 200, 217, 583; *Public Advertiser*, 5757 (11 April 1753); Francis Henry Wollaston Sheppard et al. (eds.), *Survey of London*, 53 vols (London: Greater London Council, 1900-present), 31. 169.

[24] *London Gazette*, 5375 (22–25 October 1715); *Letters of Humfrey Wanley*, ed. Peter L. Heyworth (Oxford: Clarendon Press, 1989), 459.

[25] HWC, 9. 185–186, n. 25.

Re-Inventing the Wheel

The unanticipated consequence of outlawing the dice games of hazard and passage, which punters played among themselves, was increasing recourse to games played on wheels, which were necessarily banking games. Wheels used in gaming as randomization devices do not appear in sources before the middle of the eighteenth century, and E.O., played in English resorts and in the metropolis from the later 1740s, seems to have been the first. The wheel with its forty indentations may have derived from machine parts, increasingly in evidence in an 'age of manufactures,' perhaps from a bevel gear used to turn a vertical shaft. All of the tables seized in the raid on Lord Oliphant's house were configured for games played on wheels, such as E.O. (figure 8.2), in which punters bet on letters standing for 'even' or 'odd,' and Gold and Silver, which substituted colours for

PRIVATE AMUSEMENT.

Publish'd Jan.ºt 1786, by S.W.Fores, at the Caracature Warehouse, Nº3, Piccadilly.

Figure 8.2 Thomas Rowlandson, *Private Amusement*, 1786. The Elisha Whittelsey Collection, The Elisha Whittelsey Fund, 1959, Metropolitan Museum of Art. This image depicts a game of E.O., possibly as played at Carlisle House in Soho Square, near Rowlandson's place of residence at the time.

letters.[26] The details of this last game are obscure, but documents indicate a game played at a specialized table incorporating a 'device,' and there is a reference to operational personnel 'turning the table,' supporting a conjecture that Gold and Silver was a game played on a wheel similar to E.O.[27] Significantly, unlike E.O., which continues to appear in newspapers and official documents for a period of about forty years, references to Gold and Silver were confined to about four years in the middle of the century, suggesting that it was an early, and unsuccessful, effort to evade the language of the Georgian gaming statutes. The Georgian Gaming Acts comprehended games 'determined by the Chance of Cards and Dice,' adding the dicing game of passage to faro, basset, and Ace of Hearts, and finally 'roulet' or 'roly-poly,' played with a marble on an indented board, but they had not clearly specified games played on wheels, as the probable intent of the reference to 'wheels' used to draw lots was originally to comprehend devices like Foubert's engine. It was not clear either that letters or colours could be understood as 'figures.' So effective was this stratagem that decades later the Earl of Effingham related the belief of many magistrates that E.O. was not illegal under any existing statutes.[28]

E.O. and its variants also appeared to be more equitable than other games of chance, as the 'house advantage' derived from two 'bar holes' among the forty slots on the wheel, corresponding to the house numbers in roulette, illustrating that by the middle of the century, gaming operators were finally confident that the law of large numbers would guarantee them a profit. It may simply have been that the Georgian statutes left them no choice, as the law now necessitated conformity to the doctrines of probability as surely as the Test, Corporation and Toleration Acts enjoined adherence to the doctrine of the Trinity. Games introduced later in the century were 'even money' propositions that could not be defined as unlawful lotteries, arguably, because the odds of winning or losing were readily apparent to players, and appeared to be equal or virtually so. New faith in probability most likely arose from the enhanced understanding enabled by the works of Edmund Hoyle, who beginning in 1742 published short and accessible treatises on popular card games. Unlike de Moivre, Hoyle described games from the point of view of the player, following, as Jessica Richard has pointed out, an episodic structure similar to that of the novel. Unlike Cotton or Seymour, Hoyle approached games in terms of winning strategies based on probability. While Hoyle focused almost exclusively on polite card games that depended as much on the skill of players as on chance, he deployed an entirely different approach to probability, akin to that later applied in actuarial science.[29] In 1754, he published a tract designed to explain probability 'to those who understand vulgar arithmetic only' that addressed the

---

[26] TNA SP 44/85, ff 15–18.   [27] TNA SP/36/108/2/8, 11.
[28] *Gazetteer*, 16,717 (11 July 1782).
[29] Richard, *Romance of Gambling*, 36–9; Hald, *History of Probability*, 193.

outlawed game of hazard as well as lotteries, annuities, and life insurance. It was only later in the century that writers who posthumously appropriated Hoyle's name addressed games of chance in a comprehensive way, expanding—as Hoyle had not—on the rules and procedures of such games. Nevertheless, Hoyle's was the most successful popularization of probability applied to games, outselling every writer who published on either subject over the course of the long eighteenth century.[30]

The gaming and entertainment promoter Richard Nash, the self-anointed 'Master of Ceremonies' at the resorts of Bath and Tunbridge Wells, was among those obliged to adapt to the changing legal environment. In common with metropolitan gaming operators, he quickly focused on E.O. as an expedient evasion of the new statutes. In the series of desperate lawsuits he filed in the last years of his life, Nash claimed that at the behest of Charles Simpson, John Wiltshire, Thomas Joye, and Metcalf Ashe, the proprietors of assembly rooms at Bath and Tunbridge, he had consulted attorneys about the legality of E.O. soon after the passage of the last of the Georgian Acts. Upon their advice that E.O. was outside of the language of the statutes, Nash engaged William Fenton, a cabinetmaker in London, to make four E.O. tables at a cost of £25 apiece. In exchange for these services and for Nash's continuing promotion of their venues, Nash alleged that he was promised 20 per cent of the proceeds from each of the tables. This arrangement, he further asserted, was in keeping with partnerships he had contracted in other gaming operations in Bath, such as the faro bank kept in Catherine Lindsay's assembly rooms until 1737. John Wiltshire, who was also concerned in gaming operations in London, accordingly paid Nash £170 in 1746 and 1747; Nash then claimed that when business fell off the following year, both Wiltshire and Charles Simpson offered him £100 per annum in lieu of a one fifth share, which he refused. While admitting to making payments to Nash, the defendants denied that he had a fixed share of income from any gaming, which they of course would not admit to, as it was clear to them, or so they claimed, that E.O. was unlawful under the terms of statute.[31]

An initiative against commercial gaming once again driven from Whitehall revealed details of other similar partnerships with a metropolitan nexus. After Lord Oliphant died in April 1748, his house was taken by Samuel Fisher, who lived improbably enough in rural Northamptonshire. It was known through informants that Fisher partnered with Samson Hodgson, an oilman of Ludgate, who had been apprehended in two raids on the Fountain Tavern earlier that year. Hodgson reintroduced Gold and Silver tables, so that 12 Covent Garden Piazza was once again an operational gaming house a year after it was raided, one correspondent alleging that an agreement of some sort had been negotiated with the authorities, of which arrangement the proprietors made no secret. Fisher,

---

[30] Crump, 'Perils of Play,' 3.   [31] Eglin, *Imaginary Autocrat*, 214–15.

however, kept his distance, employing a factor, Isaac Kendall, to collect his share of the take from the tables. In October 1748, the premises was raided yet again, the constables of Covent Garden perhaps predictably finding the premises nearly deserted. Three gaming tables were seized and destroyed, in the belief that it would 'be some Time before they can follow their old Practice,' notwithstanding that these tables were replacements for those seized in the earlier raid, suggesting that new gaming apparatus was easily acquired. Of the two individuals found there, Kendall, thought to be the proprietor, was committed to the Gatehouse and bound in recognizance a week later, only to be presented again near the end of the year 'for Keeping & maintaining a common Gaming house in the parish of St. Paul Covent garden,' which could have been a different venue, but was likely the same one, as Fisher was still listed as the owner in the overseer's accounts in 1749.[32]

Hodgson actively solicited partnerships in his enterprises. William Bowyer, a laceman in Holborn, was offered a share in Gold and Silver tables under the Piazza near the Covent Garden theatre for the relatively modest sum of £16. Thomas Harding, a goldsmith in the City, was also solicited. When Harding inquired whether Hodgson was not deriving sufficient income from this game, Hodgson complained that his box-keeper had acquired 'such a Method in Turning the Table that his Profit did not amount to so much as it used to do.' Hodgson was perhaps hoping to be bought out, as he seemed to complain as well of the rent he was paying on the venue, £90–£100 annually to the owner, a broker in Aldersgate Street.[33] In February of 1752, he was indicted for a Gold and Silver table, and in March was sentenced to a year in Newgate. By this point, he was already in the Fleet Prison for debt. Hodgson and Kendall appear repeatedly in sessions rolls and sessions papers, reflecting the strategy of local and national authorities targeting particularly conspicuous and recidivist operators, in the hope that these would serve as 'examples to encourage the others.' Samuel Fisher, at a safe distance in Rothwell, Northamptonshire, was thanks to Kendall's offices never obliged to set foot near any of the operations he bankrolled. Accordingly, he was not summoned, nor bound in recognizance, and was certainly never indicted.[34]

A quarter century after the passage of the last of the Georgian Gaming Acts, the jurist William Blackstone arrived at a despairing assessment of their impact:

> [P]articular descriptions will ever be lame and deficient, unless all games of mere chance are at once prohibited; the inventions of sharpers being swifter than the punishment of the law, which only hunts them from one device to another.[35]

---

[32] LMA MJ/SR/2910, r 219; MJ/SR/2912, r 141; WCA Overseer's Receipt Book, St. Paul's Covent Garden, H527; TNA SP/36/108/2/8, 88–89; *General Advertiser*, 4346 (29 September 1748); *General Evening Post*, 2345 (29 September 1748), 2355 (22 October 1748).
[33] TNA SP/36/108/2/8, 10–11, 14.   [34] LMA CLA/047/LJ/01/0860-0861.
[35] William Blackstone, *Commentaries on the Laws of England*, 4 vols (Oxford: Clarendon Press, 1769; facs. edn, Chicago: University of Chicago Press, 1979), 4. 173.

At his mention of 'devices,' Blackstone's readers would have thought immediately of E.O., which by then had proved to be the most effective of the statutory evasions that gaming entrepreneurs devised. Consequently, we will run across it again.

Ridotto Redux

One additional avenue for gaming operators to evade the Georgian statutes was of long standing. Johann Jakob Heidegger had introduced masquerade balls at the King's Theatre, Haymarket, in 1713, as a means of realizing revenue on Thursday evenings during the season when the theatre was 'dark.' Just as oratorios replaced operas for the six weeks of Lent, ridottos replaced masquerades. No alcohol was on offer, but only tea and coffee, and there was no buffet supper. There was still music and dancing, incredibly enough, and while there was no fanciful costuming or masking, the Haymarket ridotto was still a full-dress occasion. In addition to their connection to a royal patent theatre, masquerades enjoyed royal patronage, George II himself regularly attending until the death of Queen Caroline, but occasionally turning up thereafter, along with junior members of the royal family. This protection coincided with a very steep admission charge at one guinea which, even though it procured three tickets, was too exclusionary for the masquerades to be regarded as 'common,' which is to say publicly accessible, amusements. A generation of mostly literary scholars has drawn attention to masquerades, including those at Haymarket, as occasions of social inversion when social and gender hierarchies were overturned. Meghan Kobza's more recent analysis presents the London masquerade as an effort to recapture an older courtly culture.[36] As gaming was an integral part of this culture, contemporary observers more or less tacitly assumed that gaming would take place at masquerades, and at ridottos as well. Whether masquerades or ridottos, these entertainments were long thought to be 'calculated for gaming.'[37] When the Haymarket management circulated a proposal for six ridottos to be held by subscription, the grand jury of Middlesex presented them to be prosecuted and suppressed in February 1723, in part because gaming was likely to go on there.[38]

As it was an open question whether entertainments with admissions charges were 'common' according to the understanding of the Henrician statute, by the middle of the century, both Gold and Silver and E.O. had been introduced at masquerades and ridottos at Haymarket. According to a magazine writer later in the century, the masquerades at the King's Theatre 'brought together a great concourse of people who proposed to themselves no other entertainment than

---

[36] Meghan Kobza, 'Dazzling or Fantastically Dull? Re-Examining the Eighteenth-Century London Masquerade,' *Journal for Eighteenth Century Studies*, 43 (May 2020), 166.
[37] *Gentleman's Magazine*, 21 (April 1751), 185.   [38] *Evening Post*, 2116 (16 February 1723).

gaming,' initially at Gold and Silver, and subsequently at E.O.[39] Over half of newspaper accounts of masquerades in the fifteen years between 1738 and 1753 mention gaming in some connection.[40] While there were at least two raids on E.O. tables at the Haymarket masquerades in the 1750s, these were exceptions that proved the rule. In March of 1753, Henry Fielding once again raided the masquerade at the Haymarket with the intention of seizing 'gamblers and sharpers,' but considerately waited until the King, who often attended, had departed with his entourage. Although Fielding was disappointed in not being able to make any arrests subsequently, 'he obliged the persons at the gaming table to unmask, and give an account of themselves.'[41] Three years later, one periodical reported that 'houses throughout the city of London and Westminster were, at stated times, turned into gambling-shops where the whole town had access, at one shilling per head.'[42] That year John Fielding and Saunders Welch apprehended eight punters at an E.O. table at a ridotto, but did not seize the table itself.[43] After this raid, masquerades at the King's Theatre, at least, were suspended, probably for the duration of the war. When they were revived, it was in a new reign under a new monarch, and while masquerades and ridottos continued, gaming there did not, one account reporting at the beginning of 1762 that 'notorious games of hazard, such as the E.O. Tables, and the like,' had been prohibited at entertainments at Haymarket. The managers then finding that the masquerades seldom attracted 'above half the number that used to assemble' before gaming was prohibited, the admission charge was doubled.[44] The decrease in attendance may also have been due to competition from masquerades at other venues, such as Carlisle House and subsequently the Pantheon, but the increase in admission fees in place at masquerade venues by 1770 may also have been an attempt to recoup the loss of income from gaming tables.

Particularity and Deficiency

Once the Georgian Gaming Acts had been in place long enough for their effectiveness to be assessed, the verdict, in print culture at least, found them wanting. There had been scepticism in some quarters from the beginning. Three weeks after the implementation of the 1739 Act, the *Craftsman* asserted that the penalty on negligent magistrates was not stringent enough,[45] and if justices, mayors, aldermen, and others were indeed presented for this offence over the course of the next several decades, newspapers did not take notice. Other inadequacies

---

[39] *Town and Country Magazine*, 11 (December 1779), 643.
[40] Kobza, 'Dazzling or Fantastically Dull?,' 169–70.   [41] *Ladies Magazine*, 4 (March 1753), 93.
[42] *Universal Magazine*, 19 (October 1756), 165.
[43] *Read's Weekly Journal*, 2357 (3 April 1756); LMA MJ/SR/3050, rr 196, 199, 221, 261, 271–273, 277.
[44] *St. James Chronicle*, 127 (2 January 1762).   [45] *Craftsman*, 679 (14 July 1739).

soon became evident. The delay of recourse to certiorari, for example, did not stop Richard Ellah from having his case heard in King's Bench in 1747, and suing the crusading Justice Thomas Burdus into the bargain. Ellah, who kept the York Coffeehouse in Lincoln's Inn Fields, was indicted for insulting and striking Burdus ('throwing his Hatt in my face' and 'threatning to stab me with a Knife') while the latter was conducting a raid on a gaming house; Ellah subsequently spent four days in New Prison, Clerkenwell after initially refusing to give his name. Justice Burdus was in the position of having to petition the ministry for his defence to be conducted at the expense of the Crown, which fortunately for Burdus was granted.[46] In October of the same year, Burdus claimed that he was brazenly offered a bribe of £100 per annum, payable quarterly, '[i]f I would give Leave to put up two Tables for the Game of Gold & Silver.' When he detained the messenger and summoned the three perpetrators—James Wilson, Peter Fountainer, and William Piercy—they innocently told Burdus that 'they meant no harm by it, but thought that a Justice who could break Gaming Houses, could give Liberty to keep one.' Wilson, identified in his recognizance as a grocer of Russell Street, Covent Garden, had drawn up the solicitation at the request of Fountainer, a stocking-maker employed by a hosier in Piccadilly, and Piercy, listed with an address in Long Acre. Burdus reported that they were committed to New Prison for five days, then cautioned and discharged; the prison calendar, however, has Piercy and Fountainer bailed the same day they were committed, and Wilson only a day later. They may have been, as Burdus put it, 'stupid Ignorant Fellows,' but their forthrightness raises a question of whether bribery of constables and justices was not simply a routine overhead cost for gaming operations.[47] There was certainly ample reason for gaming entrepreneurs to think so.

At mid-century, a sequence of tracts appeared that drew attention both to the inadequacy of the new statutes and to the continuing misunderstanding of the mechanics of gaming concerns. The most important of these was Henry Fielding's *Enquiry into the Causes of the Late Increase of Robbers,* which among other effects, sent the metropolitan magistracy into a defensive crouch. In response to Fielding's contention that gamblers who violated the terms of their recognizances were rarely if ever made to pay the sums they were supposed to have forfeited, at least two of his colleagues issued several estreats in the very next sessions, very nearly the only examples to be found in any of the Westminster rolls in the period under examination.[48] In February of 1751, the grand jurors of Middlesex lamented to the justices of King's Bench that presentments and returns of public nuisances had 'become a mere matter of form,' lassitude that stemmed, as some constables

[46] LMA MJ/SR/2887, pc, r 93; TNA SP 44/85, f 14.
[47] TNA SP 44/85, ff 20–21; LMA MJ/SR/2887, pc, rr 63, 95–96.
[48] The justices in question were James Fraser and Thomas Lediard; the estreats were issued in April and October of 1751 (LMA MJ/SR/2951, rr 45–46, 48, 50, 54; MJ/SR/2961, rr 126–127, 129, 138–139).

admitted, 'from lewd, disorderly, and gaming houses, and unlawful places of assembly, having often been presented without effect.'[49] 'The Gaming-houses in Covent Garden are not suppressed,' one writer asserted,

> they are only removed to other places; and of what consequence is it to destroy the tables one a month, and to take a few of the poorer sort of gamesters into custody, while the wealthier sett are permitted to make their escape, and constantly evade the punishment of the law?[50]

The Westminster constabulary, asserted Saunders Welch in 1754, often despaired that their presentments had no effect but to earn them the resentment of their neighbours. Welch cited the case of a notorious brothel that was presented every sessions, yet stayed in operation, the keepers routinely dismissed with a forty shilling fine, or £8 annually, easily absorbed as a cost of doing business. Both sessions rolls and newspapers attest to gaming houses that fell into this pattern. According to one newspaper account, three successive warrants were issued for raids on the same venue near the Salisbury Stairs on the Thames, only for constables to find in each case that management had been alerted and that the players had all fled, leaving only the tables, which 'were for the third time broke to Pieces.' It was no wonder, then, that constables were reluctant enforcers, who according to Welch would often shield egregious offenders and present minor ones to create the illusion of vigilance. In these circumstances, justices and grand juries at quarter sessions were helpless:

> [C]ertain it is, in the present state of things, the solemn inquiry of twenty-four gentlemen, sworn and assembled, and convening the constables of the whole town before them, is of no manner of use. The constables of Covent-Garden, do, upon their oaths, say, there are no brothels in their parish; and that there are no gaming-houses in Westminster, the constables of that city all agree in.... [yet] houses of gaming, for all degrees, are, alas! too readily found.[51]

Perennially frustrated in their pursuit of commercial gaming ventures, or simply wishing to avoid the onus of ineffectuality, the Westminster bench, at least initially, directed its energies elsewhere, assisted by new legislation. The Disorderly Houses Act of 1751, although primarily directed at brothels, would seem to have removed a significant barrier to prosecution in stipulating that anyone who should 'appear, act, or behave...as the person having the care, government, or management' of any 'disorderly house,' including gaming venues, was liable to

---

[49] *Universal Magazine*, 8 (February 1751), 92.
[50] Sedgly, *Observations on Mr Fielding's Enquiry*, 35.
[51] *London Morning Penny Post* (3 June 1751); Welch, *Observations*, 30–2.

prosecution as such, 'notwithstanding he or she shall not in fact be the real owner or keeper thereof.'[52] From the middle of the decade, however, most of the keepers of 'gaming houses' prosecuted were publicans charged with permitting games defined as unlawful under the Henrician statute, such as bowling or tennis. In June of 1752, for example, Thomas Higginson appeared before Henry Fielding for keeping a tennis court in Windmill Street, and was ultimately indicted for operating over the course of the previous year, 'such time being no Common Tide Festival or Holliday in which by the Laws of this Land it is made Lawfull for Artificers and other Persons of Mean Estate to Recreate themselves.' Higginson was acquitted after his counsel argued that his conviction would make any coffeehouse that allowed backgammon or chess on the premises liable to prosecution.[53]

At the end of September 1757, a new statute 'for preventing Gaming in Public-Houses by Journeymen, Labourers, Servants, and Apprentices' went into effect, reinforcing the language of the Henrician Act. Publicans were not to allow members of these status groups to play cards or dice, or billiards, skittles, shuffleboard, or ninepins, whether stakes were involved or not. It sidestepped the problem of determining the duration of gaming operations, retaining the fine of forty shillings for the first offence, but increasing it to £10 for every subsequent offence. It eliminated the exception for Christmastide provided in the Henrician Act, and completely disallowed removals by certiorari, whether before or after conviction. Appeal could only be made to a future quarter sessions. Any parish resident willing to swear out a complaint could put a publican in prison overnight, as a single such complaint was sufficient to oblige magistrates to issue warrants, and the accused was not to be admitted to bail until the complainant had twenty-four hours' notice.[54] One East End victualler, convicted and fined under this statute in June 1766, complained of the hardship he was under, as his trade required him to admit clientele not known to him, and absent sumptuary legislation, 'no man's rank in life may be known by his dress.' Another writer to the same paper asserted that alehouses lacking skittles grounds were not considered worth taking, and that as long as landlords and employers were allowed to play, 'it will always be an excuse for the publicans to say they cannot tell journeymen from masters.'[55]

Henry Fielding charged grand jurors that with respect to gaming, 'there is no Reason why you should not exert your Duty as far as you are able, because you cannot extend it as far as you desire,' justifying the apparent inequity of an onus

---

[52] 25 George II c. 36, *An Act for the Better Preventing Thefts and Robberies, and for Regulating Places of Publick Entertainment, and Punishing Persons Keeping Disorderly Houses* (London: Thomas Basket, 1752).

[53] LMA MJ/SR/2982, r 140; *Old England, or, The Constitutional Journal*, 122 (28 October 1752); *Read's Weekly Journal*, 1468 (28 October 1752).

[54] 30 George II c. 24, excerpted in *The Public Housekeeper's Monitor* (London: F. and C. Rivington, 1793), 53–5.

[55] *Universal Magazine*, 21 (August 1757), 72–3; *Gazetteer*, 11,630 (20 June 1766), 11,780 (6 December 1766).

on plebeian gaming from the assumption of the Henrician statute that 'the lower Sort of People...are the most useful Members of the Society; which by such Means will lose the Benefit of their Labour.' Elite gaming, on the other hand, merely resulted in 'the Exchange of Property from the Hand of a Fool into those of a Sharper, who is, perhaps, the more worthy of the two to enjoy it.'[56] In writing of gaming elsewhere, Fielding confined his discussion to 'the inferior Part of Mankind,' as he

> was not so ill-bred as to disturb the Company at a polite Assembly; nor so ignorant of our Constitution, as to imagine that there is a sufficient Energy in the executive Part to control the Oeconomy of the Great, who are beyond the Reach of any, unless capital Laws.[57]

As Fielding probably recognized, elites were able to evade the provisions of their own enactments through the reconfiguration of what had been public space.

---

[56] Henry Fielding, 'A Charge Delivered to the Grand Jury at the Sessions of the Peace for the City and Liberty of Westminster,' in *An Enquiry into the Causes of the Late Increase of Robbers and Other Writings*, ed. Malvin R. Zirker (Middletown, CT: Wesleyan University Press, 1988), 25–6.
[57] Fielding, *An Enquiry*, 92.

9

The Pilgrimage to Saint James's, or, Clubs are Trumps

In the sixth engraving of *The Rake's Progress* of 1734 (figure 9.1), Hogarth depicted what is generally accepted to be the interior of one of the upstairs rooms of White's as it might have appeared in the small hours of the morning of 28 April 1733, when the chocolate house then tenanted by John Arthur burned to the ground. In the centre of the room sits the hazard table, at which the title character Tom Rakewell has lost his last, desperate stake. The other clientele are well-dressed if dishevelled, their wigs askew if not removed entirely, as Rakewell has done in fury. A moneylender accepts a pocket watch in pawn from a richly dressed figure. Only the box-keeper, distinguished with a croupier's rake, pays any attention to the night watchman who has intruded to alert them of the fire, from which smoke has begun to billow through the ceiling. The fire was a public spectacle that included John Arthur's spouse leaping from an upper floor onto a mattress, and the King and the Prince of Wales turning up to encourage the fire fighters. The previous proprietor's complaint of the dilapidated condition of the property in applying for a lease to rebuild in 1730 might today raise suspicions of arson, especially given the insurance settlement of £400 that Arthur received, enabling the reconstruction of all three houses by 1735.[1]

David Miers asserts that the purpose of the three Georgian Gaming Acts was to prevent sons of wealthy families from being fleeced 'by the unscrupulous managers of lower class gaming houses,' but that they were ineffectual against establishments like the recently rebuilt White's, ' houses managed by the wealthy for the wealthy.'[2] The reason was simply that elite gaming venues were able to reconstitute themselves as private subscription clubs over the course of the two decades after mid-century. Henry Fielding had dropped a hint to these proprietors in 1751 when he asked

> [w]hat Temptations can Gamesters of Fashion have, to admit *inferiour* Sharpers into their Society? Common Sense, surely, will not suffer a Man to risque a Fortune against one who hath none of his own to stake against it.[3]

---

[1] *Survey of London*, 30. 464–5.   [2] Miers, *Regulating Commercial Gambling*, 31.
[3] Fielding, *An Enquiry*, 93.

The Gambling Century: Commercial Gaming in Britain from Restoration to Regency. John Eglin, Oxford University Press.
© John Eglin 2023. DOI: 10.1093/oso/9780192888198.003.0010

Figure 9.1 William Hogarth, *The Rake's Progress: He Gambles*, 1735. Yale Center for British Art, Paul Mellon Collection. Hogarth set Tom Rakewell's undoing in the upstairs 'club room' in White's chocolate house on the night that it burned down.

John Macky had already spoken in 1724 of 'an infinity of Clubs or societies' meeting in the metropolis for either didactic or sociable purposes, while a writer in the *Gentleman's Magazine* marvelled in 1732 over 'the number of sociable assemblies' there. Public accommodations had long hired out space for private gatherings of all sorts. We have already seen, in fact, that taverns and coffeehouses hosted meetings of petty sessions called to police gaming that often took place in those very same venues. The letting of space for the regular meeting of civic and sociable groups was as important a revenue stream as the sale and service of food and drink. In a typical rowhouse with four upper floors above a basement, the street level, often with a shopfront, would hold the 'common' service area, with kitchens and storage in the basement, while the floors above that, often with the best appointments, were hired out to the entities that comprised an emerging 'associational world,' as Peter Clark called it. Mostly urban, mostly male, and mostly gathering in 'public drinking spaces,' clubs, more to the point, constituted a characteristically British species of social organization.[4]

Gaming for many of these clubs seems to have been as incidental as drinking or smoking, although there were certainly clubs as devoted to these pursuits as 'the club at White's' apparently was to games of chance. Defoe, who considered gaming 'the Bane of Conversation,' complained in 1728 that 'those who can't sit an Hour without Gaming, should never go into a Club to spoil Company.'[5] He would have been appalled to hear from observers half a century later that the most conspicuous clubs in the metropolis were entirely given over to games of chance. It would be easy to suppose that this development was one more of the evasive stratagems, described in the previous chapter, deployed in response to the Georgian gaming statutes. Elite gamblers, however, were untroubled by the legislation that some of them had a hand in enacting. The momentum for the privatization of elite gaming seems to have come from different directions, which it will be the business of this chapter to explore.

Chocolate Boxes

Francis White, born Francesco Bianchi in Genoa, opened his chocolate house in St James's Street in 1693. Like its rivals Ozinda's, Domenico Osendo's neighbouring establishment which opened the following year, and Abraham Norsa's Cocoa Tree, established in 1698, White's was a public accommodation, although an expensive one, as chocolate was a pricier commodity, given the Spanish monopoly on it. Where most metropolitan coffeehouses charged a penny for a dish of product, White's charged sixpence. After Francis White's death in 1711, his widow Elizabeth kept the chocolate house until her probable demise in 1729. At this point, Francis White the younger entered a partnership with John Arthur, who subsequently appeared as proprietor of 69 St James's Street and the two houses adjoining on either side.[6] Within its first two decades, White's was as closely associated with gaming as Lloyd's was with maritime insurance or Jonathan's with stockjobbing. These venues were not the grand and imposing structures found in 'clubland' today, but ordinary townhouses, possibly with shopfronts. The exterior of White's, as rendered in plate four of *Rake's Progress,* is unremarkable (save for the freak lightning bolt that strikes it), and no larger than the other buildings at the bottom of St James's Street, with their trademark four-storey elevation and narrow street front. While the fire destroyed the club's earliest records, so that the

---

[4] Peter Clark, *British Clubs and Societies, 1580–1800: The Origins of an Associational World* (Oxford: Oxford University Press, 2001), 1–5, 12.
[5] [Daniel Defoe], *Augusta Triumphans* (London: J. Roberts, 1728), 41.
[6] *Survey of London*, 30. 463–4.

date of its foundation is still not known for certain, Hogarth's engravings suggest that White's may already have housed a club preoccupied with gaming before the original premises burned down. In 1736, membership was by election and annual dues one guinea. It was suggested later in the century that 'the club at White's' had migrated from the Bedford Head in Covent Garden, where it had been established by at least the second decade of the century.[7] The club met in the rooms above stairs from the public rooms, creating a zone of exclusivity for a select company of fewer than a hundred members.

For a generation or more after its foundation, White's was unique. There were many sociable clubs in the metropolis, but if there were other clubs organized around gaming to the same extent, they have left no trace in the sources. Instructively, once gaming was no longer hosted in the Groom Porter's lodge after Thomas Archer's death in 1743, the club effectively expanded, when a 'Young Club' was instituted as a junior auxiliary of the original 'Old Club.' Where the elders had been preoccupied with its faro bank, their juniors added an enthusiasm for wagers, the famed White's 'betting book' marking its inception in 1743 as well. By mid-century there were 350 members of both clubs combined. While the necessity of balloting new members, and of those members paying a substantial annual subscription, presumably excluded White's from denomination as a 'common' gaming house forbidden under statute, not everyone was certain of this understanding. Erasmus Mumford declared that he could not find in any Act of Parliament 'any Exception of this same House call'd WHITE's, and the *good Company* within it,' asking its members '[i]f you have any A[c]t against *Gaming* with any such Exception in it, be so good as to produce it; for I believe…there is not a Man in the Kingdom who knows any thing of it.'[8] A writer in *The Connoisseur* in May 1754 claimed on the authority of an acquaintance in the Stamp Office that revenue from duties on cards and dice had increased sixfold in the forty-odd years they had been collected, which, he further asserted,

> will not appear very wonderful, when we consider that gaming is now become rather the business than amusement of our persons of quality; that their whole attention is employed in this important article, and that they are more concerned about the transactions of the two clubs at *White's* than the proceedings of both Houses of Parliament.[9]

It was only a year later that White's moved to new premises and adopted a new business model. In 1755, Robert Arthur purchased property on the east side of St James's Street, where the club relocated on its present site. As the neighbourhood

---

[7] *Public Advertiser*, 18,121 (3 August 1792).
[8] Erasmus Mumford, *A Letter to the Club at White's* (London: W. Owen, 1750), 9.
[9] *The Connoisseur*, 15 (9 May 1754), 85.

was already well supplied with chocolate houses in addition to Ozinda's and the Cocoa Tree, the venue 'of common resort' on the ground floor of number 69 did not reopen in the new premises across the street.[10] The chocolate house, a public accommodation that had operated under Francis White's name for six decades, was no more, the new house admitting only the duly balloted and subscribing members of the clubs that met there, so that 'White's' and 'the two clubs at White's' were one and the same.[11] The London gentleman's club was born.

Two decades after the complete privatization of White's, newspapers were reporting the names of at least ten gaming clubs in the neighbourhood of St James's and Pall Mall, charging annual subscription fees ranging anywhere from three to fifteen guineas a year.[12] Among these, Almack's (subsequently Brooks's) and Boodle's had opened as private clubs, but others, like the Cocoa Tree and White's, had once been public accommodations. While Brian Cowan has questioned the extent to which 'the relative freedom of the Augustan coffeehouse was replaced in the later eighteenth century by more restrictive gentleman's clubs,'[13] this transformation was certainly detectable in the streets and squares of St James's. Given the determination to proscribe games of chance by statute, and given the series of evasions that gaming operators immediately attempted, we might wonder why it took nearly twenty years after the implementation of the Georgian Gaming Acts for other clubs to be established following the example of White's. The original London gentleman's club had no competitors until the foundation of what became Boodle's in 1762, the same year that the Cocoa Tree incorporated as a private subscription club, followed by the opening of Almack's (subsequently Brooks's) Club in 1764. The timing of these foundations, and possibly their geographic proximity to the Palace of St James, might suggest that the sudden proliferation of subscription clubs to enable elite gaming had less to do with statute law than with the very different courtly culture inaugurated in a new reign. It is impossible to know, of course, how much high play took place at court, but if games of chance were not significant courtly pastimes, we might wonder why an exemption for the royal household was a feature of every gaming statute enacted that century, an exemption of little utility if the monarch would not permit it to be exercised. The new King's hostility to gaming was reflected soon after the accession in the removal of Robert Arthur, the proprietor of White's, as gentleman and yeoman of the cellar to the royal household, a post he had held for three years. This gesture was part of an effort to reform courtly culture that for Valérie Capdeville effectively ended White's monopoly on gaming in private

---

[10] *Survey of London*, 30. 450, 465.
[11] Algernon Bourke, *The History of White's*, 2 vols (London: privately printed, 1892), 1. 67, 112.
[12] *Middlesex Journal*, 1156 (22 August 1776).   [13] Cowan, *Coffee*, 255–6.

subscription venues.[14] The displacement, and then the exclusion, of gaming from court, however, cannot have been the sole driver of the proliferation of subscription clubs, as the apparent cessation of operations in the Groom Porter's apartments had only occasioned an expansion of the membership of White's. Commercial gaming operators sensed an opportunity to create spaces beyond the verge of the court that were nevertheless exclusive, and highly profitable. Entrepreneurs who had previously sought the protection of the Groom Porter, the verge of the court, or of other similarly ambiguous forms of privilege now found secure refuge behind the doors of subscription clubs whose exclusivity served as much to keep magistrates at bay as to bar social interlopers of dubious provenance.

The club known as Boodle's from 1768 was founded in 1762 in one of William Almack's properties at 50 Pall Mall, two years before the club that bore Almack's name opened next door. Its proximity to potentially competing clubs may explain some of the restrictions in place in its early days. Membership was limited to 250, the annual subscription set at two guineas, and initially no member of Boodle's could belong to any other club that met daily and that had at least fifty members. After a year, however, the rule was altered to strike anyone from membership who was either a candidate or a member at Arthur's, as White's was briefly known. Most importantly, its first set of rules expressly forbade games of chance, permitting only sociable games like whist, picquet, cribbage, ombre, and quadrille for relatively modest stakes, the maximum win or loss set at nine guineas in a single session, safely within the statutory threshold.[15] It is not at all clear, however, that these restrictions remained in force at Boodle's after its first two years. The second volume of the Club Book is missing its first five leaves, the club rules, apparently modified in March 1764, picking up at number '10.' There is no sign of the previous gaming restrictions, save rule 22, which stipulated

If any Gentleman plays at Cards, or is in the Card Room 'till ele[v]en o'Clock at night, & does not sup, he is to pay 2s:6d to the House: If any Gentleman plays after twelve without Supping, he is to pay the House 6s. as if he had supp'd.[16]

The stipulation that suppers be paid for whether eaten or not subsequently became a boilerplate rule for other clubs, and calls attention to the number of late-night habitués that clubs attracted. Whatever brave resolutions its founding members may have shared, competition from rival clubs together with the profit potential of gaming operations served to establish Boodle's as yet another 'gaming

---

[14] Valérie Capdeville, *L'Âge d'Or des Clubs Londoniens:1730–1784* (Paris: Honoré Champion, 2008), 199. Arthur's dismissal is documented in TNA LS 13/265, f 9v, quoted sv in Robert Bucholz's *Database of Court Officers 1660–1837.*

[15] LMA/4572/A/01/001: Club Book, Boodle's, 1762–1764; ODNB sv 'William Almack.'

[16] LMA 4572/A/01/002: Club Book, Boodle's, 1764–1770.

club' in its neighbourhood, at least as far as the press was concerned. Stephen Fox, the brother of Charles James Fox and also a notoriously deep gambler, was a member from 1768, when Almack's partner Edward Boodle took over as proprietor; William Wilberforce recalled winning twenty-five guineas of the Duke of Norfolk at Boodle's in 1780.[17] A rule adopted in 1787 decreed '[n]o Cards or Gaming to be allowed *except in the rooms upstairs.*'[18]

As for its sister club, in February 1772, George Augustus Selwyn reported that '[t]he play now at Almacks surpasses all former transactions of that kind as much as all creditibility.' Most of this play seems to have been at hazard. A series of letters written to Thomas Robinson, Lord Grantham, name sums in five figures won and lost between individuals, without any mention of banks.[19] By the middle of the decade, after complaints that the Pall Mall facilities were too crowded, grand new premises were built for the club in St James's Street, heralded in the *Morning Post* in November 1776:

> The new gaming-house, now erecting in St. James-street, is building…upon the most extensive scale, and under the protection of the first people of the *ton,* who have entered into very extravagant subscriptions, in order to support it, in a style hitherto unknown in this country.[20]

The architect Henry Holland, in designing a new clubhouse of unprecedented size and splendour, created the architectural template that the club's rivals followed over the next half century (figure 9.2). The club also acquired new management, Almack selling out to his partner, William Brooks, so that the relocated club was also renamed. Almack, who continued to keep his celebrated assembly rooms in St. James's, 'se repose sur les Rouleaux,' according to Frederick Robinson, suggesting that his profits from gaming tables at the club had been considerable.[21] In another important departure, Brooks's gaming operations were no longer relegated to the upper floors, but brazenly conducted in a ground floor room lit by large windows at street level, in plain view of the public and of local authorities.[22] The annual subscription of fifteen guineas was heftier even than White's, whose members paid ten guineas.

As one elite subscription establishment opened after another in St James's and Pall Mall, metropolitan gaming enforcement was at a standstill, the Westminster sessions rolls recording virtually no summonses for gaming for much of the 1760s

---

[17] LMA 4572/A/01/003: Club Book, Boodle's, 1770–1782; Robert Isaac Wilberforce and Samuel Wilberforce, *The Life of William Wilberforce,* 5 vols (London: John Murray, 1838), 1. 16.

[18] LMA 4572/A/01/004: Club Book, Boodle's, 1781–1791; italics mine.

[19] Wrest Park MSS, L 30/14/350/1a, 2.   [20] *Morning Post,* 1259 (6 November 1776).

[21] Wrest Park MSS L 30/14/333/151.

[22] HMC *Carlisle:* Historical Manuscripts Commission. *The Manuscripts of the Earl of Carlisle, Preserved at Castle Howard* (London: HMSO, 1897), 496.

GREAT SUBSCRIPTION ROOM at BROOKS'S,
S.^T JAMES'S STREET.

Figure 9.2 Augustus Pugin and Joseph Statler after Thomas Rowlandson, *The Great Subscription Room at Brooks's*, 1808. Yale Center for British Art, Paul Mellon Collection. Henry Holland's clubhouse for Brooks's, opened in 1776, set a new and very high architectural standard for 'clubland.'

and 1770s. While gaming continued to preoccupy the press over the course of these two decades, there were no accounts of raids, but only anecdotes of elite gaming, often recycled items that had appeared in other papers a year or two earlier. The emergence of private subscription clubs after mid-century apparently made the enforcement of gaming statutes, including the Georgian Acts, nearly impossible. A correspondent to the *London Evening Post* called the largely unenforced Gaming Acts 'libels on the Legislature, which the Legislature itself has penned.'[23] More than one writer asserted that the glaring hypocrisy of high-stakes gaming at elite subscription clubs was inevitably demoralizing to magistrates and constables. It was particularly egregious that prominent members of both houses of Parliament belonged to these clubs.[24] A satirical missive to the King purporting to come from the members of White's asked 'to acknowledge your Majesty's goodness and lenity in allowing us to break those laws which we ourselves have

---

[23] *London Evening Post*, 5333 (7 January 1762).   [24] *Reflexions on Gaming*, 11–13, 42, 45.

made and you have sanctified and confirmed.'[25] It became a cliché among newspaper writers to comment on the inconsistency of seizing 'silver tables' above or
in back of coffeehouses in Leicester Fields while gold tables operated with impun-
ity in the clubs of St James's and Pall Mall, sometimes (as was the case of Brooks's)
in plain view of the public. An epilogue to a play that premiered in 1763 put the
state of gaming enforcement neatly:

> Pray tell me, Sirs—(for I don't know)
> I Pray—is there such a thing as gaming now?
> Do peers make laws against that giant vice,
> And then at Arthur's break them in a trice?[26]

'It is not more common to see a Lawgiver shake his elbow at Arthur's, than to see
a Barber or a Shoemaker gaming in a public-house in St. Giles's,' pointed out
another observer in May 1767; 'the only difference is, that the latter are not always
secure from the unfashionable virtue of some queer neighbouring Justice of the
Peace.'[27] Until the Victorian statute was enacted decades later, it was never clear
whether gaming legislation applied to subscription clubs, and their non-
application in practice probably owed less to any contemporary reading of the law
than to the reality of a plebeian constabulary and a magistracy consisting of the
'better sort' of 'the middling sort' confronted with the activity of gamblers who
were unimpeachably elite.

The Windows of Brooks's

Defenders of subscription clubs argued that the substantial dues for membership,
augmented with a balloting procedure that required the unanimous or nearly
unanimous consent of existing members to any prospective member's admission,
excluded 'sharpers' from the premises. It was precisely the need to bar professional cheats, one newspaper writer observed in 1781, that accounted for 'the
institution of so many gaming clubs, and all the modes of ballot by which men of
known fortune and character alone are admitted.'[28] Critical commentators suggested, however, that the clubs were exclusive the better to set up nobs to be
fleeced. The gossipy *Town and Country Magazine* related the story of a young earl
returned from his travels:

---

[25] 'The Gamesters' Address to his Majesty,' by Colonel Lyttelton, 1752, from Percy Colson, *White's 1693–1950* (London: William Heinemann, 1951), 34.
[26] *Royal Magazine*, 10 (January 1764), 46.   [27] *General Evening Post*, 5230 (7 May 1767).
[28] *Gazetteer*, 16,477 (16 October 1781).

No sooner did his lordship make his appearance in this capital, than he was visited by every man of fashion, who judged he had a right to share his friendship and his purse. The connoisseurs of all the chocolate houses lay in wait for him; he was invited to and ballotted for in all the gaming societies of note about St. James's, and to his lordship's honour, he did not meet with a single black ball in any of them. A certain chocolate house in St. James's street claimed his first attention, and for some months he bled very freely in the service of this society. The other houses in the neighbourhood hearing of the chearfulness with which he parted with his cash, soon claimed him as a member, and in turn they have all shared the spoils.[29]

At its first appearance, the anecdote may have referred to Frederick Howard, fifth Earl of Carlisle, but it is worth noting that the same periodical recycled the story twice over the following decade.

As it happens, the correspondence that Carlisle received while away in Dublin as Lord Lieutenant of Ireland provides a detailed picture of the workings of faro syndicates at the clubs of St James's. Rather predictably, these very elite operations are the few commercial gaming concerns for which this kind of documentation exists. Carlisle was among a circle of politicians loosely affiliated with the ministry of Lord North, but who maintained ties with oppositionists like Charles James Fox. Fox, who emerged in the 1780s as the leader of opposition to the ministry of Pitt the Younger, was a legendarily deep gamester whose rumoured losses ran into tens of thousands of pounds. At Brooks's, gaming took place in the subscription room, the largest of the spaces in the house, at banks kept by members. In the 1780s, Fox and Richard Fitzpatrick kept the largest, which George Selwyn complained 'swallows everybody's cash that comes to Brooks's.' The restoration that the bank effected to Fox's distressed fortune was accordingly conspicuous. Selwyn recounted seeing the normally dishevelled oppositionist leader 'in a new hat, frock, waistcoat, shirt, and stockings; he was clean and smug as a gentleman, and upon perceiving my surprise, he told me that it was from the Pharo Bank.' Horace Walpole, however, wrote that Fox's success had 'awakened his host of creditors,' who by the end of May 1781 were repossessing his household goods. 'It is quite wonderful what the bank has won,' Anthony Storer remarked after describing bailiffs 'ransacking' Fox's residence; '[w]hen Charles was poor he had a comfortable house, now he is rich he is turned out of doors.' At the end of 1781, at least £6,000 was paid out to the other partners in the bank, with additional payments over the next three years, which James Hare took as a sign that 'the Bankers did not meet at the beginning of the winter in the same opulent circumstances as they had parted in at the end of the last campaign.' Nevertheless, he related, '[t]he Bank has already won considerably, and would probably have done still better if money was not very scarce, as most of the punters retain their passion without the means of gratifying it.'[30]

Computed strictly in terms of income level, the livelihood to be made from even a subsidiary connection to a gaming operation was considerable, if not respectable. Managers of venues and operations received a relatively modest cut of the proceeds, and apparently derived much of their gaming income from advancing credit. After the Fox-Fitzpatrick faro bank enjoyed a fairly successful season, Brooks complained to Fox that its partners owed him £17,000, which Hare called 'a most impudent lie,' pointing out that the faro bankers had lent Brooks £15,000 free of interest, and that Brooks 'receives at least 5 per cent for all money owing to him.'[31] Lord Robert Spencer, financially embarrassed after joining Fox in opposition and thus losing his emolument as a Lord of Trade in 1781, dealt faro at Brooks's for five guineas an hour.[32] To be sure, Spencer, who had weathered a bankruptcy, was also able to repair his fortunes as a partner in Fox's bank. George Selwyn remarked 'that I was extremely sorry that [Spencer] had quitted the *Corps de Noblesse pour se jetter dans le Commerce* [to throw himself into trade], but it is at present his only resource.' It was subsequently reported that Spencer cleared £100,000 from his share in the bank before purchasing the estate of Woolbeding in Sussex in 1791.[33] Selwyn himself kept a smaller bank at White's, confined to half a dozen punters who were forbidden to stake more than two guineas on a card. From this small enterprise he derived a steady income:

I...have picked up, by 50 l. at a time, a few hundreds. I have played at nothing else. I shall keep to this trade....as long as it is confined to such a small circle. If it is likely to proceed further, I shall cut it, as I have done all other play, and Brooks's....It is a creditable way of living, I must own; and it would be well if by robbing some you might pay others, only that *ce qui est acquis e[s]t jetté par la fenétre, et si l'on paye, on ne s'acquitte pas* [that which is gained is thrown out the window, and what is paid, is not discharged]....It is not only of course that the bank should lose sometimes, but necessary to my health. For if the punters win, they cut me, and I get a good night's rest; but if they lose, I am kept up, and then I go home rich, but *epuisé, rendu, fatigué, et je ne sai[s] pas quoi* [spent, defeated, tired, and I know not what else].[34]

Hare reported that Fitzpatrick, principal partner with Fox in the operation at Brooks's, was a suitor to Mrs Benwell, subject of a John Hoppner portrait; she

[30] HMC *Carlisle*, 476, 483, 488, 495, 554; HWC, 39. 375.   [31] HMC *Carlisle*, 554–5.
[32] HMC *Carlisle*, 489, 497.
[33] HMC *Carlisle*, 540; Rees Howell Gronow, *Reminiscences of Captain Gronow*, 4 vols (London: Smith, Elder and Company, 1862–1866), 1. 77, 3. 103.
[34] HMC *Carlisle*, 484, 755.

initially rebuffed him, until '[t]he successes of the Pharaoh Bank contributed to open her eyes, and at the end of the summer she was established as his mistress *en titre*.'[35]

Perhaps the most intriguing figure in the Carlisle correspondence is James Hare who, despite a humble background as the son of an apothecary, attended Eton and King's College, Cambridge, where he befriended Fox and other future oppositionist luminaries. His financial resources were obscure, Frederick Robinson noting his driving about town in a fashionable new carriage in the conspicuous absence of any visible means of support. Nathaniel Wraxall speculated that Hare's affluence stemmed from his marriage to Hannah Hume, the daughter of a baronet, from whom he was quickly separated. These circumstances may explain Hare's assiduity with respect to what was certainly an important source of income, his one-twelfth share in Fox's faro bank at Brooks's, augmented with the six guineas an hour he was paid for dealing. On several occasions Selwyn reported seeing Hare seated at Brooks's 'in his semicircular nitch at the Pharo table, improving his fortune every deal.' Here he kept long hours, Selwyn reporting that 'the bankers' coaches are not ordered till about six in the morning.' Consequently, Anthony Storer wrote, '[t]he Bank turns out to Hare better than an Embassy to Warsaw,' to which Hare had sought appointment, unsuccessfully. Hare was clearly very aware that the profit centre in gaming was in banking games like faro, and lay in holding the bank rather than punting. Partners in banks, of course, would periodically punt at their own tables to draw others to play, particularly if company was thin, as they would recoup any losses, since they were effectively losing to themselves. Hare notably reproached himself when, arriving in Pall Mall from the country,

> for want of any other amusement I chose to take the diversion of Hazard ... and lost near 4,000 l. in three nights to a set of fellows whom I never saw before, and have never seen since.... I knew that I deserved to be poor for having been fool enough to lose my money at Hazard instead of saving it for Pharaoh.[36]

While the clubs of St James's Street were perhaps inevitably associated with different political factions, with White's seeming to draw ministerialists, and Brooks's attracting oppositionists, these associations were not necessarily as apparent to contemporaries. Archival evidence suggests that active supporters of the ministry were no less likely to play deep at Brooks's, and indeed to play with prominent members of opposition. Grantham and his brother, Frederick Robinson, were both reliable supporters of the North ministry, but both pursued membership of Almack's and later Brooks's. Robinson urged Grantham, who was Ambassador in

[35] HMC *Carlisle*, 555.
[36] Wrest Park MSS L 30/14/333/97; HMC *Carlisle*, 497, 499, 501, 506, 540, 552, 554, 580.

Madrid for most of the decade, to retain his membership, and recounted his own efforts to be voted in:

> [S]oon after I came to England my name was put up at Almacks & I was black balld.... [W]hen the Club was removed to Brooke's in St James's street I was again put up & again put down, but being advis'd by my friends to persist, I was the night before last chosen with 36 people in the Room; an unprecedented unanimity. I have recievd the Comp[limen]ts of the Nobility upon this event, which though it will cost me some money (the subscription being 10 Guineas) I am not sorry for, as I have more than once felt the want of an open house to resort to, & as I think it worth while for a single man to pay something, to have it in his power to be acquainted with what is called the best company in London.[37]

Fox himself nominated Pitt the Younger for membership of Brooks's, to which he was elected at the end of February 1781.[38] James Hare, a member of both White's and Brooks's, noted near the end of 1781 the existence of

> two Clubs lately formed, both consisting of young men, and chiefly of different parties in politics. Goostree's is a small society of young men in Opposition, and they are very nice in their admissions; as they discourage gaming as much as possible, their Club will not do any harm to Brookes's, and probably not subsist a great while.... The other is at Welche's, in St. James's Street, consisting of young men who belong to the Government.

Hare was mistaken about Goostre's, as George Selwyn could have informed him. It was not new, having opened in 1773 at 51 Pall Mall on the same street corner with the forerunners of Brooks's and Boodle's.[39] When Selwyn was sued some years later for the arrears of his subscription, club records were produced documenting his presence in May of 1777 in Goostre's hazard room, which for the benefit of the presiding judge was immediately noted as open only to subscribing members.[40] William Pitt the Younger was a member by the time of Hare's writing, and as enthusiastic a gamester there, by his own admission, as any member of Brooks's, of which Pitt was also a member.[41] Wilberforce remembered 'the intense earnestness which Pitt displayed when joining in these games of chance,' but added that the young Prime Minister 'perceived their increasing fascination, and soon after suddenly abandoned them forever.'[42] Fox's nephew, the third Lord

---

[37] Wrest Park MSS L 30/14/333/180.
[38] Joan Winterkorn, 'The Archives,' in Charles Sebag-Montefiore and Joe Mordaunt Crook (eds.), *Brooks's 1764–2014: The Story of a Whig Club* (London: Brooks's, 2013), 68.
[39] HMC *Carlisle*, 555; *Survey of London*, 29. 335.   [40] *Morning Star*, 176 (4 September 1789).
[41] John Holland Rose, *William Pitt the Younger and National Revival* (London: G.H. Bell, 1911), 89.
[42] *Life of Wilberforce*, 1. 18.

Holland, believed that Pitt had been a partner in the faro bank at Goostre's; Holland admitted never having known Pitt, and indeed he was all of about ten years old at that time, but he may have heard gossip on that point among his family.[43] Pitt made payments to Goostre totalling £444 in 1783 and £100 in 1784, significant sums that cannot be explained as expenditures for food or drink, but might well be repayment of loans for gaming of the sort that club proprietors frequently made, or perhaps Goostre's share of proceeds from a gaming table.[44]

William Wilberforce, newly elected to the House of Commons in September 1780, joined no fewer than five clubs, including White's, Brooks's, Boodle's, and Goostre's. As a first-generation MP without family connections in Westminster, Wilberforce found gaming tables to be an easy means of making acquaintances and acquiring crucial social capital, as he recalled in his memoirs:

> The first time I was at Brookes's, scarcely knowing any one, I joined from mere shyness in play at the Faro table, where George Selwyn kept bank. A Friend who knew my inexperience, and regarded me as a victim decked out for sacrifice, called to me, 'What, Wilberforce, is that you?' Selwyn quite resented the interference, and turning to him, said in his most expressive tone, 'O sir, don't interrupt Mr. Wilberforce, he could not be better employed.'[45]

It was not until later in the decade that the established clubs came to be firmly associated with the two political parties, in large part because the reconfigured parties were themselves only just emerging. Horace Walpole, a charter member of Brooks's from 1764, recollected in the early 1790s that the prominence of Brooks's, and the pre-eminence of oppositionists within it, led Pitt the Younger to resuscitate a moribund White's, 'so that from opposite sides of the same street,' the two clubs 'were the head-quarters of the Court & Opposition Camps.'[46]

The club mentioned as 'Weltje's' under various names occupied a premises at 64 St James's Street. In February of 1782, Hare reported that the 'young Club at Weltje's' was beginning to pose a threat to Brooks's, 'as they increase in numbers, live well, and are difficult in their choice of members; it is almost entirely a Ministerial Club as Brookes's is a Minority.' The 'alarm' that Hare registered was almost certainly concern over gaming profits, as he noted only a little later in the same letter that there had recently been 'very little play at Brookes's' apart from Quinze.[47] The initial proprietor was Ludwig Weltje, a celebrated cook and confectioner, who left in 1785 to manage the kitchens at Carlton House for the Prince of

---

[43] Henry Fox, third Baron Holland, *Memoirs of the Whig Party During My Time,* 2 vols (London: Longman, 1854), 2. 32.

[44] Derek Jarrett, *Pitt the Younger* (London: Weidenfield and Nicolson, 1974), 84.

[45] *Life of Wilberforce,* 1. 16–17.

[46] Quoted in Sebag-Montefiore and Crook (eds.), *Brooks's 1764–2014,* 7.

[47] HMC *Carlisle,* 555, 575–6.

Wales. James Daubigny acquired it from Ludwig Weltje's relation Christoph two years later. Daubigny suffered a series of setbacks, including the theft of the faro bank in 1790 and the loss of a suit to recover a gaming loan in 1794, so that by the time John Baxter took over the proprietorship, the club had declined, with a membership just over two hundred, half that of White's or Boodle's and about a third of Brooks's. This club subsequently merged with the Cocoa Tree, which had opened its doors in 1698 as a chocolate house like White's, to which it was a competitor. Until it closed in 1932, it along with White's were the only private gentleman's clubs in St James's or Pall Mall that had originated as public accommodations. The original Cocoa Tree had come to be as closely associated with the Tories during the 'great age of party' as White's was with Whigs. The Loyal Brotherhood, a convivial association of Tories founded in the reign of Queen Anne, met weekly at the Cocoa Tree from 1756. Until the middle of the 1740s, it had preferred the Fountain in the Strand. The Tory 'Board' that Edward Harley founded in 1727 had met there from its inception. 'The clubs at the Cocoa Tree' were still being mentioned as 'so long and so faithfully the King's Friends' as late as 1776, the year its building was expanded with the addition of two rooms at a cost of £1,100. By 1762, it had become like White's a proprietary subscription club, and there was certainly high-stakes gaming there, as it was repeatedly mentioned as a 'gaming club' in newspaper accounts of the 1770s. Horace Walpole claimed that £180,000 had changed hands there at hazard in the course of a single week in 1780.[48] The association of supporters of the North ministry, and later those of Pitt the Younger, with an accommodation long associated with the Tory party may explain, at least partially, why this group of politicians, many from established Whig families, came to be denominated as 'Tories.'

One Device to Another

In 1769, William Blackstone's *Commentaries* attested to the futility of statutory efforts to proscribe gaming. It was also in 1769 that the state lottery abandoned any pretence of merely creating incentives for individuals to invest prudently in what in effect were government bonds. All manner of derivative enterprises had developed in tandem with state lotteries, such as lottery insurance schemes and brokerages that would purchase the eminently transferable lottery annuities for lump sums of cash, generally at great advantage to the purchaser. The cultural prejudices and stereotypes that surrounded these opportunistic ventures found

---

[48] *Survey of London*, 30. 461–2; Linda Colley, 'The Loyal Brotherhood and the Cocoa Tree: The London Organization of the Tory Party, 1727–1760,' *Historical Journal*, 20 (March 1977), 85–9; *St. James's Chronicle*, 2326 (11 January 1776); *Morning Chronicle*, 2266 (24 August 1776); HWC, 25. 12.

their way into critiques that defended commercial gaming operations as at the very least no more objectionable than the lotteries and their adjuncts:

> What will it avail to shut up the shops of Christian dealers at pharoah and bas-set, or the operators at hazard and passage; while a way remains open to a set of *Jews* to plunder thousands, in this public and outrageous manner[?][49]

From 1769, purchasing a ticket in the state lotteries was a pure gamble, entitling the holder to a chance at lump sum cash payments up to a maximum between £20,000 and £30,000, the still quite steep price of £10 to £20 per ticket offset somewhat by the relatively high ratio of winning tickets to 'blanks,' so that the 60,000 tickets sold at £13 apiece in the 1769 lottery produced only £180,000 in revenue. Just over 20,000 prizes were drawn, so that purchasers had a one in three chance at winning at least £20, for a net gain of £7. The annuities paid on 'blanks' were abandoned.[50] Speaking for opposition, Richard Brinsley Sheridan remarked on more than one occasion on the hypocrisy of a government that sponsored lot-teries for cash payouts then attempting to enact stringent gaming legislation.[51] A decade later, a correspondent to the *Morning Post* wondered

> [a]s I have frequently seen with much pleasure your strictures against Pharo, E.O. and other such games, where the odds is only about 5 per cent. against the players, it has not a little surprised me that you have not likewise issued your friendly cautions to the Public against gaming in the Lottery, where the odds against the adventurers are nearly 100 per cent.[52]

Before the American Revolutionary War broke out, Lord North had gone so far as to defend the lottery, arguing that a national 'propensity to gaming might be directed to public advantage, and as well make its way to the public coffers, as be sported away at Arthur's, Boodle's, or Almack's.' Once war was underway, he pro-posed to raise £2,000,000 with an additional tax on cards of sixpence per pack, and, extraordinarily, half a crown added to the duty per pair of dice, 'which, in this gay, gaming age, he hoped it would not be thought improper to demand.'[53] Although lottery tickets were only available to purchasers of government annu-ities between 1772 and 1784, these 'loan lotteries' were extraordinarily remunera-tive, realizing record sums in excess of £12 million in each of the last five years they were drawn.[54] The Crown was now as much a gaming operator as William

---

[49] *Universal Visiter and Monthly Memorialist*, 9 (September 1756), 422.
[50] Ewen, *Lotteries and Sweepstakes*, 199–200, 238–9.
[51] *London Chronicle*, 3816 (15 May 1781); *Scots Magazine*, 43 (September 1781), 466.
[52] *Morning Post*, 5818 (16 December 1791).
[53] *Westminster Magazine*, (July 1774), 367; *Middlesex Journal*, 1104 (23 April 1776).
[54] James Raven, 'The Abolition of the English State Lotteries,' *Historical Journal*, 34 (1991), 372.

Howell was at Belsize House decades earlier, or as Henry Martindale was to be in St James's later.

Thomas Erskine, recognizing like other writers over the previous generation the futility of gaming legislation, proposed the repeal of all penal statutes against gaming to any amount, and the expropriation of any winnings over £40 won within 24 hours. The funds thus secured would be applied either to the sinking fund 'or to the furtherance of any public object which the legislature might think fit to direct.' Charitable corporations would be able to subpoena successful gamesters to give an account of their winnings under oath. Such a measure would dampen enthusiasm for games of chance for high stakes, as '[f]ew would be so patriotic as to cock a card for the sinking fund, or so charitable as to go at every thing for Chelsea or Greenwich hospitals.' He admitted, however, that such legislation would be unlikely to pass, as

> gaming is too strongly entrenched in the houses of the great, to be thus boldly attacked in front. These appropriations would be thought to carry the air of inquisition; notwithstanding the repeal of the penal laws,...the liberty of the subject would be made use of as a popular argument against the discovery, by the oath of the defendant.[55]

Moreover, moral panic could as easily lead to moral fatigue as to reform. In satirical 'Acknowledgements to our Correspondents' in 1781, the scandal-mongering *Town and Country Magazine* listed reasons that it had not published particular submissions. '*Thoughts on the fatal Effects of Gaming,*' advised the editors, 'have no Novelty to recommend them.'[56]

Nevertheless, the recourse that elites had to private clubs, and later to aristocratic 'at-homes,' drew the attention of media, and, after political discourse was reconfigured in the tumultuous decades of the 1760s and 1770s, coverage of gaming took on a partisan cast. Fox's fellow oppositionists, according to George Selwyn, were deeply distressed at the visibility of his faro operation 'and hate[d] to hear it mentioned.'[57] Mentioned it certainly was, the ministerialist *Morning Herald* posing '[a] question for a certain *oppositionist* to answer' in September 1781:

> Is he a virtuous senator, and a real patriot, who sits up all night at a gaming table, plundering young gentlemen of their property, and who the next day, in a public assembly, arraigns the conduct of a minister for robbing the nation? The surest step that government could take in order to break the neck of opposition, and

---

[55] [Thomas Erskine], *Reflections on Gaming, Annuities, and Usurious Contracts* (London: Thomas Davies, 1776), 12–13.
[56] *Town and Country Magazine*, 13 (October 1781), 506.   [57] HMC *Carlisle*, 496.

silence all our modern patriots, would be to put a final period to gambling. Shut up the Hazard and E O tables, and the existence of the patriotic orators is no more. They live by plundering the unwary, and ruining every young gentleman of property, whom they can entice to their iniquitous schools.[58]

Soon after these accounts appeared came news that Lord Cornwallis had surrendered to the Continental Army at Yorktown, precipitating a national crisis of conscience that would once again make commercial gaming at all levels of the market a subject of public anxiety.

---

[58] *Morning Herald*, 274 (15 September 1781).

10

Harmless Amusements

High Politics and High Stakes

In October 1781, as the news of defeat and surrender at Yorktown began to circulate, so did Thomas Rowlandson's print, *E.O., or The Fashionable Vowels* (figure 8.2). Rowlandson, who would return to the subject of games of chance again over four decades of a career that was just beginning, reportedly had first-hand experience of the milieus he illustrated, having, it was said, gambled away the estate left him by a prosperous uncle and aunt, amounting to £7,000. 'He was known in London at many of the fashionable gaming houses,' ran his obituary in *Gentleman's Magazine,* probably the work of the engraver John Thomas Smith, who knew him for forty years. Rowlandson 'always played with the feelings of a gentleman,' winning and losing with equanimity, 'and his word passed current, even with an empty purse.' He once told Smith 'that he had frequently played throughout a night and the next day,' on one occasion spending almost thirty-six hours at a hazard table.[1] The punters and onlookers around Rowlandson's E.O. table are generally prosperous and genteel, their clothing fashionable and their hair neat, with the exception of the attendant who turns the wheel. While they are variously anxious, or despondent, or somnolent, or simply bored, their demeanour is polite, with the exception of a single figure, probably intended to represent an Irishman, shouting and gesticulating with a shillelagh. Rowlandson, whose early career was spent in the neighbourhood of Soho Square, and who is thought to have included at least one portrait in this print, may have intended a representation of one of the E.O. venues operating in Soho at the time, perhaps Carlisle House.

Vowel Movements

In the endgame and aftermath of the American Revolutionary War, itself the occasion of an outpouring of public anxiety, gaming became one focus of an attack on elite corruption, obliging that elite to undertake another effort at the comprehensive proscription of gaming, the first in four decades and the last until the Victorian era. This initiative was both aided and undermined by deeper and

---

[1] *Gentleman's Magazine*, 97 (June 1827), 1. 564, quoted in Bernard Falk, *Thomas Rowlandson: His Life and Art* (New York: Beechhurst Press, 1952), 25.

The Gambling Century: Commercial Gaming in Britain from Restoration to Regency. John Eglin, Oxford University Press.
© John Eglin 2023. DOI: 10.1093/oso/9780192888198.003.0011

often first-hand knowledge of the structure of commercial gaming concerns, as well as by the centrality of gaming as a cultural practice among the political elite. Renewed public anxiety over gaming was accompanied by increased public sophistication about its operation in commercial settings. An item that appeared in several papers in the spring and summer of 1781 contains what was possibly the first use of the term 'house' to refer to a commercial gaming concern, together with an analysis of the 'house advantage':

> If a man of only common sense and property were for a moment to reflect to what a disadvantage he must ever play, even where the fairness of the game cannot be suspected, or the characters of the players are indisputable, he would instantly be convinced, that in the long run he must be a considerable sufferer, as the *house* must, at all games of chance, eventually be the chief gainer; for the box (as it is called) at Hazard, or E.O. must glean the pockets of the players, and enrich the proprietors.[2]

By the beginning of the 1780s, the structure of gaming operations at different levels of the market was also clear enough to any authorities who cared to make inquiries or examine the documents available to them. The same individuals appear repeatedly in indictments and recognizances for gaming concerns in different locations. In 1781, a constable and two wigmakers in Chelsea had been bound in recognizance to prosecute one Paul Roubel for '[k]eeping a Gaming House or for suffering Gaming to be carried on and Exercised' in his residence. Two years later, Roubel (variously spelled) was indicted with four others for at least one E.O. table at Carlisle House in Soho Square, and again with four different individuals for an E.O. operation in St Alban's Street, Pall Mall. The same year, Richard Hodges faced indictments for a different E.O. concern in Pall Mall and another in Covent Garden. Roubel and his co-defendants at Carlisle House were acquitted by a jury in April 1784; the other three indictments ended in *nolle prosequi* acquittals, meaning that the prosecutor for any number of reasons had abandoned the case. John Twycross, already convicted for keeping a hazard table in February 1777, was indicted in July 1781 as one of five partners in an E.O. concern in Pall Mall; his case also ended in a *nolle prosequi* at the same time as Roubel's.[3] E.O. accounted for most of the gaming presentments made to the bench of Westminster and Middlesex over the course of the 1780s.

---

[2] The item, dated from Bath, 20 May 1781, appears in *Town and Country Magazine*, 13 (June 1781), 305; *Morning Herald*, 211 (4 July 1781); and *Hibernian Magazine* (July 1781), 376; italics mine.

[3] LMA MJ/SR/3328, r 351; MJ/SR/3405, rr lvi–lviii. Paul Roubel subsequently had a lengthy and successful career as a gaming entrepreneur, and by the middle of the decade was listed in the Westminster electoral rolls as a 'gentleman' of the parish of St George's Hanover Square with an address in Park Place. He appeared as a proprietor of a fashionable gaming venue at 40 Pall Mall in *The Greeks* of 1817. As 'old Paul Roubel' had died the previous year, the author of this exposé remembered him as 'a very good hearty fellow in his way,' further remarking that despite his occupation, 'few

Indictments for gaming at this time followed a pattern, consisting of four separate counts, two counts for keeping a gaming house followed by two for keeping a gaming *room*. This formula may reflect unresolvable confusion over the relationship between the partners in a gaming enterprise and the venue in which the gaming occurred. For the purposes of comparison, indictments of brothel keepers were one third to one half as long, usually with a single count. Authorities readily perceived that gaming concerns were much better lawyered, with counsel adept at exploiting technicalities, such as errors in paperwork. '[T]here is no law now existing, that arms the justices with sufficient power to stop this dreadful evil,' ran an open letter to the Marquis of Rockingham in April 1782:

> You may indict them at the Session, which perhaps does not commence till six weeks or two months after the complaint made—they bail it to the Session six weeks longer—then traverse it to the next six weeks more—then remove it to the next term, which probably is as long, where perhaps after all, from some defect in the proceedings or want of proof,…they are acquitted; and during all this time the nuisance continues and increases.[4]

Apparently, a move after mid-century to hearing gaming presentments at the monthly Middlesex sessions in preference to the quarterly Westminster sessions had not sufficed to address these difficulties.

Double indictments were also a means of augmenting fines if prosecutions were successful. Thus it was that Edward Burlton, in the first of his confrontations with the Westminster bench, potentially faced a total fine of £6,400 in May of 1787 for keeping a faro table for sixteen days and for keeping a room where unlawful games (i.e. faro) were played, for the same sixteen days. Additionally, unless the games in question were among those specified in the Georgian statutes as illegal lotteries, prosecutions could only go forward under the increasingly inadequate and ineffectual Henrician statute. Even those prosecutions faced insurmountable obstacles, as the language of the statute applied to any 'house, room, or place' kept for gaming, referring to immoveable 'real' property. Gaming tables, as long as they were not configured for a game denominated in the Georgian statutes, did not fall within the language of the Tudor statute. In May of 1782, three partners in an E.O. table actually sued to recover £75 from the constables who had seized it along with another table from a premises in Oxford Road. The attorney for the defendants 'admitted that there was no law which authorized any man to seize an E O table, the keeper of such table not being liable

men in higher walks of life possessed a kinder heart, or a hand which opened more freely or more liberally to the calls of humanity.' [Seymour Harcourt], *The Greeks: Being the Jeremiad of an Exiled Greek* (London: J.J. Stockdale, 1817), viii, 49.
   [4] *London Courant* (3 April 1782).

by any statute, unless he could be proved to be the keeper of the house as a gaming-house.' The plaintiffs, however, lost their suit, having 'failed in the strict proof of their joint interest either in the money or the table.'[5]

Gaming operations often lodged in once-fashionable entertainment venues fallen on hard times. Such was the case of Carlisle House in Soho Square. For a brief few seasons after its opening under Theresa Cornelys in October 1760, it was the largest and most opulent accommodation for concerts, balls, and masquerades that the metropolis could offer, until William Almack opened his assembly rooms in King Street in 1765. More serious competition arrived in January 1772, when the Pantheon opened less than half a mile away in Oxford Street. Attendance at Carlisle House fell dramatically, which halving the admission to masquerades failed to alleviate. By the end of 1772, a bankrupt Cornelys was forced to give up her tenancy. Early in the next decade, William Wade, the Master of Ceremonies at Bath, was brought in to manage entertainments at Carlisle House, of which there were steadily fewer. 'Promenades' were reduced from six per week to two, and masquerades from six every season to one or two at most. Standards had clearly deteriorated, as reports had it that visitors no longer wore full dress, that men appeared in boots, and that servants were inattentive and rude. Since the rooms were not in use for much of the week, from March 1782 space in Carlisle House was available to be let 'for respectable Assemblies.' By the end of that year, the house was empty and seeking to lure a new tenant at a discounted rent. The five men who were subsequently indicted for keeping E.O. tables at Carlisle House were in operation there, according to the bills and recognizance slips, from April 1782 until at least November 1783. It may have been Carlisle House to which George Byng, one of the members for Middlesex and a sponsor of the E.O. Bill, referred in describing a house in Soho that boasted five E.O. tables.[6]

Much the same fate overtook the Temple of Health in Pall Mall, once the focus of a popular craze, operated by James Graham, a disciple of Anton Mesmer who similarly promoted the therapeutic properties of electricity. Once public enthusiasm dissipated in the way of all popular fads, Graham found himself in debt to the tune of £2,000 due to an ill-advised effort to expand his operation, whereupon the 'electrical beds' that were let to curious couples gave way to E.O. tables that allowed Graham, in partnership with a consortium of gaming entrepreneurs, to discharge 80 per cent of his debt. This development was lampooned in a pantomime at Sadler's Wells in which Graham's 'Celestial Bed' was transformed into an E.O. table; similarly, a print of the following year depicted Graham astride an enormous and unmistakably phallic piece of laboratory equipment atop a

---

[5] *Bath Chronicle*, 1382 (17 May 1787); *London Chronicle*, 3976 (23 May 1782).
[6] LMA MJ/SR/3433, MJ/SR/3436, i 183; MJ/SR/3437, rr 227–228; *Survey of London*, 33. 73–9; *Edinburgh Magazine*, 56 (11 July 1782), 441.

gigantic E.O. wheel.[7] Savile Robinson and Humphrey Tristram Potter, who were
concerned in E.O. operations elsewhere in the City of Westminster, signed short
term leases of the property, variously £25 weekly for three weeks, and then
£35 per week for five weeks; in addition, Graham continued to receive the
admissions charge of half a crown per visitor. While he subsequently claimed that
'he had no concern whatever with the profits or losses' of the E.O. tables that his
tenants introduced, Graham admitted that he had received quite lucrative offers
for the past year from different individuals wanting to rent his premises 'for
the ... purposes of gaming,' and had only relented when unable to pay the portion
of the £12,000 he had spent fitting up his two premises in the Adelphi and in Pall
Mall. John Blissard, who acted for Graham's creditors at the Pall Mall venue, testified
that anywhere from £10 to £15 was collected in admissions on a typical evening,
from around one hundred visitors, but that some evenings as many as three
hundred were admitted. One of Graham's employees, a musician, gave evidence
that all play was for gold, and that the wheel was spun approximately three times
per minute, while a waiter at the Temple attested that as much as £50 might be
staked on a single turn of the wheel, 'particularly by a gentleman said to belong to
the bank.' The 'bank' in this case meant the Bank of England, as the individual in
question was Charles Clutterbuck, a clerk in the cashier's office who had forged
nearly £6,000 worth of banknotes before absconding across the Channel. It was
reportedly this fraud that led the bank directors to petition the Home Secretary,
Thomas Townshend, so that once again pressure from Whitehall was brought to
bear on the Westminster bench.[8]

Twice in the summer of 1782, the constables descended on Graham's property
in Pall Mall. In July, they found a crowd of three hundred on the premises, and
were only able to seize and destroy a single E.O. table. At a second raid in August,
one of the attending justices, William Addington, was bludgeoned and sustained
a serious head injury.[9] This later raid was the subject of James Gillray's print, 'The
W[e]st[minste]r Just-Asses a-Braying, or The downfall of the E.O. Table.' The
justices Addington and Sampson Wright are depicted with the heads of donkeys,
as is a third figure, representing a City financier. Addington, bleeding from his
injury and crying 'Help! Murder! help. Fire! Thieves: Popery! help!' flees a woman
brandishing a wooden mallet; the woman reproaches him for breaking down the
door: 'What, You'll open my Lock, too, without a Key, will you?' Wright and a
constable attack an E.O. wheel with instruments evoking grisly medieval

[7] Donna Andrew, '"How frail are Lovers Vows, and Dicers oaths:" Gaming, Governing and Moral
Panic in Britain, 1781–1782,' in David Lemmings and Claire Walker (eds.), *Moral Panics, the Media
and the Law in Early Modern England* (New York: Palgrave Macmillan, 2009), 187; *The Quacks,* published 17 March 1783, Frederick Stephen and M. Dorothy George, *Catalogue of Personal and Political
Satires in the British Museum,* 12 vols (London: British Museum, 1870–1954), 5. 6325.
[8] *London Courant,* (28 September, 9 December 1782); *Public Advertiser,* 15,213 (3 March 1783);
London Packet, 1893 (31 July 1782).
[9] *London Courant,* (28 September 1782).

punishments, such as the heated iron blade used to disembowel convicted traitors, while a night watchman frets that 'they'll 'dite you on Magna-Charta for breaking open their Houses! & have you before the Judges.' Wright retorts 'damn the Judges! & Magna-Charta too!! our Warrants [are] above them both.' Most intriguing of all is the suggestion of the caption that the justices would be 'indemnified for all the mischief they do, by the Bulls & Bears of the City.'[10] Gillray, at least, was of the opinion that the emerging financial sector saw commercial gaming operations as serious competition for their investment products.

Reynard and the Hounds

Thus it was that the gaming legislation proposed in 1782 and written in alignment with Blackstone's recommendation was denominated 'the E.O. Bill' in the press. In introducing the bill, George Byng echoed Blackstone in remarking that

> [i]t was in vain ... to attempt putting down gaming if the legislature should prohibit the game of E O only; for then it would shoot up again under another name; nay, there were already G R Tables; so that if the legislature did not provide an ample remedy, that would go to the very root of the disorder, the spirit of gaming would run through the whole alphabet.

This bill was drafted in coordination with the justices of Middlesex, who that April had formed an ad hoc committee to examine existing gaming legislation; they made a particular note of Blackstone's advice in the minutes of an early meeting.[11] The bill adopted language that a tract writer had recommended thirty years earlier, outlawing

> all Manner of Games, to be determined by the Chance only of Cards or Dice, of any Letter or Letters, Figure or Figures, Ball or Balls, Number or Numbers, Mark or Marks, or by any Machine, Engine, or other Invention or Device of Chance, only, by whatever Description or Denomination the same may be known or called.

The bill applied to anyone who kept 'any House, Room, or Place' for the games now classified as unlawful, or who permitted them on the premises, or who kept the game themselves, who advertised in writing or print the keeping of a game of chance, or who, in a significant departure, had a material interest in a gaming operation. The proprietor or manager in appearance or fact of a property or venue

---

[10] George, *Personal and Political Satires*, 5. 6120.
[11] *Edinburgh Magazine*, 56 (11 July 1782), 441; LMA MJ/SP/1782/04/023-024.

was to be taken as the 'keeper' as defined in the language of the bill. These two provisions were intended to eliminate much of the uncertainty that had frustrated gaming prosecutions since commercial gaming operations had begun to appear. The owner of a property might not be the keeper of a premises, who might in turn not be the manager of gaming operations within the venue. Those who supervised a table might be doing so for the partners in a 'bank,' who might never be on the premises, and some of whom might be unknown except to the other partners. It had never been clear that someone who simply had a financial interest in a gaming operation could be charged under any existing statute if they were not present at the table or even on the premises where it was located. Although the draft legislation proposed to close these and all manner of other loopholes in existing gaming statutes, there was one remarkable exception in that the exemption for the royal household was preserved.[12]

Once the draft bill was drawn up, the county's delegation in the House of Commons was consulted with a view to presenting the bill to the Speaker. The committee was advised, however, that the proper form would be a petition addressed to Parliament, which one of the members for Middlesex agreed to present. That this petitioning member was, at least initially, to be none other than the notorious John Wilkes serves to explain much of the incredulity and scepticism that greeted this effort at the improvement of public morals.[13] The justices' timing was peculiar as well, as they must have recognized. Moral panic over gaming often coincided with political crisis. The last series of Gaming Acts coincided with the gradual collapse of the Walpole ministry and the turmoil of the 'Broad Bottom' coalition that initially replaced it. Similarly, the abortive 'E.O. Bill' of 1782 was part of the background noise of the revolving-door ministries in the endgame of the American Revolutionary War. Gaming, along with sexual misconduct, was one of the cudgels used against the Foxite opposition. James Gillray's satirical print 'Banco to the Knave' of April 1782 (figure 10.1) represented the resignation of Lord North as the breaking of a faro bank, with Fox (depicted, as often, as an actual fox) announcing to the company 'Gentlemen the Bank is mine, & I will open every Night at the same hour.' After North's resignation, the ministry was in chaos, and the cabinet underwent the first of a series of reshufflings that ensued over the next two years. The new (and short-lived) government under the Marquis of Rockingham included Fox at the head of an entirely new cabinet department, the Foreign Office, an appointment that scandalized a number of newspaper writers, necessitating a public relations campaign to clear the air. Fox's enthusiasm for deep play was already notorious, his father Lord Holland already having paid off losses in tens of thousands of pounds Fox and his brother Stephen

---

[12] *Reflexions on Gaming*, 51; Fifteenth Parliament of Great Britain: second session (27 November 1781–11 July 1782), *A Bill More Effectually to Prevent the Pernicious Practice of Gaming*, 2–3, 7–8.
[13] LMA MJ/SP/1782/06/003.

Figure 10.1 James Gillray, *Banco to the Knave*, 1782. ©National Portrait Gallery, London. The breaking of a faro bank provided a metaphor for the collapse of the ministry of Lord North.

had incurred. During Fox's brief tenure as a Lord of the Admiralty when he was all of twenty-one, it was alleged that his clerks were regularly dispatched to gaming tables in St James's and Pall Mall, 'where, with a pen in one hand, and cards in the other,' Fox would sign documents 'without knowing one word of their contents.'[14]

Fox's reputation for high play concerned his allies as much as his detractors, sufficiently so that his appointment as a principal Secretary of State necessitated a public relations initiative to the effect that he had sworn off games of chance. The most conspicuous element of this campaign was Fox's resignation from Brooks's Club, which, according to one report, surprised some of the membership, 'as they considered his *post* there, at least, equivalent in point of emolument to his present place.' Selwyn reportedly quipped '[t]hat Charles had now a much deeper game to play; that he must shuffle and cut with all the world.' The *Morning Chronicle* ran an account relating that '[t]he friends of Mr. Secretary Fox assert in all companies, that his name is struck from off the books of all gaming clubs, to which he formerly belonged,' while the *Morning Herald* adverted that Fox had 'pledged to

---

[14] *London Evening Post*, 6834 (24 October 1771).

give up any sort of gaming.' Both accounts related that Fox would begin his cabinet career by introducing a bill to suppress E.O. Within several days of its initial account, however, the *Morning Herald* contended that none of these reports were true, relating an anecdote that the Foreign Secretary

> was standing near the chimney at Brooks's, with two ambassadors by him, when Mr. F[itzpatrick] called out to him from the table, *Mr. Secretary Fox, ring the bell for more cards;* the ambassadors stared with astonishment, at a minister being treated with so little ceremony.[15]

The E.O. Bill, intended to inoculate the new ministry against association with high-stakes gaming culture, backfired in that respect. In the circumstances, it was too easy to impute other motivations to the Westminster bench than sincere commitment to eradicating a social pathology.

Where any parliamentary debate over the three Georgian Gaming Acts had barely registered as Britain drifted into nearly a decade of continental warfare, gaming legislation put forward as the American Revolutionary War was winding down met with much more scrutiny. Richard Brinsley Sheridan remarked during the debate over the E.O. Bill that at least one Westminster JP was known to keep an E.O. table, while two others kept lottery offices, and wondered

> if it would not have been more proper first to regulate the police of Westminster? He begged the House to consider the authority they were going to delegate to Justices, and to the worst species of Justices, Westminster Justices.[16]

William Hyde, for example, one of the magistrates who featured most prominently in newspaper accounts of gaming raids, was a notorious 'trading justice,' meaning that reports lauding his vigilance against gaming operations were probably heavily larded with sarcasm. Admittedly, these revelations came only some years after the E.O. debacle. The *Morning Post* suggested that raids on three gaming venues in Pall Mall and St James's Street on one night in December 1791 were orchestrated by 'that *upright* and *active* Magistrate, Mr. HYDE' at the behest of rival gaming operators, possibly from the several concerns in Oxendon Street, where Hyde resided. Another item in the same issue insinuated that Hyde took bribes from lottery agents. When Hyde lost one of the prosecutions stemming from this raid (in consequence of his ignorance of how faro was played), two

---

[15] *Edinburgh Magazine*, 56 (20 June 1782), 334; *Morning Herald*, 446 (4 April 1782), 454 (13 April 1782); *Morning Chronicle*, 4029 (15 April 1782).
[16] *Public Advertiser*, 14,978 (27 June 1782); *Westminster Magazine* (October 1782), 538; Cobbett, *Parliamentary History*, 23. 110–13.

writers noted his initial failure and evident reluctance to return £276 16*s.* that had been seized.[17]

Other criticism drew distinctions between different games that might be played in the (putatively) private social gatherings now to be subject to the jurisdiction of magistrates. Sir Philip Jennings Clarke worried that the legislation 'would put an end to the harmless amusement of card-playing in private families.' Clarke had in mind fashionable card parties such as those that regularly took place in town-houses in St James's Square, arguing that 'that the present Bill would extend to every Lady who had an Assembly,' and pointing out that 'there were few Assemblies where there was not a regular Faro Bank.' The stipulated fine of £200

was as great upon those who played a sober game of whist in a corner, as on those who punted at Pharoah for thousands; and it was certain, that Pharoah was played in almost every polite house.[18]

The E.O. Bill seems to have foundered over provisions that would have allowed constables to raid private residences that were not, strictly speaking, public accommodations. Newspapers, of course, had reported a received stratagem of E.O. operators to set up in putatively private residences, and run tables in what were billed as private entertainments for invited guests. Cards of invitation were handed out to passers-by in neighbouring streets, even, it was claimed, at the door of the magistrate's office in Bow Street. The *Morning Herald* was accordingly outraged that

[t]he liberty of the subject, and the received wisdom that 'a man's house is his castle,' are now prostituted to the worst of purposes...and under the laudable pretext that private families are not to be deprived of their *innocent* amusements.

Evidently, such appeals were put forward in defence of gaming operations, a correspondent to the *Public Advertiser* one month later asking, for all of the 'noise' that had 'lately been made about certain E.O. Tables,...by what Authority any Magistrate is to interrupt the Amusement of a private Family and their Friends.'[19]

Notwithstanding these critiques, the E.O. Bill passed in the Commons, and proceeded to the upper house, where it was tepidly received. At the beginning of July 1782, Rockingham was dead of the influenza he contracted during an

[17] *Morning Post*, 5813 (22 December 1791); *Evening Mail* (5 February 1796); *New London Magazine* (January 1792), 41–2; *Oracle*, 817 (9 January 1792).
[18] *Morning Herald*, 518 (27 June 1782); *Public Advertiser*, 14,978 (27 June 1782); *Westminster Magazine* (October 1782), 534.
[19] *London Courant*, (10 May 1781); *Morning Herald*, 114 (13 March 1781); *Public Advertiser*, 14,506 (9 April 1781).

epidemic in June, prompting a precipitous reconfiguration of the cabinet. By the time the bill was debated in the Lords, Fox had resigned from the ministry, refusing to serve under the Earl of Shelburne, the new premier. Fox's departure removed the liability that the E.O. legislation was introduced to ameliorate. Several amendments were now made to the bill that the Duke of Chandos worried would cause it to be lost, as the end of the session was close at hand. The Earl of Effingham believed that the bill could still pass, but that given its flaws, it was best if it did not; the Westminster JPs had admitted to him that new powers were not necessary as long as they had enough authority to address E.O. tables.[20] The E.O. Bill ultimately passed the Lords as well, but with amendments, and as Chandos predicted, the session ended before the Commons could take up the revised bill. Observers found it hard to believe that this development was accidental. The Shelburne ministry was preoccupied in negotiating peace with France, Spain, the Netherlands, and the new United States, so the E.O. Bill plausibly got lost in the shuffle of more pressing business, both at the end of the session and the beginning of a new one, when the promised reintroduction of the legislation came to naught. The most optimistic report related that Thomas Townshend, Shelburne's Home Secretary, would propose a new E.O. bill a few days into the new session, with a view to the new legislation taking effect before Christmas, and containing a clause indemnifying magistrates from suits arising from their enforcement of the Gaming Acts during the recess. The journals of the House of Commons do not reflect that there was any such action, the last reference to the E.O. Bill occurring in July 1782. Instead of introducing revised legislation as adverted, Townshend merely urged more vigilance on the Middlesex justices.[21]

Naturally the Foxites came in for blame for the failure of the bill. Gillray published a print satire on Fox's resignation in July, in which a horned and cloven-hoofed Fox recites lines from *Paradise Lost* as he stands astride an E.O. wheel, mounted atop a globe, as Lord Shelburne personified as the sun rises over his shoulder (figure 10.2). Thomas Colley's print of that August again featured Fox, as a bewigged and frock-coated fox, presiding at an E.O. table at the moment that the gaming house is raided (figure 10.3).[22] There is no evidence that Fox himself was a partner in any E.O. operations, but as his interest in faro banks was well known and amply documented, it hardly mattered. The *Town and Country Magazine* printed a fictitious conversation between Fox and Sheridan, in which Fox revealed that he had ordered a dozen E.O. tables to support the opposition

---

[20] I have borrowed Donna Andrew's redaction of the House of Lords debate from 'Gaming, Governing, and Moral Panic,' 184.
[21] *Morning Chronicle*, 4151 (5 September 1782); *Commons Journal*, 38. 1146; *London Chronicle*, 4043 (26 October 1782).
[22] George, *Personal and Political Satires*, 5. 6012, 6119.

Figure 10.2 James Gillray, *Gloria Mundi*, 1782. ©National Portrait Gallery, London. Charles James Fox was unfairly accused of involvement in E.O. syndicates, as in this print following his resignation from the cabinet.

Justice Wrig-t's a Coming, or Secretary EO. alias Reynard put to flight.

Figure 10.3 Thomas Colley, *Justice Wright's A-Coming, or Reynard Put to Flight*, 1782. ©Trustees of the British Museum. Although Fox's partnership in faro banks is well documented, there is no evidence that he was involved in E.O. operations.

over the winter, and Sheridan related that an address of thanks would be presented to the Earl of Effingham for effectively killing the legislation.[23]

Newspapers were at variance over culpability of magistrates in the failure to contain the proliferation of E.O. and other gaming tables. There was speculation that magistrates would use the debacle of the E.O. Bill to excuse their continued inaction. One correspondent, purportedly an MP, charged that many justices relished the stature of their office without executing its duties, or were motivated in the exercise of their position by favouritism and personal interest. 'I do not mean to deny that many of you act impartially, ably, and disinterestedly,' he suggested of the Middlesex bench, 'but I am justified in saying, that none of you act firmly and vigorously.' Both supporters and detractors of the metropolitan bench believed that existing statutes either were or ought to have been sufficient to suppress gaming effectively. 'No Matter whether the Table for Gaming be a Dice Table, a Card Table, or an E.O. Table,' asserted one writer after the legislation miscarried, 'the Magistrates have a Right to enter the House, and to arrest and imprison both the Keepers and Players.' One commentator cited the vigilance of Sampson Wright against the Temple of Health, and hoped that other magistrates would follow this

[23]   Andrew, 'Gaming, Governing, and Moral Panic,' 185.

example in spite of the 'illiberal sarcasms and censures thrown out by *seceding secretaries* and others, against our police,' adding that justices should not hesitate 'to enter the very house of a Secretary of State, or any other Great Man's, upon a proper information.'[24] The *Morning Herald,* however, very tellingly noted the plea of the justices that they could not act against gaming operations without sworn depositions complaining of violations, statements that the Westminster bench had repeatedly solicited to no effect.[25]

Game On

In April 1783, Fox was back in office, having joined forces with Lord North to drive Shelburne's ministry from power. Once again, his gaming entrepreneurship was deployed against him. The Fox–North coalition was a broad target in this respect, as it included not only Fox, returning as Foreign Secretary, but Richard Fitzpatrick, his major partner in the faro bank at Brooks's, as Secretary at War. Other gaming enthusiasts included the fifth Earl of Carlisle as Lord Privy Seal and the second Lord Grantham as first Lord of Trade. Consequently, one newspaper writer could assert facetiously that

> the great and mighty coalition itself,…was brought about by *gaming.* The East-Indies is to be saved by *gaming.* And the British nation is to be restored to its antient splendour and strength by gaming. When gaming produces consequences so extensive and beneficial, who will say that *gaming* is pernicious to a state? This may be at first a paradox to the multitude; but there is not a waiter at Brookes's who could not furnish a solution.[26]

These criticisms particularly stung as the coalition did not enjoy royal support and was consequently deprived of a number of sources of patronage, obliging it to seek alternatives. As a result, even Edmund Burke, in the potentially highly lucrative post of Paymaster of the Forces, was tainted in connection with his brother Richard, who had incurred a gaming debt of nearly £7,500 in unsavoury circumstances playing hazard at Brighton. No sooner was Burke appointed than Sir Thomas Kent, one of Richard Burke's gaming creditors, proposed that Burke procure a post for a nominee of Kent's choosing, who would then pay Kent £500 per year out of the salary. Kent asserted that Burke had used his interest to secure posts or pensions for Richard and others of his relatives, including the Receivership of Window Duties for Middlesex, which cleared £1,200 per annum

---

[24] *Morning Chronicle,* 4121 (1 August 1782); *Public Advertiser,* 15,014 (1 August 1782); *Morning Herald,* 552 (6 August 1782).
[25] *Morning Herald,* (6 March 1782).   [26] *Gazetteer,* 17,065 (21 August 1783).

after the payment of a 'factor.' Noting that Burke had exposed his patron Lord Rockingham to 'opprobrium' in advancing Richard Burke 'into a conspicuous place of Public trust,' Kent wondered 'where would have been the impropriety or indelicacy of applying part of this to do an act of Justice and thereby exonerate a Brother from the Opprobrium of being held as a Cheat and a Sharper?'[27]

When Fox proposed that Whitehall take over the government of India from the East India Company, the legislation was widely interpreted as a means of creating an alternative ministerial 'slop trough.' When the India Bill failed in the House of Lords in December 1783 largely due to royal interference, the Portland ministry, the fourth in two years, was forced to resign, giving way to a new government under William Pitt the Younger. When Pitt called an election to shore up his hold on power, rhetoric against the Foxite opposition again brought gaming culture to public notice. The *Whitehall Evening Post* charged 'that three of the most assuming characters in politics' were concerned in faro and E.O. operations from which they derived their sole visible means of support. Fox was certainly comprehended in this assertion, although it was less definite which among Richard Fitzpatrick, Lord Robert Spencer, or James Hare the writer meant to exclude.[28] A writer in the *Morning Post* deployed an unusually clever metaphor, reflecting insight not only into probability but also the business model of commercial gaming:

> Gambling is now reduced to such scientific certainty, that none of the *black legs* can make a shilling, except those who play against the public. The adepts at this species of gaming, are briefly employed in seeking for *seats* in a certain assembly, where the rights, liberties, and properties of the people, have been too long the *stakes* thrown for.[29]

Sir Cecil Wray, who had supported the E.O. Bill, was angered by Fox's alliance with North, and stood against his former leader in the tumultuous Westminster election of 1784. Although Fox kept his seat, Pitt won a majority, and was in power continuously for the next seventeen years. The *Morning Post* sardonically rubbed the loss in:

> It is a ridiculous and pitiful ministerial manoeuvre, to rake up the *innocent failings* of the principal leaders of opposition, because they are inclined to unbend their burthened minds, with a harmless *game of cards*. Many of the patriots of antiquity were gamblers. Livy informs us, that...the affairs of the Senate were always discussed over a *box and dice;* and Cassius kept a *Faro* table for Brutus,

---

[27] BL Add. MSS 29,232, ff 311–312.   [28] *Whitehall Evening Post*, 5736 (25 March 1784).
[29] *Morning Post*, 3476 (30 March 1784).

while the latter was soliciting assistance for the murder of Julius Caesar. Many other instances might be brought from equally good authority.[30]

An anonymous writer, self-identified as a MP, gave voice to the crisis of confidence that historians have often described in the endgame of the American Revolutionary War, decrying the moral corruption of the political elite, of which gambling was the most conspicuous specimen: 'To this dreadful vice must the loss of America be ascribed! To this dreadful vice must every misfortune which has lately fallen on this country be attributed!' It was clear to this anonymous author in the aftermath of the bitterly contested Westminster election of 1784 that ordinary folk clearly did not seek a reform of any kind. Proposed remedies included the formation of an association of MPs who would take a sort of temperance pledge 'to play only to a *certain extent*,' which extent was instructively not defined. These members would then 'petition the King not to employ any person whatever, who belongs to a GAMBLING CLUB, or at least who has not signed the obligation.' The justification for this proposal, clearly aimed at Fox and his circle, asserted that

[t]here is no asylum for the lost and indigent GAMBLER....If he possesses powers of language and oratory, he must bully the minister for a place, or become a *mortgage* on patriotism and opposition! In his plans he will find a very powerful support, and before many years are elapsed the GAMBLING CLUBS will become *King, Lords, and Commons*.[31]

Oppositionists' supposed predilection for gaming culture made them susceptible to attack from both sides of the aisle. When Admiral Hugh Pigot's appointment to command the fleet in the West Indies coincided too closely with his alleged loss of £17,000 to the faro bank at Brooks's, the *Morning Herald* pounced on the apparent quid pro quo. Three years later, a prominent peer's crossing the aisle of the House of Lords was attributed a loss of £30,000 'at a fashionable gaming house, not White's, in St. James's-street,' probably Brooks's. Owing to this 'extraordinary run of ill luck' he 'again enlisted himself under the banners of Administration.... where the loaves and fishes are to be found.'[32]

From the eve of the general election of 1784, Pitt the Younger was aggressively positioned as Fox's moral superior in his avoidance of vice, gaming especially. 'Does Mr. Pitt blend in with the gaming clubs? No. Does he cut a figure on the turf? No,' one writer intoned, adding for good measure that Pitt possessed neither

[30] *Morning Post*, 3554 (2 July 1784).
[31] *Hints for a Reform, Particularly in the Gaming Clubs* (London: R. Baldwin, 1784), 3–5, 10, 12, 16.
[32] *Morning Herald*, 472 (4 May 1782); *Caledonian Mercury* (19 December 1785).

racehorses, nor hunters, nor dogs, nor mistresses.[33] A item that appeared in
several papers the following year claimed that 'not one of the present cabinet dif-
fers at all from the late Lord Chesterfield in his execration of Newmarket and the
Gaming Clubs, as the most infamous Seminaries of Iniquity and Ill-manners.'[34]
A comparison between Fox and Pitt that appeared repeatedly over the course of a
decade asserted that where Fox had '[e]ntered early on the turf, at gaming clubs,
&c.,' Pitt pursued 'early the painful study of the laws and constitution of his country.' Where Fox's enemies '(falsely, *we hope*) reproach him with the *excess*...of
gaming, debauchery, &c.,' Pitt's detractors '(falsely *we fear*) reproach him with the
excess of sobriety and continence.'[35]

By this time, however, Fox was a progressively less active clubman, appearing
at Brooks's less and less frequently, according to club archives, and leaving off
high-stakes play.[36] Gaming was less conspicuous across clubland as well. Clubs, as
redoubts of the political elite, were increasingly anxious to dissociate themselves
from reckless play at hazard, faro, macao, or quinze, preferring whist, regarded as
more respectable even when played for substantial stakes. By January 1787 one
daily newspaper was reporting that there was little gaming in the clubs apart from
whist.[37] Venues in Pall Mall and St James's once denominated as 'gaming clubs' in
the press began by the end of the decade to be dubbed 'whist clubs.' Goostre's was
shuttered in 1789, its proprietor obliged to file civil actions to recover arrears of
subscriptions.[38] Gold tables for faro had hardly disappeared, however, as they
were now lodged in the securely 'private' settings of entertainments in elite townhouses. Public attention was soon focused on these operations, as ours is now
as well.

---

[33] *Gazetteer and New Daily Advertiser*, 17,207 (4 February 1784).
[34] *Public Advertiser*, 15,617 (15 June 1785).   [35] *World*, 516 (23 August 1788).
[36] Leslie Mitchell, 'Charles James Fox,' in *Brooks's 1764–2014*, 28.
[37] *World*, 18 (20 January 1787).   [38] *Morning Star*, 176 (4 September 1789).

11

At Home with Faro's Daughters

George Hanger claimed in his memoirs of 1801 that when he entered metropolitan society as a young guards officer in the early 1770s, 'there was no such thing
as a Faro table admitted into the house of a woman of fashion; in those days they
had too much pride to receive tribute from the proprietor of such a machine.'[1]
Hanger, of course, referred to the heyday of the subscription clubs then emerging
in the neighbourhood of St James's. A decade later, common report had it that
high-stakes gaming was a species of the elite vice that was increasingly a political
liability during the ascendancy of Pitt the Younger, and accordingly it was put
about in the press that hazard and faro had been banished from clubland in
favour of sober and respectable whist. At the same time, there were other
emphases in print media coverage of gaming that demonstrated new awareness of
the extent to which gaming operations, the 'machines' of which Hanger wrote,
were commercial concerns organized along the same lines as 'legitimate' enterprises. By the middle of the 1780s, the fourth Earl of Cholmondeley's faro bank
reportedly took in 40,000 guineas in a particularly successful winter 'without a
single run against it that threatened its fall'; a similar sum was realized that season
at Edward Burlton's much less select venue after all expenses were discharged.[2]
Notwithstanding earlier accounts of the eclipse of gaming at Brooks's, it was
reported in 1790 that the midsummer audit of the faro bank at the club showed a
profit of over £1,000,000 since its inception, a result that was still impressive when
the figure was revised to something over £700,000.[3] The potential profit to be
realized from commercial gaming ventures, especially at the upper end of the
market, made them highly attractive to prospective entrepreneurs, and once it
became common knowledge that proprietors of metropolitan faro banks could
realize an annual return as high as 30 per cent, the banks became desirable investment opportunities. The *Morning Post* pronounced itself 'very sorry to find' in
October 1791 'that our honest cit[izen]s are beginning to dabble in the swindling
dissipations at the West end of the town,' having discovered that two City
tradesmen had put up funds 'to establish a PHARO bank in a very notorious
gambling brothel in St. James's-street.' It was perhaps inevitable, as the same paper

---

[1] George Hanger, *The Life, Adventures, and Opinions of Colonel George Hanger*, 2 vols (London:
John Debrett, 1801), 2. 6.
[2] *Public Advertiser*, 16,414 (29 December 1786).
[3] *St. James's Chronicle*, 4574 (12 August 1790); *The World*, 1130 (17 August 1790).

The Gambling Century: Commercial Gaming in Britain from Restoration to Regency. John Eglin, Oxford University Press.
© John Eglin 2023. DOI: 10.1093/oso/9780192888198.003.0012

reported in March 1794, that a prospective investor would take out an advertisement offering £1,000 'for a share in any established Pharo-bank.'[4] In April of 1793, Frederick Reynolds's comedy *How to Grow Rich* premiered at Covent Garden. In the opening scene, the country banker Smalltrade, facing a liquidity crisis, learns from his cousin Miss Dazzle that she and her brother Sir Charles also keep a bank:

> Yes, such a bank! So opposite to yours! We know nothing of notes, checks, clerks, or currency. We don't rise early in the morning to settle our accounts, or shut up before evening to prevent our customers from settling theirs. No, all our business is done in the dark....[W]hile you are satisfied with a hundred pounds of profit in a week, we are not content with a thousand in a night, and if we ever stop payment,...we have nothing to surrender but mahogany tables, wax-lights, cards, and dice-boxes.

Smalltrade immediately solicits a partnership in the Dazzle's faro operation, reasoning that 'I've so long managed a trading bank, that I must understand a gambling one.' Knowing, however, that the faro bank is unlawful, Smalltrade asks his cousin whether a magistrate might not 'send you, I, and all the noble host of Faro to be whipt at the cart's tail?' He is told simply that '[g]old makes justice blind.'[5]

Thus while Philip Jennings Clarke had asserted in opposition to the E.O. Bill in 1782 that its sponsors had not 'paid sufficient attention to the Ladies,' the press would be paying attention soon enough, as the 'Faro Ladies' of St James's Square became increasingly conspicuous in metropolitan print culture. Some contemporary newspaper coverage had it that the craze for faro, pursued as a commercial venture in aristocratic townhouses under the colour of 'at-homes,' was driven by waves of emigration from revolutionary France in the 1790s. As early as December 1789, reports circulated of a faro bank of £10,000 established in Pall Mall under two purportedly titled Frenchmen who upon examination were found to be 'Chevaliers d'Industrie, who, no longer able to execute their very honourable employment in their own country, have emigrated to this.'[6] An item that appeared in September 1792, only days after hundreds of political suspects were massacred in Paris, warned of the imminent arrival of an estimated 40,000 French émigrés,

> two thirds of them of the lowest class, who, taking advantage of the convulsed state of their native country, come over, under the plausible title of *Exiled*

---

[4] *Morning Post*, 5762 (12 October 1791), 6515 (8 March 1794).
[5] Frederick Reynolds, *How to Grow Rich* (London: Longman, 1793), 5–6, 16.
[6] *Argus*, 225 (7 December 1789); *English Chronicle*, 1595 (10 December 1789).

Aristocrats. Let our Magistrates enquire after the gaming tables nightly open to the unwary, in the houses of suspected persons of the *above description*.[7]

This convention, taken at face value, made its way into an otherwise excellent article on the prosecution of the 'Faro Ladies' in 1796.[8] In fact, the floating faro banks of St James's Square were well established at least a decade before the first guillotine blade dropped across the Channel, and were garnering significant press attention at least a couple of years before the fall of the Bastille. One correspondent asserted in June 1787 that '[t]he best place in this country, in regard to an employment of profit, under the crown, is not the Prime Minister's,...but the *keeper* of the *Faro Table,* moving about, at the different great houses of the Nobility,' referring to the gaming entrepreneur Henry Martindale, whose faro concession netted a reported £30,000 annually.[9] Correlating the emergence of faro banks at routs with the influx of refugees from revolutionary violence (taxed like present-day refugees with importing the very civil unrest that they were fleeing) was another way of attacking opposition, now politically tarred with its early applause of constitutional reforms in France.

The famously dysfunctional dynamics of the ruling dynasty also played a role in the reconfiguration of elite gaming, as well as opposition politics, with a gaming-averse monarch scolding, for example, the Archbishop of Canterbury for permitting his spouse to hold 'routs,' large card parties, in Lambeth Palace. In marked contrast to the sovereign, prominent members of the royal family were gaming enthusiasts who played, partnered in banks, and even dealt:

The Duke of Cumberland holds a Pharaoh Bank, [and] deals standing the whole night....I have always by some accident been prevented from going to the Duke's Levée, which I am sorry for, as I am told his dealing at Pharaoh is the most ludicrous thing that can be conceived.[10]

Without securing the sovereign's permission, Cumberland had married a daughter of Simon Luttrell, Earl of Carhampton, putting Cumberland and his Luttrell connections out of favour. Cumberland's sister-in-law, Lady Elizabeth Luttrell, regularly hosted Henry Martindale's floating faro bank at her house in Pall Mall. The Prince of Wales, who followed the trend of Hanoverian heirs apparent as key patrons of opposition, was notoriously connected to a number of elite gaming concerns, both in clubs and private townhouses.

---

[7] *St. James's Chronicle*, 4920 (11 September 1792).
[8] Gillian Russell, ' "Faro's Daughters": Female Gamesters, Politics, and the Discourse of Finance in 1790s Britain,' *Eighteenth-Century Studies*, 33 (2000), 481.
[9] *World*, 156 (30 June 1787).   [10] HMC *Carlisle*, 575.

A Place at the Table

William Dent's caricature *The Road to Ruin,* published in March 1792, connected various manifestations of the culture of chance with the moral corruption associated with social and political elites, particularly the rising generation of the royal family. The Prince of Wales and Duke of Clarence sit astride racehorses with their mistresses, the Prince's racer drawn to represent an unshaven Charles James Fox, while Clarence's mount, slightly ahead, probably represents Pitt the Younger. The Duke of York, on foot, throws a pair of dice. Bringing up the rear, appropriately enough on a rocking horse labelled 'Faro,' is a figure representing Albinia Bertie Hobart, who became Countess of Buckinghamshire the following year. Other elements of the scene point to the consequences of gaming culture down the socioeconomic scale. The sun, shining from one corner, is labelled 'Chance' and represented as an E.O. wheel. Three young men, in the stovepipe hats and shawl-collared coats then the height of fashion, follow; one, on a horse labelled 'Lottery Hack' tumbles into a ditch, while another exclaims 'Damn Trade! Life and a racer! That's your sort!' An elderly City couple ride behind them, she in front riding astride in breeches, he behind in a skirt, warning '[w]e're on the wrong side of Temple Bar, my dear, we are only the sort to be laugh'd at.' On the horizon, a castle floats on a cloud labelled 'Illegal Insurance,' and in the corner, a Jewish financier exults over the interest he is able to charge and the collateral he is in a position to collect.[11] Where parvenu sharpers threatened at the beginning of the century to undo the heirs of landed fortunes, by its last decade it was the middling sort who were in peril of falling into the vortex of aristocratic vice.

As Hanger suggested, however, it was the involvement of elite women that loaded these emerging gaming concerns with their greatest shock value. There had been efforts to integrate women into elite gaming circles on the same basis as men, but these were unsuccessful. William Almack, proprietor of the club that was the major rival to White's (and that Brooks subsequently acquired), from at least May 1770 leased the 'Tea Room' in one of his properties to a 'Ladies' Club,' where gaming presumably took place, but the club apparently had difficulty attracting subscribers from the outset.[12] The 'Female Coterie,' as a uniformly hostile press dubbed it, met with further challenges in procuring a venue. The Thatched House Tavern in St James's Street was to be engaged in some reports, while others mentioned a house that Sir Sampson Gideon was vacating in Albemarle Street. By February 1772, George Selwyn was writing that this facility was moribund: 'I hear no more of the Ladies Club, than if there had never been such an Institution.' A little over a year later, one of Lord Grantham's correspondents wrote of a 'Ladies Club in Albemarle Street,' distinct from any of the clubs or

[11] George, *Personal and Political Satires,* 6. 8073.
[12] *Lloyd's Evening Post,* 2010 (21 May 1770).

assembly rooms in Almack's properties in Pall Mall and King Street.[13] After this date, there is no further mention of facilities for elite women organized on the same lines as clubs for men. Male observers, faced with the prospect of accommodations for women outside of family households, were much more alarmed at the prospect of adultery than of gaming.

The alarm that greeted women's involvement in high-stakes gaming was informed by a different set of anxieties than the prospect of financial ruin that accompanied male homosocial play. Gaming had always been seen to pose an additional moral hazard for women, as gaming debts owed to men could be deployed, it was thought, to leverage sexual favours, a possibility depicted in Hogarth's painting *The Lady's Last Stake*. It was a woman's virtue that was thought to be at primary risk, and the loss of fortune, whether hers or her family's, was only incidental. The Marquis of Halifax, in his *Advice to a Daughter* near the end of the previous century, relayed an inventory of reproaches that would be levelled at a woman who played for high stakes, culminating in the assertion that a man of her class who won money of her would 'be thought no unfair *Creditor,* if where the *Estate* faileth he seizeth upon the Person.'[14] In a satire of 1728, a husband whose spouse loses five hundred guineas in a single evening is advised

> No Matter Sir,
> Your wisest Way's to pay, not question her,
> Lest by strict Honour taught, if you delay,
> This needful Debt she with her Person pay,
> And for refusing this so just Demand,
> The Sharper get an Heir to all your Land.[15]

Assumptions like these doomed the 'Female Coterie,' and subsequently dogged the 'Faro Ladies.' It did not help their case that in the 1780s, before the faro banks at their regular assemblies became common knowledge in print culture, the only metropolitan gaming concerns known to be operated by women were associated with brothels, including two high-end accommodations, 'Mother Wilden's' in Pall Mall and the 'Abbey' in King's Place. A writer to the *Town and Country Magazine* identified two brothels in the parish of St Marylebone 'where there are E.O. tables, under the auspices of two lady abbesses, where their nuns assist, and act in the double capacity of sharpers and female seducers.'[16] If women of the *beau monde*

---

[13] *Lloyd's Evening Post*, 2008 (16–18 May 1770); *Middlesex Journal*, 194 (26–28 June 1770), 209 (31-July–2 August 1770); Wrest Park MSS, L 30/14/350/1a, 196/2.

[14] George Savile, Marquis of Halifax, *The Lady's New Year's Gift, or Advice to a Daughter* (London: Randal Taylor, 1688), 160.

[15] *Marriage: A Satire*, 20.

[16] *Morning Post*, 3779 (21 March 1785), 3792 (5 April 1785); *Town and Country Magazine*, 13 (October 1781), 509.

were to gamble as high as their male counterparts, it would have to be in company with men in domestic settings. Anna Clark speculates that it was the failure of the 'Coterie' that gave rise to the gaming concerns, hosted by the celebrated 'Faro Ladies', that operated out of aristocratic households in St James's Square over the next two decades.[17]

Horace Walpole, writing to Henry Seymour Conway in March 1781, suggested that both established banks at subscription clubs and those that floated among the townhouses of St James's Square were of relatively recent origin. He naively predicted that none of these ventures would prosper for very long, as '[t]he bankers find that all the calculated advantages do not balance pinchbeck *parolis* and debts of honourable women.'[18] Other evidence suggests, along the lines of Walpole's observation, that if women without immediate access to the same resources as men could not be relied on to settle gaming debts promptly, if at all, that was simply a cost of doing business. Walpole told an illustrative story at the expense of Henry Martindale, the manager of the largest of the elite gaming syndicates. 'Pray delight in the following story,' he wrote to his literary executor, Mary Berry:

> Caroline Vernon, *fille d'honneur*, lost t'other night £200 at faro, and bade Martindale mark it up: he said he had rather have a draft on her banker—oh! willingly; and she gave him one. Next morning he hurried to Drummond's, lest all her money should be drawn out. 'Sir,' said the clerk, 'would you receive the contents immediately?' 'Assuredly.' 'Why, Sir, have you read the note? Martindale took it; it was, 'Pay to the bearer 200 blows well applied.'[19]

The anxiety induced in elite gaming circles by the compulsive gambling of the Duchess of Devonshire also bears this understanding out. Lady Mary Coke recalled the Duchess joining a faro game in progress at the Countess of Ailesbury's in May 1783, operating under the strict proviso that no player was to borrow from the bank. As she had no ready money, the Duchess begged ten guineas from Henry Seymour Conway, which she quickly lost. She then prevailed on the bank to lend her sixty guineas, against everyone's better judgement. This time she won, and was on her way out the door when she was quietly reminded of her debt to Conway, which she very apologetically paid. The rest of the company was so relieved at her departure that it was half an hour before anyone recollected that she had not repaid the bank.[20] The reported bankruptcy of a number of faro

---

[17] Anna Clark, *Scandal: The Sexual Politics of the British Constitution* (Princeton: Princeton University Press, 2004), 51.

[18] HWC, 39. 375, 377.   [19] HWC, 11. 184–5.

[20] Amanda Foreman, *Georgiana Duchess of Devonshire* (New York: Random House, 1998), 123–4.

operations in the autumn of 1797 was attributed 'to the *mauvaise foi* of the gaming Ladies, who played upon tick.'[21]

Even in these safely domestic settings, gaming women did not escape the imputation of sexual incontinence that accompanied high play. Double entendres, for example, were commonplace in press coverage of women prominent in elite gaming concerns. One writer complained in 1795 of faro hostesses luring young officers to their tables 'who have not been long enough in the army to wear out their first cockades.'[22] Sarah Archer (figure 11.1) was a particular target during the last decade of the century. According to Charles Pigott, she was 'a perfect mistress of all our *polite, fashionable arts*,' including '*raising a cock* at Faro (an expression much used at the intricate and pleasant game..., and a *practice never omitted, when an opportunity offers*).'[23] After Major Baggs, a gaming enthusiast fallen on hard times, died in custody after a gaming-house raid, the *Oracle* related that '[t]he *Muff* which MAJOR BAGGS used to wear when playing at *Pharo,* and which he found to be so lucky, he has bequeathed to Lady ARCHER, her Muff being old, and a good deal out of repair.'[24]

Figure 11.1 James Gillray, *Modern Hospitality*, 1795. ©National Portrait Gallery, London. Sarah West Archer was one of the most prominent of the 'Faro Ladies.'

[21] *Times*, 4000 (16 September 1797).   [22] Quoted in Ashton, *Gambling in England*, 80.
[23] Charles Pigott, *The Female Jockey Club, or a Sketch of the Manners of the Age* (London: D. L. Eaton, 1794), 101.
[24] *Oracle*, 817 (9 January 1792).

Rouleaux and Routs

By the beginning of the 1780s, these free-floating commercial concerns were already finding their way from subscription clubs into domestic entertainments. 'The Pharaoh bankers are in excessive great fashion,' Storer informed Carlisle in May of 1781; '[t]hey are sent for to hold banks, and as much interest is made to have them as there ever was to have Texier,' referring to Antoine Le Texier, a theatrical manager who was famous for dramatic monologues. One faro banker, Sir Willoughby Aston, circulated 'with his Strong box and his memorandum book. Each lady has her day set down in his book, exactly as if he was the physician, to wait upon them at such a particular hour.' Another was reportedly 'worn out in being kept up at one Lady's house or another till six in the morning.' Several months later, Storer related that '[t]here are now so many banks that the market is overstocked.' George Selwyn was much in demand as a faro banker for a time, reporting two requests to hold banks at entertainments hosted by a Mrs St John and a Mrs Crewe, which he begged off:

> *Je renonce à tout cela; les inconvéniens en sont innombrables* [I have renounced all that; its disadvantages are innumerable]; all my play at present is confined to a rubber at whist, and a little Pharo with Ailsford, and perhaps two or three more. *Le grand évènement c'est la perte or la gain de* [the great result is the loss or gain of] 50 or 80 guineas.[25]

By the momentous year of 1789, the presence of high-stakes faro operations in domestic settings under elite hostesses was public knowledge. 'You have heard of public gaming houses, against which there are so many laws,' a magazine piece had a fictitious young lady in town write to her correspondent in the country, speculating on her reaction to 'a Pharo-table established in a private house' with a hostess who 'appears in the two-fold character of Lady of Quality, and principal partner of a Pharo-Bank.'[26] Alongside the private subscription clubs that became a staple of elite sociability structured around gaming were the putatively domestic gaming venues constituted in the at-homes in elite households superintended by socially conspicuous hostesses. Unlike Ladies Mordington and Casillis decades earlier, the faro hostesses of St James's Square possessed unimpeachable social credentials.

---

[25] HMC *Carlisle*, 485–7, 582. The 'Sir William Areton' mentioned in the HMC volume is a mistranscription; there is an earlier reference to a bank kept by 'Sir W. Aston.' Aston married a daughter of Lord Chancellor Northington, and later merited an entry in Pigott's *Jockey Club* (Cokayne, *Complete Baronetage*, 2. 49); Charles Pigott, *The Jockey Club, or a Sketch of the Manners of the Age* (London: D.H. Symonds, 1792, 113–15).
[26] *Walker's Hibernian Magazine* (December 1789), 712.

Lady Archer, the former Sarah West, was one of the four most prominent 'Faro Ladies' by the 1790s. She was a widow, her husband, Andrew, second Lord Archer of Umberslade, having died in 1778. Coincidentally, he was the grandnephew of Thomas Archer, the Groom Porter. Charles Pigott related that Lady Archer's income had been reduced significantly at the marriage of her eldest daughter to the fifth Earl of Plymouth in 1788, which resulted in the bulk of the Archer estate being transferred to the new Countess. This circumstance explained Lady Archer's recourse to hosting faro banks as well as her notorious parsimony, guests at her routs complaining 'that when lemons are dear, she makes her *lemonade* of *cream of tartar,* which is apt very much to agitate their noble intestines, and to produce a most *unpleasant* effect in the company.'[27] Sarah Archer was the most frequently caricatured of the 'Faro Ladies,' along with Albinia Bertie, granddaughter of the Duke of Ancaster, married to the Hon. George Hobart, who succeeded his elder half-brother as third Earl of Buckinghamshire in 1793. While the second Earl's title was transferred, his estates passed to his daughters, and while George Hobart had inherited an estate in Lincolnshire from a distant relative, his spouse reportedly found its income insufficient to support her new title. Lady Buckinghamshire was coincidentally the sister-in-law of the faro entrepreneur Lord Cholmondeley, who had married Georgianna Bertie in April 1791. At 33 St James's Square, spectacularly rebuilt and expanded by Robert Adam, the Buckinghamshires were next-door neighbours to Beilby Porteous, the Bishop of London.[28] Among the 'Faro Ladies,' Sarah Richmond Concannon was overshadowed somewhat by her husband, Lucius, an Irish half-pay officer, and according to the scandalmongering *Town and Country Magazine* an archetypal gaming parvenu, identified as the son of a Dublin tobacconist (when he was actually a nephew) who arrived in England 'a stranger without friends, money, or expectations.' His present circumstances belied that inauspicious beginning, as Concannon rented a house at £200 a year, kept a fleet of sleek new carriages, and 'though no more than a dealer at Pharo, gives the most princely entertainments of any man in this kingdom.'[29] The fourth was Mary Pitfield Sturt, another wealthy widow who had inherited a large estate in Shoreditch and in 1756 had married Humphrey Sturt, MP for Dorset, who died in 1784. Her son Charles was MP for Bridport, a member of the Foxite opposition, and a friend of the Prince of Wales.[30]

As was the case with subscription clubs, these domestic entertainments were profitable enterprises overseen by commercial gaming entrepreneurs and bankrolled, for the most part, by elite males. A typical faro bank, one tract helpfully explained, would be established by one or more individuals, 'who deposit between

---

[27] Pigott, *Female Jockey Club*, 102, 106–7.   [28] *Survey of London*, 29. 205–7.
[29] *Town and Country Magazine*, 22 (July 1790), 308.
[30] *Complete Peerage*, 1. 188, 2. 403; Roland G. Thorne, *The House of Commons 1790–1820,* 5 vols (London: History of Parliament Trust, 1986), 3. 491, 5. 317; Lewis B. Namier and John Brooke, *The House of Commons 1754–1790,* 3 vols (London: History of Parliament Trust, 1964), 3. 507.

them from five hundred to a thousand guineas, agreeing to bank again in case that should unfortunately be lost.'[31] In May of 1787, Daniel Pulteney requested a loan of £1,000 from the Duke of Rutland toward the £1,500 he needed for a one quarter stake in a faro bank; in this case, the other partners included three women, namely the Duchess of Devonshire, her sister Lady Duncannon, and Lady Harrington. This exception proved the rule, however, in that other faro partnerships were reluctant to admit these three, as it was known that the Duchess was in debt to most of the fashionable faro banks in the metropolis. Pulteney apparently received the loan, as he was thanking Rutland for his assistance a month later.[32] About two years later, Thomas Meyrick, an army officer, 'put a small sum of money into a faro Bank with Lord Cholmondely, Lord Hampden and Mr. Concannon,' as Meyrick subsequently confessed to the Earl Fitzwilliam. In 1787, Meyrick had married the natural daughter and sole heir of Admiral Keppel, which 'brought him a handsome acquisition of fortune.'[33] The same type of gaming entrepreneurship prevailed in these settings as in the private men's clubs of Pall Mall and St James's. If faro banks in clubs or private households in the parish of St James were not bankrolled by the same investors, they were administered by the same personnel. The pseudonymous writer 'Charles Sedley' evoked the atmosphere of an at-home in St James's Square in *The Faro Table, or The Gambling Mothers* of 1808:

> After Supper, the company began to retire; when FARO was announced. A celebrated dealer had been transported, from Saint James's Street, with his Bank and train — his croupiers, his figures, his livrets, his blue crosses, his yellow cards, his red cards, and his black lozenges — and, thus marshalled,...he invited the punters to take seats: assuring them, that the bank — which, by the bye, was the joint property of some of our first nobility — would answer the punter to any amount.... The long green table was adorned with packs of sealed cards, and the bank was filled with rouleaus of twenty-five, or fifty, guineas each.... 'Ace wins' — 'king loses' — were the monotonous, and only, tones heard round the table.[34]

The career of Henry Martindale, the best known of a family of gaming entrepreneurs, bears this reality out. His brother John Martindale appears in August 1775 as the 'Master' of White's, and by the next decades White's was often known

[31] *Faro and Rouge et Noir* (London: John Debrett, 1793), 30.   [32] HMC *Rutland*, 3. 388, 393.
[33] Sheffield Archives, Wentworth Woodhouse Muniments WWM/F 27/80, reproduced with permission from the Milton (Peterborough) Estates Company and the Director of Communities, Sheffield City Council; the Wentworth Woodhouse papers have been accepted in lieu of Inheritance Tax by HM Government and allocated to Sheffield City Council; *Gentleman's Magazine*, 100 (July 1830), 2. 87.
[34] Charles Sedley, *The Faro Table*, 2 vols (London: J.F. Hughes, 1808), 1. 88–9, 2. 74–5. 'Sedley' was possibly the publisher J.F. Hughes, who was threatened with litigation by John King, born Jacob Rey, the financier who was the second husband of the faro hostess Lady Lanesborough.

interchangeably as 'Martindale's.'[35] In addition to the gaming tables at White's, Martindale ran a floating gaming operation through private residences in and adjacent to St James's Square. By 1787, he was said to derive an annual income of £30,000 from this concession.[36] At an assembly at Carlton House hosted by the Prince of Wales in January 1790, Martindale's faro bank reportedly netted £2,000, notwithstanding John Willett Payne, the Prince's private secretary, winning a thousand guineas.[37] At the end of the following year, there were plans to expand operations into Bath, in the form of a subscription club in Laura Place, to be equipped with tables for faro, hazard and E.O.[38] So well established was the Martindale operation that the faro concern comprised of the brothers and their underwriters came to be known in the London press as 'the Firm,' and over the course of the decade, that term was applied widely to partnerships in gaming concerns in upmarket venues in St James's and Pall Mall as well less upscale operations in Oxendon Street and elsewhere.[39] Other clubs pursued this arrangement as well, Griffiths, the manager at Brooks's, receiving twenty-five guineas a night to run the faro tables at Mary Sturt's twice-weekly assemblies in St James's Square, club staff presiding as dealers.[40] '[A]n *itinerant* Faro bank' operated by a gaming concern, readers of the *Gazetteer* were informed,

> is as pretty a device, and as honest a calling, as any in the world; for it eases ladies and gentlemen of a great deal of trouble, and is besides mighty convenient, as it is the cheapest treat that a lady can give.[41]

There were suggestions that even lower-end gaming concerns in Covent Garden had a stake in elite townhouse operations, one observer relating that much of the material apparatus of gaming, such as the specially configured tables for faro, were 'provided by a set of *gentlemen* in the other end of the town, who make a comfortable livelihood by lending out their furniture *per* night.'[42]

The coordination of gaming operations between clubs and at-homes was conspicuous enough that a commentator in March 1791 could assert that '[p]rivate houses are now become *public places* under the name of *routs*.' Given considerable doubt that the magistracy of St James's would obtrude itself in this traffic, there was speculation that social sanctions might succeed where legal consequences were unlikely. Queen Charlotte was rumoured to have considered barring from Court 'all notorious female gamblers,' only to be advised 'that very thin

[35] Wrest Park MSS L/30/14/361/8; HMC *Carlisle*, 458; *Morning Post*, 5793 (19 November 1791).
[36] *World*, 156 (30 June 1787).   [37] *Whitehall Evening Post*, 6467 (14 January 1790).
[38] *Morning Post*, 5793 (19 November 1791).
[39] *Morning Post*, 5806 (2 December 1791); *World*, 2110 (2 October 1793); *Morning Post*, 7518 (5 April 1796).
[40] *Evening Mail*, 461 (6 February 1792).   [41] *Gazetteer*, 19,085 (5 February 1790).
[42] *St. James's Chronicle*, 4667 (15 March 1791); *Universal Magazine*, 89 (July 1791), 29.

Drawing-rooms would be the result.' The *Morning Post* in particular promoted this approach to suppressing elite gaming, at least among women, throughout the year 1791. The newspaper recounted rumours of the refusal of a faro hostess's effort to arrange a court presentation for her croupier, perhaps the same hostess subsequently rumoured to be *engaged* to her croupier.[43] Readers of the *Post* were regaled that same summer with the story of a maid of honour in disgrace at court after pawning a diamond necklace 'to pursue her ill luck at the Pharo table of a well-known lady of fashion,' who again may or may not have been '[t]he *Maid of Honour* who got the *black eye* last winter, in a fracas at a fashionable *Pharo table*.' *That* courtier, the *Post's* readers were informed, 'received intimation, that if she ever *cocks* or *punts* again, that she shall be forbid the Royal Presence!' The timing of these rumours was instructive, as the King's younger brother, Henry, Duke of Cumberland, known to keep a faro table at which he dealt himself, had died in September 1790, before which it may have been awkward to banish faro operators from court. It was still uncomfortable enough that Cumberland's widow continued to keep her late husband's bank, and that her sister, Lady Elizabeth Luttrell, was also a noted faro hostess. Caroline Vernon, whom Horace Walpole placed at a faro table operated by Henry Martindale around this time, continued in attendance on the Queen until Charlotte's death in 1818; whether she mended her ways, or no royal ultimatum was delivered, is not known.[44]

Pigott related that while Cumberland House was 'not so extensive, or magnificent' as Carlton House, the residence of the Prince of Wales, under the widowed Duchess it was still 'the receptacle of all the elegance and fashion in town. Her Faro Table is the best attended; consequently, the profits arising from it the most considerable.' The Duchess and her sister managed the operation 'with all imaginable decorum.' Within two years, however, Pigott was reporting that Cumberland House was 'shut up, and the faro bank, over which Lady El[i]z[a]b[e]th was wont to preside, either entirely annihilated, or removed to a more obscure corner of the town, where persons of her *elevated* condition cannot often appear with *consistency* or *propriety*.' Thomas Nelson, whom rumour related had gotten his start as coachman to the famed courtesan Charlotte Hays, was successively proprietor of gaming operations in Soho and the vicinity of the Strand, and had by 1791 taken over what had been Almack's at 56 Pall Mall. The cessation of faro at Cumberland House presented an opportunity Nelson was quick to seize, illuminating his front windows 'to decoy the refuse of the Cumberland House Party, several of whom condescended to mix with the very *lowest* description of Greeks about town.' Several days earlier, Sarah Archer had purchased the Duchess of Cumberland's faro bank.[45]

---

[43] *Morning Post*, 5581 (17 March 1791); 5615 (25 April 1791); 5650 (4 June 1791); 5661 (17 June 1791).
[44] *Morning Post*, 5658 (14 June 1791); 5719 (23 August 1791); HWC, 11. 184.
[45] Pigott, *Jockey Club*, 3. 82–3; *Female Jockey Club*, 182–3; *Morning Post*, 5813 (22 December 1791); *Star*, 1132 (12 December 1791).

Despicable Exhibitions

Lord Kenyon, Chief Justice of the Court of King's Bench, confronted (as a later chapter will show) with a number of unsuccessful gaming prosecutions, as well as with his own problematic rulings on gaming credit in civil actions, threatened in May of 1796 to put anyone convicted before him of violations of the Gaming Acts in the pillory, 'though they should be the first ladies in the land.' Around the same time, John Tobin's play *The Faro Table* was read in the green room of Drury Lane and received favourably, Richard Brinsley Sheridan as manager tentatively approving it for production the next season. It was subsequently withdrawn, however, over concerns that it was too similar to Sheridan's own *School for Scandal,* but also from a worry that the character of Lady Nightshade, an aristocratic widow who is a faro hostess, might be taken to represent Sarah Archer, whom Tobin protested he knew neither personally nor by reputation. Since Lady Nightshade in the course of the action is implicated, among other things, in the theft of a diamond necklace, the Drury Lane management ostensibly feared exposure to litigation.[46] As an MP, Sheridan had been a conspicuous opponent of the E.O. Bill and other efforts to proscribe gaming, citing the government's hypocritical sponsoring of lotteries. He had also been accused of being concerned in faro operations himself. 'What an assurance in Mr. Sheridan to oppose lotteries,' one correspondent had exclaimed in 1790; '[l]et him look to his Pharo Table!'[47] It also happened that Kenyon's threat, it seemed, was very nearly made good when Lady Buckinghamshire reported the theft of the faro bank from her house (figure 11.2). This was not the first such instance, as she had reported the bank stolen in 1792; Sarah Concannon reported a similar theft in 1795. These reports were greeted sceptically, as it was suspected that a run of luck for the punters or other financial contingencies would result in the partners pocketing the bank. In this case, however, the theft resulted in the prosecutions of the bank's operators. About six weeks after the theft was reported, the two footmen whom Lady Buckinghamshire had identified as the suspects informed against her and against Lady Elizabeth Luttrell, Mary Sturt, Lucius Concannon, and Henry Martindale before Justice Conant.

The informations were heard in court on 14 March 1797, and were excerpted in several newspapers. Lady Elizabeth Luttrell was charged with playing faro at the Earl of Buckinghamshire's on 30 January. George Evett, one of the Buckinghamshires' dismissed servants, testified that faro had been played there every Monday and Friday from the beginning of the season, after the middle of November, that Lady Elizabeth had played on the day in question as well as on 27 January, when Lady Buckinghamshire had managed the faro table. Evett

---

[46] Elizabeth Benger, *Memoirs of John Tobin* (London: Longman, 1820), 67–9, 157–8.
[47] *Public Advertiser*, 17,408 (23 April 1790).

Figure 11.2 James Gillray, *The Loss of the Faro Bank*, 1796. ©National Portrait Gallery, London. Albinia Bertie Hobart, Countess of Buckinghamshire, another faro hostess, depicted with her husband George Hobart, third Earl of Buckinghamshire, Sarah Richmond Concannon, Lucius Concannon, Richard Brinsley Sheridan, Charles James Fox, and Lady Archer.

disclosed that there was also an E.O. table operating. The defence attorney noted that the witness was a suspected felon, and that Thomas Kennet, Lady Elizabeth's manservant, had testified that Lady Elizabeth was not at Lady Buckinghamshire's at all on the night specified in the information. Henry Martindale stood charged with keeping the faro table at the Buckinghamshires, Joseph Burford testifying that four or five croupiers and tellers were each paid ten shillings a night to super-intend the table, at which 'there were frequent quarrels and wranglings...about cheating.'[48] The guilty parties were chiefly players, according to a report in the *Times,* which related that '[t]hough every table has four croupiers, yet the Bank holders find that double that number are necessary to watch all the little tricks and artifices of some of the *fashionable punters.*'[49]

The end result was a summary conviction before Justice Conant in the magis-trates' offices in Marlborough Street. Lady Buckinghamshire, Lady Archer, and

---

[48] *General Evening Post*, 10,044 (11 March 1797); the same account appeared in *Lloyd's Evening Post, London Chronicle, Whitehall Evening Post,* and the *Star.*

[49] *Times* (4 April 1794), quoted in Ashton, *Gambling in England,* 81.

Lady Elizabeth Luttrell were each assessed £50, the statutory fine for gaming, and Martindale was fined £200 for keeping a gaming table. At this point, of course, these very well-connected gaming operators could have appealed their case into King's Bench, but in the circumstances, they didn't dare appear before Lord Kenyon. The months between Kenyon's warning and the final resolution of the case witnessed a spate of caricatures, showing various of the Faro Ladies in the pillory, and comparing them with street prostitutes in St Giles, and being flogged at the cart's tail by Lord Kenyon himself. In one caricature (figure 11.3), four of the faro hostesses stand in the pillory, while Fox sits in stocks underneath one, suggestively shrouded in her skirts. Gillian Russell argues that these images effected what they depicted in the public humiliation of 'Faro's Daughters.' At least one newspaper report supported this contention, relating that 'Lady B[uckinghamshire] has expended the whole profits of her Faro-table in suppressing her likeness in the pillory,' despite Lady Elizabeth Luttrell having 'advised her friend to despise the exhibition.'[50]

Kenyon's threat was all the more remarkable given that highly placed individuals known to him, even the judiciary elite, stood to be tarred in the prosecution of the 'Faro Ladies.' Among those implicated by the Buckinghamshires' footmen

Figure 11.3 Isaac Cruikshank, *Faro's Daughters*, 1797. ©Trustees of the British Museum. Lord Kenyon's threat to put gaming operators in the pillory, 'though they be the first ladies in the land,' resulted in a number of prints on this theme.

---

[50] Russell, 'Faro's Daughters,' 490–6; *Evening Mail* (3 September 1796).

was Matthias O'Byrne, who was presented both for keeping a faro bank, and for playing at St James's Square. He denied ever having kept a faro bank, and denied playing on the night mentioned in the information, but admitted that he had played within the last six months, 'and he should, no doubt, amuse himself in the same manner again.' When queried whether he was aware that playing faro was unlawful, O'Byrne professed ignorance, remarking only that both the current and former Lords Chancellor 'had stood at the back of his chair while he was at play' without either of them offering any admonition, nor was O'Byrne certain that the Prime Minister had never seen him play. He did not fail to note, either, that he had regularly played hazard with one of the presiding magistrate's fellow justices.[51]

The case of the 'Faro Ladies' resulted in an exposé of metropolitan gaming operations that focused unprecedented attention on their structure as commercial enterprises. Although faro hostesses in St James's Square continued to be the public face of the scandal, it was clear to many observers that their spouses were the active partners in these operations (although Lady Buckinghamshire's contention that she should be spared a fine as a *femme couverte* unable to pay was dismissed). The prologue to Frederick Reynolds' *The Will*, which opened at Drury Lane shortly after the trial, made this arrangement plain to its audiences:

> Still the High Gamester and obedient Mate
> Veil deep-laid schemes in hospitable state;
> Pharo, though routed, still may Justice dare,
> Fine a few pounds, and many a thousand share.[52]

Similarly, in Gillray's print *The Loss of the Faro Bank, or, The Rooks Pigeon'd*, it is Lord Buckinghamshire who reports the theft of the bank to his spouse, who deals at a table at which the Concannons, Fox, and Lady Archer sit.[53]

Neither the conviction of Henry Martindale nor those of 'Faro's Daughters' put an end to gaming operations in St James's. One of the hostesses was said to have paid her fine out of the proceeds of a single night's winnings, and dropped her appeal. This may or may not have been Sarah Archer, who reportedly planned to reopen her faro bank for the approaching winter season, 'in open defiance of Lord K[enyon] and the *pillory*.'[54] George Hanger attested in 1801 that

> [i]f a gentleman in these days has but a few guineas in his purse, and will walk directly up to the Faro table, he will be the most welcome guest in the house; it is

---

[51] *London Chronicle*, 5899 (14 March 1797). The Chancellors in question were Alexander Wedderburn, Lord Loughborough (subsequently Earl of Rosslyn), in office from 1793 to 1801, and Edward, Lord Thurlow, who served from 1778 to 1792.

[52] Frederick Reynolds, *The Will: A Comedy in Five Acts* (London: G.G. and J. Robinson, 1797), v–vi.

[53] George, *Personal and Political Satires*, 7. 9078.

[54] *St. James's Chronicle*, 6136 (18 April 1797); *Observer*, 305 (8 October 1797).

not necessary for him to speak, or even bow, to a single lady in the room, unless some unfortunate woman at the gaming-table ask him politely for the loan of a few guineas: then his answer need be but short – 'No, Dolly, no; can't;' for this ever will be received as wit.[55]

John Tobin's play *The Faro Table* was proposed again at Drury Lane in 1806 after Sarah Archer's death, and two years after Tobin's own demise, only for its rejection to be repeated on the grounds that it might still be read as an actionable attack on the now dowager Countess of Buckinghamshire, still an active faro hostess. In 1813, Tobin's brother James wrote the Drury Lane management that as there were 'no more peeresses or ladies of quality standing in the way,' his deceased brother's play might finally be staged. In November 1816, after Lady Buckinghamshire's death, it finally premiered at Drury Lane, twenty years after its initial 'table read,' but under a different title, *The Guardians*. It was not a success, having only nine performances, and the houses were too thin for the management to justify 'the customary remuneration' to Tobin's estate.[56] As *au courant* as it may have been when Tobin finished it, by the time it was performed it was a comedy of manners that targeted habits long out of fashion. One reviewer remarked that Tobin 'might as well have produced the wigs, ruffs, and hoops which we remember our fathers to have described as the daily costume of their youth,' adding for good measure that no character like Lady Nightshade was 'ever beheld in the present day, or in any time near the present day.'[57] Faro's Daughter was as much a museum piece as any of the artefacts that Napoleon had appropriated from Egypt, having disappeared as elite sensibilities around games of chance had shifted. We will return to explore the character of this transition and the reasons for it, but the still-thriving gaming culture outside the rarefied atmosphere of St James's Square requires our attention once again.

[55] Hanger, *Life and Opinions*, 2. 5–6.   [56] Benger, *Memoirs of John Tobin*, 157–8.
[57] *Bell's Court and Fashionable Magazine*, 86 (November 1816), 233.

12

Breaking Even

Gaming Entrepreneurship at Century's End

While Thomas Rowlandson's 1791 watercolour purports to show hazard played in
a 'subscription room' (figure 12.1), it is safe to say that he was not depicting one of
the elite venues in the parish of St James Piccadilly. The players and onlookers in
Rowlandson's picture are a motley collection, some better dressed than others,
some presentable and others grotesque, like the pockmarked and toothless standing figure, whose shillelagh is probably intended to stereotype him as Irish.
A portrait of Hoyle overlooks the room, as do representations of a winning caster
('The Caster In') and a losing one ('The Caster Out'). Above the door is an
ostensible calculation of the odds at hazard that reads

Figure 12.1 Thomas Rowlandson, *The Subscription Club Room*, 1791. The Clark Art
Institute, Williamstown MA. A number of down-market gaming venues in
neighbourhoods like Leicester Square coexisted with upscale operations in clubs and
townhouses in St James's.

The Gambling Century: Commercial Gaming in Britain from Restoration to Regency. John Eglin, Oxford University Press.
© John Eglin 2023. DOI: 10.1093/oso/9780192888198.003.0013

5 to 4 That you get [stripped] of all your Property
4 to 3 That you endeavor to recruit upon the Highway
2 to 1 That you come to be Hanged.

It is more likely that Rowlandson intended one of the more modest establishments enumerated in Patrick Colquhoun's 1796 census of the criminal under-
ground of the metropolis. Apart from the clubs of St James's and the Faro Ladies'
'at-homes,' Colquhoun counted around thirty gaming houses, defined as 'houses
opened for the express purpose of play,' in the City of Westminster.[1] These more
publicly accessible gaming venues were concentrated in the streets between
Haymarket and Leicester Fields, in streets north and south of the latter, and, as
always, in and around Covent Garden, in addition to a few more modest venues
in St James's Street, operating in the shadow of the clubs. One small-scale operation, consisting of a single faro table, occupied a room above a china shop in
St James's Street, while at another, that of the gaming entrepreneur Augustus de
Heine at the corner of Pall Mall, the bank was established at a relatively modest
£250.[2] When Thomas Moore was tried before Lord Kenyon in December 1799 for
keeping a gaming house at 6 Oxendon Street, the prosecution brief reported no
fewer than five such operations in that street, along with 'two or three' in Panton
Street which bisected it, and others scattered between Haymarket and Leicester
Fields. They were open at all hours, 'assembling Persons of every description' to
play mostly at Rouge et Noir, 'being very profitable to the Keepers of the Tables,'
and not one of the games enumerated in the first Georgian statute, so that 'the
Penalties of that Statute cannot be recovered against them.' When the constables
initially arrested Moore in November of 1796, they found two French emigrants,
both priests, who were only in the house to sit by the fire, and cadge a meal from
'the Viands at the Side-Board with which these Houses are always furnished gratis'; Moore was 'in the Act of turning them out, because they would not play.' In
addition to the hapless priests, Moore's clientele was very socially heterogeneous.
Apart from one punter purported to be 'a notorious Highwayman,' there were
also 'some Gentlemen of Character,' in addition to a couple of merchants, an
attorney, an ambassador's secretary, and a captain of dragoons; the artisanal class
was represented by a shoemaker and a breeches-maker, along with a number of
apprentices. There were also several valets, a hairdresser, and 'a Black Musician.'[3]
In August of 1796, constables visited 6 Lisle Street, listed as the property of Henry,
Jonathan, and William Oldfield on the warrant issued when an informant
disclosed that it was 'a notorious gaming house.' The house was distinguished

[1] Patrick Colquhoun, *A Treatise on the Police of the Metropolis* (London: H. Fry for Charles Dilly,
1796), x.
[2] *Morning Post*, 5800 (25 November 1791), 5803 (29 November 1791), 5807 (3 December 1791),
6460 (3 January 1794).
[3] TNA TS 11/931/3301, ff 1–4.

only by its number plate, mounted on a swivel so that the porter could observe any visitors to the house through an aperture in the door. This porter received weekly wages of one guinea from a Mr Jones in the City, who was probably an underwriter of the bank. After being admitted 'with great difficulty,' the constables found only two other men in the house apart from the porter: a Frenchman claiming to be an exiled count, and a merchant's clerk who asserted that 'his only business in the house was to see a lady.' The officers seized tables for hazard, E.O., and Rouge et Noir, and also a table for a game called Russian War, as well as 'a great quantity of playing cards' and a number of gaming tokens, redeemable at the house for crowns and half-crowns. The information on 6 Lisle Street stated that notwithstanding its security measures, it was 'a common gaming-house, open to all parties.'[4]

As ever, these middle-range establishments strove to attract an affluent clientele. Newspapers described lavish amenities on offer even away from the charmed precincts of St James's. Patrons of establishments in Oxendon Street and vicinity, it was reported, 'live in a stile of unprecedented luxury and dissipation,' court testimony relating that dinners offered at these eight or nine venues cost an estimated £150,000 annually.[5] In the Court of King's Bench in November 1797, Joseph and Mary Atkinson were identified as the proprietors of many years' standing of a gaming house at 15 Covent Garden Piazza, where 'different games at cards, dice and E.O. were continually going on' from dusk until dawn:

> They, daily, gave magnificent play dinners; cards of invitation for which were sent to the clerks of merchants, bankers and brokers in the city. Atkinson used to say he liked citizens…better than any one else, for, when they had dined, they played freely; and, after they had lost all their money, they had credit to borrow more.[6]

As the verdicts on the 'Faro Ladies' were handed down, an analysis of the 'Rise and Progress of the Present System of Gaming' appeared in newspapers that pointed to an 'extensive system of Gaming in the metropolis' that had emerged over the course of the previous two decades, and was now in a position 'to threaten to draw into its vortex a very considerable portion of the circulating property of the metropolis.' News media were now sounding the alarm, decades, of course, after the fire had started:

[4] *London Packet*, 4209 (5 August 1796); *Lloyd's Evening Post*, 6078 (8 August 1796); *Oracle*, 19,394 (8 August 1796); *True Briton*, 1129 (8 August 1796). In Rouge et Noir, played with cards, punters staked on which of two sequences of cards, labeled 'red' and 'black,' would reach a point total equal to or exceeding thirty-one, without going over forty. Strictly speaking, wagers were placed on colours, rather than the 'numbers or figures' stipulated in the statutes.

[5] *London Packet*, (27 May 1796).   [6] Ashton, *Gambling in England*, 87.

The mind shrinks with horror at the existence of a system in the metropolis, unknown to our ancestors, even in the worst periods of their dissipation;...for then no regular establishments—no systematic concerns for carrying on this nefarious trade, were known. Partnerships in Gaming-Houses, conducted on the principles of commercial establishments, is a new idea in this country; and, until the last seven or eight years, had very little footing in the metropolis.

Prior to 1777, the writer claimed, gaming operations did not *appear* 'to have been conducted upon the methodized system of partnership-concerns, wherein pecuniary capitals are embarked.' The proliferation of E.O. tables, and the negligence of authorities in policing them, allowed their proprietors to acquire real estate. Consequently, a sum 'little short of *One Million Sterling*, is said to have been acquired by a class of individuals originally (with some few exceptions) of the lowest and most depraved order of society.'[7] After John Twycross and Richard Wetenhall were fined £1,800 for keeping gaming tables in Bath in April of 1787, a writer remarked that although the fine was 'seemingly a large sum,' it was 'a mere trifle' in consideration of the enormous profits of gaming ventures, noting that 'the present culprits are only the ostensible members of a numerous co-partnership, *amongst whom the money may be easily raised*.'[8] Gaming establishments operating completely outside the statutes were less numerous than those catering to other illicit vices, such as the 2,000 brothels and 50,000 prostitutes that Colquhoun estimated were operating in greater London, but they were much more commercially sophisticated and, as we shall see, better equipped to face down legal challenges. For all of Kenyon's posturing, the high courts in Westminster Hall flailed just as ineffectually in the face of emboldened gaming entrepreneurship as had the Westminster magistracy for the last several decades.

Honourable Debtors

Where gaming at the Groom Porter's lodge earlier in the century had been 'for ready money only,' credit was as crucial to other gaming operations as it was to any other commercial enterprise. Observers who favoured legalized gaming subject to regulation pointed to credit advanced at gaming tables as the real source of trouble. One writer proposed, in addition to a central licensing authority and the prohibition of all but 'gold tables,' that credit be disallowed, as it was 'when the losing gamester is drained of cash and notes, and plays upon tick, [that] the black storm arises.'[9] Another writer asserted that there was little 'deep play' when play

---

[7] *Monthly Visitor*, 1 (March 1797), 251–6; extracts appeared in the *Times*, 3965 (5 August 1797).

[8] *Universal Magazine*, 80 (April 1787), 213; italics in original.

[9] *Gentleman's Magazine*, 30 (February 1760), 90.

was for 'ready money,' and recommended the repeal of all gaming legislation, to be replaced with a statute requiring the discharge of all gaming debts within twenty-four hours, under pain of the penalties for debt.[10] Credit was even more essential to the elite gaming establishments in St James's. James Hare cocked an eyebrow at the Duke of Cumberland's decidedly unprincely behaviour in not only dealing at faro himself, but imposing a betting limit of ten guineas, and perhaps worst of all, forbidding credit.[11] At the other end of the scale was the dowager Countess of Lanesborough, who seems to have run a faro bank at least briefly that acquired a reputation for lending money to punters at exorbitant interest rates. Whether this reputation was justified is uncertain. She had taken as her second spouse John King, sixteen years her junior, disparagingly known as 'Jew King,' a Sephardic financier who had been born Jacob Rey.[12] Anti-Semitic stereotypes had always been present in public discourse over gaming, Thomas Erskine remarking that '[a] gamester without his jew, is... [a] lamp without oil, or... [a] ship without water.'[13] These analogies were echoed by a newspaper writer during the debate over the E.O. Bill, asserting that 'Jews are no inconsiderable support of the E. O. Tables' as they would reportedly 'fix themselves near the capital Tables, for the Purpose of unstringing their Purses, and throwing Folly into a high Fever' by making usurious loans for play.[14]

One component of the 'black legend' of unwonted social mobility from gaming was the body of anecdote involving waiters, bootblacks, and other menial staff of subscription clubs acquiring fortunes from lending at gaming tables. Newspapers recounted anecdotes of staff at subscription clubs who amassed considerable sums of capital from advancing short-term loans to elite punters. Some of these accounts were clearly inflated, such as the report of the head waiter of one establishment who retired with £10,000 a year, the proceeds of loans at the rate of 'half a crown in the pound,' or 12.5 per cent, payable in forty-eight hours, advanced to members 'at late hours in the night, when they were run out of cash at the gaming table.'[15] A recapitulation of the same story in a different paper a year and a half later revised the figure to a more plausible £1,000 per annum.[16] Another such tale related that two waiters of an establishment in St James's had each acquired capital of £5,000 over the preceding four years through making overnight loans of up to £500 'to broken gamblers of quality, and receiving so many guineas instead of pounds.'[17] Rumour had it that Sir Thomas Rumbold Bt., an MP and a notorious East India nabob, had begun his career as a bootblack at White's.[18] The election of Robert Mackreth as member for Castle Rising in 1774 was accompanied by multiple accounts of his origins as a waiter at White's, where he allegedly raised a

[10] *Lloyd's Evening Post*, 1894 (23 August 1769).   [11] HMC *Carlisle*, 575.
[12] *Morning Post*, 5785–6, 5792 (8–9, 16 November 1791).
[13] Erskine, *Reflections on Gaming*, 14.   [14] *Public Advertiser*, 14,978 (27 June 1782).
[15] *London Evening Post*, 6612 (24 March 1770).   [16] *Middlesex Journal*, 393 (5 October 1771).
[17] *General Evening Post*, 5871 (30 May 1771).   [18] Bourke, *History of White's*, 1. 142.

fortune from lending small sums at exorbitant interest.[19] It is difficult to know how plausible these stories were. Wait staff at clubs were in a position to lend as much as ten guineas, small change for an aristocratic punter but a considerable sum for a waiter, and could derive significant income from the interest. At the most prestigious establishments, staff could receive generous gratuities, especially at Christmas, when one waiter in a subscription house in St James's Street reportedly got over £500 in 'boxes.'[20] There was certainly a wildcat atmosphere, in which junior personnel might engage in their own individual speculations, at some risk, admittedly, since they clearly did not themselves command the sums they were advancing. These accounts may merely be folklore generated by anxiety over undeserved social mobility, or they may point to another possibility, that gaming as a commercial venture had assumed the characteristics of other commercial enterprises.

There was certainly risk involved in credit advanced for gaming, which probably accounted for the exorbitant rates of interest mentioned in newspapers, as much as 30 per cent in some cases. High-born punters were not always above defaulting on 'debts of honour,' especially when their creditors were merely the managers of gaming concerns. The club proprietor William Brooks had died in relative poverty in 1782, contemporaries noting his excessive alacrity to advance credit to members, accompanied with a corresponding diffidence over collecting loans that were due, as Richard Tickell's verses suggested:

> [L]iberal Brooks, whose speculative skill
> Is hasty credit, and a distant bill;
> Who, nursed in clubs, disdains a vulgar trade,
> Exults to trust and blushes to be paid.[21]

When a punter at Daubigny's in St James's Street refused to repay a loan of 350 guineas advanced from the house 'for the purpose of continuing his play,' the proprietor sued. The Caroline and Queen Anne statutes had invalidated securities given for sums lost at gaming, but were silent on the subject of money lent for play. The court in this case ruled for the defendant,[22] and Daubigny was ultimately forced to give up his tenancy.

Daubigny notwithstanding, gaming proprietors who advanced credit at their tables stood a good chance of 'making bank,' given conventions that had evolved stipulating the prompt repayment of 'debts of honour,' which, according to one critic, had 'such an Influence on the Minds of most Gentlemen, that they think it scandalous...not to be punctual in the Discharge of Gaming Debts, in Preference

[19] *Westminster Magazine* (November 1774), 583.
[20] *Gentleman's Magazine*, 55 (January 1785), 70.
[21] Quoted in *Survey of London*, 29. 331.
[22] *Morning Post*, 6578 (20 May 1794).

to their honest Creditors.'[23] Other observers had long noted how the notion that gaming debts were to be discharged first burdened tradesmen who were obliged to wait.[24] '[T]housands are cheerfully paid as a debt of honour,' lamented the barrister Benjamin Sedgly at mid-century, while honest tradesmen owed legitimate debts were forced into bankruptcy as their high-born creditors enriched sharpers. 'This ought to be considered…as a principal branch of national corruption,' he continued, as it reduced nobility and gentry 'into such a necessitous condition' that they would be forced to recoup their fortunes by prostituting themselves to the ministry in power. Continental nobility had already been corrupted in this way.[25] Another commentator around the same time wondered '[w]hether in order to suppress *Gaming* effectually, it would not be proper to make it disgraceful and dishonourable to pay what is falsely called a *Debt of Honour*?'[26]

A solution along these lines was proposed in 1776. Thomas Erskine was not yet called to the bar when he published his *Reflections on Gaming*, which appeared in three editions over the next two years. High-stakes gambling, Erskine wrote as American colonists rose in revolt, was nothing less than a threat to national security. A member of Parliament, a gentleman of property who held his seat by birthright, was 'a mill-stone about the neck of his country' when encumbered with gaming debts, and 'the man who has dismembered his fortune, will dismember the empire to recover it.' Existing gaming legislation was futile, as it depended on informers, already 'detestable in a free country,' who stood to lose 'more in being excluded from so lucrative a society, than [they] can gain by the conviction of an offender.'[27] In lieu of statutory proscriptions, Erskine proposed measures to attack credit advanced for gaming, specifically outlawing the sale of annuities payable for the life of the seller, a particularly common financial instrument deployed by gaming lenders like Robert Mackreth and John King. The purchase price was typically six years' worth of income from the annuity, so that in exchange for £3,000, for example, a purchaser would receive £500 annually for the life of the seller. Even if a 'life' were delimited to thirty-three years from date of purchase, as was standard practice, such a contract was clearly usurious, the more so the longer the annuity was due. Erskine further proposed to limit the payment of such annuities already contracted to a term of seven years and ten months, which was more consistent with conventional rates of interest.[28] When legislation to this end was introduced in 1778, one newspaper reported '[c]ash runs at present so very small at the West End of the Town, as to have occasioned an almost total stand-still' of high-stakes gaming, another explaining that 'now the Usurer is

[23] *The Historical Register*, 92 (July 1738), 270; *Craftsman*, 633 (26 August 1738).
[24] *The Museum*, 3 (26 April 1746), 83.
[25] Sedgly, *Observations on Mr Fielding's Enquiry*, 30–1.
[26] *London Evening Post*, 3783 (16 January 1752).   [27] Erskine, *Reflections on Gaming*, 14.
[28] Erskine, *Reflections on Gaming*, 7–8, 10–11, 14.

no longer at Hand with his Annuity Bond,' funds could not be raised to pay gaming debts.[29] There is no indication, however, that this legislation passed.

Fifteen years later, Erskine, by then a distinguished barrister, was establishing himself as an able defender of gaming entrepreneurship, with particular regard to the vexed issue of credit. A high court ruling in the 1755 case *Barjeau v. Walmsley* held that while the Queen Anne statute had invalidated securities advanced for gaming loans in excess of £10, it had not invalidated contracts for those loans. Although a gaming creditor could not seize collateral, nor, under the ruling in *Young v. Moore* two years later, imprison the borrower for debt, he could still file a civil action.[30] Decades later, Erskine convinced none other than Lord Kenyon to issue a series of rulings upholding these judgments, and the rights of gaming creditors, including notorious gaming operators, on the eve of his threat to put the 'Faro Ladies' in the pillory. In May 1793, the gaming proprietor Richard Wetenhall pursued one Wood, who was advanced credit to continue play at Wetenhall's establishment, all the way to King's Bench. William Garrow protested on his client's behalf 'that the Plaintiff kept a common gambling house' and that 'money lent knowingly to game with, was not recoverable,' effectively asking the court to overturn *Barjeau*. The court declined, with Kenyon reiterating the earlier ruling that the Queen Anne statute 'only avoided *securities* for money lent to play with, and did not extend to cases of mere loans without any security taken.' A year later, it was Garrow's turn to appear for the plaintiff, one Bulling who had won the comparatively modest sum of £3 10*s.* from a Mr Frost. Kenyon remarked that he had never seen such a case brought, but as play appeared to be fair and the total sum well under the £10 threshold set in statute, he instructed the jury to find for the plaintiff if they found his witnesses credible.[31] Asked for a third time to overturn *Barjeau* the very next year in the case of *Leapridge v. King*, the celebrated jurist doubled down:

Lord Kenyon said that he had once, from memory only, without looking into the Act of Parliament (9 Anne c14), held that money lent at the time of play could not be recovered back; but that he was mistaken in that decision, for...the Act of Parliament only enacted that the security should be void, but did not say that no action should be maintained for the money.

In this case, however, the jury was plainly put off by the plaintiff's operating an E.O. table at Ascot, and gave a verdict for the defendant.[32] Nevertheless, the

[29] *Public Advertiser*, 13,707 (14 September 1778); *St. James's Chronicle*, 2774 (22 December 1778).
[30] John Strange, *Reports of Adjudged Cases in the Courts of Chancery, King's Bench, Common Pleas, and Exchequer*, 2 vols (London: Henry Lintot, 1755), 2. 1249; George Wilson, *Reports of Cases Argued and Adjudged in the King's Courts at Westminster*, 3 vols (London: J. Worrall and B. Tovey, 1770), 2. 67–8.
[31] Isaac Espinasse, *Reports of Cases Argued and Ruled at Nisi Prius in the Courts of King's Bench and Common Pleas*, 6 vols (London: Andrew Strahan, 1796), 1. 18–19, 235.
[32] Thomas Peake, *Additional Cases at Nisi Prius,* 2 vols (London: J. and W. T. Clarke, 1829), 2. 32–3.

rulings in *Barjeau v. Walmsley* and *Wetenhall v. Wood* stood, and were not defini-
tively overturned until 1838. The judiciary had ensured that credit remained an
important profit centre for gaming proprietors.

Turning the Tables

Where gaming legislation early in the century had been drafted explicitly to protect the young heirs of landed estates from sharpers who lurked at gaming tables,
by the end of the century the main character of the melodrama of moral corruption around gaming was recast as a junior clerk, working his way upward in a
commercial concern, tempted to steal from his employers. Up to a dozen establishments in the vicinity of Leicester Fields, one newspaper report warned, were
'open to all young men from the city, to bankers' clerks, and to all persons whom
it was necessary to trust with considerable sums of money.'[33] The Bank of England
had already sounded the alarm in advance of the abortive E.O. Bill when a clerk
cashier named Charles Clutterbuck forged £6,000 in banknotes, staking much of
the proceeds at gaming tables in the Temple of Health. Another such clerk was
John King, who in 1795 absconded from his employer with a banknote for £1,000,
which was made over to Augustus de Heine, who cashed it in payment of King's
losses at de Heine's Rouge et Noir table in Pall Mall. King's employer, Godwin and
Company, then filed suit against de Heine and his partners.[34] In June of 1796, an
émigré named Badioli, who kept an 'Italian warehouse' for imported goods such
as olive oil, filed suit in King's Bench against Francis Oldknow, who had been
fined £200 a year earlier for keeping a faro table at his house in Conduit Street
near Hanover Square. Badioli employed his grandson, John Wilson, as a clerk,
who rewarded his grandfather's solicitude by embezzling £500, and losing £161
14s. playing Rouge et Noir at a table that Oldknow kept at the Tun Tavern in
Oxendon Street. Neither for the first nor the last time, the celebrated barristers
William Garrow and Thomas Erskine appeared for plaintiff and defendant.
Erskine made much of Wilson's having embezzled from his own grandfather,
arguing that no one would be safe from the accusation of someone so devoid of
moral sense. Garrow carried the day, however, postulating that the keepers of the
table 'must have known' that one so young as Wilson, who looked to be about
seventeen, could not have acquired such a sum by honest means.[35]

The debacle of the Faro Ladies had been precipitated by the *cause célèbre* of
Henry Weston, Kenyon's pledge to pillory convicted gaming operators coming
two days before Weston's trial for forgery. Weston was a 'very elegant and

---

[33] *London Packet*, 4336 (2 June 1797).   [34] *Morning Chronicle*, 8027 (7 July 1795).
[35] *London Packet*, 4187 (15 June 1796); *Evening Mail*, (15 June 1796); *Gazetteer*, 21,066
(17 June 1796).

handsome young man' with seemingly impeccable social credentials, hailing from Anglo-Irish gentry and having an uncle who was a baronet, a retired admiral, and the governor of Greenwich Hospital. Even at his trial, he had an eminently trust-worthy appearance, one newspaper report commenting on his 'suit of black' and his 'very handsomely dressed' hair.[36] At the age of eighteen, Weston came to London and 'went into trade,' entering the firm of a Mr Cowan, who managed the capital of a number of retired army officers. In a very short time, Weston so impressed Cowan and his partners that the affairs of the firm were left completely in his hands while his employer attended to pressing business that took him out of town for several months. Weston then embezzled an estimated £30,000 and obtained another £16,000 by forgery, for which he was arrested in April 1796 and convicted at the Old Bailey a month later. Much of the proceeds of Weston's lar-ceny were lost at gaming tables at Phillip's and Nelson's in Pall Mall, and at Searle's in Covent Garden, where he reported losing £7,000.[37] Although it was not the only such case to make the papers in that decade, Weston's case was the most tragic, resulting in the evisceration of a firm's entire capital, the defrauding of the Army, the Navy, and the Bank of England, and ending in a hanging. In common with the earlier cases of King and Wilson, it also represented the violation of a cordon sanitaire between the vice of a dissolute aristocracy and the virtue of a sober and respectable grand bourgeoisie. In focusing attention on these cases, print media strengthened that distinction. However, while it was all very well to try gaming entrepreneurs in the court of public opinion, it seemed clearer than ever that trying them in courts of law was a still very much a lost cause.

This reality was evident in the debacle that faced the Westminster JP Sir Robert Taylor. In common with Thomas Archer the Groom Porter, Taylor's primary vocation was architecture. He was particularly celebrated for his London town-houses, but he was as well known as a metropolitan magistrate, his work as Sheriff of London earning him a knighthood in 1783. Four years later, however, Taylor was under pressure as a Westminster justice with oversight of the wealthy and fashionable parish of St James Piccadilly. In May of 1787, one John Tipping sued in the Court of King's Bench for a writ of mandamus against Taylor, who had refused to hear Tipping's information against Edward Burlton (coming to the magistrates' attention neither for the first nor the last time) and a partner named Bishop for keeping a faro table. At the same time, reports surfaced of gaming operations proliferating in Spring Gardens at the east end of St James's Park, which appeared to be within Taylor's jurisdiction. The latter circumstance was easily dealt with, as the street that took its name from the gardens and the

---

[36] *Oracle*, 19,321 (16 May 1796).
[37] OBPO t17960511-27; Gillian Russell repeats Frank McLynn's proofreading error in reporting the sum of Weston's initial forged note at £100,000; Russell, 'Faro's Daughters,' 490; Frank McLynn, *Crime and Punishment in Eighteenth-Century England* (Oxford: Oxford University Press, 1991), 135.

buildings on it properly belonged to the Park and consequently fell within the verge of the court, placing it under the jurisdiction of the Board of Green Cloth. The suit in King's Bench was another matter. Taylor argued that jurisdiction over 'lotteries,' which statutorily included faro under the first Georgian Gaming Act, had been removed from Commissions of the Peace under a subsequent statute. Tipping's attorney pounced on this transparently specious contention, pointing out that the statute in question only applied to lotteries authorized by acts of Parliament. The writ was issued, although there is no record of the result; in any case, another information was lodged against Burlton and another partner (possibly Robert Bullock, a brewer in Whitechapel) for a faro operation, for which Burlton appeared at the rotation office in Litchfield Street.[38] Taylor does not seem to have been a 'trading justice' engaged in petty peculation, but he seemed to be availing himself of any excuse he could find not to pursue gaming operations within his purview. His reluctance to pursue gaming operators reflected the increasing confidence on the part of gaming entrepreneurs that their social aspirations were legitimate as their business was legitimate, to the extent of employing every commercial and legal means to advance these assertions.

William Addington, who had been attacked during the raid on the Temple of Health in 1782, similarly found himself before the Court of King's Bench on a writ of mandamus fourteen years later, charged under the statute of 1739 for declining to proceed against a gaming house in Lisle Street, Leicester Fields, 'because the complainants were two common informers.' The informers in question were John Shepherd and Theophilus Bellasis, a pair of disreputable attorneys who ran what can only be described as a protection racket for gaming establishments. In one cryptic newspaper item, there were identified as

> *Squinting Jack Qui Tam,* and the *Lanky Theophilus,*...the present Receivers General of the Gaming House *hush money,* from such black leg proprietors as wish to decline the honour of paying their respects to the *Full Bottom Quartetto* in *Banco Regis.*[39]

Another report estimated their annual income from this enterprise at £1,800. Joseph Atkinson, who with his spouse operated a gaming venue in Covent Garden Piazza, admitted to paying Shepherd and Bellasis £80 on one occasion and £100 on another.[40] Under pressure, Addington apologized, stating the reasons for his caution his having 'twice been materially injured' in course of proceeding against gaming houses, the first being his injury at the Temple of Health, and the second

---

[38] *World,* 123 (23 May 1787), 129 (30 May 1787), 130 (31 May 1787); *Bath Chronicle,* 1382 (17 May 1787).

[39] *Morning Herald,* 5778 (9 October 1797).

[40] *Morning Post,* 9008 (22 November 1797).

a case where 'an action was brought against him, which cost him a considerable sum of money.' In the present case, he understood that Shepherd and Bellasis had attempted to extort money from the proprietors. Addington dutifully issued a warrant for a second raid on the premises at the corner of Lisle Street and Leicester Street, and several individuals were seized playing hazard. Accounts differed of what happened next. According to one report, the apprehended punters, citing self-incrimination, refused to give evidence against each other or against the proprietors. Another related the opinion of the Bow Street magistrates 'that the evidence of any of the parties against each other is inadmissible.' Whatever occurred, the prosecution once again was dropped.[41]

Newspapers did not fail to notice raids conducted on gaming operations in St James's Street in the same two city blocks as White's and Brooks's, and at most two or three streets away from Cumberland House, the Sturts, and the Hobarts. A raid on Edward Burlton's premises seized £276 16s. from a table in an upstairs room. Burlton, who had appeared on similar charges before, was ultimately able to have his conviction quashed upon turning up at quarter sessions with William Garrow as his counsel in January 1792. Garrow cornered the arresting justice and the high constable of St James's into admitting that they did not know how faro was played, and consequently could not prove that it was being played in Burlton's house on the evening of the raid.[42] Stung, perhaps, by the incongruities of enforcement that newspapers noted, or emboldened, perhaps, by Lord Kenyon's threat to pillory gaming operators of whatever station or sex, the magistrates of St James's dared in the summer of 1796 to move against the subscription house of Captain Charles Wheeler at 65 St James's Street. At trial, the informant on whose testimony warrants were issued was pointedly asked

> how he could possibly state in his Information that it was a common gaming-house, when it was impossible for any person to go into it excepting a Subscriber, much more a man with such an appearance as he was[?]

The charges against Wheeler, whom the constables had found on the roof hiding behind a chimney during the raid, were dismissed. Incredibly, a faro table seized during the raid was returned, 'as no play was going forward' when the constables entered. Because Wheeler's premises was 'supported by the subscription of a number of gentlemen,' it therefore could not 'be deemed a common gaming-house.'[43] All the raid on Wheeler's accomplished was to inscribe in case law the

---

[41] *Whitehall Evening Post*, 7716 (21 April 1796); *Gazetteer*, 21,019 (23 April 1796); *Lloyd's Evening Post*, 6039 (9 May 1796); *Evening Mail* (16 May 1796); *Morning Herald*, 5353 (18 May 1796). Regrettably, the sessions rolls for this period are in very poor condition and unfit for consultation.

[42] *New London Magazine* (January 1792), 41–2.

[43] *Morning Post*, 7610 (1 August 1796); *London Packet*, 4206 (29 July 1796); *Oracle*, 19,388 (1 August 1796).

understanding that all-male subscription clubs were not comprehended under gaming statutes and were accordingly invincible against law enforcement.

As gaming enterprises became larger, more sophisticated, and more prosperous, gaming entrepreneurs seized their advantage, levelling charges of extortion, a criminal offence, against informants, creating a legal stalemate with the frequent result of all parties dropping their prosecutions. From the 1780s, it was more and more common for gaming operators to respond to prosecutions with civil actions alleging extortion. The Atkinson family, who ran one of many long-running gaming concerns in Covent Garden Piazza, deployed this strategy repeatedly. In December 1783, Mordaunt Atkinson and Peter Wilder were indicted with three others for keeping a gaming house in St Alban's Street, Pall Mall, where E.O. was played. The following April, all of the defendants were acquitted *nolle prosequi*. One reason became clear the same day, when John Worley appeared at the Old Bailey on an indictment 'for fraudulently extorting and obtaining monies and a promissory note' from Atkinson and Wilder 'by threatning to prosecute [them] for keeping a gaming house. There being no evidence he was acquitted.'[44] In another of these prosecutions, William Garrow moved that Thomas Holbrook, an informer against Joseph and Mary Atkinson's establishment in Covent Garden who had been arrested for a civil debt in retaliation, be discharged upon finding bail. Atkinson had threatened to proceed in this way against anyone who informed against his house. Erskine, appearing for the Atkinsons, asserted that Holbrook and others had extorted money from the Atkinsons and other gaming operators, and that correspondence from the defendant corroborating this charge was in the possession of the court.[45] Gaming entrepreneurs' resort to this and other vexatious tactics may explain the unusual number of gaming prosecutions before the Court of King's Bench in the last decade of the century.

The attention of King's Bench was turned to gaming operations after the Pitt ministry had been unsuccessful in the prosecution of members of the London Corresponding Society for high treason, which might seem merely coincidental except for the remarkable fact that William Garrow and Thomas Erskine, celebrated barristers who had faced each other during the trials of John Thelwall, Thomas Hardy, and John Horne Tooke, now found themselves on opposite sides of gaming prosecutions. This initiative was heralded in August of 1794, when Thomas Rennell, a clerical client of Pitt the Younger, delivered a sermon entitled *The Consequences of the Vice of Gaming* at Winchester Cathedral. This sermon was published that year and, unusually for polemics against gaming, reprinted twice over the course of the decade. Rennell connected gaming not only to political corruption, a fairly standard conclusion, but to political and religious radicalism as well, an implicit indictment of the Foxite opposition. This intention was

[44]   LMA MJ/SR/3436, f 183; OBPO t17840421-142, 143.
[45]   *Courier*, 1644 (10 November 1797); *Evening Mail* (15 November 1797).

probably clear to the reviewer who remarked that 'the mischievous consequences produced by this practice are sufficiently numerous, without imputing to it effects with which it has no apparent concern.'[46] The ground for Rennell's attack had already been prepared in the priming of suspicion of French émigrés, as unjustly taxed with importing faro and Rouge et Noir as they were with introducing the same ideological toxins that had occasioned their exile.

Rex v. Miller in December 1796 was the first such prosecution ever to be tried before a jury. Erskine instructed Thomas Miller, charged with keeping a gaming house at 4 Leicester Street, Leicester Fields, to plead guilty in order to preclude the testimony of the Crown's witnesses. Garrow asked to call his witnesses anyway, to satisfy the minds of the jury, and the judge, Lord Kenyon, agreed. In his opening statement, Garrow cast Miller as an audacious and unrepentant serial violator of the gaming statutes. Miller had been before lower magistrates more than once, and had stated his income from his gaming house at £2,000 per year. John Shepherd, who as an accused extortionist was not an entirely credible witness, testified that Miller had boasted to him that he was not concerned about standing in the pillory as '[e]very body who knew him would know what it was for... and there was no disgrace in standing in the pillory for such a thing.' Moreover, if he were at any time fined as much as £500, he would not miss the sum. Magistrates had previously seized and destroyed two of his gaming tables, which Miller had no trouble replacing; one of the new tables was large enough to seat thirty punters. Frequently there were over forty in attendance at this table, more than could sit down, so that it was not uncommon for half a crown to be offered for a seat. In addition to this potentially suspect testimony, Shepherd also produced material evidence in the form of gaming tokens issued bearing Miller's name, which were sold at the rate of a guinea for eight, and redeemable for half a crown apiece, netting the proprietor a 5 per cent profit.[47]

An identical arrangement had existed at John Listor's gaming concern in Norris Street, Haymarket, a few years earlier. Michael Finagan, a surgeon, testified before petty sessions that he had frequently played hazard at Listor's house, and that Listor issued silver counters with his initials on them, selling eight for a guinea, each counter passing as half a crown.[48] In this and other respects, Miller's operation illustrated the optimal monetization of a hazard table. In addition to the profit from the sales of tokens and charges for seats when the house was at capacity, there was also the traditional collection of 'box hands' after every three 'mains' thrown. In this case half a crown was due, one witness estimating that the 'box' would collect a token six or seven times in the course of an hour. Miller indignantly denied, however, that he, acting on his own, had cheated an

---

[46] Crump, 'Perils of Play,' 17; Analytical Review, 19 (August 1794), 477.
[47] Oracle, 19,492 (1 December 1796); Weekly Entertainer, 28 (12 December 1796), 473, 475–6.
[48] Lloyd's Evening Post, 5498 (21 September 1792).

inebriated player of £70 with false dice, described in one information as loaded to favour 'seven,' and in another as pasted together with wax. This charge, significantly, was not included in the indictment, notwithstanding Garrow's opinion, and Kenyon's concurrence, that the Crown had incontrovertible proof of a clear violation of the Caroline statute. Kenyon, clearly affronted by Miller's cavalier stance toward the sanctions he faced, kept him in prison for nearly a year while considering the sentence. Erskine asked the court to consider that '[t]he defendant had totally given up all connection with gaming-houses, was married to a very respectable woman, and if not deprived of liberty, would be able to support himself and family with credit.' In the end, Miller was sentenced to one year in the house of correction in Cold Bath Fields, fined £500, and thereafter bound in recognizance for good behaviour for seven years.[49] Miller subsequently filed an unsuccessful petition for clemency in part from a contention that Shepherd, known to be a professional informant, had perjured himself.[50]

A gaming operator who had the undivided resources of the Crown brought to bear against him could be crushed under its weight, but the central government was never in a position to exert such formidable pressure consistently. It could only hope to generate examples 'to encourage the others.' Generally, 'the others' paid little attention. William Oldfield, named with his brothers as proprietor of a gaming venue at 6 Lisle Street, was subsequently convicted for another operation at 26 Oxendon Street. He pleaded for clemency on the grounds of having been injured while serving in the Navy, which plea the prosecuting magistrate supported. Shortly afterward, however, Oldfield was seized at a gaming table at Searle's in Covent Garden and, unable to persuade the court that he was only there to collect a debt that Searle owed him, was sentenced to a year in prison. After Oldfield served his term, the cook at the house of correction in Cold Bath Fields sued him for £5 1s. 8d. 'for some provisions...furnished to the defendant beyond the gaol allowance.' The suit was dismissed, as Oldfield had been provided items such as porter, which inmates were forbidden to have, except in cases of illness. The cook also took in a newspaper for him, as Oldfield, like a merchant banker following markets in securities, 'was anxious to see how the games of Faro and of Rouge et Noire were going on, while he was in custody.'[51]

[49] *Weekly Entertainer*, 30 (20 November 1797), 401–2.
[50] TNA Judge's Reports on Criminals HO 47/22/30.
[51] *London Packet*, 4336 (2 June 1797); *Observer*, 291 (2 July 1797); *London Chronicle*, 6036 (7 November 1797); *Courier*, 1644 (10 November 1797); *London Packet*, 4412 (24 November 1797); *Evening Mail* (1 December 1797); *Mirror of the Times*, 95 (20 January 1798); *Evening Mail* (24 January 1798); *Albion*, 233 (6 June 1800).

Polite and Commercial People

As a new century loomed, metropolitan readers were more aware than local authorities had been at mid-century of the arrangements that had enabled commercial gaming in the metropolis and beyond since the beginning of the century now ending. More to the point, gaming entrepreneurs were asserting in various ways their standing as solid citizens as respectable as anyone else 'in trade,' or even as those engaged in more prestigious sectors of the economy. In counterpoint to admonitions about the disrepute of gaming entrepreneurship, toward the end of the century gaming operators and their functionaries, to the real or apparent astonishment of the judiciary, often behaved as if there was nothing untoward about what they and much of the public viewed as business concerns no less respectable, for example, than banks or brokerage houses in the City. Partnerships in banks kept by elite operators, and the provision of credit to high-stakes players, supported by high court rulings, served to buttress these pretensions. Thomas Erskine, representing a concern in the City against the gaming proprietor Augustus de Heine and his partners, compared his clients, 'known to most of the gentlemen of the jury,' to the defendants, who also 'were in partnership, but not in any trade which the law would recognize.'[52] Gaming operators increasingly begged to differ, and were willing to wager that there were features of their business that any number of potential jurors *would* have recognized.

In 1791, James Nicholson of Leicester Fields appeared as a character witness for Daniel Hopkins, an accused art thief. Despite claiming to have known the defendant for ten to twelve years, Nicholson was ignorant of defendant's felony convictions, or his having been imprisoned. When queried about his own occupation, the witness stated 'I live on what I have, I do not follow any business.' When it was suggested that his business was a gaming table in Whitcomb Street, one of a number kept in the streets between Haymarket and Leicester Fields, Nicholson wondered aloud '[w]hat has my keeping a gaming-table to do with it?...I do keep a gaming-table, I do not deny it.'[53] In May 1796, one Frost, by trade a 'whitesmith' who worked in lighter-coloured metals such as nickel or tin, was identified as a one-half partner in an E.O. table at 20 Oxendon Street, from which he was sufficiently prosperous that he had lived 'upon his property' for the previous seven years.[54] William Cocksedge and Charles Maitland, partners in a gaming concern in Leicester Street that operated under Cocksedge's name, were sufficiently confident of their invulnerability in February 1798 to prosecute

---

[52] *Town and Country Magazine*, 27 (April 1795), 128–9.   [53] OBPO t17910216-40.
[54] *London Packet*, 4177 (23 May 1796).

Bernard Huet, an émigré, for passing a forged banknote on them.[55] One witness
before Lord Kenyon identified himself without hesitation as

> a *Groom-porter* at Stacie's, the Bedford Head, Covent Garden, where Faro, and
> other unlawful games are played every night, and where he officiated...so lately
> as the night before....Lord KENYON observing the witness to be a well-dressed,
> genteel-looking young man, very strenuously recommended to him to seek
> some other means of livelihood.[56]

The most successful gaming entrepreneurs could aspire to the same path to gentility that sugar planters, slave traders, and East India 'nabobs' had blazed before
them. One commentator complained as early as 1788 that there was 'not a keeper
of a pharo bank or E. O. table, or gaming house of any kind, but would be
affronted if not dubbed *Esquire*.' Another newspaper reported a witticism at the
expense of gaming entrepreneur John Twycross, a proprietor of concerns in
London and Bath, who notoriously gave himself airs of superiority despite his
origins as a box-keeper. When an Ascot box-keeper pointedly deferred to
Twycross's more extensive experience in that capacity, it 'set the whole Table in a
horse laugh, as Mr. Tw[ycross] much piques himself upon his *blood*.'[57] Robert
Mackreth, who took over the proprietorship of White's from his father-in-law,
Robert Arthur, in 1761, transferred the proprietorship to John Martindale in
1772, and then successfully stood for Parliament. He sat in the House of
Commons through the last quarter of the century and was knighted in 1795. That
year, John Martindale and William Phillips, another gaming operator in
St James's, were said to be aspiring to seats in Parliament; Martindale stood
unsuccessfully for Ilchester in 1796, garnering only sixteen votes from the two
hundred-odd enfranchised householders.[58]

Mackreth was concerned with the Martindales in a number of other properties
in London and the home counties. In 1789, Mackreth sold Martindale the freehold of the house in St James's Street. About the time that the freehold of White's
changed hands, John Martindale also acquired the manor of Purley Magna in
Berkshire from Mackreth. By September 1793, this estate had been sold to
Anthony Storer, a habitué of the more fashionable faro tables of St James's, who
built the manor house that still stands on the property. Mackreth also assisted the
Martindales in securing a loan from the fourth Duke of Queensberry, in the form
of an annuity payable for the life of the purchaser, in this case Queensberry, who
was to have £2,000 per annum in exchange for the income of seven years. As 'Old
Q' was nearly seventy when this transaction occurred, it may have looked like an

[55] OBPO t17980214-70.   [56] *Oracle*, 19,966 (30 June 1798).
[57] *Weekly Entertainer*, 12 (6 October 1788), 323; *Morning Star*, 111 (22 June 1789).
[58] HMC *Kenyon*, 544; Thorne, *House of Commons 1790–1820*, 2. 347.

advantageous wager, but Queensberry in fact lived to the age of eighty-six, and in any case, John Martindale defaulted on the annuity after only three years.[59] John Martindale's obvious social ambition turned out to be his undoing, which became clear after his filing for bankruptcy in 1798. Among the documents turned over to his assignees were promissory notes for outstanding gaming debts dated some years earlier from Richard Fitzpatrick, an MP and senior military officer who had been the major partner in Fox's faro bank at Brooks's. When pressed for payment, Fitzpatrick claimed that the assignees had refused payment of similar claims against Martindale, citing the Queen Anne Act's invalidation of securities for gaming debts. Fitzpatrick pledged to pay his 'debt of honour' only after Martindale's creditors had been satisfied. Martindale asserted that no claims against him had been refused on the grounds of the gaming statutes, as none of his outstanding debt at the time of his filing had stemmed from play. That was not to say that his gaming operations had nothing to do with his bankruptcy. It was noted that while Martindale accepted unenforceable promissory notes for his punters' losses to his tables, he paid their winnings in cash on the spot, 'a custom eventually so destructive of his property as to cause his bankruptcy.' Fitzpatrick's contention that the refused claims were for gaming debts, and the assignees' counter that they rather arose from 'gross and distressing contracts, for excessive and usurious remuneration' in the form of 'exorbitant portions of the presumed gains of the gaming table,' suggests that these rebuffed creditors were partners in Martindale's faro banks.[60]

Bankruptcy was no barrier to Martindale's opening a new subscription club, much to the dismay of Lord Kenyon, underwritten by the Prince of Wales. Under pressure from Kenyon, the heir apparent admitted that he had allowed his name to be circulated as a prospective member of Martindale's new club, which was founded 'merely for the usual purposes of social intercourse, to which I can never object to be a promoter,' on the understanding 'that the object of this institution was to enable [Martindale's] trustees to render justice to various honorable & fair claimants.' Kenyon replied that he 'thought it my duty to recommend to the Magistrates not to grant a licence to Mr. Martindale, considering what had passed, respecting him, before me judicially.' The new club occupied a 'magnificent' townhouse in New Bond Street where the second Earl of Buckinghamshire had lived until his death in 1793, and had opened by February of 1800, '*malgré* all the

---

[59] *Survey of London*, 30. 451; Estate memoranda and accounts of Anthony Morris Storer of Purley Park, 1793–1822, Berkshire Record Office D/EX 2006/73–74, 91–92; John Bernard Bosanquet and Christopher Puller, *New Reports of Cases Argued and Determined in the Court of Common Pleas* (Hartford: Hudson and Goodwin, 1811), 4. 214–15.

[60] *Observations on Two Letters Addressed by General Fitzpatrick to Lord Kenyon* (London: H. L. Galabin, 1800), 4–7; *True Briton*, 2295 (30 April 1800).

legal denunciations that have been issued against it.'[61] Martindale was listed as a vintner at the same address in 1819, still paying bankruptcy dividends to his creditors.[62]

It was perhaps testimony to the developments described in this chapter that the 1790s witnessed a flurry of speculation about measures to address the numerous problems that subscription gaming venues were thought to pose. Alongside rumours of legislation to suppress subscription gaming houses were proposals to tax them. Recommendations of this kind with reference to gaming and public revenue were certainly not new. The Scottish jurist and philosopher Henry Home, Lord Kames, recommended in 1774 that gaming houses 'be heavily taxed' to prevent 'poverty and idleness.'[63] Either Kames was oblivious to the statutory restrictions that gaming concerns lay under, which seems incredible, or he considered the gaming statutes so ineffectual as to be negligible. One writer estimated at the beginning of the decade that a tax on gaming houses would produce £10,000 per annum, while another suggested that licensed faro banks would by themselves 'produce an increase to the Revenue of almost any amount.'[64] Another correspondent proposed a capitation tax of a sort on gaming rooms of five guineas per punter per night, arguing that '[w]hoever is determined to *game high,* will not be debarred therefrom, if the fine was ten times as heavy.'[65] A taxation proposal in 1795 proceeded from the mistaken assumption that gaming establishments were *already* licensed.[66] During his defence of the informer Thomas Holbrook in 1797, Garrow in exasperation proposed in court that

> it would be much better that these gaming houses should be licenced under certain limitations, than that they should continue in their present state. They would in that case contribute a little to his Majesty's revenue; and by a badge or mark, the keeper of an infamous gambling-house might be distinguished in his appearance from a member of the highest rank and consideration in the country.[67]

In short, Garrow, who had appeared as counsel in a number of high-profile gaming cases by this point, and had prosecuted prominent gaming operators, was admitting that it had become difficult to distinguish gaming proprietors from their more respectable peers.

[61] *The Correspondence of George, Prince of Wales 1770–1812,* ed. Arthur Aspinall, 8 vols (Oxford: Oxford University Press, 1967), 4. 95–6; *Oracle,* 22,143 (15 November 1799), 22,156 (30 November 1799); *Lloyd's Evening Post,* 6623 (5 February 1800).
[62] *New Monthly Magazine and Universal Register,* 11 (February 1819), 79.
[63] Henry Home, Lord Kames, *Sketches of the History of Man,* ed. James A. Harris (Indianapolis: Liberty Fund, 2007), 534.
[64] *World,* 1233 (14 December 1790); *Argus,* 518 (4 November 1790).
[65] *Public Advertiser,* 17,612 (17 December 1790).
[66] *Whitehall Evening Post,* 7661 (17 December 1795).   [67] *Evening Mail* (15 November 1797).

Figure 12.2 Thomas Rowlandson, *Gaming House*, 1808. Courtesy of the Lewis Walpole Library, Yale University. The clientele of this gaming venue contrast with its luxurious appointments.

Rowlandson's depiction of another gaming house interior from 1808 (figure 12.2) suggests that little had changed after decades of legislation and policing. A placard advertises hazard four days a week, Sundays included, and faro every night. The battered headgear, gaping expressions, and unrestrained gestures of the figures around the hazard table suggest a socially mixed clientele, as does the somnolent trio seated in front of the fire as an uncouth waiter, pawing at his scalp, ineptly tumbles a dram from a tray. The room, however, boasts upscale appointments: high ceilings with elegant moulding, a carved chimney piece, posh wall sconces and window treatments. Rowlandson may very well have intended one of the less exclusive gaming houses of St James's, identified only with a street number. As well-furnished as this interior appears, neither the room nor its occupants are as grand as those Rowlandson depicted in his rendition of the Great Subscription Room at Brooks's from the same year. By this time, the hue and cry over gaming had dissipated once again, the Napoleonic Wars having chased anecdotes of high play from newsprint. It was only after peace broke out that print culture turned again to the subject of gaming concerns as demobilized officers, among others, returned to gaming tables. They did so, however, in an altered moral atmosphere.

13

Toward the Victorian Reconfiguration
of Gaming, and Afterward

The Victorian Gaming Act was essentially the same legislation that had been proposed in 1782 and then aborted by parliamentary manoeuvre. In considering the
reasons that the sort of comprehensive proscription of gaming proposed in 1782
finally passed in 1845, the obvious answer would seem to be 'Victorianism': a
wider acceptance of a commercially-oriented values system among the political
and cultural elite, with a cult of work replacing a culture of leisure and an ethic of
fiscal prudence supplanting an aesthetic of luxury and refinement. In the words of
David Miers, '[t]he social and economic conditions that prevailed in Victorian
Britain were simply not conducive to excessive gaming.'[1] A mercantile and industrial bourgeoisie emerged that distinguished itself by eschewing the vices of either
the class below it or that above it, that prided itself on the avoidance of irrational,
unmanageable risk, and that had increasing political leverage, accelerated by the
reforms of 1832. As it happened, the new statute was only the latest in a series of
legislation that demonstrated the redistribution of political power to new economic elites whose wealth was grounded in industry and commerce. By 1845, a
traditional landed elite saw reason to ally itself with this emerging cohort and its
sensibilities. It would probably require another lengthy and detailed study to do
justice to these developments as they may have impacted metropolitan gaming
culture. It would be worthwhile, however, to advance some suggestions about the
changing position of commercial gaming in the Regency metropolis.

Janet Mullin suggests that a divide had already opened up across 'playing for
money' between the middling sort playing whist and other games for modest
sums, and high-stakes gaming, something associated with a morally compromised elite.[2] The financial sector, whose public image had significantly altered in
the decades since the South Sea Bubble, absorbed this ethos of sobriety and fiscal
prudence. At the beginning of the period, contemporaries viewed brokers who
trafficked in shares of joint stock companies as little different from those who
wagered on the blood sports of bull and bear baiting. A clear distinction could
now be drawn between the reckless because unpredictable risk of punting at roulette and the responsible because manageable risk of short selling securities.

---

[1] Miers, *Regulating Commercial Gambling*, 61.   [2] Mullin, *Sixpence at Whist*, 174.

The Gambling Century: Commercial Gaming in Britain from Restoration to Regency. John Eglin, Oxford University Press.

The gambling that was business was finally in a position to look down upon the business that was gambling.

Drawing Blanks, and Filling Them In

Donna Andrew suggests that while gaming certainly didn't decline in the early nineteenth century, newspapers, which had been major drivers of public concern, were no longer as interested in it. The French Revolution, and the wars it occasioned, drove gaming houses out of the papers. Andrew notes that between 1800 and 1810 there were three stories a year about gaming in the *Times;* in the previous two years, there had been twenty-six. It was only in 1817, well after the end of the Napoleonic Wars, that the *Times* covered gaming to the extent it had in the 1790s. Most of these newer stories, however, were about lotteries, or about thefts or frauds perpetrated to support gaming. Andrew suggests that it was concerns about political radicalization, which had seen elite gaming excesses used for polemic effect, that tempered coverage.[3] As Fox had gone into retirement, and the administration of Pitt the Younger had effectively neutered its opposition by fair means and foul, ministerialists found that the stereotype of the oppositionist as gambling reprobate was less necessary. Radical oppositionists, however, had also enjoyed some success in giving the ministry a taste of its own medicine.

In this connection, it is useful to compare two compendia of gamester lore, both published in multiple editions either side of the French Revolutionary and Napoleonic Wars. Charles Pigott's *Jockey Club* (1792) and *Female Jockey Club* (1794) exposed elite vice toward an expressly ideological end, in line with Pigott's political radicalism. Pigott was an insider, a product of Eton and Trinity Hall, Cambridge, attached to Fox and his circle. He was sympathetic to the French Revolution, authoring in common with other radical reformers his own response to Burke's *Reflections*, and including in his addenda to *The Jockey Club* entries for Burke as well as Pitt the Younger, and for Louis XVI, Marie Antoinette, Lafayette, and other French notables, making explicit the parallel between a morally vicious British ruling class and a corrupt French elite. 'The late titled debauchees of Paris and Versailles, have paid dearly for their insolent barbarous excesses,' he remarked, with reference to the Duchess of Cumberland; '[l]et the grandees of this country look to themselves and tremble.'[4] Pigott deployed first-hand knowledge of the private lives of the political elite across the partisan spectrum 'with devastating effect.' In one scholar's assessment, *The Jockey Club* rivalled Thomas Paine's *Rights of Man* 'in the alarm it spread among the government's law officers.'[5]

---

[3] Andrew, *Aristocratic Vice*, 215–17.   [4] Pigott, *Jockey Club*, 3. 83.
[5] Jonathan Mee, *Print, Publicity, and Popular Radicalism in the 1790s* (Cambridge: Cambridge University Press, 2016), 131–5.

All three instalments of the book saw multiple printings, including transatlantic imprints, and provoked the publication of indignant rejoinders. One of these, with a view to defending the characters of those impugned, helpfully filled in the blanks that Pigott had left in the names of his subjects.[6]

Twenty-five years later, another collection of scandalous anecdotes focused on gaming in a way that Pigott had not. *The Greeks* and *The Pigeons*, both of 1817, and *The Gaming Calendar* of 1820, are all possibly the work of Seymour Harcourt, probably a pseudonym, which only appears on the last of these compendia. All appeared from the same publisher, Harcourt's *Gaming Calendar* making repeated reference to the earlier works. The brief preface to *The Greeks* incorporated subtle blackmail, adverting that a sequel would soon appear with compromising addenda solicited from readers, to which end the author requested 'that all communications respecting either...the plunderers or the plundered, may be addressed to his publisher.' He boasted that 'even the bare announcement' of the imminent publication of *The Greeks* had prompted two elite gaming venues to close their doors from fear of exposure.[7] The preface to *The Gaming Calendar* suggests that it was compiled from material thus solicited in the front matter of *The Greeks*. It cast more opprobrium on gaming than its predecessors, but little of this material was original, repeating verbatim observations that had appeared in newspapers twenty years earlier. As was commonplace among admonitory writers, Harcourt claimed that gaming was at an unprecedented height, and repeated the convention that gambling dens were a foreign innovation introduced by 'the hordes of emigrants, consequent on the French revolution, whose vices contaminated the very atmosphere.' He contended that prior to 1789, there were no more than half a dozen gaming houses in greater London, apart from long-established subscription clubs. 'Should it become necessary to publish the continuation of this work,' he adverted in concluding *The Gaming Calendar*, 'I shall, most probably, insert every name at length, and *fill up the Blanks* (left as a warning) *in the present Volume*, to which it will, of course, be a *most interesting Key.*'[8] Military and naval officers were especially numerous among the gamblers identified with the customary blanks left in their names, opening an avenue to speculation that the recently demobilized were unable to meet Harcourt's price. Whether Harcourt was a sincere moral reformer or merely an extortionist, he acted from a belief that sufficient opprobrium was attached to gambling that his subjects would balk at telling him to 'publish and be damned,' as they might have when Pigott was writing.

---

[6] *An Answer to Three Scurrilous Pamphlets, Entitled 'The Jockey Club'* (London: J. S. Jordan, 1792).
[7] *The Greeks*, iv.
[8] Seymour Harcourt, *The Gaming Calendar* (London: J. J. Stockdale, 1820), 15, 179; italics in original.

The Shoes of the Fishmonger

The once ambivalent judiciary had also turned a corner on the subject of gaming, most critically on the issue of credit. Two decisive rulings were handed down from King's Bench in 1819. In *Sigel v. Jebb*, overturning centuries of understanding of gaming as a status offence, the court ruled that games of any kind were unlawful if anyone played them for money. In *Cannan v. Bryce*, it held that if money were lent for an unlawful purpose, and the lender was aware of that purpose at the time of the loan, the loan was an illegal transaction and not recoverable at law.[9] While this turnabout did not eliminate high-end commercial gaming, it was sufficiently curtailed for a single operator to dominate the market. By the 1830s, gaming in clubland had been absorbed into William Crockford's establishment, known informally under his name despite its official designation as the St James's Club (figure 13.1). The political journalist James Grant wrote in 1837 that gaming had practically ceased at the three established clubs of White's, Brooks's, and Boodle's, and that almost all of the others had rules against gaming, forbidding dice and restricting stakes at cards. Consequently, in *The Great Metropolis*,

Figure 13.1 Thomas Rawlins, *The Hazard Room at Crockford's*, 1837. Yale Center for British Art, Paul Mellon Collection. William Crockford's St James's Club was the epicentre of high-stakes play as the Victorian era dawned.

---

[9] Thomas Starkie, *Reports of Cases, Determined at Nisi Prius, in the Courts of King's Bench and Common Pleas,* 3 vols (London: Andrew Strahan, 1823), 3. 1–2; House of Lords, *The Three Reports from the Select Committee of the House of Lords Appointed to Inquire into the Laws Respecting Gaming* (London: House of Commons, 1844; facs. edn, Shannon: Irish University Press, 1968), 46.

Grant discusses 'gaming houses,' chiefly Crockford's, in a separate chapter from the clubs of St James's and Pall Mall. Crockford, a fishmonger by upbringing, had none of the social ambition that was the undoing of the Martindales, making no attempt to burnish his working-class vowels and consonants, and nonchalantly tolerating references to the club as 'Fishmonger's Hall.' Although he sent his sons to Eton, Harrow, Oxford, and Cambridge, he was content for his eldest to enter the wine trade, and for his daughters to marry respectable clergymen. The origins of Crockford's original fund of capital are murky. His early success was anecdotally attributed to an extraordinary head for figures, and the ability to calculate odds rapidly. Observers also noted Crockford's encyclopedic knowledge of his clientele and their assets, one describing him as 'a walking Domesday Book.' Sometime around the turn of the century Crockford acquired at the discounted price of £200 a one-quarter share of a gaming concern at 5 King Street, near St James's Square. He purchased 50 St James's Street in 1823 for the subscription club that opened there under his name, purchasing in rapid succession two neighbouring houses. All three were torn down in 1825 to build a new clubhouse of unprecedented size and magnificence, which opened in 1828.[10]

'One of the greatest evils of gambling,' a polemic of 1837 ran, 'is the introduction, through its means, of improper persons into society, from which they otherwise would, and ought to be, excluded.'[11] Crockford's detractors suggested that the club was notably less exclusive than its neighbours, purpose-built for gambling, and open to anyone, regardless of parentage or education or association, who was capable of paying the entrance fee of twenty guineas and the annual subscription of ten. When the club opened in 1823, membership was offered to anyone belonging to White's or Brooks's or Boodle's without balloting, and even after a selection process was instituted, Grant reported that no applicant with Crockford's support was ever refused. A remark from the bench, after Crockford's widow sued Viscount Maidstone for outstanding debts, supported this contention. The court accepted that subscription clubs were not 'common gaming houses' if members were balloted and subscription fees charged. If, however, 'the rules are a mere sham, and no one is called on to pay if he plays, while all who choose to go there gain access, then the case is different.'[12] William Heath's satirical print from around the time that Crockford opened his new and expanded premises depicts him as an elegantly attired shark attempting to lure an apprehensive John Bull up the front steps, as sinister tentacled crustacean figures peer from the front windows. 'Pray walk in Mr Bull — you will find the Company

[10] James Grant, *The Great Metropolis* (New York: Theodore Foster, 1837), 93–95; 'Crockford and Crockford's, *Bentley's Miscellany* 17 (1845): 257; sv 'Crockford, William, *Oxford Dictionary of National Biography Online.*

[11] [Charles James Apperly], 'The Anatomy Of Gaming,' *Fraser's Magazine*, 16 (1837), 15.

[12] George Henry Hewit Oliphant, *The Law Concerning Horses, Racing, Wagers and Gaming* (2nd edn, London: S. Sweet, 1854), 331–2.

select, I assure you,' offers the shark unctuously, 'at least allow me to present you with a Card.'[13]

Crockford's real innovation was a business model for commercial gaming that optimized the law of large numbers. James Grant described in tones of wonder the apparent novelty of the arrangements for gaming at Crockford's, which in Grant's estimation set it apart 'from all other gaming houses in the metropolis':

> I allude to the circumstance of all the members or strangers introduced by the members, playing against the house or bank.... What is meant by the house, or bank, is Mr. Crockford himself, as represented by the inspector or some other friend, for he never handles a card or throws a die personally.... The club was formed on the principle of not allowing any two members, or any two strangers, to play at hazard together, because it was deemed unbecoming in noblemen and gentlemen to run the risk of breaking in on the friendship assumed to exist between them, by gaining money of each other.... It was therefore resolved that an establishment should be opened in which all the members might play against the proprietor, who not being of their own class, but simply a tradesman, they could cheerfully fleece.[14]

By Crockford's day, faro and macao, the latter a prototype of baccarat, had gone out of fashion, to be replaced with Rouge et Noir, also known as trente-et-un. Crockford, however, capitalized on a predilection for hazard, which was nearly always played for 'ready money,' was believed to be an 'English' game, and was thought to be the 'fairest' of all games of chance, statistically speaking, as the odds between 'setter' and 'caster' were reckoned to be *nearly* even.[15] In fact, as Arbuthnot and de Moivre had demonstrated over a century earlier, the 'setter' enjoyed an advantage of around 1.5 per cent over the 'caster,' which perhaps did not register when players exchanged the roles of 'setter' and 'caster' in 'English hazard.' If, however, the role of the 'setter' were entirely subsumed in the 'bank,' as was the case in 'French hazard,' Crockford's introduction if not his invention, the bank according to one estimate would realize a 100 per cent profit every sixty-three casts.

If it is debatable whether Crockford's had really absorbed all or most of the gaming in 'high life,' it certainly drew most of the attention, standing proxy for every gaming venue in the metropolis, high or low. Writers like Charles Apperly, James Grant, and Henry Luttrell mentioned other gaming 'hells,' such as those that still proliferated around Leicester Square, only in passing. The twenty-odd venues in the streets between St James's Square and Green Park generally did not pass under names, but only addresses. Luttrell identified one house, at 81

[13] George, *Personal and Political Satires*, 11. 15,935.   [14] Grant, *The Great Metropolis*, 86.
[15] *The Annals of Gaming* (London: G. Allen, 1775), 31.

Piccadilly, that rivalled Crockford's in the depth of play, sponsoring like its neighbour a bank of £10,000 for French hazard with minimum and maximum stakes set at ten shillings and £200. Even this upper crust neighbourhood hosted downmarket concerns, such as the 'hell' in tiny Pickering Court with a £50 bank; the one or two Leicester Square operations that made Luttrell's list confined themselves to English hazard.[16] In attesting to the continuing difficulty of policing gaming, writers pointed to the attempt to convict Crockford under the Georgian statutes, when he stood liable for a fine of £162,000, meaning that two residents of the parish of St James Piccadilly would have to attest to unlawful games played at Crockford's on each of 810 different days. As had become standard operating procedure in gaming prosecutions, on the day Crockford was summoned to 'try his traverse,' the *qui tam* prosecutor did not appear.[17]

As Crockford gained ascendancy among metropolitan gaming entrepreneurs, the groundwork for their undoing was being laid. One figure of the political establishment who conspicuously did not join Crockford's when invited was Robert Peel. Peel was the dedicatee of Henry Luttrell's *Crockford's, or Life in the West*, an attack on elite gaming culture and a sequel to Luttrell's satirical poem *Crockford House*. Charles Apperly, whose pieces on field sports as well as an *Anatomy of Gaming* appeared under the pseudonym 'Nimrod,' reported that Peel 'could not be persuaded' to join Crockford's and declined to play hazard when pressed, and speculated that because '[h]is fortune was made by the persevering industry of his father, . . . he intends letting it descend to another generation.'[18] As Home Secretary in the reformist Tory cabinet of Lord Liverpool, Peel was the force behind measures such as the Metropolitan Police Act of 1829, which finally replaced the archaic and eminently corruptible unpaid parish constables and watchmen with salaried professional police. This development certainly contributed in no small way to the disappearance of commercial gaming, at least in public awareness. A year earlier, the duty on a pack of cards, which had reached the astronomical level of half a crown in 1801, was reduced to one shilling, the sum enacted in 1756. These duties had neither generated very much revenue for the Crown, nor had they deterred gaming, even after rising to a shilling sixpence in 1776 and two shillings in 1789.[19] Perhaps the most important reform with respect to the culture of chance was the ending of state lotteries in Britain in 1826, from concerns about their fiscal inefficiency rather than any moral objections.[20] One consequence was that a governing elite that could no longer be taxed with the hypocrisy of profiteering from a form of gambling that was particularly pervasive because it was legal would now have a freer hand to regulate gaming effectively once it chose to do so. Peel as Prime Minister witnessed the passage of the

[16]   Henry Luttrell, *Crockford's, or Life in the West* (New York: J. J. Harper, 1828), 61.
[17]   Grant, *Great Metropolis*, 108–9.   [18]   Apperly, 'Anatomy of Gaming,' 16.
[19]   Berry, *Taxation on Playing Cards*, 40.   [20]   Raven, 'Debating the Lottery,' 93.

Victorian Gaming Act, one year before the momentous repeal of the Corn Laws under his leadership fundamentally reconfigured British politics.

Select Companies and Select Committees

Renewed concern about gambling arose in the context of an economic downturn after the global financial panic of 1837, leading to moral panic over gambling generally and wagering in particular, as race meetings had become less socially exclusive. A final, fateful ruling issued from the Barons of the Exchequer in *McKinnell v. Robinson* the following year, when the opinion in *Cannan v. Bryce* was specifically applied to gaming, the court stating that the plaintiffs, who operated 'a common gambling house,' could not recover money 'lent for the express purpose of a violation of the law, and enabling the borrower to do a prohibited act.'[21] Nevertheless, the failure of legislation to regulate wagering, together with a perception that 'common gaming houses' had once again proliferated, led Parliament to launch an unprecedented investigation in 1844.

In the six decades since the collapse of the E.O. Bill, the world had changed. Select committees of both houses of Parliament investigated the need for new legislation, summoning expert witnesses and compiling minutes of evidence with supporting documentation in appendices, all printed and bound in folio volumes. The hearings themselves were remarkable theatre, with aging dandies on both sides of the interrogations, witnessing and bearing witness to altered sensibilities. Lord Palmerston, for example, sat in the chair of the Commons committee, but yielded it and refrained from questioning when William Crockford was summoned, as he was a member of the club and no stranger to its hazard room. Frederick Byng, a man about town in the Prince Regent's day but on the threshold of sixty in 1844, was to contemporaries a figure of fun, subsequently never rating an entry in any edition of the Dictionary of National Biography. He had never outgrown the nickname of 'Poodle' that the Duchess of Devonshire bestowed on him as a child on account of his head of curls. Asked if he remembered 'when gambling-tables were kept in private houses,' he recalled being at Mrs Sturt's 'during the gambling, as a boy.'[22]

Clearly, not everything had changed. Even after the Police Act of 1839 gave law enforcement enhanced powers to act against gaming venues, and enacted stringent penalties against violators, police complained of the same impediments that had hobbled magistrates and constables a century earlier. One police

---

[21] Roger Meeson and William Newland Welsby, *Reports of Cases Argued and Determined in the Courts of Exchequer and Exchequer Chamber,* 16 vols (London: S. Sweet, Stevens and Sons, and A. Maxwell, 1838), 3. 441–2.

[22] House of Commons, *Report from the Select Committee on Gaming* (London: House of Commons, 1844; facs. edn, Shannon: Irish University Press, 1968), 77, 171–82.

superintendent advised the committee of the preparations that were necessary in advance of a raid. After an investigation that left 'no doubt' that a premises was a gaming venue, he would make a report to the police commission, circulate the report to householders of the parish and secure affidavits from them, sworn and signed in the presence of magistrates, present the affidavits to the commission and secure a warrant from them, and finally 'to endeavor if possible, to get an officer in disguise into the gaming house to witness play being carried on, previous to my entry,' a significant obstacle, as gaming venues would not admit visitors not accompanied by regular habitués of the house.[23] Only seven gaming operations had been raided since the new legislation went into effect; only two of sixty-seven individuals seized were imprisoned, and only after failing to pay their fines; only one individual was fined the maximum of £100.[24]

Police officials, magistrates, and jurists alike were queried about the definition of a common gaming house, and specifically whether or not subscription clubs fell within that definition. Witnesses either categorically claimed that they did not, or noncommittally suggested that they might. The police commissioner Richard Mayne regarded a 'common gaming house' as one 'to which anybody is admitted' to play any game of chance. Thomas Hall, the chief magistrate at Bow Street, stated decisively that a gaming venue had to be 'kept as a place of public resort' to fall within the statutes, and that 'generally speaking, a club would not be considered a common gaming-house.' John Adams, a sergeant at law and the chair of the Middlesex Sessions, declared that

[a] common gaming house is a house to which any persons may have access, with the permission of the owner of it, for the purpose of playing at unlawful games, and for the lucre and gain of such owner; it does not extend to subscription houses, or to a private house.

The questioner pressed Adams on the point, asking if he really thought that a club, however large its membership, could not be prosecuted even if gaming were proven to go on there. 'Certainly not,' came the reply, as gaming operations therein would have to result in the 'lucre or gain' of the occupants, a club being 'merely the joint occupancy of a thousand people.' Frederick Byng, alone among the witnesses, would not accept that a private club did not fall within the gaming statutes. When a questioner noted that Crockford's was a private club, unlike 'a common gaming-house, into which every person that pleases may enter,' Byng was adamant:

---

[23] Quoted in Ashton, *Gambling in England*, 148.   [24] House of Lords, *Three Reports*, 64, 66.

But the one is the offspring of the other. The taste acquired at the table of the club gives a desire of gambling to all manner of persons who enter the club, who never dreamed of gambling before.

In its final report, the Commons committee admitted that it had not been able to devise any formulae to proscribe gaming in clubs 'without any violation of the general principle which protects private houses from intrusion.'[25]

As had been the case a century earlier, the police took decisive action as a result of pressure applied from the select committee, which had pressed police on their contention that raids on gaming venues exposed them to civil liability for trespass. In May 1844, just over two months after his initial appearance, Commissioner Richard Mayne of the Metropolitan Police announced that '[t]he night before last an entry was made into all houses known to be gaming houses in town,' seventeen in all.[26] Just over £3,000 was seized from six individuals found playing hazard at 46 Albemarle Street, but that was an anomaly, as little or no cash was found in the fifteen other venues raided. In November, six months after the hearings had concluded, most charges were dismissed for want of proof that gaming was taking place at or near the time of the raids, even the recovery of gaming equipment not sufficing. It was precisely these sorts of evidentiary standards that the 1839 statute had expressly voided. Of the eighty suspects seized, only nine were assessed fines, almost all of which were modest, the majority in the amount of three pounds.[27]

Byng testified as a Westminster magistrate, supporting a perception of a marked decrease in gaming at the older subscription clubs, other than Crockford's, which was not founded until 1823. He readily accepted a suggestion that clubmen inclined to play for high stakes had depleted their resources, even as he insisted that Crockford's had spawned imitators, deluxe gaming venues that lured elite males who would otherwise never have frequented them. The relatively modest wagers in the Betting Book at White's compared to those of earlier decades might support this perception, but the select committee report related that wagering, commonplace in the previous century, was by 1844 confined to sporting events, especially racing. The report reflected many of the same anxieties that had conditioned earlier proscription efforts, including concern over cheating, with accounts of rigged wheels and false dice introduced by both players and management in establishments like Crockford's. By the Victorian era, however, even a magistrate like Byng, asked whether Crockford's croupiers cheated at the hazard tables, was

---

[25] House of Commons, *Select Committee on Gaming*, viii, 9, 46, 82. Byng's great uncle, George Byng, had introduced the E.O. Bill as M.P. for Middlesex in 1782.
[26] House of Commons, *Select Committee on Gaming*, 209.
[27] Miers, *Regulating Commercial Gambling*, 57–9.

able to reply that it was not necessary, as the house advantage in perfectly fair play at 'French hazard' would generate a 100 per cent profit in about two hours.[28] It was no wonder that at his retirement in 1840, two years after the Exchequer Court pulled the rug from under gaming credit, William Crockford was reported to be worth £1,200,000. Crockford began to speculate rather less successfully, but more respectably, in real estate. Called as a witness before the select committee, Crockford replied evasively that he was not at liberty to discuss what 'gentlemen' did in what he and they regarded as a private space; what happened at Crockford's, stayed at Crockford's.[29]

In 1890, at least two periodicals ran what purported to be an interview with an anonymous retired MP, who claimed to have sat on the select committee in 1844. This piece disparaged the view of elite gaming put forward in works like Luttrell's 'silly' novel of 1828, countering that such material was either deliberately sensational or was produced by those like the hapless MP informed by one of the select committee's witnesses that 'his lordship knows what he is talking about, and you do not.' The interview asserted that it had always been quite difficult to be chosen a member of Crockford's, that gaming took place in a single room accessible only after passing through the length of the building, and that any number of members never set foot there. It was admitted, however, that the club's lavish amenities, including its legendary dinners provided free of charge after midnight, would have been unsustainable without the profits from 'French hazard,' Rouge et Noir, and other games. While Grant had allowed that there were members, most famously the Duke of Wellington, who never entered the 'hazard room,' he left a detailed description of the interior of the club that made the prominence of its gaming facilities apparent. Viscount Palmerston, a member of Crockford's, had tried to save it, arguing that gaming at the club was always 'on the square' and that, contrary to what Grant had reported, credit was seldom advanced for play. As was the case a century earlier on the passage of the Georgian statutes, Palmerston and others warned that gaming would be much more dangerous and damaging once it was driven from public view. Defenders of commercial gaming could argue from enhanced public understanding of the operation of gaming concerns, suggesting, for example, that play against a 'public bank' removed any grounds of personal animosity.[30]

The statute of 1845 effectively outlawed commercial gaming when it erased problematic distinctions and finally recognized and addressed the structure of gaming operations. Acknowledging that it had never been determined 'whether certain Houses, alleged or reputed to be opened for the Use of the Subscribers

---

[28] House of Commons, *Select Committee on Gaming*, 76, 82.
[29] House of Commons, *Select Committee on Gaming*, 171.
[30] *Blackwood's Magazine*, 891 (January 1890), 56; *Littell's Living Age*, 2379 (1 February 1890), 308–9; Grant, *Great Metropolis*, 81–2.

only,...are to be deemed common Gaming Houses,' the 1845 statute simply put the nettlesome question of publicity or privacy aside. Instead, it would suffice to prove 'that a Bank is kept there by One or more of the Players exclusively of the others,' or that one or more players, including the bankers or managers of games, enjoyed a statistical advantage over the others. It repealed the provision of the Henrician Act that allowed landed gentry to license their servants to game for the entertainment of their guests, and made the presence of 'instruments of gaming' on a premises prima facie evidence that unlawful gaming took place there, whether or not it could be established that money was staked. These provisions removed obstacles that persisted even after the Metropolitan Police Act of 1839 expanded the power of the police to raid suspect premises.

Under the terms of the 1845 Act, then, police were empowered to enter any suspected gaming venue, by force if necessary, and search for gaming apparatus, the presence of which would suffice to prove that unlawful gaming took place there. David Miers, however, argues that 'any connection between the enactment of the 1845 Act and the decline in public gaming is coincidental rather than causal.'[31] Remarkably, for some decades after 1845, the same constraints operated on the Metropolitan Police that had applied to parish constables over a century earlier. Police, for example, continued to fear that civil litigation for trespass would ensue if no evidence of gaming was found on a premises raided on the deposition of householders. For their part, residents in the neighbourhood of a gaming venue were as reluctant as ever to inform the police. Instructively, the warrants of all seventeen raids undertaken in May 1844 were issued on the affidavits of the same two householders, although the raided venues were spread across four parishes. The security precautions that gaming operations had always taken also remained a significant obstacle. Fifteen of the sixteen houses raided in May 1844 clearly had advance notice of police action, while fourteen required forced entry, to which end the Gaming Houses Act of 1854 outlawed the bolting of the exterior doors of any house named in a warrant. Magistrates were still in thrall to legal folklore, continuing to believe, for example, that private subscription clubs were exempt from the provisions of gaming statutes, including the 1845 Act.[32]

There was one significant departure from the E.O. Bill of 1782, as well as all of the gaming legislation of the old century, in that it was not thought necessary to exempt the royal household, the home of a devoted couple with four children and more on the way, the subsequently scandal-prone heir apparent turning all of four years old that November. This omission by itself spoke volumes about the normative shifts that distinguished a new epoch from 'Old Corruption.'

---

[31] Miers, *Regulating Commercial Gambling*, 61.
[32] House of Commons, *Select Committee on Gaming*, 210; Miers, *Regulating Commercial Gambling*, 58–9, 62–3.

The Tragedy of the Common Gaming House

Take my advice – when deep in debt,
Set up a bank and play Roulette!
At once distrust you surely lull,
And rook the pigeon and the gull.
The bird will stake his every franc
In wild attempt to break the bank –
But you may stake your life and limb
The bank will end by breaking him!

By the end of the nineteenth century, when William Gilbert composed these lines for *The Grand Duke,* the last of his collaborations with Arthur Sullivan, the presence of 'house advantage' large enough to guarantee significant profits to gaming entrepreneurs was widely recognized even if never properly understood. Gilbert and Sullivan's Grand Duke was based on the Grimaldi Princes of Monaco, the Mediterranean microstate whose independence had been recognized in 1861. Soon afterward, Louis and François Blanc, owners of casinos in the resorts of Wiesbaden and Bad Homburg, won from Carlo Grimaldi the concession to build what became the Grand Casino on an undeveloped promontory they named 'Monte Carlo' in honour of the Prince. The Blancs were drawn both by the sunny climate of the Riviera and by 'the imminent arrival of the railways.' Their Grand Casino was such a success that the two hotels that served Monaco in 1868 had been joined by 46 others only two decades later.[33] Monaco and other gambling havens on the continent would become steadily more accessible to British visitors as steam ship travel and rail networks expanded.

Later in the century, the leisured and monied could still find play for high stakes without traveling abroad, but it became increasingly difficult as the police, emboldened by judicial rulings and empowered by new tactics, were able to capitalize on increasing social opprobrium toward upmarket gambling and act against even the most socially exclusive venues. One was the Park Club in Park Place, St James's, which had only been open two years when it was successfully prosecuted in 1884. Jenks, the proprietor, appealed, on the grounds that the club was open only to subscribers, and that club rules forbade dice, permitting only baccarat, a game recently introduced from the continent that was not named in any statute. In *Rex v. Rogier* in 1823, Justice William Best had ruled that any game, though lawful in itself, was unlawful if played for excessive stakes. However, as any statutory limits on stakes had been repealed under the 1845 Act, there was no longer any legal standard for determining 'excess.' Nevertheless, Sir Henry Hawkins,

---

[33] Peter Thorold, *The British in France: Visitors and Residents since the Revolution* (London: Continuum, 2008), 131.

Chief Justice of Queen's Bench, decided against the appellant across the board in a ruling astonishing both for its breadth and for its peremptory redefinition of terms. The designation of a 'common' gaming house had for centuries been taken to denote an accommodation open to the public. Hawkins now declared that the adjective 'common' referred to the function of a premises and not to its accessibility. Because gambling was the primary purpose of the Park Club, it was a 'common' gaming house irrespective of its exclusivity. As for baccarat, Hawkins ruled it an unlawful game on two grounds: that it was played in an unlawful gaming house, and that it was played to excess or in any other way that was damaging to public morals. As circular as this reasoning may seem, it carried the day and hardened into precedent.[34]

Consequently, it was no longer unheard of, as it had been a century or even half a century earlier, for private clubs to be raided, however socially elevated their clientele might be. The protocol that evolved in response to this reality was for club management to take the fall if an establishment were prosecuted. When a club was raided as a common gaming house, as the Park Club, renamed the Field Club, was only five years after Hawkins's ruling in *Jenks v. Turpin*, the proprietor and his staff would plead guilty to all charges, sparing members the embarrassment of being summoned, for which favour they were happy to discharge any and all fines assessed. These might amount to as much as £500, but in some cases were still calculated according to the formula stipulated in the Henrician Act of a paltry six shillings and eightpence per day. The police, however, with the acquiescence of the magistracy, increasingly deployed civil forfeiture as a deterrent to high-stakes play. Along with gaming paraphernalia, police would seize any cash found on a raided premises, including any discovered on the persons of members present. Sums as high as £3,500 were seized from members of the Field Club in 1889. They could, of course, file a request for the police to return their property, provided they were willing to disclose in a publicly accessible document that they had been apprehended in a gaming venue playing for high stakes.[35] The police were willing to bet that clubmen would cut their losses in these circumstances, the social opprobrium that now attached to deep gaming at the high tide of Victorianism tipping the odds in their favour.

Private residences were still sacrosanct, for the time being. In February of 1891, Sir William Gordon-Cumming sued the Prince of Wales and four others for slander after it became common knowledge that Gordon-Cumming had been accused the previous September of cheating at baccarat played at a private house party at Tranby Croft in Yorkshire, the country estate of the parvenu shipping magnate Arthur Wilson. The Scottish baronet was observed surreptitiously altering his bets, adding or removing counters after games were decided, but before stakes

---

[34] Miers, *Regulating Commercial Gambling*, 66.
[35] Miers, *Regulating Commercial Gambling*, 68–70.

were collected or paid, a manoeuvre known in casino parlance as 'la poussette.' The resulting trial was yet another public scandal involving the heir apparent. Although this royal scandal uniquely did not involve adultery, and although the court found for the five defendants (the once socially conspicuous Gordon-Cumming, after resigning from his regiment and all of his clubs, was forced into seclusion on his Scottish estate), the opprobrium on the Prince of Wales was considerable. A cartoon was published substituting his crest motto of 'Ich Dien' with 'Ich Deal,' as it was known that he had kept the bank at Tranby Croft, and he was hooted in public, ironically enough at Ascot.[36]

The first decades of the twentieth century witnessed 'little parliamentary concern with gaming' from a perception by the beginning of the century 'that high play had "burnt itself out."' This indifference carried through the First World War and remarkably enough through the 'roaring twenties.'[37] During the next decade, however, police became concerned that private residences were being rented out for continental-style casino gaming for the ostensible purpose of charitable fundraising. In November of 1935, police in evening dress attended one quite legitimate function at Sunderland House that raised £100,000, but adverted that there were other houses, including six in Bayswater Road, where the pretext of philanthropy was a sham. Tabloid coverage of 'charitable' gaming parties fed public outrage, and the Ivory Cross, a beneficiary of the Sunderland House galas that provided dental treatment to the indigent, announced that it would decline all such donations. While it seems to have been accepted by this time that private residences were not exempt from the attention of the police enforcing gaming statutes, eighty of the ninety-four raids in 1937 and 1938 were directed at gaming machines, a down-market amusement that had arrived in Britain around the time of the First World War. Courts were still unsure at that late date if roulette and *chemin de fer* were comprehended under the 1744 statute still in force.[38]

The Defence Regulations issued during the Second World War were particularly draconian with regard to gaming, permitting the prosecution of any and all gaming for money, and reversing the burden of proof if ten individuals were found playing for gain on any premises. These regulations remained in force after the war, resulting in over four hundred convictions in just two years. Concerns that these measures were excessively harsh led the post-war Parliament for the first time to contemplate seriously the permitting of commercial gaming under a regulatory regime involving licensing, a measure first advocated two centuries earlier. To this end, the Royal Commission on Betting and Gaming began its inquiries in 1949. In its final report in 1951, the commission concluded

[36] Michael Havers, Edward Grayson, and Peter Shankland, *The Royal Baccarat Scandal* (London: Souvenir Press, 1988), 28–30, 236, 243, 262.
[37] Miers, *Regulating Commercial Gambling*, 71–3 and n. 50.
[38] Miers, *Regulating Commercial Gambling*, 78–81.

that gambling as a factor in the economic life of the country, or as a cause of crime, is of little significance, and that its effects on social behaviour, insofar as these are a suitable object for legislation are in the great majority of cases less important than has been suggested to us by some witnesses. We therefore consider that the object of gambling legislation should be to interfere as little as possible with the individual liberty to take part in the various forms of gambling, but to impose such restrictions as are desirable and practicable or prevent excess.[39]

The commission recommended that games be unlawful if firstly, chances were unequal among players, or between players and the bank, and secondly if players paid any surcharge (akin to the 'box money' collected in hazard) as a condition of staking. The Betting and Gaming Act of 1960, however, only adopted the first of these recommendations. Under this legislation, 'a club could in theory play any game, which satisfied the criterion that the "chances" in it were equally favourable to all the players, including the banker,' meaning, potentially, that roulette could only be played without the green 'house numbers.' As it was the practice in some games, most notably baccarat, for the bank to rotate among the punters, it was possible to offer players the opportunity to hold the bank, ostensibly evening the odds. Entrepreneurs quickly seized on this expedient as well as the collection of 'cagnottes,' as 'box money' was known in continental casinos, so that gaming clubs proliferated in London and elsewhere in Britain during the 'swinging sixties,' such as the fictitious example visited by Wilford Bramble's character in the 1964 Beatles vehicle *A Hard Day's Night*. Order was imposed on seeming chaos when the Gaming Act of 1968 enabled the implementation in 1970 of the Gaming Clubs Regulations, which permitted play at four 'banker's games,' namely roulette, baccarat, dice, and blackjack, 'specifically designed to be favourable to the bank,' in licensed clubs. Taking on the traditional role of the Groom Porter, the regulations also encoded the rules of those games.[40]

Rien Ne Va Plus

The twenty-first century has witnessed a further settling into ambivalence about various species of gambling in Britain and elsewhere. The United Kingdom revived its national lottery in 1994, three hundred years after Thomas Neale's, perhaps ironically in support of National Heritage. In the United States, casinos

---

[39] Quoted in Neil Fagan, 'Enforcement of Gaming Debts in Britain,' *New York Law School Journal of International and Comparative Law*, 8 (Winter 1986), 10, as well as in Miers, *Regulating Commercial Gambling*, 81.

[40] Miers, *Regulating Commercial Gambling*, 84–5; Frank Downton and Roger L. Holder, 'Banker's Games and the Gaming Act 1968,' *Journal of the Royal Statistical Society*, 135 (1972), 336–7, 340.

once confined to the state of Nevada have spread nationwide on the lands of indigenous tribes, often operated by casino chains headquartered in Las Vegas. The gaming houses of twenty-first century London savour of the ersatz elegance of the old Las Vegas strip, located adjoining the premises of middle range hostelries, such as the St Giles in Great Russell Street over the London Central YMCA, or the Imperial in Russell Square, in the shadow of the grander accommodation formerly known as the Russell Hotel. Critics admired Mike Hodges' 1998 film *Croupier*, with Clive Owen in the title role, for its convincing simulation of the atmosphere of these clubs. William Crockford's name once again dignifies an appropriately louche venue in Mayfair, as well as another location atop the newly constructed Las Vegas Hilton. In the oldest redoubts of St James's Street, a once-energetic gaming culture survives only in the odd relic, such as the E.O. table rumoured to sit among the artefacts of Boodle's, or the glass-covered faro table found in the library of Brooks's.

As a new millennium dawned, legislation with a mind to both public welfare and public revenue still struggled to craft an effective regulatory regime that addressed games of chance. Debate over the Gambling Act of 2005 focused on the licensing of face-to-face gaming in brick-and-mortar venues, and a proposal for eight 'supercasinos' in former industrial centres like Manchester and struggling seaside resorts such as Blackpool was ultimately jettisoned as a result. Online gaming, operating in exempt jurisdictions such as Gibraltar and Malta, was ignored, setting the stage for its rapid expansion upon the introduction of the iPhone two years later. Consequently, '[w]here once devotees of casino games may have stood at the roulette or baccarat table, they now play the same games on a laptop or mobile phone.'[41]

These are the circumstances that form the context of our conclusions about Britain's 'gambling century.' Eighteenth-century gaming culture perhaps encapsulates as nothing else the tensions that draw so many scholars to the period. The society that was confronted with faro, hazard, and E.O. was also coming to grips with unprecedented social mobility, floated by new wealth from new sources. Tales of former household servants, for example, wearing silk brocade and riding in private carriages gained credence from the reality of individuals of relatively humble origin making fortunes from overseas trade in sugar, cotton, ivory, silk, tea, or enslaved human beings. Likewise, play for money was prominent in the public imagination because money itself, deployed through an ever expanding and ever more sophisticated range of mechanisms, was increasingly pervasive culturally. We have only to think of an elite marriage market in which prospective spouses were rated in pounds per annum, as if they were municipal bonds.

Gambling may have been more conspicuous less because of any popular mania than from the efforts of the state to assert a monopoly over the operations of

---

[41] Davies, *Jackpot*, 15, 39–41.

chance as absolute as its hold over the legitimate use of violence. In Britain, the complicity of the state in the culture of chance was long-standing. The lotteries that proliferated everywhere in Europe and its imperial holdings were increasingly state enterprises that could brook only so much competition. In Britain, more to the point, those with resources and connections were able to speculate profitably in tickets ultimately acquired by a wide socioeconomic swath of their less affluent countrymen and women, including quite humble folk purchasing shares of single tickets as small as one sixty-fourth. If the stewards of the fiscal-military state did not want potential 'adventurers' frittering away disposable cash at E.O. tables that might augment the public purse via state lotteries, still less did wealthy and prominent 'scalpers' in a position to purchase tickets by the hundreds at the point of issue for later sale at a mark-up.

Conflicting signals from Whitehall and Westminster contributed to the absence of clarity that dogged any efforts to regulate, contain, or police commercial gaming concerns, confusion that prevailed to different extents through to the middle of the twentieth century. The official imperative to police gaming emerged just as the mechanisms to do so were under unprecedented strain due to population growth and the declining stature of the magistracy. The admonitory literature produced over several decades from outside of gaming culture had conditioned official responses in ways that were often counterproductive. The uneven enforcement of the law meant that it was not enhanced constraints that finally contained gaming culture, but a new moral economy introduced in consequence of the transformations of industry and commerce. It clearly became less permissible for an expanding commercial 'middling sort' to engage in other than sociable play for other than modest stakes. As Charles II settled into his restored throne, it was still taken for granted that the propertied could gamble recreationally if they chose, while those in trade were to be discouraged and workers absolutely forbidden. As a young Queen Victoria succeeded her scandal-prone predecessors, the hypocrisy that tolerated gaming among nobs while subjecting plebs to the full rigour of the law became too much even for elites to bear. The commodification of respectability meant that the assumptions that guided two centuries of polemics against gaming were finally hardwired into the attitudes and values of their intended audience.

Bibliography

Manuscript Sources

Bedfordshire and Luton Archives:
Wrest Park Manuscripts (L 30/14).

British Library (BL):
Add. MSS: Additional Manuscripts.

Cambridge University Library:
Cholmondely Houghton Manuscripts.

Huntington Library:
Stowe Manuscripts.

London Metropolitan Archives (LMA):
Boodle's Club, Club Books, 1762–1791 (LMA/4572/A/01/001-004).
CLA/047/LJ/01: Sessions Files, London Sessions of Peace and Gaol Delivery.
CLA/047/LJ/11: London Peace and Gaol Delivery Instruction Books.
COL/WD: City of London, Wardmote Returns.
MJ/SP, MSP: Middlesex Sessions Papers.
MJ/SR: Middlesex and Westminster Sessions Rolls.
(i-ii: indictments; pc: prison calendar; r-rr: recognizances).
SM/PS: Justices' Working Documents.WJ/SP: Westminster Sessions Papers.
WJ/OC: Westminster Sessions of the Peace: Orders in Council.

National Archives, Kew (TNA):
Chancery Proceedings: Six Clerks Series.
Entries of Presentments and Orders, Stamp Office, 1707–1714.
HO 47: Judge's Reports on Criminals.
LC 3: Lord Chamberlain's Appointment Books.
LC 5: Lord Chamberlain's Warrant Books.
PC: Privy Council Correspondence.
SP: State Papers.
T1/431: Treasury Papers, Stamp Office.
TS 11: Treasury Solicitor's Papers.

Sheffield Archives:
Wentworth Woodhouse Muniments (WWM).

Westminster City Archives (WCA):
Church Rates, Pall Mall Ward, St. James's Piccadilly.
Examination Papers, St Clement Danes.
WCB: Minutes of the Court of Burgesses, 1705–1709.

Overseers Accounts, St. James's Piccadilly.
Overseers Receipt Book, St. Paul's Covent Garden.
Vestry Minutes, St Clement Danes.
Watch Rates, Pall Mall Ward, St. James's Piccadilly.

Printed Primary Source Collections

CSPD Charles II: *Calendar of State Papers, Domestic Series, of the Reign of Charles II*, 28 vols (London: Public Record Office, 1860–1939).
Calendar of State Papers Relating to Ireland [of the Reign of Charles II], ed. Robert Pentland Mahaffy, 4 vols (London: HMSO, 1905–1910).
Calendar of State Papers, Colonial Series, America and West Indies, 1685–1688, ed. J. W. Fortescue (London: HMSO, 1899).
Calendar of Treasury Books, ed. William A. Shaw, 32 vols (London: HMSO, 1904–1961).
Calendar of Treasury Books and Papers, ed. William A. Shaw, 5 vols (London: HMSO, 1900).
HMC *Buccleuch*: Historical Manuscripts Commission. *Report on the Manuscripts of the Duke of Buccleuch and Queensberry, Preserved at Montagu House, Whitehall*, 3 vols (London: HMSO, 1899–1903).
HMC *Carlisle*: Historical Manuscripts Commission. *The Manuscripts of the Earl of Carlisle, Preserved at Castle Howard* (London: HMSO, 1897).
HMC *Kenyon*: Historical Manuscripts Commission. *The Manuscripts of Lord Kenyon* (London: HMSO, 1894).
HMC *Ormonde*: Historical Manuscripts Commission. *The Manuscripts of the Marquis of Ormonde, Preserved at the Castle, Kilkenny*, 2vols (London: HMSO, 1895–1899).
HMC *Rutland*: Historical Manuscripts Commission. *The Manuscripts of the Duke of Rutland, Preserved at Belvoir Castle*, 4 vols (London: HMSO, 1889).
HWC: *The Correspondence of Horace Walpole*, ed. Wilmarth Sheldon Lewis, 48 vols (New Haven: Yale University Press, 1937–1983).
Journal of the House of Commons, 85 vols (London: HMSO, 1802–1830).
Statutes of the Realm, 11 vols (London: HMSO, 1810–1828).

Electronic Resources

OBPO: Old Bailey Proceedings Online
ODNB: Oxford Dictionary of National Biography

Newspapers and Periodicals

Albion
Analytical Review
Annual Register
Applebee's Original Weekly Journal
Argus
Athenian Mercury
Athenian Oracle
Bath Chronicle
Bee, or Literary Weekly Intelligencer

Bell's Court and Fashionable Magazine
Bingley's Journal
British Apollo
British Journal
British Magazine
Caledonian Mercury
Champion
Common Sense
Connoisseur
Courier
Covent Garden Journal
Craftsman
Daily Advertiser
Daily Courant
Daily Gazetteer
Daily Journal
Daily Post
Diary or Woodfall's Register
Echo
Edinburgh Magazine
English Chronicle
English Post
English Review of Literature
Evening Journal
Evening Mail
Evening Post
Express
Farley's Bristol Journal
Fog's Weekly Journal
Freeholder's Journal
Gazetteer
General Advertiser
General Evening Post
General Magazine
Gentleman's Magazine
Grub Street Journal
Hibernian Magazine
Historical Register
Independent Chronicle
Intelligencer
Ladies Magazine
Lloyd's Evening Post
London Chronicle
London Courant
London Daily Advertiser
London Daily Post
London Evening News
London Evening Post
London Gazette
London Journal

London Magazine
London Morning Penny Post
London Packet
London Post
London Recorder
Magazine of Magazines
Middlesex Journal
Mirror of the Times
Monthly Miscellany
Monthly Review
Monthly Visitor
Morning Chronicle
Morning Herald
Morning Post
Museum
New London Magazine
New Monthly Magazine and Universal Register
New Morning Post
Newcastle General Magazine
Observator in Dialogue
Observer
Old England, or, The Constitutional Journal
Oracle
Original Weekly Journal
Oxford Magazine
Parker's General Advertiser
Pasquin
Penny London Morning Advertiser
Penny London Post
Post Boy
Post Man
Public Advertiser
Public Ledger
Public Register
Read's Weekly Journal
Royal Magazine
St. James's Chronicle
St. James's Evening Post
St. James's Journal
Scotchman
Scots Magazine
Sentimental Magazine
Star
Sun
Telegraph
Times
Town and Country Magazine
True Briton
Universal Magazine
Universal Spectator

Universal Visiter and Monthly Memorialist
Walker's Hibernian Magazine
Weekly Entertainer
Weekly Journal or Saturday's Post
Weekly Miscellany
Weekly Packet
Weekly Register
Westminster Journal
Westminster Magazine
Whitehall Evening Post
World

Printed Primary Sources

Anon., *An Account of the Endeavours that have been Used to Suppress Gaming Houses, and of the Discouragements that have been met with* (London: n.p., 1722).

Anon., *The Annals of Gaming* (London: G. Allen, 1775).

Anon., *An Answer to Three Scurrilous Pamphlets, Entitled 'The Jockey Club.'* (London: J. S. Jordan, 1792).

Anon., *The Arraignment, Trial, and Condemnation of Squire Lottery, Alias Royal-Oak Lottery* (London: A. Baldwin, 1699).

Anon., *The Art of Engaging the Affections of Wives to their Husbands* (London: Jacob Loyseau, 1745).

Anon., *The Character of the Beaux* (London: n.p., 1696).

Anon., *A Collection of Statutes that Relate to the Office of Justices of the Peace* (London: n.p., 1727).

Anon., *The Comical Pilgrim* (London: S. Briscoe, 1722).

Anon., *Considerations Critiques et Politiques sur la Défense et sur la Tolerance des Jeux de Hazard* (Cologne: n.p., 1764).

Anon., *The Country Gentleman's Vade Mecum* (London: John Harris, 1699).

Anon., *Court Poems* (London: J. Roberts, 1716).

Anon., *A Digest of Adjudged Cases in the Court of King's Bench* (London: W. Strahan and M. Woodfall, 1775).

Anon., *Faro and Rouge et Noir* (London: John Debrett, 1793).

Anon., *The Gamester's Law* (London: Arthur Collins and Samuel Butler, 1708).

Anon., *The Greeks: Being the Jeremiad of an Exiled Greek* (London: J. J. Stockdale, 1817).

Anon., *Hints for a Reform, Particularly in the Gaming Clubs* (London: R. Baldwin, 1784).

Anon., *The History of Jasper Banks* (Dublin: G. Faulkner, 1754).

Anon., *La Maison Academique, Contenant les Jeux* (Paris: Etienne Loison, 1659).

Anon., *Marriage: A Satire* (London: J. Roberts, 1728).

Anon., *A Modest Defence of Gaming* (London: R. and J. Dodsley, 1754).

Anon., *A New Voyage to the Island of Fools* (London: John Morphew, 1713).

Anon., *The Nicker Nicked, or the Cheats of Gaming Discovered* (London, n.p., 1669).

Anon., *Observations on Two Letters Addressed by General Fitzpatrick to Lord Kenyon* (London: H. L. Galabin, 1800).

Anon., *The Pleasures of Matrimony* (London: Henry Rhodes, 1688).

Anon., *The Public Housekeeper's Monitor* (London: F. and C. Rivington, 1793).

Anon., *Readings upon the Statute Law* (London: D. Brown, T. Osborn, W. Mears, and F. Clay, 1724).

Anon., *Reflexions on Gaming, and Observations on the Laws Relating Thereto* (London: J. Barnes and R. Corbett, 1751).

Anon., *The Vices of the Cities of London and Westminster* (Dublin: G. Faulkner and R. James, 1751).

Anon., *A View of Paris, and Places Adjoining* (London: John Nutt, 1701).

Anon., *The Whole Art and Mystery of Modern Gaming Fully Expos'd and Detected* (London: J. Roberts and T. Cox, 1726).

[Apperly, Charles James], 'The Anatomy Of Gaming', *Fraser's Magazine*, 16 (December 1837), 9–24.

Argenson, René d', *Notes*, ed. L. Larchy and E. Mabille (Paris: Émile Voitelain, 1866).

Argenson, René d', *Rapports Inédits de René d'Argenson*, ed. Paul Cottin (Paris: Librairie Plon, 1891).

Auckland, William, Lord, *The Journal and Correspondence of William, Lord Auckland* (London: Spottiswoode, 1861).

[Balmford, James], *A Short and Plaine Dialogue Concerning the Unlawfulnes of Playing at Cards or Tables* (London: Richard Boile, 1593).

Barlow, Theodore, *The Justice of Peace* (London: Henry Lintot for John and Paul Knapton and John Nourse, 1745).

Benger, Elizabeth, *Memoirs of John Tobin* (London: Longman, 1820).

Berkeley, George, *Alciphron, or, The Minute Philosopher* (London: Jacob Tonson, 1732).

Blackerby, Samuel and Nathaniel, *The Justice of Peace his Companion*, 2 vols (London: E. and R. Nutt and R. Gosling, 1734).

Blackstone, William, *Commentaries on the Laws of England*, 4 vols (Oxford: Clarendon Press, 1769; facs. edn, Chicago: University of Chicago Press, 1979).

Bosanquet, John Bernard and Christopher Puller, *New Reports of Cases Argued and Determined in the Court of Common Pleas* (Hartford: Hudson and Goodwin, 1811).

Boswell, James, *The Life of Samuel Johnson*, ed. Marshall Waingrow, Bruce Redford, Elizabeth Goldring, and Thomas Bonnell, 4 vols (New Haven: Yale University Press, 1995–2020).

Brown, Thomas, *Amusements Serious and Comical, Calculated for the Meridian of London* (London: n.p., 1702).

Bulstrode, Whitelocke, *The Charge of Whitelocke Bulstrode, Esq., to the Grand Jury and Other Juries of the County of Middlesex* (London: J. Browne, 1718).

Bulstrode, Whitelocke, *The Second Charge of Whitelocke Bulstrode, Esq., to the Grand Jury and Other Juries of the County of Middlesex* (London: Elizabeth Nutt and R. Gosling, 1718).

Bulstrode, Whitelocke, *The Third Charge of Whitelocke Bulstrode, Esq., to the Grand Jury and Other Juries of the County of Middlesex* (London: D. Brown and R. Gosling, 1723).

[Burgh, James], *Political Disquisitions, or, An Enquiry into Public Errors, Defects, and Abuses* (London: Edward and Charles Dilly, 1775).

Centlivre, Susanna, *The Gamester, A Comedy* (London: William Turner and William Davis, 1705).

Centlivre, Susanna, *The Basset Table* (London: William Turner and J. Nutt, 1706).

Collier, Jeremy, *An Essay on Gaming, in a Dialogue* (London: John Morphew, 1713).

Cobbett, William, *Parliamentary History*, 36 vols (London: T. C. Hansard, 1806–1820).

Cokayne, George Edward, *Complete Baronetage 1611–1800*, 5 vols (Exeter: William Pollard, 1900–1909).

Cokayne, George Edward, and Vicary Gibbs, eds., *The Complete Peerage of England, Scotland, Great Britain and the United Kingdom*, 12 vols (London: St. Catherine's Press, 1910–1959).

Collins, Arthur, *The English Baronage* (London: Robert Gosling, 1727).

Colman, George, *The Nabob* (London: T. Cadell, 1778).

Colquhoun, Patrick, *A Treatise on the Police of the Metropolis* (London: H. Fry for Charles Dilly, 1796).

Cotton, Charles, *The Compleat Gamester* (London: R. Cutler and Henry Brome, 1674).

Cotton, Charles, *The Compleat Gamester* (London: Charles Brome, 1709).

Cowper, William, *The Charge Delivered by the Honorable William Cowper at the Sessions of the Peace and Oyer and Terminer to the Grand Jury and Other Juries of the County of Middlesex* (London: John Stagg, 1730).

[Defoe, Daniel, attributed], *The Gamester: A Benefit-Ticket for All that are Concern'd in the Lotteries* (London: J. Roberts, 1719).

[Defoe, Daniel], *Augusta Triumphans* (London: J. Roberts, 1728).

Dolins, Daniel, *The Charge of Sir Daniel Dolins, Kt., to the Grand Jury and Other Juries of the County of Middlesex* (London: Samuel Chandler, 1725).

[Erskine, Thomas], *Reflections on Gaming, Annuities, and Usurious Contracts* (London: Thomas Davies, 1776).

Espinasse, Isaac, *Reports of Cases Argued and Ruled at Nisi Prius in the Courts of King's Bench and Common Pleas*, 6 vols (London: Andrew Strahan, 1796).

Evelyn, John, *The Diary of John Evelyn*, ed. Esmond S. de Beer, 6 vols (Oxford: Clarendon Press, 1955).

Farington, Joseph, *The Diary of Joseph Farington*, ed. Kenneth Garlick and Angus MacIntyre (New Haven: Yale University Press, 1978).

Fielding, Henry, *An Enquiry into the Causes of the Late Increase of Robbers and Other Writings*, ed. Malvin R. Zirker (Middletown, CT: Wesleyan University Press, 1988).

Fox, Henry, third Baron Holland, *Memoirs of the Whig Party During My Time*, 2 vols (London: Longman, 1854).

Frain du Tremblay, Jean, *Conversations Morales sur les Jeux et les Divertissements* (Paris: André Pralard, 1685).

[Gildon, Charles], *The Post-Man Robb'd of his Mail* (London: A. Bettesworth and C. Rivington, 1719).

[Giles, Jacob], *The Compleat Parish Officer* (London: Elizabeth Nutt and R. Gosling for Bernard Lintot and W. Mears, 1718).

Giles, Jacob, *A New Appendix to the Modern Justice* (London: Bernard Lintot, 1722).

Goldsmith, Oliver, *The Works of Oliver Goldsmith*, ed. Arthur Friedman, 5 vols (Oxford: Oxford University Press, 1966).

Gonson, John, *A Charge to the Grand Jury of the City and Liberty of Westminster* (London: J. Lewis, 1729).

[Goodall, William], *The Adventures of Captain Greenland*, 4 vols (London: R. Baldwin, 1752).

Grant, James, *The Great Metropolis* (New York: Theodore Foster, 1837).

Gronow, R. H., *Reminiscences of Captain Gronow*, 2 vols (London: Smith, Elder and Company, 1862).

Halifax, George Savile, Marquis of, *The Lady's New Year's Gift, or Advice to a Daughter* (London: Randal Taylor, 1688).

[Hammond, Charles], *The Loyal Indigent Officer* (London: E. C., 1670).

Hanger, George, *The Life, Adventures, and Opinions of Colonel George Hanger*, 2 vols (London: John Debrett, 1801).

Harcourt, Seymour, *The Gaming Calendar* (London: J. J. Stockdale, 1820).

Hausmann, Friedrich (ed.), *Repertorium der Diplomatischen Vertreter aller Länder*, 3 vols (Zurich: Fretz und Wasmuth, 1950).

Hervey, John, *Letter Books of John Hervey, First Earl of Bristol*, ed. Sydenham Hervey, 3 vols (Wells: Ernest Jackson, 1894).

House of Commons, *Report from the Select Committee on Gaming* (London: House of Commons, 1844; facs. edn, Shannon: Irish University Press, 1968).

House of Lords, *The Three Reports from the Select Committee of the House of Lords Appointed to Inquire into the Laws Respecting Gaming* (London: House of Commons, 1844; facs. edn, Shannon: Irish University Press, 1968).

Hoyle, Edmund, *An Essay toward Making the Doctrine of Chances Easy to Those Who Understand Vulgar Arithmetick Only* (London: J. Jolliff, 1754).

Hunt, Edward, *An Abridgement of all the Statutes in Ireland, in the Reigns of Queen Anne and King George, in Force and Use* (Dublin: A. Rhames and E. Dobson, 1718).

[Huygens, Christian], *Of the Laws of Chance, or, A Method of Calculating the Hazards of Game*, tr. attributed John Arbuthnot (London: Benjamin Motte for Randall Taylor, 1692).

[Jones, Charles], *Hoyle's Games Improved* (London: Thomas Davies and others, 1775).

Kames, Henry Home, Lord, *Sketches of the History of Man*, ed. James A. Harris (Indianapolis: Liberty Fund, 2007).

Kilburn, Richard, *Choice Precedents upon all Acts of Parliament, Relating to the Office and Duty of a Justice of Peace* (London: J. Nutt for Jacob Tonson, 1715).

Le Blanc, Jean-Bernard, *Letters on the English and French Nations*, 2 vols (London: J. Brindley, R. Franklin, C. Davis, and J. Hodges, 1747).

Limojon de Saint-Didier, Alexandre Toussaint, *The City and Republick of Venice*, tr. unknown, 3 vols (London: Charles Brome, 1699).

Lucas, Theophilus (pseudonym), *Memoirs of the Lives, Intrigues, and Comical Adventures of the Most Famous Gamesters* (London: Jonas Brown, 1714), reprinted in Cyril Hartmann (ed.), *Games and Gamesters of the Restoration* (London: Routledge, 1930).

Luttrell, Henry, *Crockford House: A Rhapsody* (London: John Murray, 1827).

Luttrell, Henry, *Crockford's, or Life in the West* (New York: J. J. Harper, 1828).

[Macky, John], *A Journey through England in Familiar Letters* (London: J. Roberts, 1714).

Meeson, Roger, and William Newland Welsby, *Reports of Cases Argued and Determined in the Courts of Exchequer and Exchequer Chamber*, 16 vols (London: S. Sweet, Stevens and Sons, and A. Maxwell, 1838).

Misson, Maximilien, *A New Voyage to Italy*, 2 vols (London: R. Bently, M. Wootton, T. Godwin, and S. Manship, 1695).

Moivre, Abraham de, *The Doctrine of Chances, or, A Method of Calculating the Probability of Events in Play* (London: W. Pearson, 1718; 2nd edn, London: Henry Woodfall, 1738).

Montmort, Pierre Rémond de, *Essai d'Analyse sur les Jeux de Hazard* (Paris: Jacques Quillau, 1708).

[Mumford, Erasmus], *A Letter to the Club at White's* (London: W. Owen, 1750).

Namier, Lewis B. and John Brooke, *The House of Commons 1754–1790*, 3 vols (London: History of Parliament Trust, 1964).

Nemeitz, Joachim Christoph, *Séjour de Paris* (Leiden: Jean van Abconde, 1727).

Odingsells, Gabriel, *The Bath Unmask'd: A Comedy* (London: John Walthoe, 1725).

Oliphant, George Henry Hewit, *The Law Concerning Horses, Racing, Wagers and Gaming* (2nd edn, London: S. Sweet, 1854).

Ozell, John, *The Art of Pleasing in Conversation* (London: W. Feales, F. Clay and R. Wellington, J. Brindley, and C. Corbett, 1735).

Parliament of Great Britain, 12 George II c. 20, *An Act for the More Effectual Preventing of Excessive and Deceitful Gaming* (London: John Baskett, 1739).

Parliament of Great Britain, 18 George II, c. 34, *An Act to Explain, Amend, and make more Effectual the Laws in Being, to Prevent Excessive and Deceitful Gaming, and to Restrain and Prevent the Excessive Increase of Horse Races* (London: Thomas Baskett, 1745).

Parliament of Great Britain, 13 George II, c. 19, *An Act to Restrain and Prevent the Excessive Increase of Horse Races, and for Amending an Act Made in the Last Session of Parliament, Entitled 'An Act for the More Effectual Preventing of Excessive and Deceitful Gaming'* (London: John Baskett, 1740).

Peake, Thomas, *Additional Cases at Nisi Prius*, 2 vols (London: J. and W. T. Clarke, 1829).

Pepys, Samuel, *The Diary of Samuel Pepys*, ed. Robert Latham and William Matthews, 11 vols (Berkeley: University of California Press, 2000).

Pigott, Charles, *The Jockey Club, or a Sketch of the Manners of the Age* (London: D. H. Symonds, 1792).

Pigott, Charles, *The Female Jockey Club, or a Sketch of the Manners of the Age* (London: D. L. Eaton, 1794).

Pope, Alexander, The Poems of Alexander Pope, ed. John Butt (New Haven: Yale University Press, 1963).

Préchac, Jean de, *La Noble Venitienne, ou La Bassette: Histoire Galante* (Paris: Claude Barbin, 1679).

[Préchac, Jean de], *The Disorders of Basset*, tr. unknown (London: John Newton, 1688).

Reynolds, Frederick, *How to Grow Rich* (London: Longman, 1793).

Reynolds, Frederick, *The Will: A Comedy in Five Acts* (London: G. G. and J. Robinson, 1797).

Rutledge, Samuel John James, *The Englishman's Fortnight in Paris* (London: T. Durham and G. Kearsly, 1777).

Ryder, Samuel, *The Charge to the Grand Jury of the City and Liberty of Westminster* (London: J. Roberts, 1726).

Salkeld, William, *Reports of Cases Adjudg'd in the Court of King's Bench* (London: Elizabeth Nutt and R. Gosling for J. Walthoe, 1717).

Savile, Henry, *Savile Correspondence*, ed. William Durant Cooper (London: Camden Society, 1858).

Sedgly, Benjamin, *Observations on Mr Fielding's Enquiry into the Causes of the Late Increase in Robbers* (London: John Newbery, 1751).

Sedley, Charles, *The Faro Table,* 2 vols (London: J. F. Hughes, 1808).

Seymour, Richard, *The Court Gamester* (London: J. Wilford, 1732).

Sheppard, Francis Henry Wollaston, et al., eds., *Survey of London,* 53 vols (London: Greater London Council, 1900–present).

Smollett, Tobias, *The Adventures of Ferdinand, Count Fathom,* 2 vols (London: W. Johnston, 1753).

Southerne, Thomas, *A Maid's Last Prayer, or Any, Rather than Fail* (London: R. Bentley and Jacob Tonson, 1693).

Stanhope, Philip Dormer, *The Letters of Philip Dormer Stanhope, Earl of Chesterfield,* ed. Philip Stanhope, Viscount Mahon, 5 vols (London: Richard Bentley, 1845).

Starkie, Thomas, *Reports of Cases, Determined at Nisi Prius, in the Courts of King's Bench and Common Pleas,* 3 vols (London: Andrew Strahan, 1823).

Steele, Richard, et al., *The Tatler,* ed. Donald Bond, 3 vols (Oxford: Oxford University Press, 1987).

Strange, John, *Reports of Adjudged Cases in the Courts of Chancery, King's Bench, Common Pleas, and Exchequer,* 2 vols (London: Henry Lintot, 1755).

[Swift, Jonathan], *A Poem on the Erecting a Groom-Porter's House Adjoining to the Chapple, in the Castle of Dublin* (Dublin: n.p., 1725).

Swift, Jonathan, *Directions to Servants* (London: Hesperus, 2003).

Thorne, Roland G., *The House of Commons 1790–1820*, 5 vols (London: History of Parliament Trust, 1986).

Urfey, Thomas d', *A Fool's Preferment, or the Three Dukes of Dunstable* (London: Joseph Knight and Francis Saunders, 1688).

Vanbrugh, John, and Colley Cibber, *The Provok'd Husband, or A Journey to London* (London: J. Watts, 1728).

Wales, George, Prince of, *The Correspondence of George, Prince of Wales 1770–1812*, ed. A. Aspinall, 8 vols (Oxford: Oxford University Press, 1967).

Wanley, Humfrey, *Letters of Humfrey Wanley*, ed. P. L. Heyworth (Oxford: Clarendon Press, 1989).

[Wanley, Nathaniel], *The History of Man, or the Wonders of Humane Nature* (London: R. Basset and W. Turner, 1704).

Ward, Edward, *A Walk to Islington* (London: n.p., 1699).

Ward, Edward, *The World Bewitch'd* (London: n.p., 1699).

Welch, Saunders, *Observations on the Office of Constable* (London: Andrew Millar, 1754).

Wilson, George, *Reports of Cases Argued and Adjudged in the King's Courts at Westminster*, 3 vols (London: J. Worrall and B. Tovey, 1770).

Wright, Edward, *Some Observations Made in Travelling through France, Italy, etc., in the Years 1720, 1721, and 1722*, 2 vols (London: T. Ward and E. Wicksteed, 1730).

Secondary Works

Akkerman, Nadine, *Invisible Agents: Women and Espionage in Seventeenth-Century Britain* (Oxford: Oxford University Press, 2018).

Andrew, Donna T., '"How frail are Lovers Vows, and Dicers oaths:" Gaming, Governing and Moral Panic in Britain, 1781–1782,' in David Lemmings and Claire Walker (eds.), *Moral Panics, the Media and the Law in Early Modern England* (New York: Palgrave Macmillan, 2009).

Andrew, Donna T., *Aristocratic Vice: The Attack on Duelling, Suicide, Adultery, and Gambling in Eighteenth-Century England* (New Haven: Yale University Press, 2013).

Ashton, John, *A History of English Lotteries* (London: Leadenhall Press, 1893).

Ashton, John, *The History of Gambling in England* (London: Duckworth, 1898).

Beattie, John, *The English Court in the Reign of George I* (Cambridge: Cambridge University Press, 1967).

Bellhouse, David, 'A Manuscript on Chance Written by John Arbuthnot,' *International Statistical Review*, 57 (December 1989), 249–59.

Bellhouse, David, 'The Role of Roguery in the History of Probability,' *Statistical Science*, 8 (November 1993), 410–20.

Bellhouse, David, 'Banishing Fortuna: Montmort and De Moivre,' *Journal of the History of Ideas*, 69 (October 2008), 559–81.

Belmas, Élisabeth, *Jouer Autrefois: Essai sur le Jeu dans la France Moderne* (Seyssel: Champ Vallon, 2006).

Berry, John, *Taxation on Playing Cards in England from 1711 to 1960* (Colchester: International Playing Card Society, 2001).

Blyth, Henry, *Hell and Hazard: William Crockford versus the Gentlemen of England* (London: Weidenfeld and Nicolson, 1969).

Bourke, Algernon, *The History of White's*, 2 vols (London: privately printed, 1892).

Brenner, Reuven and Gabrielle, *Gambling and Speculation: A Theory, a History, and a Future of Some Human Decisions* (Cambridge: Cambridge University Press, 1990).

Caillois, Roger, *Man, Play and Games*, tr. Meyer Barash (Urbana: University of Illinois Press, 2001).

Capdeville, Valérie, *L'Âge d'Or des Clubs Londoniens (1730–1784)* (Paris: Honoré Champion, 2008).

Clark, Anna, *Scandal: The Sexual Politics of the British Constitution* (Princeton: Princeton University Press, 2004).

Clark, Geoffrey, *Betting on Lives: The Culture of Life Insurance in England, 1695–1775* (New York: St. Martin's, 1999).

Clark, Peter, *British Clubs and Societies, 1580–1800: The Origins of an Associational World* (Oxford: Oxford University Press, 2001).

Colley, Linda, 'The Loyal Brotherhood and the Cocoa Tree: The London Organization of the Tory Party, 1727–1760,' *Historical Journal*, 20 (March 1977), 77–95.

Colley, Linda, Britons: Forging the Nation (New Haven: Yale University Press, 1992).

Colson, Percy, *White's 1693–1950* (London: William Heinemann, 1951).

Cotton, Hope Donovan, 'Women and Risk: The Gambling Woman in Eighteenth-Century England,' Unpublished Ph.D. dissertation, Auburn University, 1998.

Cowan, Brian, *The Social Life of Coffee* (New Haven: Yale University Press, 2005).

Crump, Justine, 'The Perils of Play: Eighteenth-Century Ideas about Gambling,' (Centre for History and Economics, Cambridge University, April 2004).

Dagnall, H., *Making a Good Impression: Three Hundred Years of the Stamp Office and Stamp Duties* (London: HMSO, 1994).

Dalton, Charles, *English Army Lists and Commission Registers, 1661–1714*, 6 vols (London: Eyre and Spottiswoode, 1892–1904).

Dasent, Arthur Irwin, *The History of St. James's Square* (London: Macmillan, 1895).

Daston, Lorraine, *Classical Probability in the Enlightenment* (Princeton: Princeton University Press, 1988).

David, Florence Nightingale, *Games, Gods, and Gambling: A History of Probability and Statistical Analysis* (London: Charles Griffin, 1962; repr. edn, Mineola, NY: Dover Publications, 1998).

Davies, Rob, *Jackpot: How Gambling Conquered Britain* (London: Faber and Faber, 2022).

Deutsch, Phyllis, 'Moral Trespass in Georgian London: Gaming, Gender, and Electoral Politics in the Age of George III,' *Historical Journal*, 39 (September 1996), 637–56.

Downton, F., and R. J. Holder, 'Banker's Games and the Gaming Act 1968,' *Journal of the Royal Statistical Society*, 135 (1972), 336–64.

Dunkley, John, *Gambling: A Social and Moral Problem in France, 1685–1792* (Oxford: Voltaire Foundation, 1985).

Eglin, John, *The Imaginary Autocrat: Beau Nash and the Invention of Bath* (London: Profile, 2005).

Evans, James, '"A Sceane of the Uttmost Vanity": The Spectacle of Gambling in Late Stuart Culture,' *Studies in Eighteenth-Century Culture*, 31 (2002), 1–20.

Ewen, Cecil L'Estrange, *Lotteries and Sweepstakes: An Historical, Legal, and Ethical Survey of their Introduction, Suppression and Re-Establishment in the British Isles* (London: Heath Cranton, 1932; repr. edn, New York: Benjamin Blom, 1972).

Fagan, Neil, 'Enforcement of Gaming Debts in Britain,' *New York Law School Journal of International and Comparative Law*, 8 (Winter 1986), 7–31.

Falk, Bernard, *Thomas Rowlandson: His Life and Art* (New York: Beechhurst Press, 1952).

Foreman, Amanda, *Georgiana Duchess of Devonshire* (New York: Random House, 1998).

Freundlich, Francis, *Le Monde de Jeu à Paris 1715–1800* (Paris: Albin Michel, 1995).

Gigerenzer, Gerd, Zeno Swijtink, Theodore Porter, Lorraine Daston, John Beatty, and Lorenz Krüger, *The Empire of Chance: How Probability Changed Science and Everyday Life* (Cambridge: Cambridge University Press, 1989).

Grussi, Olivier, *La Vie Quotidienne des Joueurs sous l'Ancien Régime à Paris et à la Cour* (Paris: Hachette, 1985).

Hacking, Ian, *The Emergence of Probability* (Cambridge: Cambridge University Press, 1975; 2nd edn, Cambridge: Cambridge University Press, 2006).

Hald, Anders, *A History of Probability and Statistics and Their Applications before 1750* (New York: John Wiley and Sons, 1990).

Harris, Bob, 'Lottery Adventuring in Britain, c.1710–1760', *English Historical Review*, 133 (April 2018), 284–322.

Harris, Bob, 'The 1782 Gaming Bill and Lottery Regulation Acts (1782 and 1787): Gambling and the Law in Later Georgian Britain', *Parliamentary History*, 40 (October 2021), 462–80.

Harris, Bob, *Gambling in Britain in the Long Eighteenth Century* (Cambridge: Cambridge University Press, 2022).

Hartmann, Cyril Hughes (ed.), *Games and Gamesters of the Restoration* (London: Routledge, 1930).

Havers, Michael, Edward Grayson, and Peter Shankland, *The Royal Baccarat Scandal* (London: Souvenir Press, 1988).

Holland Rose, John, *William Pitt the Younger and National Revival* (London: G. H. Bell, 1911).

Jamieson, Ross, 'The Essence of Commodification: Caffeine Dependencies in the Early Modern World', *Journal of Social History*, 35 (Winter 2001), 269–94.

Jarrett, Derek, *Pitt the Younger* (London: Weidenfield and Nicolson, 1974).

Kavanagh, Thomas, *Enlightenment and the Shadows of Chance: The Novel and the Culture of Gambling in Eighteenth-Century France* (Baltimore: Johns Hopkins University Press, 1993).

Kavanagh, Thomas, *Dice, Cards, Wheels: A Different History of French Culture* (Philadelphia: University of Pennsylvania Press, 2005).

Kobza, Meghan, 'Dazzling or Fantastically Dull? Re-Examining the Eighteenth-Century London Masquerade', *Journal for Eighteenth Century Studies*, 43 (May 2020), 161–81.

Landau, Norma, *The Justices of the Peace, 1679–1760* (Berkeley: University of California Press, 1984).

Landau, Norma (ed.), *Law, Crime, and English Society, 1660–1830* (Cambridge: Cambridge University Press, 2002).

Lecky, William Edward Hartpole, *A History of England in the Eighteenth Century* (London: Longman, 1878).

Lemmings, David, and Claire Walker (eds.), *Moral Panics, the Media, and the Law in Early Modern England* (New York: Palgrave Macmillan, 2009).

Lillywhite, Bryant, *London Coffee Houses* (London: George Allen and Unwin, 1963).

McLynn, Frank, *Crime and Punishment in Eighteenth-Century England* (Oxford: Oxford University Press, 1991).

Mee, Jonathan, *Print, Publicity, and Popular Radicalism in the 1790s* (Cambridge: Cambridge University Press, 2016).

Miers, David, *Regulating Commercial Gambling: Past, Present, and Future* (Oxford: Oxford University Press, 2004).

Mitchell, Leslie George, *Charles James Fox* (Oxford: Oxford University Press, 1992).

Molesworth, Jesse, *Chance and the Eighteenth-Century Novel: Realism, Probability, Magic* (Cambridge: Cambridge University Press, 2010).

Morris, Marilyn, *Sex, Money, and Personal Character in Eighteenth-Century British Politics* (New Haven: Yale University Press, 2014).

Mullin, Janet E., 'Cards on the Table: The Middling Sort as Suppliers and Consumers of English Leisure Culture in the Eighteenth Century,' *Canadian Journal of History*, 45 (Spring/Summer 2010), 49–81.

Mullin, Janet E., *A Sixpence at Whist: Gaming and the English Middle Classes 1680–1730* (Woodbridge and Rochester, NY: Boydell and Brewer, 2015).

Munting, Roger, *An Economic and Social History of Gambling in Britain and the USA* (Manchester: Manchester University Press, 1996).

Murphy, Anne L., 'Lotteries in the 1690s: Investment or Gamble?,' *Financial History Review*, 12 (2005), 227–46.

Netchine, Ève (ed.), *Jeux de Princes, Jeux de Vilains* (Seuil: Bibliothèque Nationale de France, 2009).

Parlett, David, *A-Z of Card Games* (Oxford: Oxford University Press, 1992).

Raven, James, 'The Abolition of the English State Lotteries,' *Historical Journal*, 34 (1991), 371–89.

Reith, Gerda, *The Age of Chance: Gambling in Western Culture* (London: Routledge, 1999).

Richard, Jessica, *The Romance of Gambling in Eighteenth-Century Britain* (New York: Palgrave Macmillan, 2011).

Richard, Jessica, ' "Putting to Hazard a Certainty": Lotteries and the Romance of Gambling in Eighteenth-Century England,' *Studies in Eighteenth-Century Culture*, 40 (2011), 179–200.

Russell, Gillian, ' "Faro's Daughters": Female Gamesters, Politics, and the Discourse of Finance in 1790s Britain,' *Eighteenth-Century Studies*, 33 (2000), 481–504.

Sebag-Montefiore, Charles, and Joe Mordaunt Crook (eds.), *Brooks's 1764–2014: The Story of a Whig Club* (London: Brooks's Club, 2013).

Shepard, Alexandra, *Accounting for Oneself: Worth, Status, and the Social Order in Early Modern England* (Oxford: Oxford University Press, 2015).

Shoemaker, Robert, 'Crime, Courts and Community: The Prosecution of Misdemeanors in Middlesex County, 1663–1723,' Unpublished Ph.D. dissertation, Stanford University, 1986.

Shoemaker, Robert, 'The London "Mob" in the Early Eighteenth Century,' *Journal of British Studies*, 26 (July 1987), 273–304.

Shoemaker, Robert, *Prosecution and Punishment: Petty Crime and the Law in London and Rural Middlesex, c.1660–1725* (Cambridge: Cambridge University Press, 1991).

Steinmetz, Andrew, *The Gaming Table: Its Votaries and Victims* (London: Tinsley Brothers, 1870; repr. Montclair, NJ: Patterson Smith, 1969).

Stephen, Frederick, and M. Dorothy George, *Catalogue of Personal and Political Satires in the British Museum*, 12 vols (London: British Museum, 1870–1954).

Street, Howard, *The Law of Gaming* (London: Sweet and Maxwell, 1937).

Thomas, Keith, 'Numeracy in Early Modern England,' *Transactions of the Royal Historical Society* 37 (1987), 103–32.

Thompson, Francis Michael Longstreth, *Hampstead: Building a Borough, 1650–1964* (London: Routledge and Kegan Paul, 1974).

Todhunter, Isaac, *A History of the Mathematical Theory of Probability* (London: Macmillan, 1865; repr. edn, New York: Chelsea Publishing Company, 1949).

Tosney, Nicholas, 'Gaming in England, c. 1540–1760,' Unpublished Ph.D. dissertation, University of York, 2008.

Tosney, Nicholas, 'The Playing Card Trade in Early Modern England,' *Historical Research*, 84 (November 2011), 637–56.

Walker, Jonathan, 'Gambling and Venetian Noblemen c.1500–1700,' *Past and Present*, 162 (February 1999), 28–69.

Whiffen, Marcus, *Thomas Archer: Architect of the English Baroque* (Los Angeles: Hennessey and Ingalls, 1973).

Wilberforce, Robert Isaac and Samuel, *The Life of William Wilberforce*, 5 vols (London: John Murray, 1838).

Zollinger, Manfred (ed.), *Random Riches: Gambling Past and Present* (London: Routledge, 2016).

Index